DYNASTY

DYNASTY

The Stuarts 1560-1807

JOHN MACLEOD

Hodder & Stoughton

First published in Great Britain in 1999
by Hodder and Stoughton
A division of Hodder Headline PLC

10 9 8 7 6 5 4 3 2 1

British Library Cataloguing in Publication Data

A CIP catalogue record for this title
is available from the British Library

ISBN 0 340 70766 6

Typeset by Hewer Text Ltd, Edinburgh
Printed and bound in Great Britain by
Clays Ltd, St Ives plc

Hodder and Stoughton
A division of Hodder Headline PLC
338 Euston Road
London NW1 3BH

for

Alasdair Dan MacKinnon

and Alistair Martin

. . . is lionaidh an cuan do-thuigsinn
le làn-mara 's mìle seòl,

Falaichear cladach na trioblaid
le bhodhannan is tiùrr a' bhròin
is buailidh an tonn gun bhristeadh
mu m'chasan le suathadh sròil . . .

(bho 'Reothairt', Somhairle MacGill-Eain)

CONTENTS

LIST OF ILLUSTRATIONS

PREFACE

This is a popular history of the house of Stuart, with special emphasis on their lives and reigns from Mary, Queen of Scots' accession to personal rule in 1560 to the overthrow of James VII and II in 1688. The first chapter is devoted to the rise of the dynasty in Scotland – Stewarts, as they then called themselves, in the Scots spelling – and the last to the efforts, unsuccessful, of the exiled Stuarts to recover their thrones, as well as examining the personalities of the quasi-Stuarts, William and Mary, and Anne, who took their place. The mass of the book, then, concentrates on the Stuarts who exercised powerful and at times near-absolute monarchy, in the teeth of turmoil, change, Reformation, and homicidal doctors. The book makes no pretence to original scholarship, but is drawn from a huge variety of other writers. The most helpful are listed in the bibliography. Within the text I have attributed as many insights as possible to their original authors.

The history, of course, has a special frisson: it is launched on bookshops as Scotland, for the first time since 1707, regains its parliament, under another executive monarchy from that of Queen Anne.

The sharp will notice my special debt to Lady Antonia Fraser, in my studies of Mary and Charles II, though I do not follow her in every conclusion, and the latter biography struck me as excessively lenient. The work of Barry Coward and John Miller was a most useful guide to the tortured politics following the Restoration. Stewart Ross's entertaining history of the line concentrates much more on the early Scottish kings; his outline of the origins of the Stewart family is invaluable, and his book is one of those rare historical works you can enjoy reading in bed.

You may detect a certain bias, in the direction of Protestantism and especially its Scottish, Presbyterian form. This is, however, rather a corrective to the mass of popular writing in this field, in an age when monarchy and religion were inextricably intertwined. I was surprised, in the course of executing this work, how many of my preconceptions and opinions were successfully challenged. I concluded with a much more favourable view of James VI and Charles II than when I began; Charles I and William of Orange sank sharply in my esteem. With the exception of the Old Pretender, however, none of the Stuarts is dull, and I have enjoyed spending much recent time in their company.

There are points to clarify. I have used the French spelling, Stuart, from the reign of Mary onwards; she, and her husband, Henry Stuart, Lord Darnley, both adopted that style. When we come to the joint rule of Scotland and England, with competing numerals – James VI and I; William II and III – I have adopted the higher numeral for general reference: hence, James VI, William III. I owe this solution, in fact, to Winston Churchill, who as a young member of parliament, in 1901, suggested the government justify the new king's title of Edward VII – which caused great offence in Scotland, which had never had a previous King Edward – by making it known that, should a monarch accede to the British throne with the name of a previous Scottish king, the higher numeral would be taken for title. But our present sovereign made the same mistake in 1952; and neither she, nor her son, have named their princes Robert, James, Malcolm, David or Alexander . . . A notorious problem for history in this period is dates: Britain had not adopted the Julian calendar in the Stuart era, and by 1745 there was an eleven-day difference between old-style British dates and new-style Continental ones. I have adopted the general convention of dating an event in, say, Paris, by the new style, but a battle or whatever in England by the old style.

I am indebted to Roland Philipps, Angela Herlihy and all at Hodder & Stoughton for their help, criticism and enthusiasm. I thank my agent, Robert Kirby, and those who have granted access to libraries: my father, Rev Professor Donald Macleod,

MA, of Edinburgh; my minister, Rev Roderick MacLeod, BA, of Tarbert, Harris; and Dr James A.D. Finlayson, MB ChB, of Tarbert, Harris.

Mrs Marsaili MacKinnon, MA LLB, of Scadabay, Harris, read an early typescript, swooping ruthlessly on errors of type or grammar, and made many useful and encouraging remarks. But this book bears my name and any eluding mistake is my responsibility. Murdo Morrison, of Tigh na Mara, Tarbert, Harris, intervened in a critical computer crisis, amid chapter ten, and spared me death by hyperventilation.

I am grateful to Mr Scott McNally who saved the entire project from premature death in the Kelvin.

Only last week I met the Prime Minister, the Rt Hon Tony Blair MP, as he made an official visit to Harris. I enjoyed pointing out to him a site where for some nights Charles Edward Stuart hid on the run after Culloden. Mr Blair's visit, the first of a governing Prime Minister to the Outer Hebrides, was in its own way a symbolic gesture of reconciliation and goodwill to a part of the British Isles which, in 1746 and for too many years ever since, has been deemed remote, barbarous and alien.

History is not inevitable. It was never certain that Britain would not evolve into an absolute monarchy, such as those in France, Prussia and Austria-Hungary. We went, rather, by a road less travelled, to forge a state and a Union of remarkable stability and social peace. This was very much the inadvertent fruit of Stuart rule. How we started our road from James VI, who bewailed the Outer Hebrides for their 'bluidie and wiket Hielandmen', but tried sincerely to unite his kingdoms, to the democratically accountable Tony Blair, virtual monarch of a land enjoying, still, parliamentary sovereignty, free exercise of the franchise, and religious toleration – and, moreover, who can show himself in the far Highlands, striving to preserve the Union – is the Stuart story and the story of this book.

JOHN MACLEOD
Isle of Harris
September 1998

1

BEGINNINGS

The Early Stewarts

The Stuarts began with a queen and her second husband. She grew tired of him and, probably, was part of the successful plot to blow him up. But their descendants – she was Mary Stewart, Queen of Scots; he was Henry Stuart, Lord Darnley – held the throne of Scotland from 1567, and from 1603 those of England and Ireland. They were twice overthrown and, in 1688, permanently deposed. In exile, though, Stuart princes made repeated efforts to recover their crown. A serious attempt could still be mounted as late as 1745; in 1788, the year in which Charles Edward Stuart died, officials of state were still obliged, amid oaths of office, to forswear any effort to restore him to his throne. His brother Henry, a cardinal of the Church, died, the last of the male line, only in 1807, twelve years before the birth of Queen Victoria and but two lifetimes beyond living memory.

Their glamour endures.

The years of Stuart reign were marked by squalor, turbulence, civil war, disorder at home and decline of English and Scottish influence abroad. They presided over religious repression. They came to repudiate the faith of the great majority of their subjects. Stuart kings were repeatedly at odds with their parliaments. They made secret treaties with foreign powers. They reneged on ministers; they reneged, on occasion, on their closest friends. They sought the powers of absolute monarchy, but lacked the skills either of conciliation or plain government. They were, for the most part, a line of incompetents; one proved so foolish, so untrustworthy, and so dangerous that at length an exasperated country cut off his head. Of their native land, the seventeenth century – when, most of the time, Stuarts held the throne – must be reckoned the most miserable night in Scottish history. The last defeat of the Stuart cause, at Culloden, in 1746, proved the key catastrophe of modern Highland history.

But they were also brave. They tended, unlike their Hanoverian successors, to have happy marriages and be good parents. They were, for the most part, sincerely religious; in two cases, so adamant in their faith they ruined their reigns. More: the Stuarts had exquisite good taste. Charles I, especially, endowed the country with beautiful buildings and built up a priceless collection of painting and sculpture, much of which is in royal hands to this day, in trust for the nation.

And yet this line, this dynasty of Stuart, continues to fascinate. After their final extinction, Jacobitism – their cult, from Jacobus, the Latin for James, the name of the most stupid and unpleasant Stuart king of all – became fashionable. Sir Walter Scott romanticised it; noble ladies wrote sweet songs about the 'Bonnie Prince'; Queen Victoria – another of the Stuarts' pudding-faced German successors – actually declared, with no evident sense of the ridiculous, that she herself 'was a Jacobite at heart'. Songs, novels and in our own day the motion picture and small screen continue to exploit the Stuart romance. The Scottish tourist industry draws heavily upon it; Culloden, and such sites as the Palace of Holyrood house, the Jacobite monument at Glenfinnan, and so on draw many thousands of visitors each year. And even the most hard-headed and Protestant of Highlanders, studying what happened after the Jacobite defeat, can find himself wishing Charles Edward had succeeded – knowing full well that, when it was a matter of life and death, in 1745, most Scots actually fought against him.

Why, for all the havoc they wrought, do we have an enduring affection for those blundering kings and princes?

In Scotland their cult is fuelled by a certain emotional nationalism. They were a Scottish house; until Charles II, their monarchs were Scottish-born. Under the Stuarts Scotland retained its own parliament and a measure of independent government. But most of this Scottish sentiment is, at bottom, irrational, founded upon ignorance.

More important: the Stuarts had a genuine charisma. Some,

of course, more than others; there can have been little aesthetic or social pleasure in dining with James VI and I, with his
filthy table manners, crude jokes and foppish favourites. But
his mother, Mary, was a woman of outstanding beauty, tragic
fortune, and gentle virtue. She was a hopeless queen. But she
abides as perhaps the most romantic, forlorn figure in European history. Charles Edward Stuart, her great-great-great
grandson, is also an appealing figure (and, indeed, rather
resembled her in appearance: both were tall, and red-headed,
and fair of face). He had considerable accomplishments; he
had verve and dash. Until failure and drink ruined him, there
is abundant evidence of ability and humanity. Like most of
the line, too, he was physically very brave.

They also exercised power. This is one excellent reason for
studying the decades of Stuart reign, for it was in those years
that modern institutions moved to birth and modern political
concepts – freedom of worship, limits on executive authority,
the sovereignty of parliament, constitutional monarchy, the
establishment of religion – were hammered forth, not least in
response to Stuart despotism and failure. James II and VII
was, in truth, the last king who attempted to rule by un-
trammelled, direct power. His daughter, the obese and rather
forgettable Queen Anne, was the last monarch who dared to
deny an Act of Parliament the royal assent. The Hanoverian
monarchs who followed her are dull not least because they
never (though George III genuinely tried) wielded serious
power. Victoria could still influence. George V could reconcile
and cajole. In the reign of the present queen the last vestige of
real – as opposed to nominal – royal prerogative has quite
vanished.

They presided over – well, excitement. Most of it was
excitement their kingdoms could well have done without.
Many of these excitements ended in great bloodshed: Mary's
attempt to recover her Scottish throne: the Babington conspiracy; the horrible end of those plotting, and her own
decapitation; the Gunpowder Plot; the English Civil War;
the Battle of the Covenants; and the repeated skirmishes of the
Jacobite risings. (Culloden, in fact, was the last battle fought

on mainland Britain, though no regiment now boasts it among its battle honours.) The years of Stuart hegemony were scarcely dull.

And there was that monstrous ill-luck. One may not go as far as the Skye cleric who wrote, in our own century: 'by the very intensity of their desire to break down the carved work of the Church of Scotland, the Lord hurled the Stuart dynasty off the Throne of Britain, and left them ultimately without issue to occupy that Throne again.' But the Stuarts were, time and again, benighted by military defeat; ill-timed storms; premature death; murder; conspiracy; the sword and the axe. They were a ruling house who, latterly, could win glory only in the last stand; the forlorn hope; the lost cause. At the last even their fecundity failed. The legitimate male line perished, ending in two practically estranged brothers: one a terminal alcoholic, the other a homosexual prelate.

Stuart courts, too, were in one or two reigns most glamorous. Charles I patronised great painters such as Van Dyke. Charles II reigned over Dryden, Congreve, and other playwrights and writers of the Restoration. Dull Queen Anne certainly was; but her reign – the 'Augustan Age' – is still regarded as a glorious epoch in English literature. Even in their troubles – especially in Scotland – the Stuart era gave birth to some of Gaelic's finest verse, and some key political texts still studied today, such as Samuel Rutherford's *Lex Rex*, though that was an intellectual exercise in countering the Stuart tyranny. Charles II, in England, is perhaps the only Stuart monarch remembered with any affection; the 'Old Rowley' who caroused and wenched incognito; in whose reign London was burned down, then largely rebuilt by Wren; on whose deathbed asked fondly for his favourite mistress, the orange-selling Nell Gwyn. (There seems to be a tradition in England of venerating rascally monarchs, if their carnal appetites are big enough: the dreadful, bloodthirsty Henry VIII, cruel and capricious as he was, is likewise a folk hero.)

Nor can we underrate the power of religious faction. In the Roman Catholic districts of the Highlands a certain, genuine Jacobitism still simmers. Charles I was posthumously elevated to martyrdom by the High, Catholic faction of the Church of England. (He is still venerated by that section of the Church today.) Likewise the Scottish Episcopal Church was practically a Jacobite sect, and thus toiled for much of the eighteenth century against prejudice and inconvenience.

And today, in horrid shadow-effect, the politics of Northern Ireland, and indeed the terraces of Scottish football, are still blighted by a post-Christian Protestant exultation in Jacobite defeat at the Boyne in 1690.

Stuart males were vigorous in libido, with the odd homosexual prince, like James VI, or the terminal cardinal. (William III should be acquitted of that aspersion.) The line also spawned feline, if generally hapless, women. The Tudor streak lent them a capacity for showmanship: they built grand palaces, and great ships. They also had a tendency to die prematurely, often violently; so their history is agreeably splattered in blood. And there are wonderful what-ifs; questions we can never now answer. What if Mary had fled straight to France, rather than decide to seek refuge in England? What if Oliver Cromwell had lived another five years? Was the Duke of Monmouth really – as many believe – issue of a legitimate marriage of Charles II, rather than one of many Stuart bastards? And if he was, was it some black pact with the Pope that made his father deny it? What if, early in the eighteenth century, the Old Pretender had embraced the Protestant faith, deciding that, as Henri of Navarre had thought Paris worth a mass, London was worth doing without one?

And what if – the biggest question of all – Charles Edward Stuart, the Young Pretender, had pressed on from Derby?

Incompetent. Untrustworthy. Spectacularly unfortunate. Yet, say what you might about this extraordinary family, they were anything but dull.

There is, besides, the odd edge of piety. The Stuarts were incurably religious. Their tragedy was that, as well as being for the most part devoid of basic political skill, they clung to a view of monarchy – the divine right of kings – which sat ill at ease with the emerging democracy of Protestant and especially Presbyterian faith; this drove them, inevitably, first to Episcopacy and then to Roman Catholicism, and thus at last cost them all save the occasional favour of Popes. The Stuarts believed – and James VI actually taught, and wrote – that kings ruled not by the will of men, but by the will of God. To Him alone, the Most High, the king had at last to make account. And in God's providence, by primogeniture, thrones were attained; and by primogeniture, the right of the first-born, were thrones occupied, and not by any issue of competence or expediency or popular will.

Thus true Jacobites ridiculed the usurping Hanoverians; after all, when George I succeeded Anne in 1714, there were literally dozens alive with a better claim by blood to the crown than he. And, even in the 1970s, a female demonstrator had to be arrested at the House of Commons; she was petitioning, and screaming, that nothing lawful could be enacted, nothing at all, until the true sovereign (in most neo-Jacobite eyes, the present Duke of Bavaria) was restored to the throne.

The trouble is that the second House of Stuart won the English throne by virtue of Tudor descent, James I being a great-grandson of Henry VII, whose blood claim to England's throne was most dubious. And their claim even to the throne of Scotland was, by strict primogeniture, equally invalid by the tenets of later Jacobite ideology. Others had a better claim by blood; the Stewarts held it because of descent from one man who had defended Scots independence – Scots sovereignty – and was thus preferred as king to one who had compromised it.

The Scots made this plain in the 1320 Declaration of Arbroath, addressed to Pope John XXII – such a depraved pontiff that it was 1958 before there dared to be a XXIII. The barons gathered to sign this in the name of their sovereign, Robert I, sometime Robert the Bruce, who had led the Scots to victory at Bannockburn six years before, and freed them of subjugation to the English crown. They petitioned the Pope because the crown of England was loth to acknowledge the fact; and, England being of more weight in Christendom than Scotland, Rome likewise refused to recognise Robert as lawful king. So the barons sternly intimated, in dog-Latin: 'So long as a hundred of us remain alive we will never be subject to the English King. It is not for glory, riches or honours that we fight, but for liberty alone, which no worthy man will lay down save with his life.'

Robert was a true nationalist. An early and important concession from Rome was the king's veto over clerical appointments; Robert was anxious to avoid the insinuation of English clergy into the Scots Church. It meant, then, that the Reformation came to Scotland late – it took root earlier in England – but, when it came, it came as a thunderclap, and with much more sweeping success. It also set a precedent: that religion in Scotland was to be distinctively Scots. The repeated efforts of Stuart kings to impose English practices on the Scots Kirk would create serious trouble.

Present that day at Arbroath was Walter FitzJames Stewart, Baron Renfrew, High Steward of Scotland, widower of the king's late daughter.

It was 1328 before the Treaty of Northampton secured an end to twenty-two years of war and the turmoil that had seized Scotland since 1286, when on a wild night King Alexander III was found dead at the bottom of a cliff.

Alexander III was one of Scotland's ablest kings. His triumph at the Battle of Largs had secured the Hebrides from the Norwegian king, a highlight of a reign afterwards wistfully recalled as an 'age of wine and wax, game and glee'. At his death he was only forty-five years old. Yet he had outlived all his children; his sole descendant and heir was his granddaughter in Norway, a child of three. Queen Margaret never saw her native land. She was not brought to Scotland until 1290, and was no nearer than Orkney (then a Danish possession) when she sickened and died.

The six guardians, who had acted as a council of regency for the little girl, were caught up in vicious argument, claim and counter-claim as to who was now rightful King of Scots. They sought a disinterested judge, and rather too readily accepted Edward I, King of England, as umpire in the difficulty, even conceding Edward's demand that only candidates acknowledging him as overlord would qualify for the Scots crown.

There were thirteen claimants, of whom only two were important. One was the old Lord of Annandale, Robert de Brus; the other was John de Balliol. Both were grandsons of King William the Lyon, and second cousins to the late Alexander III. Balliol had the stronger claim, though, being descended from the older sister of de Brus's mother. Edward I went by strict law and chose John de Balliol. But he could not resist testing his new authority: repeatedly he sought to embarrass and humiliate the new monarch, demonstrating his docile vassalage to the world, thus making plain Edward had in truth conquered Scotland without sword leaving scabbard. Balliol's subjects were encouraged to appeal to Edward I for satisfaction of any grievance. Balliol suffered slight upon slight; he was even, on one occasion, summoned south to explain why he had not paid his wine merchant's bill.

In 1295 he finally rebelled and made separate treaty with the King of France. The following spring Edward I invaded, in a spectacular campaign of triumph spiced with atrocity. Berwick was sacked. Dunbar fell. The great castles of Scotland surrendered; Balliol sued for peace, and formally ceded his kingdom to Edward. The rest of the campaign was but triumphal march for the English monarch. He went north as far as Elgin; returned by Scone (pausing to collect the Scots' Coronation Stone: it would not return until 1996) and, at Berwick, called the Scots parliament before him. Anyone who was anybody in Scotland came and duly grovelled.

There followed the Wars of Independence. Balliol, discredited as weak and incompetent, sank without trace. There was the heroic, ultimately hopeless crusade of William Wallace. Then there rose (having in the most sleekit fashion ducked and dived between the varying camps of Balliol, Wallace and Edward) the younger Robert de Brus.

Bruce died of leprosy in 1329. He was succeeded by his son, David II, who died – after a long but weak, chaotic reign – without issue. He was in turn succeeded by his nephew, Robert II. A Stewart.

And he came of a line not lost in the mists of Scottish history, not a race of noble Highlanders, but from a family who had been in Scotland less than two centuries and whose origins were Norman-French; the trail of blood is lost in Brittany.

Robert II was the great-great-great-great-great-great-great-great-grandson of one Flaald, who flourished about 1050, in Dol-de-Bretagne, and was the seneschal at the Breton court; the word, of Germanic origin, means 'old servant'; and the office was most honourable: something between a butler and a trusted manservant, the man who personally served the duke himself at the formal, near-ritualistic dinners of that day; a man of authority in the household, almost certainly literate. It was hereditary; Flaald's son and grandson followed him, in the title of 'dapifer', which means more or less the same thing. They must have been reliable, stolid people, of noble bearing, fit for the company of kings and princes, discreet and loyal.

Flaald was followed by his son Alan as dapifer at Dol; his grandson, Alan, in turn succeeded the father, but joined the Holy Crusade, and died by some infidel sword. *His* son, Flaald II, made a shrewd career move. He left Brittany for England, and cultivated friendship with Henry, third son of King William the Conqueror, who was feuding bitterly with his brothers: Robert, Duke of Normandy, and William II – 'Rufus' – the King of England. In 1100 William II was conveniently killed in a hunting accident. Henry promptly seized power and proclaimed himself king. The coup did not go unchallenged. Some of the nobles revolted and appealed to Normandy; after all, Robert was the older of the Conqueror's sons. It is a mark of how little England mattered those days, and how widely disdained it was abroad as a barbarous dump, that Henry I was able to cut a deal. In exchange for generous annual tribute, Duke Robert relinquished any claim to the English throne. King Henry could now establish his authority and bestow title and favour on his cronies – mostly Bretons, like Flaald II.

It was his son Alan, though, who benefited most, for his

father did not long survive Henry's accession. By 1116 this Alan was a grand English gentleman, owning huge tracts of land. In Shropshire alone – where he was sometime sheriff – he owned no fewer than seventy manors, and was generally called Lord of Clun and Oswestry. He mattered to King Henry because he was well placed, and with sufficient men and horse at his call, to guard the Welsh Marches and watch the king's back. Like the Border between Scotland and England, it was a turbulent frontier, with repeated raid and counter-raid and cattle-rustling and rapine and sacking and burning and so on.

To cap everything, Alan Fitz Flaald even married a very rich heiress, one Avelina de Hesdin, who brought him more estates in ten other English counties. It made Alan, Lord of Oswestry, more of a force than ever; it is a sign of the trust Henry had in him that the marriage was permitted at all. Avelina bore her lord three surviving sons; and, when her good man died about 1120, his titles and wealth were divided between them. Jordan Fitz Alan, the eldest, inherited the family holdings in Brittany and the dapifership of Dol. William Fitz Alan became the new Lord of Oswestry and, using his father's wiles of wit and marriage, continued the traditions of men on the make. He established a new, grand family: the Fitz Alan line, first Earls, then Dukes of Arundel. Walter, the third son, was left with little: two small Shropshire manors, one held by grace and favour from his elder brother. Walter Fitz Alan had little wealth, no significant vassalage, no great status, and no fine prospects.

There were three avenues for the upwardly mobile, of good birth and family, in the Middle Ages. One was the Church, offering a hierarchy of advancement and ever more gracious living. One was marriage, to a good-blooded and immensely wealthy woman. Walter seems to have had little taste for a religious life; and his genteel poverty made him a poor catch for a rich family. 'That left him with only one viable option,' writes Stewart Ross. 'He had to attach himself to a feudal superior who was prepared to recognise and reward his talents.' Walter's plight had another element of desperation.

King Henry was dead and the country was torn in war between his daughter, Matilda, and his nephew, Stephen of Blois. (Walter's brother William prematurely backed Stephen and had to flee for his life; it was some years before he recovered his inheritance.)

Then, in the winter of 1135–6, Walter Fitz Alan had an offer he could not refuse, from King David of Scotland.

This David had inherited the crown of his father, Malcolm III – 'Canmore'; his mother was the famous Queen Margaret, of Saxon royalty, a descendant of King Alfred. Margaret is to this day rather demonised in folklore as a major anglicising influence in Scots life. She was a woman of fanatical piety, who greatly disliked both the Gaelic language and the surviving traditions of the Celtic Church. She encouraged rich cloth and fine manners at court; she made her husband drink French wine, not rude ale. Worse: she dragged him into English concerns. In 1072 Malcolm unwisely marched south to wage war against the Norman usurper. The Conqueror beat him back, then marched himself into the heart of Scotland, forcing Malcolm to humiliating homage at Abernethy. In 1092 William Rufus seized Carlisle, and Cumbria – hitherto part of Malcolm's realm – was permanently lost to Scotland. In 1093, raiding back, Malcolm was killed at Alnwick. His brother Donald Bane took control, reversed much of Margaret's innovation, and for some years held it against the claims of Malcolm's sons, until he was finally deposed in 1097 by David's half-brother, Edgar. At his death in 1107 he was followed by David's full brother, Alexander.

It was on Malcolm's sons by Margaret that her influence was most significant. And that influence was compounded by the marriage of her daughter, Matilda, to Henry I, so that the young Prince David spent most of his time at the English court and became a veritable Englishman himself. He was a baron, lord of the two counties of Huntingdon and Northampton, fully ten years before he became King of Scots in 1124. When he came back it was with a great host of English friends, acquaintances, and hangers-on, all of the Norman noble blood, who saw little prospect of fortune in England but had high hopes of winning a place in Scotland. The émigrés in this peaceful Norman conquest included Walter, whom David made High Steward of Scotland; and the first Robert de Brus, whose father had arrived in England with William the Conqueror.

The advent of these nobles – in great number – had a serious impact on Scots order, for they were granted great Scottish estates, held by written charter from the king, and displaced much of Scotland from the old Celtic concept of landholding and authority. It would survive, for centuries yet, in the Highlands, where chiefs lived and governed in paternalist, heritable jurisdiction over land which, in a sense, all clansmen felt was theirs as much as his. In southern Scotland, though, these lackeys of King David brought English-style feudalism.

Walter Fitz Alan most loyally served his king, and in time David's grandson, Malcolm IV. As the boy was only eleven at accession in 1153, there was a prolonged period of minority, in which Walter played a leading role. Perhaps his most signal triumph, in over thirty years of service, was his 1164 defeat of Somerled, first Lord of the Isles. Somerled had driven the Norse from the Hebrides. He then unwisely tried to drive the Anglo-Norman nobles from Scotland, for Malcolm IV was demanding that Somerled cede his mainland territories to the crown. He launched attack upon Renfrew, at the very heart of Walter's territory. The enterprise ended with Somerled's forces routed and Somerled himself slain.

So Walter amassed land and honours; the main estates were in Renfrewshire, and to this day Baron Renfrew is a junior title of the Prince of Wales. In a most unusual mark of the king's favour, Walter Fitz Alan was granted that borough of Renfrew: usually, the monarch kept Scotland's towns for himself, as the crown's main source of cash income. And David II bestowed yet another honour, the title of Steward. This office was one of direct, close service to the king. It combined administrative and courtly duties. The Steward was a fixture at court. Where the king went, he went. He witnessed the royal seal on documents; he was confidant, *aide de camp*, and private secretary. More, as the Breton post of dapifer, the office was hereditary. Within three generations Stewart was the family surname.

Stewart fortunes prospered. They amassed land in Lanarkshire, Berwickshire, East Lothian, and built their power base. They were tied, by blood and marriage, to most of Scotland's nobility, including the house of Bruce. Above all, they were close to the throne.

Alan Fitz Walter, second High Steward, lacked his father's caution but was a gifted if impetuous soldier. His son, another Walter, was a prudent influence in royal diplomacy; he also had the role of justiciar, highest office in the crown's gift, supervising dispensation of the king's justice and taking personal charge in cases of particular delicacy. Alexander, fourth High Steward, survived the turbulent politics of Alexander III's long minority with some skill, and his military expertise – and patience – won him some glory at the Battle of Largs in 1263, when Norway at last lost even nominal sovereignty over the Hebrides. His son James, fifth High Steward, was a slippery, low-profile, cunning sort of fellow, who did his duty by the crown – whoever wore it in the difficult years after Alexander's death – and avoided committing himself too plainly to any given faction.

The Stewarts – as they now signed themselves – were a Scottish institution. And Walter Fitz James, sixth High Steward, proved perhaps the first real hero of the line. He was a jolly, bold, swashbuckling type, of undoubted courage and gallant loyalty. He single-handedly raised the family profile, changing their image – as Ross puts it – 'from cautious administrators to proud warriors worthy of marriage into the royal family'. Walter was only twenty when he fought at Bannockburn, yet with sufficient brio to win these lines of Barbour:

> Walter Stewart of Scotland fine
> Who was then but a beardless youth
> Came with a group of noble men
> That might by countenance be known . . .

The following year, Walter won the highest prize: the hand of the king's daughter in marriage.

Marjorie was nineteen years old: her life was short and, for the most part, wretched. She could scarcely remember her mother and, due to his many flights and vicissitudes, hardly saw her father until he triumphed at Bannockburn. She spent eight years herself as a prisoner of the English. Nor did she long survive marriage to Walter Stewart. She bore Walter a son, Robert, in 1316 and died the following year, only twenty-one. (A tradition that she was killed by a fall from her horse is now doubted.) No doubt Walter grieved correctly, but such bereavement was commonplace in the fourteenth century. (His first wife, Alice, had died too.) It was not long before he married again; in 1319 he scored a spectacular personal triumph as warden of Berwick, when he successfully beat off a mighty English siege.

But he was fully aware of his son's importance. After King Robert himself, and his brother Edward – acknowledged by the Bruce as heir-presumptive – Marjorie had been formally recognised as next in line. The king had still failed to beget a male heir. (David was at last born in 1324, in the curious position of being eight years younger than his nephew.)

By the time young Robert Stewart was ten, both his parents were dead. It seems he was then brought up at court and, after Prince David and his grandfather, his claim to succession was plainly acknowledged. He had the blood of Bruce and the name of Stewart, and bore the rank of one from a noble line of royal servants, hardy in battle and skilled in statecraft. Naturally, from early manhood – and especially when David II took the throne – he was prominent in Scots affairs. The years of the new king's minority were probably the happiest of his life.

Robert 'was a comely young man,' writes John of Fordun, 'tall and strong, modest, generous, high-spirited and well-mannered; and the innate sweetness of his personality ensured that he was loved by all true-hearted Scots'. But, genial as this prince may have been, he lacked either steel, self-discipline or any evident ability. He spent much of his time wenching. His amours were legion. He married young – and rather suddenly – one Elizabeth Mure, of genteel but undistinguished blood; it was not an ideal match politically, and the bond has more than a hint of shotgun wedding. What was worse was that Elizabeth had been betrothed before; in Scots law, this would make any children by her marriage to Robert illegitimate. Still worse, the couple were within the fourth degree of affinity and, in canon law, the union was therefore incestuous. A papal dispensation was eventually sought, after Elizabeth had borne Robert eight children; and the position was now serious, for it was becoming less and less likely that King David would beget an heir-apparent.

Widowed about 1355, Robert married again – a much more sensible match, to one Euphemia, daughter of the Earl of Ross. She too fell within forbidden degree of blood-relation, but Robert now had the wisdom to apply for prior dispensation from the Pope. Euphemia gave him another five children. He also begot a good few bastards. He is said, in all, to have fathered at least twenty-three offspring, and no doubt there were liaisons without issue. As the king toiled fruitlessly for an heir of his own, Robert's fecundity did little to improve their strained relations.

In 1346 there was another foolish Scots foray over the Border, which ended in the customary rout and – worse – the capture of their king. (David II boasted before joining arms that he 'might well march all the way to London'; and so he did, but as a prisoner.) He was in English hands for a decade, a hostage to support many delightful schemes and deals. Robert was left in the unenviable position of monarch *de facto*, without a monarch's authority; indeed, he was not even an earl. His emollient personality precluded him, happily, from alienating the nobility and perhaps jeopardising his prospects. But the effective regency exposed him as a weak, ineffective ruler. He balanced this faction and flattered that one. The Treasury suffered. Power slipped from court to the periphery. The rule of law faltered.

In 1357, the English duly placated, King David returned. He continued, unavailingly – encouraged for a time by widowhood and a new, nubile queen – to try to beget a child. Relations between him and Robert chilled yet further. Robert unwisely winked at an uprising in 1363, by the Earls of Douglas and March. The rebellion failed and he was lucky to survive. He was fortunate, too, to survive insistent English pressure upon David to recognise the English king, or one of his heirs, as successor should he die without issue: this was part of the tedious debate over David's hefty (and still unpaid) ransom. The Scots parliament rejected the deal in 1364. In 1368, somehow, Robert caused the queen offence and he and some sons did a stretch in an island prison, on Loch Leven. This gaol figured again in Stewart fortunes.

Still childless, King David divorced his second queen (she fled to Avignon to plead with the Pope) and sought to marry yet again. The affair was still in legal confusion – and poor David was still as sterile as ever – when, on 22 February 1371, he fell ill at Edinburgh Castle and died the same day.

Robert Stewart was King of Scots.

It is the tragedy of Robert II that, by the standards of the day, he was an old man when at last he won the crown. He was already in decline, physically weakening, his judgement faltering. Though he lived, in fact, to be the oldest of all Scots monarchs, he is remembered as a weak ruler incapable of administering the firm, decisive government Scotland sorely needed. Further, he had two serious handicaps. The long, complex politics of his long, long wait had enmeshed him inextricably with certain great Scottish families, such as the Douglases, thus restricting his independence; what were the Stewarts, they could say, but just such a noble baronage who had got lucky? The Earl of Douglas actually challenged Robert's right to the throne. Robert I would have had his head for it. Robert II bought him off, granting Douglas high honours and his son the king's own daughter in marriage. Such a show of weakness boded ill for the reign.

Worse, there was the fruit of Robert's exuberant loins, complicated by a web of wider Stewart relations. Scotland had but sixteen earldoms: yet seven of these were held by

Stewarts. And there were his wild, indisciplined sons, all too happy to feed the image of a family who believed themselves above the law. Most notorious was Alexander, Robert's fourth son, who so abused office as the king's lieutenant in the Highlands he won the soubriquet, 'Wolf of Badenoch': by 1388 there was such a scandal the king was compelled to deprive him of office. The Wolf took not the slightest bit of notice. By this time, in any event, the king was virtually senile. He was almost stone-deaf; his sight was failing, and melancholy overwhelmed him.

In 1388, when his eldest son John, Earl of Carrick, heir-apparent, was ill and feeble, and the second son, Robert, was determined to gain power before something dreadful happened to cost the dynasty everything, Robert II effectively abdicated, signing his prerogatives over to the three estates in General Council – a very grand convocation of the Scots parliament. In turn they obediently appointed Robert Stewart, Earl of Menteith, as governor of the realm. In May 1390 Robert II died, peacefully and largely forgotten, at Dundonald. 'A more tender heart might no man have,' wrote one loyal contemporary. But a later Scots historian, John Major, said bluntly: 'I cannot hold the aged King to have been a skilful warrior or wise in counsel.' Robert II was a nice man and a bad king.

His successor, though, plumbed new depths of pathos. John, Earl of Carrick, took the throne as King Robert III. 'He was not the worst monarch to wear the Scottish Crown,' writes Ross drily: 'his shortcomings were far too passive to merit such an ignominious accolade.' It seems the prince had never been bright and was always somewhat deficient of personality. He had the same generous, affable, easy-going nature as his father; worse, in 1388 John had been kicked by a horse. The accident left him crippled, practically housebound, and prone to dreadful depression.

Of Robert III, Mackie says he was one whom, 'ill-luck had pursued from his cradle'. He was quite at the mercy of his formidable, scheming brothers, and of the abiding Douglas. He was fifty-three at succession and already a broken man.

His physical incapacity weakened him in one regard then crucial for a Scots monarch: he had the utmost difficulty in travelling. But it was his fearsome melancholy – a near-maniacal, religious self-abasement and self-loathing – that ruined his reign. He lacked the confidence even to be crowned king in his own given name. (In fairness, the name John was – and has, in fact, remained – as unpopular with European monarchs as with Popes; by 1390 Scotland, England and France had all suffered dreadful or embarrassing King Johns.)

Stories are legion of meek, mild, self-flagellating Robert III who accepted the blame for everything and failed to make any effective use of the power vested in him. During his reign, wailed one contemporary writer, 'there was no law in Scotland. The strong oppressed the weak and the whole kingdom was a den of thieves.' He was really king in name only; Earl Robert's guardianship had to be repeatedly renewed. Earl Robert, of course, had more interest in building a personal fortune than in falling out with big nobles. So Scots barons scrapped, feuded, looted, and squabbled without restraint. The Wolf of Badenoch and his 'wild wickit Hielan men' burned Forres, to remind the Earl of Moray just who was boss in the north. The Earl of Moray was slow on the uptake, so they burned Elgin next. 'Homicides, robberies, fire-raisings and other misdeeds remained unpunished, and justice seemed banished beyond the kingdom's bounds,' wrote the Moray chronicler.

Robert III and his queen, Annabella, had seven children. Three of the four daughters were married to Douglases. One of male twins, born in 1384, survived. His elder brother, the Earl of Carrick – born in 1378–was thought by 1398 sturdy enough to lead an expedition against the Lord of the Isles. This earl, David, was also foolish enough to alienate Robert, Earl of Menteith, his uncle and Scotland's general guardian. A vicious family struggle developed. Poor Robert III tried to sweeten things with new titles. His son became Duke of Rothesay and, on the same day, the Earl of Mentieth was elevated to Duke of Albany. (Typical of Robert III's judgement, the latter title sounded much grander to Scots: 'Albany' evoked 'Alba', the ancient name of all Scotland, while Rothesay was but the king's holiday home.

Rothesay proved headstrong, reckless and foolish, and was soon in open rebellion. The Duke of Albany was instructed by King Robert, at length, to arrest him; that he be 'put in custody for a time until, after punishment by the rod of discipline, he should know himself better'. It is doubtful if Rothesay had sufficient time in prison to profit spiritually. He was seized in January 1402, jailed in Falkland Castle, and there died in late March. Officially he died of dysentery. It is more likely his uncle had him deliberately starved to death. (One of Rothesay's gaolers, a John Wright, was much later granted lucrative revenue by Albany, during the exile of James I and his time of regency. It has the smell of hush money.)

Between Albany and the throne stood only his unhappy brother the king and the eight-year-old Prince James. By 1404 Robert III was fearful of what his brother might scheme next, and Albany was now quite beyond anyone's control. Friends of the late Rothesay were dying mysteriously. The earldom of Mar was seized for the son of the Wolf. The king, determined to protect his surviving son, now Earl of Carrick, declared all royal Stewart possessions an independent territorial jurisdiction – a regality – and began to pension a separate, loyal court around the young earl. By 1406, though, Robert III was so alarmed he despatched the earl to France for his own safety. Officially it was said that James was merely going to acquire 'good habits'. But everyone knew the real reason.

The prince never saw finishing school. It is possible that Albany alerted Henry V; it is certain that, on 14 March, the ship and its cargo were seized by English sailors off Flamborough Head, and the eleven-year-old heir to Scotland's throne was borne to London. Henry sagely declared that England offered quite as good an education as France. So the prince was welcomed into the Tower.

King Robert had once dictated his own epitaph: 'Here lies the worst of kings and the most wretched of men in the whole kingdom.' The news from London was the finish of him. 'His spirit began immediately to fade, his bodily strength ebbed away, he grew pale and such was his sorrow that he ate nothing more until he yielded up his soul to his Creator.' Robert III died on 4 April 1406.

His son proved a much better king, and a very much nastier man.

James I, when at length the English suffered him to return – he was thirty before he could assume personal reign – proved a worthy successor to the mighty Bruce. He was athletic, cultured, dashing. We have poetry too, such as the *King's Quair*, with its lament for the long wasted years of England. In truth James was well cared for by the English, comfortably housed and richly fed. He was of much more value alive. Of his eighteen years in exile, only three were spent in the Tower; most of the time the Scots king enjoyed salubrious castles, including ten years at Windsor itself.

Henry V kept his promise. The King of Scotland was given the best of education. James I took power fluent in English, French, Scots and Latin. He had beautiful handwriting; samples of it are the first from a Scots king to survive. He was by contemporary accounts an agreeable singer, harpist and piper. He was frequently brought to court. Twice he actually campaigned in France with Henry. He was made a Knight of the Garter in 1421. He was an honoured guest at the coronation of Henry's new bride, Queen Catherine. And he excelled in the arts of manhood: archery, wrestling, horsemanship, fencing. One does not have the impression that James was closely guarded or close-confined. That he never tried to escape suggests, perhaps, unhappy memories of childhood; or that high living in England suited him much better than he would later admit. (The Scots had, until his death in 1420, to endure the gentle regime of Albany.)

He fell in love with, and won the hand of, Lady Joan Beaufort, daughter of the Earl of Somerset and a granddaughter of John of Gaunt, fourth son of Edward III. It was a genuine love-match; from the day of their marriage, James seems never to have looked at another woman. Within months of their wedding, in 1424, they were resident as king and queen in Scotland.

James proved a king of courage – and ruthlessness. He moved rapidly to assert his authority, increasing tax, manoeuvring with determination to curb the power of the nobility. In an early sign of Stewart contempt for the Highlands, James I strove too to smash the power of the Lordship of the Isles, the Clan Donald fiefdom which effectively ran the Hebrides as a separate kingdom.

For all his gifts, though, there was brutality too. He was given to summary executions. When Inverness resisted him, the town was burned to the ground. Most unwisely, he broke deals. Highland chiefs were summoned for friendly discussion, and clapped in irons as soon as they arrived. James proved himself unworthy of trust, and so forfeited the loyalty of the ruling class. In 1437 he pushed the barons too far: a plot hatched, and James I was savagely murdered in his apartments at Perth. He was succeeded by his son, James II, a boy of six.

There is a depressing similarity to the Stewart century that followed. Stewart rulers continued to die young, usually violently, and leave infants on the throne, with years to go before they themselves could assume personal rule. Nobles vied for supremacy. Wicked uncles sought it, including physical possession of the young monarch. There was a plethora, of course, of Albanies and Douglases; the abiding power of such Scots robber-barons was dented. Feuds and plotting persisted. Stewart sovereigns continued to fight and tangle with England, to intrigue with France, to smash any independent power in the Hebrides and the Highlands.

James I bequeathed a dark legacy to the dynasty. Decisive he might have been. But he also demonstrated an arrogance that was increasingly to mar Stewart – and Stuart – monarchs; a reluctance to consider any interest other than their own, an inability fairly to consider an opposing point of view. Also, with more and more recurrence, the melancholy of Robert III was to make appearance. The die was cast for a line of thrawn, implacable, and largely gloomy rulers. Five more would meet violent deaths. Virtually all had wretchedly unhappy childhoods.

Four more Jameses followed in immediate succession. The century is too complicated, too repetitive, and too depressing to want to study in very great detail. It was 1444 before James II seized power in his own right, having enjoyed long protection by his formidably clever mother and survived many a machination by yet blacker Douglases. His immediate need was money (especially as he had rather the worse of the bargain in his July marriage to Mary of Gueldres; her uncle, Philip the Good, Duke of Burgundy, demanded an annual settlement upon her of £5,000 (no doubt to keep her in the style to which she would like to become accustomed) and then took his sweet old time paying the dowry. Queen Mary, after all, had married a man with striking deformity: James II had a large prominent port-wine birthmark, and was nicknamed 'Fiery Face' by the disrespectful.

There were also old scores to settle. The Douglases were too mighty to confront. So James II struck at their cadets, the Livingstones. Two of the line were executed. Two were jailed. All Livingstone land was forfeited. The charges – of plotting against James and his 'dear mother' – mattered less than the display of power and the substantial land and cash now seized by the crown. The Douglases were progressively isolated; James moved directly in 1452, killing William Douglas, with his own hand, in a grotesque *auto-da-fé* at Stirling. There followed virtual civil war between Douglases and the king, with much bloodshed and suffering. Scotland further endured bad harvests and endemic plague.

But James II won the war; systematically, too, he gathered earldoms, lands and revenue for the crown. By careful patronage, he built up great support amid state and Church; he even conciliated the Earl of Ross. His mistake, as others before and since, was to take on England. He dreamed of seizing Roxburgh Castle, firmly in English hands, and to this end raised a massive force, equipped with mighty guns, in which James took obsessive interest. He was a soldier at heart, a warrior, and fascinated by artillery. Which was why, on 3 August 1460, he was standing right beside a cannon, happily bombarding the Roxburgh ramparts, when it exploded and killed him.

His son, King James III, was eight. He has been described by Michael Lynch as the most gifted – and most unpleasant – of Scots kings. The country was better governed in his minority than it was under his personal rule. He may well have been homosexual. Certainly he favoured the company of low-born, good-looking young men; he preferred music to athletics, religion to warfare. He particularly shocked the old nobility by his indiscriminate honours. A blacksmith, a tailor and a musician won titles from him. A mere architect was made an earl. He was incompetent as a ruler, milking the country for every tax and duty and emolument imaginable; daft enough deliberately to debase the coinage. He warred with his brothers. One royal earl was imprisoned, and there died; men spoke of murder. The Earl of Albany fled to exile. All the time, somewhere in Scotland, trouble brewed. The year 1472 saw the one abiding achievement of James III: he had been granted Orkney and Shetland as surety by his father-in-law, the King of Denmark, against a promised dowry; the Danes defaulted and, that year, the islands were permanently annexed to the Scottish crown.

In 1488 the nobles revolted. They had, incredibly, James's fourteen-year-old heir as their willing figurehead. The king lost a critical battle, at Sauchieburn, and took refuge in a barn, where he was killed by an assassin posing as a priest. Naturally, once James IV was safely installed as king, there had to be some show of enquiry into this regicide. Parliament, though, reached no conclusion more convincing than that 'the King happinit to be slane.'

The new regime's position was uncertain. It was two years before James IV felt secure enough to have a coronation. But he rapidly matured and quickly cast off the restraints of minority. He was ruling in his own undoubted right by 1491. In 1493 he boldly seized, tried and executed the Lord of the Isles. The dominion was broken, the title taken for the heir to the Scots throne. As a man, though, James IV is remembered as generous, genial and sophisticated. He was haunted, to a degree, by the betrayal of his father; all his days he wore a spiky iron chain by his bare skin, in penance. He was the last Scottish monarch who could speak Gaelic. And he made a most significant marriage.

Scotland's relations with England were never easy. There were repeated cross-Border incursions. In 1496 James IV even aligned himself with the cause of Perkin Warbeck, who claimed to be one of the lost 'Princes in the Tower' and thus rightful King of England. Warbeck was to him but a pawn, something with which to taunt the English; a Scots force headed south and there was some enjoyable if inconclusive fighting, with James startling observers by his courage: bold to the point of foolhardiness. 'I saw him throw himself into the most dangerous situations . . . He doesn't take the slightest care of himself,' said a bewildered Spanish observer. Ominous words.

The raids did no great harm and were popular in Scotland. Warbeck at length broke the Scottish connection, sailed south to renew his enterprise on a freelance basis, failed, and lost his head. The Spanish mediated and cajoled, impressed by the young Scots monarch and eager that he align his cause with them and not with France; they themselves were already tied to England by the recent marriage of Catherine of Aragon to Prince Arthur. An Anglo-Scots truce was brokered in 1497; the following year saw further negotiation to seal this unusual amity by a royal wedding. How seriously James took this treaty is debatable – he demanded trivial amendments and signed the lot in most casual fashion – but none could doubt his delight in his marriage, in 1503, to the Princess Margaret, daughter of Henry VII, allying the Stewarts to the House of Tudor. The wedding celebrations were the most lavish Scotland had ever seen; Edinburgh fountains ran with wine, and William Dunbar composed a poem, 'The Thistle and the Rose'.

The match of James and Margaret had far-reaching consequences. As a bond for peace, though, it lasted a bare decade. Relations between the two realms deteriorated anew. English diplomats barely troubled to hide their contempt for Scotland's second-rate court. Margaret herself was unhappy. She wrote homesick letters to her father. James himself took solace in the bed of one Janet Kennedy. Still, both James and Henry were genuinely eager to avoid war. The Queen of Scots was not openly humiliated. Henry paid the dowry in full and on time. It was his death in 1509 that brought serious trouble, for Henry VIII was a very different man to his father. Aggressive, headstrong, lacking either caution or skills of emollition, disagreement became conflict and crises became drama. What was all the more serious was that, until Henry and his queen had issue (and the Princess Mary was not born until 1516) the Scottish queen was heir-presumptive to the English throne. Nor was James slow to hint at her importance. Their second son, born the year Henry succeeded, was named Arthur. The insinuation was obvious.

In August 1513, as Henry VIII prepared to invade France, James made ready to invade England. He had the backing of the French king: promises of cash, weaponry, even acknowledgement of his aspirations to the English crown itself. France badly needed a back-door domestic crisis in England. And a good serious pillaging raid was always popular in Scotland. Secret treaty had been made with France in 1512. It promised hard benefits; Henry VIII offered no inducement whatever to abide by the 'Perpetual Peace' made with his father. And Henry had left England in June, with most of his army.

The largest Scottish force ever assembled invaded on 22 August, readily took this garrison and that market town, achieved all that James needed to do. But the king, who had never fought a major battle, could not resist the heady glory of a real showdown with an English army – like the one rushing north under the Earl of Surrey, who sent baiting messages ahead to the King of Scots. James took up the challenge and did battle at Flodden Field. By sundown his army had been smashed, the cream of Scotland's nobility slain, and the king himself – who had led the last charge in person – lay dead, shot with an arrow and smashed by an axe. Dead besides were the Archishop of St Andrews, nine earls, fourteen lords of parliament, assorted chiefs, two abbots, and one bishop, and thousands of Scotland's bravest men.

The new king, James V, was nineteen months old. He was a

new and deadly combination, Stewart and Tudor. He also suffered an appalling liability: his mother. Queen Margaret was a wilful, selfish woman with overweening confidence in her political judgement (which, in fact, was woeful). Within four months of Flodden she married again, to the Earl of Angus. The marriage failed. She made a fool of herself in Europe, striving for divorce, and took a lover. Her son did not have the domestic serenity he required for final maturity. He grew up, as Ross writes, to be 'the most insecure and unpleasant Stewart of all'. In the meantime Queen Margaret lost control of James, who fell into the hands of the Red Douglases, the family of Margaret's estranged husband. Angus spoiled the prince so shamelessly it is a wonder he did not turn out much worse than he did. Whatever James asked for, he was given. First it was horses, fine clothes; later, as James grew to pubescence, Angus supplied him with whores. This was meant, of course, to keep the king a foppish and obedient creature under the Douglas leash. But time passed and James grew. He grew, too, to detest his captor. In 1528 the king escaped, disguised, to reunite with his mother (now divorced and remarried) and begin personal rule. Angus was lucky to escape with his life.

James V was of odd appearance, unhandsome rather than ugly. He had fine Stewart features and bad, pallid Tudor colouring. Observers commented on his eyes: they were cold, flickering, and reminded some of a snake. He was a sickly child and never, in fact, of robust health. He was prone to collapse in crisis. Some have subsequently spoken of psychosomatic illness. He may well, though, have had porphyria; another addition to the Stuart (and, indeed, Hanoverian) inheritance. His daughter, and grandson, certainly had. The king had another problem: his woeful education. Angus had done little more than provide for the gratification of lust. His Latin and Italian were deplorable; his French hesitant. Much more significant, he was the first King of Scots unable to speak Gaelic. He showed aptitude only in music. He was prone – even as king – to disguise himself and go about his subjects incognito, as the 'Goodman of Ballanbreich'. Fornication, as much as privacy, was his motive.

In noble family tradition James managed to beget at least seven illegitimate children – three before he turned twenty. (Three won benefices in the Church; another was made Earl of Moray, and put his own mark on history.) He did not marry until 1537, and his first queen – Madeleine of France – died only seven weeks after her arrival in Scotland.

King James V had a mean, vindictive streak. He was also greedy. He taxed and extorted without mercy; he spent grotesquely. The court became spectacular in furnishings and apparel. He built grandly: Linlithgow, now ruinous, is his most celebrated folly. 'This King inclineth daily more and more to covetousness,' wrote an English agent in 1539. But, more significant for his own people, was the grand Palace of Holyroodhouse, still a royal residence today, with its Renaissance spires and graciousness of the Loire. Here his daughter, heavily pregnant, would watch in terror as an aide was stabbed to death before her eyes; here, in the happiest weeks of his life, the Young Pretender threw parties, with music and dancing, in his 1745 occupation of Edinburgh.

James V also began vigorously to persecute the rising Protestant movement. He was well aware of the corruption in the Scottish Church. But his private debauchery went alongside conspicuous public piety. James V did toil hard for Scottish interests abroad. And he does seem genuinely to have cared for the poor, who did remember him with affection; they perceived him as one out to protect them from noble depredation. The Scots nobles all feared him; most detested him. He moved with vicious speed and malice against any family who offended him – or any family the king plainly did not like. He had some zest for showmanship. He made a spectacular Highland cruise in 1540, right round Cape Wrath and the Pentland Firth, circumnavigating Scotland, in twelve mighty armoured ships, collecting hostages – sons of chiefs – for education in the south. There is no doubt, for all his nastiness, James V firmly imposed the rule of law.

But his second marriage, to Mary of Guise – and, of course,

by this time religion, for Henry VIII had broken with Rome –
drove him to renew the Auld Alliance with France. His
mother though was still about, complicating everything.
The Church was so unpopular in Scotland, too, that many
tacitly admired the English king. James made one dreadful
mistake. Having agreed to meet – and treat – with Henry, at
York, in 1536, he simply stood him up. Henry VIII arrived
but James V did not. It was a slight the old monster never
forgot.

Nemesis struck James V with awful haste. In 1540 he had
everything: a secure realm, a secure succession (two infant
sons by his new queen), much wealth and great standing at
home and abroad. Then, in April 1541, both his sons died.
European politics suddenly marginalised Scotland, as France
and the Holy Roman Empire fell out, and both appealed to
the English for support. Henry VIII's stock recovered in
Europe. By the end of the year James V had lost the initiative.
If Henry now raided, no foreign power would come to his aid.
In October the dowager queen, Margaret, died: another
weapon against Henry now gone. James was sick. His judgement faltered. Henry VIII was insulted again. There were
more cross-Border skirmishes, followed by what was fast
becoming a Scottish tradition: humiliating defeat, by a smaller
English force, in set-piece battle. At Solway Moss, in November 1542, the Scots were routed by an army a quarter their
number.

James V simply collapsed. He retreated to Peebles, then
Linlithgow – where his queen was fast approaching another
confinement – and at last to Falkland, where he took to bed
and stayed there, in the blackest and most despairing melancholy. The King of Scots simply turned his face to the wall and
willed himself to die.

They brought him word, a few days before, that a princess
had been born to his queen. 'It cam wi' a lass; it'll gang wi' a
lass,' murmured King James V. He died on 14 December, only
thirty years old.

2

DAUGHTER OF DEBATE

Mary, Queen of Scots

Mary, Queen of Scots, is one of the most celebrated women in history and a central figure in the traditional pageant of Scottish history; a tradition in which writers and scholars, till very recently, described the past of Scotland in terms of soap opera and stubbornly glamorised thugs, failures and losers.

Hollywood now engineers Scotland's past as romance. But the romance of Mary still enchants, in the most pernicious sense of the word. The queen is both exalted (as tragic heroine, Roman Catholic martyr, a woman of spellbinding personality and beauty) and belittled, by general failure to take her seriously. Mary was, after all, Queen of Scots, though her direct personal reign lasted a mere five years. As queen her judgements, decisions and actions mattered greatly to her country and her subjects. The drama of the lady, her husbands, her dresses, her jewels, her songs and poems, her lapdogs, is but sideshow to the only question that matters: was she a good queen?

A 'daughter of debate', Elizabeth I tartly called her cousin, and in the centuries since her death Mary Stuart has been no stranger to controversy. Her enemies had all the best titles. Mary's execution inspired one to write: *An excellent dyttye made as a generall rejoycinge for the cutting of the Scottishe queene*; another: *Marie Stewarde late Quene of Scotland hath defiled her owne bodie with many adulteries*. The most important, politically, was George Buchanan's *Ane detectioun of the doinges of Marie quene of Scottes*, a sustained diatribe rushed forth, at the behest of Scotland's new regime, to assuage English opinion in the wake of Mary's deposal and, critically, to stop Queen Elizabeth from attempting her restoration. On the other hand, there were Mariolaters, such as the French author who produced *L'Histoire et Martyre de la Royne D'Ecosse*. At least, in her own century, the poor woman was taken seriously; her reign highlighting tensions then tearing Christendom, her life and prospects critical in European affairs. The starry-eyed twaddle came much later, Mary herself being shrunk in scale from the queen who may or may not have been a disastrous sovereign to the woman who may or may not have flirted with Rizzio; connived in the murder of her second husband as she romanced with the man who was briefly to be her third.

And still it pumps out: the books, booklets, the films and dramatisations. Jenny Wormald acidly notes that, in one edition of the British Library *Catalogue of Printed Books*, 455 titles were devoted to Mary Stuart. Only another Mary, the Blessed Virgin herself, won more. Mary Tudor, a much more important figure, had inspired but seventy-three.

The story of Mary, Queen of Scots, is indeed one of glamour, romance, passion, courtly splendour, rise and fall and tragedy.

It is, arguably, the story of a ruler of demonstrable incompetence, a Queen of Scots who disliked her own country more than any of her predecessors, never in truth knew it or understood it, proved a calamitous judge of character, and spent most of her life ignoring the throne of Scotland (which she actually held) and dreaming of the throne of England; a dream which, in the end, cost the queen her head.

It is also, arguably, the tale of an intelligent, enthralling and beautiful queen, who in the early years of personal rule governed with skill and cunning, until derailed by infatuation and marriage to a boorish, drunken, inadequate cousin. She spurned the only man, perhaps, who truly loved her for herself; he went mad, and died held close-confined by his appalled relations.

The life of Mary is one of romance, tragedy and mystery. Yet the whole period of her reign spans decades of great historic importance. To her womb we trace all subsequent monarchs; to understand the compounding disaster of her

Stuart successors, we must study the life, reign and times of Mary in some depth.

Mary was born in the Palace of Linlithgow on 7 or 8 December 1542. (It is typical of her enigma that such a straightforward detail of biography remains uncertain. She herself always insisted it was the 8th; it suited her, because that is the Feast of the Immaculate Conception.) She was the daughter of James V, who never laid eyes on her. A week later he was dead and she was Queen of Scots. Scotland faced another dreadful minority reign, with all its instability and terrors. The infant queen's own son would one day write righteously of his grandfather's end, punished by God for his fornications, bereft of two heirs male, leaving only 'a double curse behind him to the land, both a Woman of Sex, and a new borne babe of age to rule over them'.

James VI did not exaggerate. This was an age when the concept of a queen regnant was, to most, ludicrous, even alarming; an age when women were viewed purely in terms of relation to men, when wives were absolute subjects, in thrall-dom to their husbands. Henry VIII had fought a frantic – indeed, homicidal – marital campaign in desperate effort to beget a lawful male heir; he had to divorce one wife, behead another, and break with Rome to achieve it. The infant Mary's succession was an occasion for alarm and fear throughout the land. Scots had good reason to be afraid. Henry VIII, now old, alcoholic, bloated and vicious, was not slow to exploit the situation.

The little queen was crowned on 13 September 1543, at the unprecedented age of nine months: itself an indication of the panicked atmosphere. (It was also the thirtieth anniversary of the Flodden disaster.) One can imagine the concern for her wellbeing. Stuart prospects hung as a thread on this infant's life, and her survival – in such a time of high infant mortality – was much doubted. In March her mother deliberately ordered the child unswaddled and displayed to the English ambassador, Sir Ralph Sadler, winning his optimistic report to London: 'it is as goodly a child as I have seen of her age, and as like to live, with the grace of God.' In July panic struck, when the infant fell ill. But Mary recovered, teethed, and grew.

Scotland had survived a good few minority reigns. But Mary's sex put its infant sovereign in a most difficult position. She was a star prize in the cynical marriage games of European royalty. If she married a foreign prince, Scotland could be subjected to an alien crown. If she was betrothed to some native Scots aristocrat, there were all the associated perils of faction, alienation and civil war. The matter was complicated, too, by religion, for the Protestant party was gaining strength, and the Reformation well under way in England. And Mary – most awkward of all – was more than Queen of Scots; only the lives of King Henry's children, and the old brute himself, stood between her and England's throne. In her person she would bring to her husband a kingdom as well as a dowry and, in real possibility, those of England and Ireland.

Her accession was the signal for England and France to seek, with new skill and energy, a decisive part in the affairs of Scotland. France had a natural ally in the queen dowager, Mary of Guise; her cardinal brother was a personality of force in the French state. Mary, too, had hardly settled in Scotland; she had been its queen for barely four years. In previous minorities the queen dowager, whoever she was, enjoyed great influence. But the part had been badly damaged by the antics of Queen Margaret, widow of James IV, whose colourful personal life (and utter lack of political judgement) caused chaos both in Scotland and England. Nor had Queen Mary enjoyed the time to establish her own presence on the national consciousness. Largely ignored by the Scots nobility, locked out of high counsels, entrusted with nothing more than the safe custody of the infant monarch (and even that under close supervision), the new queen dowager naturally looked to France.

If France had this important ally, England had a powerful motive. Henry VIII saw his chance to force a marriage, of the infant Mary to his own heir-apparent, the little Prince Edward. The Earl of Angus, the most Anglophile of all Scots nobles – he had been exiled to England since 1528 – was called to Hampton Court, and groomed for his part as an ambassadorial Cupid. So he travelled north with other 'English lords', Scots nobles of Protestant sympathies, such as the Earl of Bothwell, or Lord Maxwell (captured by the English at Solway Moss, but swiftly returned to push Henry's agenda), and other Solway Moss hostages.

Against them was the queen dowager, and David, Cardinal Beaton, a debauched prelate of great guile, long informal diplomat for James V – a Catholic, pro-French party. Between them all, unconvincing and unfeared, so irresolute no one took him very seriously, was the new heir-presumptive, James Hamilton, Earl of Arran. As a great-grandson of James II, the tiny queen's death would make him King of Scots. It was this uninspiring fellow – the queen dowager described him as 'the most inconsistent man in the world; for whatever he determineth today, he changeth tomorrow' – was made governor-general of Scotland and tutor – or guardian – of the little queen; an astonishing slight on the queen dowager. Mary of Guise was a smarter politician than him, or the rest of the pack: her fierce Catholicism apart, she deserves more regard than she has generally enjoyed.

Morale, and ethics, at the Scots court sank low. Bribery, gossip, back-biting, treachery, and endless intrigue left the nation sorely led. The governor-general, in the whole nest of lies, was presently in the thrall of the English lords. In 1543 Arran followed the Henrician example and permitted production of the Bible in the common tongue, rather than in the hitherto exclusive Latin Vulgate: a major Protestant advance, and the first concession to an ever more vociferous Reformation lobby, which saw each such yielding as an excuse to press for more. But Arran's own religious conviction was as muddy as the rest of the man. In the reign of James V he had been blacklisted as a heretic. Arran, among other crimes, had dismissed the Pope as a mere bishop, and that 'a very evil bishop'. But, now he and his sons stood so close to the throne, he was loth to part with Catholic sympathy. Some disputed Arran's legitimacy: there were grounds for doubt about the validity of his parents' marriage. The Church – the Roman

Church – could alone judge the question, to the satisfaction of what was still, save England, a generally united Christendom.

Yet Arran signed Scotland to the Treaties of Greenwich, which, sealed by the intended marriage of Queen Mary to Prince Edward, proclaimed peace between Scotland and England throughout the reigns of Henry and Mary; further stipulating that, after her tenth birthday, the queen should remove to England to complete her education. It was not the best of deals for Scotland, but it promised precious peace to the Borders, and some stability for the realm; the treaties would have held had not old Henry started to push his luck.

The English king began to demand Mary's transfer to England as soon as possible. Further, he pointedly failed to ratify the Treaties of Greenwich within the agreed two months. Some Scottish ships, sailing forth innocently in the belief their country was at peace with England, were seized by Henry's navy. The result, of course, was to rouse nationalist pride. Henry had exposed himself as treacherous, even belligerent. So the regime of the English lords, quite discredited by events, collapsed. Cardinal Beaton, and his faction, seized control of affairs. Arran weakly trimmed his sails and kept his titles. The Treaties of Greenwich were repudiated. And the Queen of Scots was hastily bundled away from Linlithgow to the fastness of Stirling Castle. By the end of 1543 Scotland and France had renewed the Auld Alliance.

Henry VIII was furious. As always, in any frustration in reign or life, he resorted to violence. (This was the man who, for no particular reason, had executed his sixty-seven-year-old Plantagenet cousin, the Countess of Warwick; the executioner, inexperienced, panicked when the first axe-stroke failed, and rained blow upon blow on the wretched old lady's head, neck and shoulders before at last she died. It was but one of many grotesque cruelties in the Great Harry's life.)

There followed the Rough Wooing: one of the most vicious assaults on the Scots Lowlands ever launched by the English. Henry, determined on his matchmaking enterprise, sent forces north with murderous orders of fire and sword. The instructions were most detailed. Maximum damage was to be wrought on Scots property, livestock, standing crops, stores and goods. The campaign endured two years. Villages, market towns, churches and abbeys were razed. Many hundreds of innocent people were slain. Edinburgh Castle barely failed to yield to a ferocious English siege. One particularly mean incursion was deliberately timed around a season's harvest, when ripe, brittle corn was fired by the acre. By the end of 1544, as violence and terror spread through the realm, the Queen of Scots had been taken to still further refuge, at Dunkeld; as the crisis grew still further, the child was removed again, to the island refuge of Inchmahome, on a Perthshire loch.

Such rapine and bloodshed did not, of course, encourage the Scots to think again; rather, it inflamed the land in anti-English sentiment. But their sufferings also began to discredit the power, and judgement, of Cardinal Beaton. King Henry, too, rightly saw Beaton as his principal opponent in Scotland, and Roman Catholicism with him. Two further streams of English policy fast developed, on top of brutal warfare: to foster the Reformation movement in Scotland, at any cost; and to remove Cardinal Beaton. In 1544 the order was expressly given to the English forces to 'turn the Cardinal's town of St Andrews upside down, leaving not one stone upon another'. And English agents fostered and abetted assorted plots to remove Beaton by assassination.

Yet it was now that the queen dowager began at last to win real influence. Her goals were secret, but to posterity plain: to secure a French marriage for her daughter; to remove the child from Scotland as quickly as possible; and to persuade the Scots that fast, abiding alliance by marriage to France, even if wounding to national pride, was preferable to extinction at the arms of England. The queen dowager had the disadvantage of her sex; but, in subtlety, she was more than a match for Arran, the main advocate of a Scots marriage for the queen, and too guileless to hide the hope that his own son and heir might be the husband.

In any event, as the English harried the Lowlands still, fewer and fewer greatly cared whom their infant monarch might marry; Scotland, on top of everything else, was on the brink of civil war over religion.

It is fashionable today to deplore the Scottish Reformation. Wild images are peddled of crazed mobs smashing up cathedrals, destroying priceless and beautiful art, demagogue preachers at their head. Four hundred years on, Lord Boothby proclaimed the Reformation a national disaster; a cousin of our present queen, Lord Harewood, has dismissed John Knox as a 'tiresome old thunderer'.

What nothing can deny is the appalling state of the unreformed Church in Scotland. One need not resort to contemporary Protestant tracts. T.C. Smout says bluntly of this period: 'Scotland had been a Catholic country with peculiarly close links to Rome for five hundred years . . . the Scottish Church had long been remarkable for the depth of its corruption.' Examples abound: he cites them. An incumbent priest at Linlithgow, in 1456, was obliged to declare that he would 'neither pawn the books, plate and vestment of the town kirk nor maintain for his enjoyment "a continual concubine". It does not sound somehow as if his sponsors would have had much objection to his enjoyment of an occasional concubine.'

Many monastic houses, convents and so on, had a bad reputation for licentiousness. By the mid-sixteenth century, with the exception of the Carthusian order (deliberately imported by James I in a desperate effort to lend holy men some respectability in his realm) Scots monasteries had 'long since ceased to be the vehicles for spirituality. They had become nothing more than property-owning corporations.' There abounded men best described as secular clerics, who had won – or bribed to obtain – abbotships, so winning the revenues of the relevant monastic lands. Nor had the royal house set an example. James V, in 1532, had taken advantage of Rome's struggle with Henry VIII to win, from the Pope, titles of titular abbot for his three illegitimate baby sons, thus securing each land and wealth for life.

Friars roamed the land, begging for a living, hugely resented by the unordained poor. Most monks were lazy, many illiterate, though, by and large, their lives were less scandalous than those of their abbots. The lewdness of Scots nuns – not that there were many of them – was notorious; Rome, in 1556, was sufficiently concerned to commission a graphic report of their prostitutions. Most nuns could not write their own names. Discipline had so collapsed in Scots orders that few nuns even bothered to live within a convent's walls. Nor was the regular parish priesthood much more respectable; great damage had been wrought by the Scots crown winning, from the 1300s onwards, power of patronage over the Scots bishoprics. No Pope dared oppose a King of Scots in filling a diocese. So Scotland soon had plenty of wicked placemen bishops. Along with abbots and other prelates, they made merry, and lived most well, on the revenues of their spiritual office. Monies due to parish priests, for their own support, never reached them.

As a result the priests, denied any alternative for survival, preyed rapaciously on the poor people of Scotland. Some won or haggled their way to possession of several livings at once. Some started businesses. Some screwed every last penny out of parishioners for the most elementary ecclesiastical services; commonly, a priest demanded a cow as price for conducting a service of burial. Nobody, in this mean culture of religion, spent much money on buildings, many of which slid into deplorable disrepair. And there were untold abuses of power, high and low: many a recorded instance of priests saying mass half-drunk; priests scarcely able to read; priests begetting bastard children. A Jesuit, no less, woefully reported to Rome in 1562 that the Catholic clergy of Scotland were 'extremely licentious and scandalous'. Cardinal Beaton himself exemplified the state of affairs. He held three rich livings at the same time, and had fathered – and openly supported – twenty illegitimate children.

'The destruction of parish churches and abbeys which popular legend blames on the followers of John Knox,' writes Smout, 'is only partly attributable to the Protestants. More is due to the shameful negligence of the old Church, to the savagery of English armies, particularly . . . in the Rough Wooing, and to prolonged neglect of landowners whose property the fabric of the abbeys often became.'

There were two strands to this movement of Reformation. One was the development of a radical force, taking the doctrines of Luther to their logical conclusion: they – men such as John Knox – sought to create an entirely new Church in Scotland, a whole new order, autonomous in its affairs, national in its bounds, owning no head but Christ himself, no statutes but those of its own courts, no doctrine but those supportable in Scripture, and in no sense professing allegiance to the Pope of Rome. The second strand was a movement of counter-Reformation: to reform and renew the Church, within the Roman order, and purge it of its notorious corruptions. But such an internal renewing could not be launched until the removal of Beaton, and by then – not least because of the political situation in Scotland as a whole – it was far too late.

We might also, in passing, demolish another myth: that the Scots were a people of peculiar intolerance, who fought out their religious disputes by sword, prison, torture and fire. In fact, in this terrible era of Christendom, as Europe shook to its foundations, as thousands (on both sides) were slain on charges of heresy, the Reformation era in Scotland was one of remarkably low bloodshed. When the Reformation at last triumphed, in 1560, only twenty-one Protestants had been martyred; at the very most (and that is giving Catholic claims the benefit of the doubt) there were but three Roman Catholics, ever, put to death for their faith in Scotland. Scotland saw no Smithfield; no Massacre of St Bartholomew's Eve; nothing was inflicted on Scots Catholics as befell their English brethren in the last decades of the sixteenth century.

Yet, whatever the land, it was still an age of bloody cruelty, of violence. In March 1546 George Wishart, leading Protestant preacher, most gentle of men, was burned at the stake in the castle of St Andrews; watching the spectacle, comfortably cushioned, were Cardinal Beaton and his bishops. Three months later a band of Protestant lairds, disguised as stonemasons – Beaton, in these increasingly uncertain days, was refortifying his base – burst in upon the cardinal as he lay recovering from a night of exertion with his present amour, Marion Ogilvy.

Beaton was held at swordpoint. He was pressed to repent of the slaying of Wishart. Then he was hacked to death. His butchered body suffered untold indignities – 'ane callit Guthrie loosit done his ballop's poynt and pischit in his mouth that all the people might see', a detail best left in its original Scots – before the assassins hung Beaton's remains from a castle tower. Whether acting in concert with England, or not, they now occupied the castle and appealed to England for help. England was slow to act; at length, France intervened. Besieged, the assassins retrieved Beaton's corpse, pickled it in salt, and stored the barrel in the castle's celebrated Bottle Dungeon.

At last, in January 1547, Henry VIII went to meet his God. Edward VI was only nine years old: both realms had child sovereigns. A council of regency was established in England, headed by the Earl of Hertford, who had led much of their force through Scotland in the Rough Wooing. As Lord Protector, and further ennobled to the honour of Duke of Somerset, he pursued the wooing with still more vigour. Somerset was too late to save the reformers at St Andrews – they were besieged and overcome by the French – but, in September 1547, he inflicted crushing defeat on the Scots army at Pinkie Cleugh, near Musselburgh. Thousands were killed. Some 1,500 Scots were taken prisoner. What remained of the Scots army was chased to the very gates of Edinburgh; only the continued stronghold, still fast, of the city's castle blocked further English triumph.

England went from the success of Pinkie Cleugh to pursue a policy of strategic occupation. Assorted strong positions on the east coast of Scotland – in Berwickshire, Lothian, Fife – were seized and fortified. A standing army was established at Haddington, south of Edinburgh, able to dominate the capital. It was the final disaster for Arran: he had lost Beaton; he had presided over the Pinkie débâcle. In the meantime he and his house had shamelessly feathered their nests. Arran, in six years as governor-general of Scotland, tutor of its queen, had brought the realm to humiliating lows. Support for a marriage between his heir and the queen fast evaporated. The Scots wanted the English out. The only source of succour was France. And France would demand but one price: the marriage of the Queen of Scots to the heir of their own throne. A Scots council of war gloomily accepted this reality in November 1547. The queen's exile to France seemed likely; the occupation of Scottish strongholds by French forces seemed their best guarantee of national survival.

By year's end fifty French captains had reached Scotland. In the Scots camp outside the fortifications of England's Haddington garrison, negotiations were made and a deal was at last signed between Arran and the envoys of Henri II in January 1548. Arran committed himself to summon the Scots parliament, and gain its assent: Mary, once betrothed to a Prince of Wales, was now instead engaged to marry the Dauphin Francis. She was to be taken to France as soon as possible. French forces would occupy key fortresses and strongholds in Scotland. Arran's reward for this would be a French duchy – that of Chatelherault – but he was forced to allow his heir, the Master of Hamilton, to depart for France with the queen. He knew the lad was to all intents and purposes now made hostage; a measure certain to assure Arran's continued compliance with French policy. The hapless Master of Hamilton was well used to this role: he had, in the previous two years, been hostage both of Cardinal Beaton and, later, Beaton's murderers.

By June the French were in Scotland in force: a well-equipped army of 6,000 men, including Italian and German mercenaries, well armed, with skilled engineers. In July parliament met and endorsed Arran's compact, asking only that the French king should defend Scotland as he defended his own realm, without compromising its independence. It was the best deal on offer: the Scots knew it.

In March Mary had almost died: the illness is unknown, but it was probably measles. The French already had a dim view of Scotland's healthiness for a little queen. To them it was a grim, dark, damp, backward little place, rude of custom and squalid of abode. Now that all else was in place, it was time to sweep her to France. Henri II sent his own royal galley.

On 7th August, at Dumbarton, after what must have been an emotional farewell for the queen dowager, the little girl set sail, accompanied by her three bastard brothers, and her guardian, Lord Erskine, and her governess, Janet Stewart, Lady Fleming, an illegitimate daughter of James IV.

She was also joined by a personal train of noble children, about her own age, of whom Mary Fleming, Mary Seton, Mary Beaton and Mary Livingston are remembered as 'the Queen's four Maries'. (In fact the tale told in the traditional Scots song of that name – Joan Baez memorably recorded it, three decades ago – has nothing to do with Mary, Queen of Scots: it conflates the Four Maries with the tragedy of Mary Hamilton, a Scots lady-in-waiting executed at the Russian court in the eighteenth century.)

It was a perilous journey. There was a real chance – as had befallen James I – that the English would capture the convoy and its precious cargo. Nor could anyone take storm and sea, wind and tide, for granted. Storms, in fact, chased the queen all the way. There was a nasty moment off Lizard Point, when the ship's rudder disintegrated and had to be hastily replaced. Everyone (except the small queen) was horribly seasick.

On 13 August the Queen of Scots landed at France. (There is still much confusion as to where; it was probably on the coast of Brittany.) John Knox – who detested the French, and sought at all times a pro-Reformation, pro-English policy – saw her departure for France as a national betrayal: worse, a move of deliberate Continental corruption 'to the end that in her youth she should drink of that liquor, that should remain with her all her lifetime, for a plague to this realm, and for her final destruction'. His queen was five years, eight months old.

The French kept their side of the Haddington bargain. English forces fighting in France were pressed all the harder; in the meantime, the French gave the invaders a miserable time in Scotland. In 1549 alone the French spent 2 million livres on their Scottish operations. The English had built a line of forts through Border passes and along the east coast; the French countered by building a line of their own. The French could devote more men and more money; they also had better guns. In the meantime the English will to fight fast drained away. The council in London were distracted by two rebellions on their own soil, in Cornwall and East Anglia. Then the Protector fell; Somerset lost power, and in due time his head. Further, the health of Edward VI was now faltering; around this time, he contracted the tuberculosis that would kill him, and the succession was a cause of serious worry.

England was at length compelled completely to withdraw from the south-east Lowlands. Perfidious diplomacy had served England ill, in the end: it had only resulted in the swift flight of the Scots queen to a hostile court, and so defeated its own ends. England made peace with France in March 1550, and with Scotland in June 1551. The latter is of historic importance because it settled, finally, the disputed Border between Scotland and England. The 'Debatable Lands' ceased to be an issue: Berwick, lost to Scotland in the reign of James III, was never restored.

But the French did not leave Scotland. To many – especially the Protestant leaders – it seemed they had but exchanged English occupation for a French one. Arran remained in power, compelled to follow a pro-French policy. His half-brother was made Archbishop of St Andrews. Nobles thought likely to dissent were lured to France, brainwashed and bribed. It seemed that Arran and the general influence of the Hamilton family depended wholly on French goodwill. But matters were not that simple. Arran could not, in law, be readily removed as the queen's tutor until her 'pupillage' expired, on her twelfth birthday. Further, he had shown already his ability to switch when threatened. Whether his son was hostage, or no, it was widely suspected that, should the French strip him of office, Arran would appeal to England, seeking their help 'on grounds of religion'. For, under Edward VI's council, Protestantism was taking firm hold in that land, the Reforming party winning advance upon advance in Church and state.

All this changed dramatically in 1553, when Edward VI died, unmarried, childless. Protestant efforts to alter the succession quickly came to nothing and, in the terms of Henry VIII's will, Mary Tudor became queen. She was the most ardent of Roman Catholics, for whom piety went before any political reality; there was no further question of English support for a putative Protestant Scotland. In 1544 the Queen of Scots turned twelve. Arran was allowed to go quietly, and resigned office rather than face uncomfortable investigation of his stewardship. Mary of Guise, queen dowager, became regent; and from that point all Scots government followed obediently the interests and dictates of French foreign policy.

Mary Tudor's ill-conceived marriage to Philip of Spain led England to renewed war with France. Scotland acquired importance as a second front, and, though the war with England and Spain at first went badly for France, by 1558 it had won the offensive. There was talk of combining a French attack on Calais (England's last foothold on mainland France) with a Scots attack on Berwick. For this the Scots had no enthusiasm. Besides, so heavy now – and so prominent – was the French presence in Scotland that the Auld Alliance had become seriously unpopular. Scotland was under a French regent. A French minister, ever present to guide her hand in the service of France, seemed almost her equal in power. High offices in Scotland were held by French. Scots fortresses were garrisoned by the French. And all those important sons of France were, of course, accompanied by their wives, children and mistresses.

Gordon Donaldson doubts if, after 1550, there were ever more than 4,000 of a French force in Scotland. But it still amounted to what was, effectively, a professional standing army, something hitherto unknown in Scotland. And that same army that vouchsafed protection from England might, on French orders, be turned with equal effect on serious Scots resistance to French whims. More: if France seriously proposed to invade England from the north, that would mean the raising of a Scots army; since Flodden, Scots loathed the very notion of raiding England in the service of France. A rush of volunteers was out of the question and the Scots nobles made plain their lieges would defy all threat or coercion. If a Scots army were to be raised, it would have to be on a mercenary basis – a paid army. But who would pay for it? The French sought a national census, an evaluation of all Scots gentlefolk, and their wealth in heritable or movable estate – as a prelude, of course, to heavy taxation. This amazing scheme was rejected by parliament. France had made itself seriously unpopular.

So stood her realm; how fared the queen? On 24 April 1558 she was married, in the splendour of Notre-Dame, and in a ceremony of grotesque magnificence, to the Dauphin Francis, and enjoying easily the happiest years of her life. By now she was herself, to all intents and purposes, French; French in interests, affection, religion and outlook, and showing little interest in the land which looked on her as its queen. She had been near-idolised in France, even on her arrival from Scotland as a child of five, widely hailed as a pertly glamorous child-queen, seeking refuge in fair France from grim Scotland and the dastardly English. Little as we know of Mary's early childhood, we know that by five three things were established: she was most biddable in temperament; she was charming; and, physically, she was very pretty.

In France her dominant influence was Antoinette of Guise, her grandmother, a tough, kindly, most clever lady who enjoyed astonishing longevity; Mary survived her by only four years. Then there was the queen, Catherine de Medicis herself; most loving of mothers, most deadly of rulers. There was the king's mistress, Diane de Poitiers. And there was Mary's uncle, Cardinal Guise, who would be a leading light in the Council of Trent. It was not long, either, before the Queen of Scots met her betrothed: the Dauphin Francis. The contrast struck many. She was a lively, ruddy, healthy little girl: the Dauphin was a thin, ailing, puny thing, never strong. Courtiers sighed romantically over them, and there was much sentimental twaddle concerning the childish pair: it is plain, though, that both children liked each other, and Francis – at least – was brought to genuine love of his wife.

It was also apparent that, by the standards of her day, the

Queen of Scots was considered a great beauty. She had very fine skin, and the white complexion thought fitting, and magnificent, very fair hair: as a grown woman, it was auburn. Her features were well defined, almost sharp; her nose, late in life, appeared rather too long. Her grandmother wrote admiringly of Mary's well-formed mouth and chin, her almond-like eyes. Famously, Mary grew to be extremely tall. She stood five feet ten inches as an adult. Even today, this is thought a lot of woman: then, it was a proud (and unusual) height for a man.

It was in France that the queen seems first to have enjoyed any formal education. When she landed she could speak nothing but Scots, a tongue the French thought barbarous, though she was wise enough never to lose it. She was not long resident when King Henri, eager to Frenchify his charge as fast as possible, sent away her Scottish suite, including even the four Maries, and surrounded her with gilded French children, of which his own daughter, Elisabeth, became perhaps the closest friend Mary ever had. By adulthood she spoke French with great skill and eloquence, and it was the language she naturally thought in – and spoke – for the rest of her life.

She was not given the firm, bluestocking education that honed the fine intelligence of her English cousin, Elizabeth. Mary, though, was not a fool: she was bright, eager to please, and naturally curious, and thus most easy to teach. She learned Latin, Spanish, and Italian, to fine fluency; she also seems to have known some Greek, for she had Greek texts in her Scottish library. She learned to draw. She danced, brilliantly – it was probably her finest skill – and she mastered the usual accomplishments, singing, needlework, lute-playing and so on. Her handwriting is neat, legible, very rounded; it changed hardly at all from her childhood to the end of her life, save that the letters grew much larger – a disconcerting feature, that.

Her passions, too, were formed in France. She doted on dogs, little ones. She enjoyed physical activity, and had the Stewart love of the hunt and the chase. She liked to gamble.

She had a sunny nature, never keen on confronting reality whenever reality became unpleasant. She detested violence. She loathed ingratitude. In an intolerant age she herself was remarkably tolerant. Mary loved going to weddings, and loved being with children. She was prone to extravagance. She had, on occasion, a witty tongue.

Perhaps her real problem was that Mary's upbringing was too sunny, cossetted and happy altogether. This was scarcely in the family tradition. Her father, and his fathers before him, had endured turbulent and miserable years of childhood. Certainly Mary was separated from her mother (and only once met her again after quitting Scotland for her education). But her years in France were serene and pampered in the extreme. She was surrounded by an army of servants. Life was a constant progress from palace to palace. (In those days, before sanitation, a much ruder age, even the most noble relieved themselves in whatever corner or nook of a grand dwelling was immediately to hand; the houses, soon utterly fouled, were regularly vacated for intensive cleaning.) And the palaces of France, its châteaux and mansions, were a far cry from the much smaller castles and palaces of Scotland.

Every whim of childhood was indulged. In 1551 Mary and her little companions had no fewer than twenty-two lapdogs. There were four big hounds, to boot; there were singing birds and falcons, and the finest horses. (The young queen's favourites were Bravane and Madame la Réale.) Horses were a frequent present to the royal nursery: more exciting (though they did not last long, being destructive and unruly) were two mighty bears, from the Marshal de Saint-André. The king provided the children with one of Paris's finest dancing-masters. They regularly saw wild-animal shows, jugglers, jesters, acrobats, performing players of every variety. There was, of course, much music. There were constant parties and balls.

And then, as the future bride of the Dauphin, Queen Mary was furnished with the richest of wardrobes. Her household accounts show the astonishing fabrics and opulence of attire considered fit even for a little girl: yards of damask, taffeta, satins and silks; colours from the most formal to the most vivid: black, white, orange, red, silver thread and gold thread. She had purses and pearls, shoes by the dozen, furs and gloves and ribbons and collars and chains and belts of gold and fine combs. At the age of nine, three mighty brass chests were already crammed with jewellery.

The household was of considerable size; King Henri was always trying to reduce the pay-roll. By 1558 the Queen of Scots enjoyed ten chamberlains, seven *maîtres d'hôtel*, five doctors, thirty-seven pages of honour, two general controllers, four masters of the wardrobe, twenty-eight *valets de chambre*, twenty-two noble ladies (to help care for the babies of the household), four barbers, three apothecaries, six pantry aides, but only one water-bearer and two laundresses, 'leading one to suppose,' writes Fraser tartly, 'that the royal nurseries were more luxurious than they were hygienic'. And how they ate, all of them! On a single day in 1553 the household munched through some 250 loaves of bread, eighteen good joints of beef, eight sheep, four calves, 120 chickens and pigeons, twenty capons, six geese, three deer and four hares.

In such a fantasy, it is hard to imagine that the Queen of Scots long pined for her native land. Nor is there any evidence that her tutors – or anyone else – sought to instruct her in its history, traditions and problems. She was being groomed, most intensely, as fair and fit consort for the next King of France; he, presumably, would have effective charge of Scotland on her behalf, and the queen's northern kingdom would be bound to France, perpetually. And, if any further proof of Mary's lack of commitment to her own people were needed, it would be furnished dramatically at her wedding.

Yet so much hinged on the life of this girl that her health and welfare were a matter of obsession to her guardians. From Scotland, the queen dowager fussed incessantly; the surviving correspondence of mother and daughter shows that, even amid all the burdens of the Scottish state, Mary of Guise found time to fret about the tiniest details of her daughter's routine and habits. She was most concerned, perhaps, with the queen's religious instruction, but even her counsel on this betrayed awareness of the fragility of life in that era. Wherever the court went, for instance, the queen's own private communion vessels went, lest she be infected by some loathsome disease from a common chalice.

Mary's health deserves more attention than it has often received; in the personal, near-absolute reigns of those days, any illness or vulnerability of a sovereign had major political significance. She had a robust childhood; the first sign of trouble ahead appeared in her adolescence, and, apart from the onset of puberty, with its complications, may have owed something to the situation in Scotland. From 1554 her mother was regent. Affairs in that land became more vivid to Mary, and – guided especially by her uncle, Cardinal Guise – she was manoeuvred into some bizarre constitutional games. In 1556 she signed a quite improper Instrument of Revocation, effectively putting off her majority and prolonging the regency. At Guise's specific suggestion, too, she began to send her mother the equivalent of political blank cheques – plain sheets of paper with her regal signature, Marie, penned at the bottom. (All her life, in fact, the Queen of Scots signed in the French form.)

What exacerbated the strains on her was a household crisis between 1556 and 1557. It was a tedious domestic drama, at first, not untypical of an overwhelmingly female establishment where some very clever women are trapped in a situation little better than common domestic service. There were arguments over spending. The queen's governess was distrusted widely in the household. There was much begging for funds to spend on yet another lavish royal dress. Finally queen and governess – a prim, self-important woman called Mme de Parois; she had replaced a predecessor disgraced by an improper liaison – fell out. This Mme de Parois saw it as her prerogative to distribute to the deserving, at her own discretion, the queen's outworn, cast-off clothing. The young queen saw otherwise. The queen dowager was dragged in to the dispute. Cardinal Guise became involved. Mme de Parois now began to cause a great deal of bad blood. The queen's letters to Scotland at this time show an increasing hysteria; worse, for a queen, wild overreaction to slight or criticism. She assured her mother that de Parois had nearly been the cause of her death, 'because I was afraid of falling under your displeasure, and because I grieved at hearing through these false reports so many disputes and so much harm said of me'.

The queen, not yet sixteen, seems to have had something close to a nervous breakdown. And there is evidence that others worried overly about her health. There were, of course, fears of assassination, and these were well-founded: in April 1551 a mysterious plot to poison her was uncovered, perhaps at English instigation. But, when the queen was only thirteen, Cardinal Guise was already sending irate letters to Scotland, trying to play down tales that his niece was constantly ailing. In truth – and his letters betray as much – Mary was already plagued by stomach troubles, which would assault her all her life: bouts of abdominal pain, indigestion and vomiting, sitting oddly alongside an undiminished, even fierce appetite. From 1556 she was prone to odd fevers. And, as the de Parois episode illustrates, she formed a habit of responding to situations of extreme pressure by virtual prostration. This was serious.

Mary, like her father, was a hysteric: a queen who would meet psychological stress with physical illness, 'subject to the fatal political weakness of collapsing in time of trouble,' writes Jenny Wormald, '. . . what effect did it have on her kingdom, in this age of religious and political upheaval and trauma, to be saddled with a ruler who shut herself off from reality whenever reality became difficult?'

Contemporaries would describe her as 'melancholy'; say she suffered the 'spleen', 'rheum' and 'fits of the mother'. Modern medicine translates these maladies into gastric ulcer, rheumatism and hysteria. From her teens onwards, certainly, Mary had frequent episodes of illness; her son likewise suffered, and – though he never knew his mother – her ailments were so notorious that he was able to describe her attacks to his own personal physician. Her worst attacks came in later life, and Mary described the sensations of 'the accustumat dolor of oure syde' in pathetic words which still survive. 'Ane rewme that troublis our head gritalie with an extreme pane, and discendis in the stomack, sa that it makis us lately to laik appetite . . . vexed by sickness, with a great vomisement . . . flewme, and colore, the dolour of my syde.' There was also odd, short-term palsy; sometimes she could not use her right hand; sometimes she bewailed 'not being suffered the command of my legs'.

> Attacks often confined her to bed [write two medical historians], and she was melancholy, excitable or distracted. This mental 'instability' together with her recurrent invalidism and inability to move her limbs, her 'grievous pain in her side', and her equally inexplicable recoveries, impressed those around her as histrionic and put on, and she was believed to feign illness as occasion demanded to gain her ends. Mary, Queen of Scots, shares with many sufferers from her illness, living and dead, the fate of being judged 'hysterical'.

Ida MacAlpine and Richard Hunter, in *George III and the Mad Business*, leave the reader in little doubt that Mary – and James VI, and certainly George III, and several of his sons, including George IV – all suffered from porphyria, a rare metabolic disorder, identified only in the 1930s. Attacks can be avoided, by shunning certain triggers: various drugs, large quantities of alcohol; or a diet deficient in protein. But porphyria has no cure. And the disorder is hereditary.

His contemporaries, of course, thought George III was insane; the king suffered cruelly at the hands of barbarous physicians, and history – seeing in his own psyche the roots of these episodes of instability – has, despite MacAlpine and Hunter, cast him in the reviled part of the Mad King Who Lost America. Yet the stability and safety of his country, a constitutional and most limited monarchy, was never imperilled by George III's rare bouts of serious illness; at most, in 1788, his illness might have triggered a change of government. Mary's collapses, on the other hand, risked the gravest consequences.

It is hard not to feel, studying her letters and conduct at this time – and subsequently – that this was a queen with very little sense of self; very little psychological autonomy. She was quite in thrall to her mother, to her uncle, to the French court. Again and again she is described, by approving contemporaries, as 'biddable', 'willing', 'placid', docile', and so on. These might be admirable qualities in a debutante, whose sole aspiration was a good marriage; whose most demanding chore, in subsequent life, would be the hiring of a decent nanny. In a queen regnant, such passivity could spell disaster.

And so we come to Mary's wedding, on that spectacular day in April 1558. There was the setting of the cathedral of Notre-Dame. There was a grand, canopied extension outside, including a twelve-foot arch. The procession was headed by liveried Swiss guards; there marched the heads of France's noblest houses. Musicians, gaily arrayed in red and yellow, entertained on the trumpet, the sackbut, the violin and flageolet. There came a hundred gentlemen-in-waiting of King Henri; grandly dressed princes of the blood; and the princes of the Church, in jewelled and magnificent vestment. There came the groom, the fragile but happy Dauphin; he was quite upstaged, though, by the bride. She wore white – then a daring innovation: in French tradition, it was the colour of court mourning. She wore diamonds, pearls, jewels, a magnificent crown; this included one splendid carbuncle valued in excess of 500,000 crowns.

After the nuptials, most formal and solemn, gold and silver coin was thrown by the basketful to the vast crowd of common people waiting outwith. There followed, later, a 'long and Lucullan banquet'; there was only one jarring note, which might seem ominous, when the bride's head began so greatly to ache under the heavy crown that a lord-in-waiting was called to hold it. Jousting followed, and games, and a grand ball, and then a magnificent supper, followed by a still more magnificent ball, even grander than the first; it featured artificial horses, of gold and silver cloth, and gliding imitation barques, six of them, with rich sails, each carrying two noblemen and seeming to float on the floor as on a real if most celestial sea . . . and so on. Apart from the pother of the crown, and that the Dauphin's favourite horseman had lost an eye in the jousting, it was – no doubt – the biggest day of Mary's life.

But it was underscored by reprehensible diplomacy.

There were two marriage treaties agreed, between Scotland and France, in the months before this extravagance. One was open and one was secret. The official treaty was quite satisfactory to the Scots. Their queen pledged herself to uphold her realm's ancient freedoms, liberties and privileges. As long as she stayed furth of Scotland, the queen dowager was to serve as regent. In the event of her own death, and that without issue, the King of France – and the Dauphin – bound themselves to support the succession of her throne by the nearest heir of blood; which was still the Duke of Chatelherault, sometime Earl of Arran. The Dauphin would, on marriage to the queen, enjoy the title of King of Scotland – and not merely as king consort, but the 'crown matrimonial', giving him full rights in government and regency, equal with the queen. On his accession to the French crown, both nations would be united under a common monarchy; it was agreed fitting, then, that there should be naturalisation of both peoples in anticipation of this. So all Frenchmen were recognised as Scots; all Scots, as Frenchmen. If she were widowed, Mary would have free choice whether to remain in France or return to Scotland. She would in that doleful situation, and whatever she chose to do, inherit the fortune of 600,000 livres. Their eldest male child would inherit both crowns; should there be no sons of their union, the eldest surviving daughter would inherit the Scots crown only.

Such terms were standard of that time in the match of a female heiress to a still more powerful heir. The only thing the Scots refused to swallow was King Henri's request for the crown of Scotland, that it be sent to France for the wedding ceremonies and used for a Scots coronation of the Dauphin. They were probably fearful it might be lost – or kept.

The second treaty – had the Scots lords known of it – would have brought on apoplexy. But its details were kept from them. Mary signed three separate deeds, giving away things that were in no sense, and by no law of God or man, hers to give. The first agreed that, in the event of her death without issue, Scotland – and Mary's claim to the throne of England – passed absolutely to the French crown. The second made over Scotland, and its revenues, to the King of France and his heirs, until France was fully compensated for its expenses recently incurred in Scotland's defence. And, in the third, Mary renounced – in anticipation – any agreement made by the Scots parliament which contradicted or interfered with the foregoing.

This deal is an astonishing indictment of a sovereign queen. She may have been some months short of her sixteenth birthday. She was certainly eager to please; her mother, and her uncle, were delighted with the dispositions. But, in truth, she had consigned her kingdom – the kingdom of which she was queen in her own right – to the status of a French dominion; even a French chattel. She had abolished the lawful Scots succession. She had put Scotland in French pawn. She had repudiated the authority and rights of the Scots estates, her own parliament. 'Young as she was,' seethes Wormald,

> these might be considered the most revealing political acts of her life. They stand as a devastating comment on her view of Scotland, the one kingdom which was actually hers to govern . . . In an age when personal monarchy was the motivating force of government, and kings were straining every nerve to increase their power and authority, she provides the unique spectacle of an adult reigning monarch who did not want to reign.

In England, meantime, Queen Mary was sick, still childless, and in visible decline. A programme of murderous religious persecution – Protestants from every status in life burned at the stake by the hundred, from children as young as twelve to mothers big with child, from meat-porters to a sometime

Archbishop of Canterbury – left her hated and despised by the great mass of her subjects. Even her husband, who had led her into calamitous war with France – and cost England Calais – had coldly deserted her. In October, poor Mary Tudor – in person, the kindest and most religious of women – died. She was succeeded by the sister she detested, Elizabeth, daughter of the 'whore' Anne Boleyn.

King Henri, in France, at once declared his son and daughter-in-law King and Queen of Scotland, England and Ireland. In strict canon law of Rome, he was right. Catholic Christendom had never acknowledged the divorce of Catherine of Aragon by Henry VIII; therefore, the new Queen of England was but the bastard Elizabeth. Her claim was not helped by her birth only a few months after the wedding; clearly, Elizabeth was conceived out of wedlock. And she herself, in an English affectation, claimed to be Queen of France, a status stubbornly proclaimed by every English sovereign since Agincourt, a pretence kept up as recently as the coronation of George III in 1761. There was, in truth, much legal confusion: England's parliament had in times past pronounced Elizabeth illegitimate, but the will of Henry VIII specifically forbade the crown to pass to a foreigner, which Mary certainly was.

Such details, though, were irrelevant. King Henri's action ignored political reality; insulted the new Queen of England; and immediately cast Mary, Queen of Scots, in diabolical light in English eyes. To the end of her days she was regarded with profound suspicion by Queen Elizabeth. For the rest of her life, barring a minority of a Roman Catholic minority in England, the English hated – and feared – the docile, dolorous Queen of Scots.

Her French career rapidly flowered, and fell. In June 1559 King Henri was horribly injured, jousting; his opponent's lance shattered, and shards shafted through the king's throat, and through his visor and through one eye to his very brain. For days he lay, sometimes in stupor, sometimes in agony, sometimes lucid and sometimes not. Infection set in, and after untold suffering Henri II died on 10 July. Francis was king;

Mary, Queen of Scots, was Queen of France. Francis was little more than a boy, and troubled himself little with matters of state. As king, he used the new authority to spend more time hunting and hawking than ever. He probably had not even attained puberty; if the marriage was consummated at all, it remained childless. Many observers of the king – a strange, puny figure – doubted he would ever be capable of begetting children; there are hints he was in some way genitally defective.

In the meantime Scotland was, once again, in mounting chaos. The Protestant party was stronger than ever, and openly soliciting support from England; in October 1559 they were joined by none other than Chatelherault, who could credibly claim the Scottish throne. That same month they briefly occupied Edinburgh, in defiance of a weary, ageing queen dowager. In February 1560 the Protestant 'Lords of the Congregation' made formal treaty with England: the new Treaty of Berwick gave England legal basis for decisive intervention in Scots affairs, and soon English forces besieged Leith, held by the regent and her French troops. (In England, significantly, the stramash was called the War of the Insignia, because of the French king's usurpation of their own royal arms.) It reduced the regent to distraction. Mary of Guise was already very ill; she died on 11 June 1560. When news of her passing at length reached the Queen of Scots, she collapsed, and was ill for days.

The government of Francis could send no further military support; there was enough trouble going on in France. Francis resorted to diplomacy, in his queen's name. Both England and France at length agreed to vacate Scotland, leaving only tiny token forces – sixty troops apiece; in return, Francis and Mary would recognise Elizabeth as Queen of England and give up her arms. The Treaty of Edinburgh was concluded on 6 July 1560. It was on the point of ratification by Francis and Mary when, on 11 August, the Scots parliament embraced the Reformation. In one dramatic week, a Protestant Confession of Faith was promulgated; the Pope's jurisdiction abolished; the celebration of mass utterly prohibited, on pain of death for a third offence. It was revolution; it was the Reformation.

Mary's interest in Scotland and its affairs was likely little enough; it was her husband's problem, the government of France's problem. Then, one Saturday in November 1560, King Francis returned from a hard day's hunting complaining of earache. The following day he collapsed in a dead faint while hearing vespers. Swelling appeared behind his left ear; there was a deep-rooted middle-ear infection, probably a secondary infection from his bad eczema. For days the boy-king suffered and suffered, as much at the hands of his doctors as of his ghastly illness. Soon the infection was in his brain. On Thursday 5 December, a month short of his seventeenth birthday, King Francis died.

Mary, Queen of Scots, was now a mere widow. She hung about France for a few months, lost, grieving, denied influence or much standing. Within the year she would return to Scotland, to rule in her own name and in her own right.

3

MONSTROUS REGIMENT

Mary: The Personal Rule

Previous Stewart sovereigns – enduring tedious and turbulent minorities, or, like James IV, seeing his inheritance threatened by an incompetent parent – had struggled to win direct personal power as soon as possible. We have already seen that Mary was of a most different stamp. Her mother's death effectively paralysed Scots government; yet for fourteen months Mary dallied in France – as queen, as widow – and so laid up a heap of trouble for herself. In her absence the Reformation triumphed. With a sympathetic Protestant sovereign in England, Scotland rapidly cast off the yoke of France. A stable government quickly asserted itself, even in the continuing absence of the lawful sovereign. It mattered not that Mary herself refused to endorse the revolutionary acts on things spiritual; nor that she likewise refused to ratify the Treaty of Edinburgh. She exposed herself as irrelevant; worse, dispensable.

Now she was a widowed queen dowager herself; worse, one without issue, and thus of no political importance in France. She briefly entertained hopes of regaining her position by marriage to the new king, Charles IX, though the match would have required a papal dispensation. It became clear such a restoration was not on offer. The new king was only eleven years old; power effectively resided in the queen mother, Catherine de Medicis, who had little time for Mary and none at all for the house of Guise. So Mary's status and importance in the French court ceased to be. She had, too, her claim to the throne of England. To this the Catholic powers paid lip-service; but neither they, nor any significant bloc of opinion in England itself, were willing to back her bid with force. She was indisputably Queen of Scotland. It was a land she had no real desire to see nor to inhabit again. At the same time it was the best kingdom she had.

There remained the question of marriage. Though Mary cast a hopeful eye about Christendom, no prince showed interest in a slightly used queen dowager; the real prize on offer was Elizabeth, in England, confidently expected to take husband in the near future. Elizabeth was a threat in a more direct sense to Mary: in their present state of relations, Mary's passage by sea to Scotland – or passage by sea anywhere – would certainly invite interference by the English navy. On the other hand, return to Scotland would see Mary under great pressure to marry the Earl of Arran; not Chatelherault, but his son. The Hamiltons remained a powerful faction, balanced only by the house of Lennox. Besides, such a Scottish match would be hugely popular in Scotland. Cardinal Beaton himself had favoured the union. There was an additional – and, in these cynical days of the royal marriage game, most unusual – complication: the Earl of Arran was genuinely in love with her.

They had sailed to France together in 1548 as children. And there seems to have been some kind of flirtation – an understanding – between them that, should Mary fail after all to win the Dauphin's hand, Arran would certainly be head of the list of alternative spouses. She had even given him a ring, which the poor youth took to be a token of pledge; and, when word came that King Francis was dead, Arran lost no time in despatching the pathetic reminder to her. This was all very sweet. But, in the new climate of Anglo-Scottish amity, many in Scotland's ruling establishment – not hitherto sympathetic to Hamilton aspirations – saw advantage to the match. Arran was a gentle, biddable thing most unlikely to wield significant power over his wife, far less the kingdom. Elizabeth herself had declined his hand in marriage; but she, too, was eager to see him bound with Mary. Such a match, surely, would gently guide the Queen of Scots to embrace the Reformation and repudiate the French alliance.

But there was another faction in Scotland too, Protestants in name but moderate in religion, and of more pragmatic temper, who saw it to the realm's best advantage if, first, Mary married almost anyone but a Hamilton; and, second, if she played a more complex, teasing game with the English queen, the better to advance Scottish interests. There was also the passion of the age: this age of Reformation, when men of God spoke in the most intemperate terms; when men of Rome happily burned scores alive to save their immortal souls from heresy. Even John Calvin, that most scholarly and gracious man, had triumphantly hailed the death of Francis in words that still make one wince. 'Did you ever read or hear of anything more timely than the death of the little King?' he wrote gloatingly. 'There was no remedy for the worst evils when God suddenly revealed himself from Heaven, and He who had pierced the father's eye, struck off the ear of the son.'

Mary's immediate response to widowhood was violent grief; it seems to have been entirely genuine; and almost no one else at the French court managed a convincing show of sharing it. And she wrote a poem of genuine power on her loss, of which some lines are worth quoting:

> Le regret d'un absent
> Si je suis en repos
> Sommeillant sur ma couche
> J'oy qu'il me tient propos
> Je le sens qui me touche
> En labeur et requoy
> Tousjours est prez de moy . . .

> The regret of one lost
> As I slide into sleep
> The absent is near
> And alone on my bed
> I feel his touch dear
> In toil or in play
> We are near every day . . .

As Mary left the death-chamber, demoted, she had to dip curtsey to the queen dowager; Francis had been dead but one day when Catherine demanded the return of the crown jewels.

The rest of Mary's time in France passed in a flurry of plot, intrigue and high diplomacy. Much speculation centred on her next marriage. Don Carlos of Spain? The Archduke Charles? The King of Sweden? Arran, of course, was a high favourite. In the meantime some distance appeared, for the first time in her life, between Mary and her Guise uncles. It may be that they now lost interest in her; as they themselves had lost their key role in French political life. But it may also be that Mary was, for the first time in her days, striving genuinely to think for herself. She made a striking impression on some who now dealt with her in her own right, who had long thought her nothing more than a pretty consort. Even William Throckmorton, now Elizabeth's wily ambassador to France – and who had seen Mary as an infant in Scotland – left a meeting much taken by the demeanour of Mary the widow:

> both a great wisdom for her years, modesty, and also of great judgement in the wise handling herself and her matters . . . I see her behaviour to be such, and her wisdom and kingly modesty so great, in that she thinketh herself not too wise, but is content to be ruled by good counsel and wise men (which is a great virtue in a Prince or Princess, and which argueth a great judgement and wisdom in her).

It was, as historians have noted, not just a eulogium to the Queen of Scots but a quiet rebuke to his own queen, whose court was then a byword for frivolity, and who was notoriously loth to trust the judgement of mere men. Only a few months before Throckmorton wrote, Amy Robsart, wife of Elizabeth's favourite, Lord Robert Dudley, had been found dead in mysterious circumstances; there was scandalous talk all over Europe, that 'the Queen of England is to marry her horsekeeper; and he has killed his wife to make room for her!' Mary, hard as it now is to credit, was seen, by contrast, as the model of decorum and good judgement.

Don Carlos of Spain, heir to the Spanish empire, was a tempting match in terms of future status and wealth, though he himself was a puny, feeble, stunted, lisping epileptic of a man. But Catherine, and France itself, opposed the match; the betrothal never came. England was worried too: envoys came and went, sniffing the air anxiously and pressing hopefully for ratification of the Treaty of Edinburgh. Elizabeth and Mary graciously exchanged portraits. There was a much more significant visitor, though, in the spring of 1561: Mary's cousin, Henry, Lord Darnley. He was a grandson of Margaret Tudor, widow of James IV, by her marriage to the Earl of Angus; her daughter of that match had married Matthew Stuart, the Earl of Lennox, who could claim descent (through the Hamiltons) from James II. But Darnley, still only a youth of sixteen, had been raised entirely in England, where his mother's fortunes had been turbulent; she was, indeed, no stranger to the Tower. He was also Roman Catholic. As a resident of England, and so not debarred by Henry VIII's will, he was favoured by England's Catholic party for the succession, should anything untoward become of Elizabeth. Darnley was also very tall and, by the standards of that day, very handsome, with a long oval face and soulful eyes. Certainly Darnley's family hoped he would catch Mary's eye. She graciously received him, and did not forget him; but she still aspired to the Spanish match.

Mary took vacation from court to holiday around her Guise relations (and take advantage of their counsel, away from the baleful gaze of her mother-in-law). It was spring 1561, and on a leg of her travels she met two important Scottish visitors: rival ambassadors, from rival camps.

One was John Leslie, Bishop of Ross, who led Scotland's Roman Catholic party; the other was Lord James Stewart, Mary's half-brother, who spoke for the provisional, Protestant government in Mary's realm. Leslie bent Mary's ear first: he wanted her to *detain* Lord James in France, and then set sail for Aberdeen, where he vowed to have 20,000 men levied and at the queen's service, able to seize Scotland by storm and impose the old religion by force. Mary, who detested violence, refused to listen to a word of it: she saw more importance in Leslie's insistence – and he was right – that her own people longed for her return and that the Scots, of both creeds, would for the greatest part delight to see her home.

Next she met her brother. Lord James Stewart – Mary later elevated him to the title of Earl of Moray – was one of the ablest and most attractive scions of the dynasty, and one of the more impressive Scots of this turbulent period. He was twelve years older than the queen, son of James V by his tryst with Margaret Erskine. Moray was a bastard: but it was conceivable, in real crisis, that the Scots might prefer a strong king of dubious birth to a weak queen of undisputed legitimacy. It is to James's credit that, until she had destroyed herself, he showed unflinching loyalty to Mary, as he afterwards showed to her son. He cared more for power than status. He cared, above all, for order. James was a solemn, unsmiling figure, showing neither his father's charm nor his fierce appetites. But his gravitas made him a most effective man of affairs. He had a subtlety of touch and speech – of course, there was Tudor guile in his blood – and, above all, he could deal well with the English, who thought highly of him. He also had, if not quite a tolerance, a generally moderate outlook on religion; in this he closely resembled his cousin Elizabeth.

Lord James, more than anyone else, prepared the way for Mary's homecoming. Naturally – he had stopped first by the English court to confer with William Cecil and other key ministers – he pressed Mary to embrace the Protestant faith. This she utterly refused to do; she urged him, instead, to change his, proferring fat benefices in France and even a cardinal's hat. James did not push the issue; he declined the Catholic blandishments. (He already had his sights on Moray.) He counselled, before everything, circumspection. 'Buiff all things, madame, for the luif of God presse na matters of religion, not for any man's advyse on the earth!'

The queen declared that she had but one demand: the right to celebrate her own religion in private, including the celebration of mass. Granted that, she would come home without an armed force; she would accept the new religious establishment in Scotland. It was, from the queen's point of view, a successful and encouraging meeting, for her brother saw no credible objection to her enjoying private mass, though he knew many other Scots would be of less temperate outlook. And he impressed his sister as a man of statecraft and judgement, an ally and confidant she could trust. (She might have trusted him less had she known, within days of their meeting, that he had passed on all their conversation – and details of other French dealings – to the English.) It has been suggested he was even trying to set up Mary for seizure at sea, and detention in England. More likely – and with guile rather than dishonesty – he wanted to be on good terms with both queens.

In May Mary had one of her collapses: the strain of the Spanish negotiations weighed heavy on her. By the time she returned to court, in June, she knew any realistic hope of marriage to Don Carlos was gone. And she seems, by the end of her travels, and fortified by her meeting with Lord James Stewart, to have made up her mind: she would return to Scotland. It is worth noting that she did not have to go at all. She was only eighteen years old. The chances were excellent, yet, of a glamorous suitor. Though denied influence at court, she had yet an honoured place, from which it would have been difficult to dislodge her. The Guises might yet regain influence. She had a comfortable French inheritance: much money, and lands. But she was a Stewart by blood, with a zest for adventure, even danger: the same gambling quality that led James II to cannon, James III to low-born company, James IV to Flodden. And, from Scotland, she was well placed to pursue her claims for England; if not to its throne in place of Elizabeth, then certainly to recognition as Elizabeth's heir.

On 10 June the Protestant lords formally invited Mary to Scotland, themselves impressed by the advantages of a malleable, glamorous queen, easy-going in public religious affairs, by birth and blood well suited to worry England, while prepared to support a new ruling order in Scotland the English had approved. Lord James wrote the formal letter. And the most wily William Maitland of Lethington, a close associate of James, wrote in his own stead, promising the queen he would do all he could for her service. Both men had another agenda: they were eager to prevent a marriage of Mary to the Earl of Arran, another of the over-mighty Hamiltons. To that end they wanted the queen back in Scotland, in their own camp and on their own terms. The Treaty of Edinburgh was still a problem, but one best dealt with once Mary had returned. The English, by contrast, were obsessed with it. In July, frustrated, Elizabeth was so angry she launched into one of her toe-curling, ear-burning, fishwife outbursts, humiliating Throckmorton before court, and declaring that in no circumstance whatever would she grant the Queen of Scots safe-conduct past her coasts. It was a foolish tirade. It was even more foolish, as wiser heads saw, to keep Mary on the Continent, where she was far more apt to be enmeshed in popish, anti-Elizabeth intrigues than in her own Scotland.

Mary rose well to this crisis – after another bout of prostrating illness. She responded with dignified and gracious words. She amazed Throckmorton (and onlookers) with several pretty, dramatic speeches, more in sorrow than in anger, speaking well of her queenly cousin; reminding him that she had sailed thirteen years before to France despite the real danger of English interception; that she would sail fearlessly forth again on those high seas, safe-conduct or no safe-conduct, and:

> I trust the wind will be so favourable as I shall not need to come upon the coast of England; and if I do, Mr Ambassador, the Queen your Mistress shall have me in her hands to do her will of me; and if she be so hard-hearted as to desire my end, she may then do her pleasure, and make sacrifice of me; peradventure that casualty might be better for me than to live . . . In this matter, God's will be fulfilled!

It was histrionic, grandiloquent, over the top; it was magnificent, and enthralled all who heard of it.

Calmly, without safe-conduct, Mary made ready to part from France. There were fêtes, parties, tearful farewells; she travelled to Calais, continued to charm Throckmorton on their last French meeting – even sent his wife little presents, of gilt; and pressed once more, ever so gently, for a safe-conduct. Elizabeth, at the very last moment, finally assented; but Mary was off French soil by the time the letter reached Calais. The voyage started badly: a fishing boat sank in the harbour as the queen prepared to sail, and its crew drowned before the horrified eyes of the royal party; and the queen broke down completely as her vessel left the French coast behind, weeping inconsolably, crying, '*Adieu, France, adieu, France . . . adieu donc ma chère France . . . Je pense ne vous revoir jamais plus.*' And, indeed, she never did.

On 19 August 1561 Mary, her retainers (including the four Maries) and party landed at Leith. (An east-coast voyage, and port, were deliberately chosen; a Dumbarton landing would have led her straight into the hands of the Hamiltons, with their own firm plans for her life.) She was met by Lord James Stewart, and her Secretary of State, Maitland of Lethington. So began the personal reign of Mary, Queen of Scots.

Now, horribly as it all fell apart in the end, many historians insist that for the first three years or so Mary presided over a government that ran Scotland's affairs, and defended Scottish interests, with high political intelligence. The keynote was conciliation. It is worth remembering what did not happen. Scotland was not again brought to Border warfare with England. Nor was it caught up in the schemes of France, or Spain, or other Catholic powers. Nor – which could so easily have happened – was the realm torn in civil war over religion. Nor was there an outbreak of persecution, by either Reformers or Romanists. These were stable years; 'amity' was maintained with England, and, guided by the Earl of Moray (as he became in 1562) and Lethington, the queen was cleverly presented, and for the most part acted, as all things to all men.

There is no doubt that one main interest dominated her thoughts and administration: her hope of the English throne. But this could also be played to Scotland's advantage. So, on the one hand, Elizabeth had to be agreeably impressed by Mary's reign over a stable Protestant realm: that meant, as far as possible, coexistence with the Reformed settlement and the Protestant majority. On the other hand, Mary was cleverly advised not to forfeit the support of English Catholics; nor to shun communication with the Pope, and the Catholic powers in Europe. So Mary had mass in her private apartments. But mass was nowhere else permitted in Scotland; more than once, by her proclamation, priests were prosecuted – jailed – for saying mass beyond the bounds of court. She did not ratify the Reformation Acts of 1560. But she did nothing to reverse them. She might – and the crown was desperately hard up – have commandeered the greater part of the wealth of the old Church. But she let by an arrangement dividing those riches, not really to her advantage, between the crown and the new Kirk. And she assented to new legislation which, ratification of 1560 or no, made plain her endorsement of the new order.

Mary, too, following these policies, used all her charm, and striking physical presence, to win support, loyalty. It had been two decades since the Scots had last looked on an adult sovereign. Her height and beauty – and that enchanting, magnetic quality on which so many contemporary writers exclaim – lent added interest; the outdoor pursuits she naturally favoured, course and field and so on, gave her abundant opportunity to show herself before her people. She also travelled, to a remarkable extent, about her realm. She spent five successive springs in Fife. On two summers, 1562 and 1564, she visited Aberdeen, and went as far north as Inverness. She visited Argyll in 1563; she toured widely in the Lowlands. Most of the time she lived at Holyrood; sometimes, though, Mary lived for lengthy spells at Stirling.

Unlike her father, Mary built nothing. No palace, house or lodge lasts as a physical mark of her reign. But her court was one of high culture. The gifted humanist George Buchanan, who would, in time, be her chief vilifier, now wrote Latin songs – *pompae* – and masques for the Scottish court. There were musicians in number: sweet singers, English, Italian and

French. The great James Lauder began his musical career under Mary; and even spent some years with her in English captivity, before returning to adorn the court of James VI. She danced, of course; and, like a true medieval monarch, was concerned to put on great show of magnificence as occasion demanded. It is too easy, learning of Elizabeth's close questioning of visitors to the Scottish court about details of Mary's appearance, dress and accomplishment, to see petty feminine jealousy. The splendour of court, a sovereign's skill in pomp and circumstance, was then a vital element of statecraft.

It was not long before Mary, Queen of Scots, enjoyed considerable popularity. She was keenly tested within days of her arrival, when mass was celebrated in her chapel at Holyrood. Protestant demonstrators sought to break in and disrupt proceedings: Lord James himself barred the door, defying them to lay a hand on his person. Edinburgh folk rioted in the streets; the next Sabbath, in St Giles' – the historic High Kirk of Edinburgh – John Knox delivered a powerful sermon, declaring that he feared one mass in Scotland more than 'ten thousand armed enemies'. He had a point, by his own light: for one, the restoration of Catholic Scotland would, as elsewhere, be the return of fire, faggot and all the most violent implements of repression; and, for another, the queen's chapel did rapidly become a focus for Roman Catholics in Edinburgh and elsewhere.

John Knox and Mary never quite hit it off. Even his loyal biographer, Thomas McCrie, candidly regrets the intemperance of the Reformer's language; but, as he fairly points out, these were intemperate times. Certainly Knox spoke of the queen with ugly words, declaring that she was 'indurate against God and His truth', and once and again proclaimed her certain doom, to the point where even Protestant ministers wondered, sarcastically, if Knox was of 'God's privy council', and forewarned of Mary's destiny. (The antipathy was mutual: Mary described Knox as 'the most dangerous man in the kingdom'.)

Knox and his queen met on one or two occasions, to argue ferociously on religion. To this day folk-myth remembers him as the bounder who made poor Mary cry. This conveniently ignores the reality that Mary herself called him in for these audiences (which was naïve: she had nothing to gain from granting him the royal presence; and Knox made the most of the privilege) and, indeed, that Mary stood a foot taller than her turbulent preacher, and can scarcely have been intimidated. Knox is a complex character. He was a visionary, a revolutionary, something of a nationalist. He made no bones about his conviction that to kill an immoral or godless ruler was, in certain circumstances, justifiable. He had a keen skill in argument and a rough, earthy humour. Knox, in some ways, was centuries ahead of his time: he dreamed, for instance, of creating an order of free parish schools throughout Scotland, and was keenly disappointed that the wealth of the old Church was not collared to such an end.

His great virtue was his courage: at his burial, one rightly eulogised him as 'one who never feared the face of man'. His great fault, like many brave and strong-willed people, was a blatant egotism. Knox seems to have regarded Edinburgh as his personal domain; perhaps he felt upstaged by the pretty young queen. Certainly his contempt for women in power was notorious. In 1558, appalled by the atrocities under the regime of Mary Tudor, and with Mary of Guise in his sights too, Knox had issued the magnificently titled *First Blast of the Trumpet Against the Monstrous Regiment of Women*. 'To promote a woman to bear rule, superiority, dominion, or empire, above any realm, nation or city, is repugnant to nature, contumely to God, a thing most contrarious to His revealed will and approved ordinance; and, finally, it is the subversion of all equity and justice.' In this view he was a man of his age; the Salic Law of France, for instance, expressly excluded women from succession to the throne. But it can scarcely have excited the admiration of his queen.

Lord James was at their first meeting. Mary launched an attack on Knox, for inciting subjects to rise against her late mother and herself, for producing the *First Blast*. Knox graciously allowed that, should she herself rule well, he would not oppose the queen on grounds of her sex alone. On religion, of course, they were irreconcilable. Nor would he retreat from the position that subjects might rightly rise against an ungodly ruler, though, as he charmingly put it, he himself would be 'as well content to live under Your Grace as Paul was to live under Nero'.

'Well, then,' retorted the queen, 'I perceive that my subjects shall obey you, and not me; and shall do what they list and not what I command: and so must I be subject to them and not they to me!'

Knox assured her that, should she subject to God as upheld by his Church, Her Grace would be brought to everlasting glory.

'Yea,' said the queen, 'but ye are not the Kirk that I will nurse. I will defend the Kirk of Rome, for, I think, it is the true Kirk of God.'

'Conscience requireth knowledge,' retorted Knox, 'and I fear right knowledge you have none.'

They met again, some eighteen months later, after Knox had preached against the queen's love of dancing; the Scots court had become a lively place, full of gaiety and merriment, and in dancing the queen fully displayed her natural exuberance. And there were other interviews. The meetings achieved little. The queen had never a hope of gaining the Reformer's love or trust; he himself was less than fair, preaching and writing against her court and hinting at untold depravities. On the other hand, she did win a certain respect: Knox did not again consider her an empty-headed fool, but subsequently spoke darkly of her 'great craft'. Both gave as good as they got in those encounters; both, one suspects, rather enjoyed them.

There were only two serious episodes, in this generally sunny period, threatening the stability of the realm. In Mary's Highland tour in August 1562 she was entertained by the Earl of Huntly, head of the Gordons and the premier Catholic magnate of Scotland. This Huntly lived in the most grand state, and appeared almost to aspire to monarchy. Certainly he was immensely powerful, and rich. The queen had inadvertently crossed him, earlier that year, by granting her brother the earldom of Moray; hitherto, Huntly had administered these rich lands for himself. But he, too, troubled her: not just by his formidable might in the north, but by the disgraceful conduct of his third son, Sir John Gordon, who feuded bitterly with Lord Ogilvie, and seized his lands, and then fled the queen's justice. This Ogilvie, who had been most unjustly disinherited – his stepmother had accused him of making unwanted advances, to his late father's wrath – was a favourite of the queen; now his oppressor enjoyed Huntly's protection.

Further, Huntly made plain his regal disapproval of the queen's cool policy towards Scots Catholics; further still, in an act of near-calculated insult, he had invited the queen to celebration of mass on his territories, though that Eucharist was her sole personal prerogative in the kingdom. Huntly had Stewart blood, too, being a grandson of James IV by a bastard daughter. Huntly was a dangerous man: only the fact that he was universally distrusted gave the queen, and Scotland's order, any measure of safety. At any rate, he now launched a most dangerous plot: he began to harry Mary's progress through the north, and pressed the queen hard to stay with him at Strathbogie where, in all probability, he would have seized and murdered her ministers (including Moray and Lethington), married the queen off to his son, and executed a Roman Catholic *coup d'état*.

He had gone too far, though, in his impudent attentions: the queen swept west, well clear of Strathbogie; publicly announced Moray's earldom; gave out orders against Sir John Gordon; and then, finally, had her flabber utterly gasted at Inverness, where the keeper of the royal castle – another son of Huntly's, Alexander Gordon – denied his sovereign admission. This was more than insolence: this was treason. The Highlands now rallied to their queen; Huntly panicked, for the first time, and ordered Alexander to admit her. The royal party swept in, took control, and hanged the man off the battlements for his defiance. Huntly's last chance – his only chance – was now full-scale rebellion. For some weeks, queen and earl played an uncertain game of brinksmanship. He was too powerful to attack; he was too scared to move. He dodged about his estates, sleeping in different lodgings each night, trying to evade capture. On 16 October Huntly and Sir John Gordon were outlawed – 'put to the horn' by order of the Privy Council. Huntly retreated to the hills, and might have got away with everything, had not his imperious wife urged him to abandon guerrilla warfare and Highland skulking for open attack. (She was following the counsel of local witches: they assured her that, by nightfall, Huntly would be lying in the Tolbooth of Aberdeen, without a wound on his body.)

Huntly duly took to battle with the queen's forces at the Hill of Fare, above Corrichie in Aberdeenshire; his indecision, though, frustrated the potential of his force, and when the fight was at last waged it soon went very badly for the Huntlys. Trapped in a swamp, riven by cannon and arquebus fire, the great bear of the north was captured, with Sir John and another of his sons; Huntly was being led, on horseback, towards a triumphant Moray when he crashed, quite dead, to the ground, probably of a massive heart attack. That night, indeed, his vast unmarked corpse did lie in the Tolbooth of Aberdeen; in short order it was stuffed, salted and embalmed, and, in May 1563, the ridiculous mummy was solemnly put on trial in Edinburgh, and convicted of treason. The earldom of Huntly was attainted; the riches of the Gordons were forfeit. Sir John Gordon, later that same year, was tried and condemned to death. Political reality – there were rumours flying about that he had been 'familiar' with his monarch – compelled Mary herself to attend and watch the beheading. It was a botched, messy job; the queen collapsed in tears, and spent the next day or so in her chamber, in characteristic prostration.

It was a short-term triumph for the crown. But it may be argued that, by so comprehensively destroying the earldom of Huntly, largely to the enrichment of Protestant lords such as Moray, and by dividing this considerable Catholic power base, Mary had sealed her future doom. When crisis came, there was no great Catholic magnate to come to her aid; no friendly north to play off against a hostile, near-revolutionary south. (Mary restored the earldom of Huntly in 1565: but the new earl was Protestant, and scarce likely, in a crunch, to fight for the queen who had destroyed his father.)

The other episode was a sad incident of soap opera: the languishing, lovelorn Arran. By the end of 1562 his passion for the queen had become a full-blown neurosis, and he had won the enmity of James, Earl of Bothwell, who hated the Hamiltons anyway. Arran became the victim of various bawdy practical jokes, designed to sully his reputation; the rumour was deliberately circulated that he had hatched a plot to abduct the queen. Arran, highly strung (he was already generally thought to be deranged), hit back with counter-accusations and wild letters; he tried to persuade John Knox that Bothwell and Lethington – not he – had designs on the queen's liberty. Frightened of the peril Arran's follies threatened to inflict on the family, old Chatelherault locked him up. Somehow, though, Arran smuggled out a wild letter, duly passed to the queen. A desperate kinsman, Gavin Hamilton, dashed to court to try and persuade Mary not to believe a word Arran said.

But she was thoroughly alarmed. Gavin Hamilton and Bothwell were promptly arrested on suspicion of conspiracy. Meanwhile, the incorrigible Arran managed to escape, half naked, from the window of his cell, fashioning his bedding into ropes. He made his way to a fine house in Stirling, by which point he was a pitiful spectacle, and his mental condition beyond dispute. Arran screamed of devils, witches; he spoke of sinister plots on his life; he insisted that he was already husband of the queen, and that she shared his bed. He clung to his delusions even before the Privy Council, accusing Bothwell of high treason. There was no point putting the poor wretch on trial. He spent some years confined, in miserable and grim lodgings, at Edinburgh Castle; in 1566 he was delivered into the care of his mother, and locked up for the rest of his life, ill and demented. He died in 1609, long surviving the other actors in the drama of Mary's court.

The queen was still popular; she was in office, but was she in power? Somehow, subtly, her authority ebbed in court and beyond. One emerging factor was her uninterest in affairs – or perhaps laziness. She seldom bothered to attend meetings of her council, and delegated much authority and administrative exercise to clever men. So she began to appear, at least to the ruling nomenklatura of the Scots court, as something of a cipher: a queen who thoroughly enjoyed being royal, who delighted in grand jewels and gowns, and who surrounded herself with sports, merriments and music, but who had no real interest in exercising a queen regnant's authority.

It was also quite apparent that the queen took no pleasure in Scotland: was unhappy being in Scotland, and – insofar as she exercised political muscle at all – planned for nothing as much as to be out of Scotland, enthroned in England or at least somewhere on the Continent. Here she may be instructively contrasted with her mother. Mary of Guise had also disliked her adopted land: resented its climate; hated its customs; chilled in its palaces; and thoroughly pined for the elegance of France. But Mary of Guise had exercised a strongly developed sense of duty. She had toiled not merely to safeguard her daughter's inheritance in Scotland, but toiled as a necessary extension of her own professional ethic: the good rule of good sovereigns. Her daughter, for all her beauty, her charm notwithstanding, comes across as a rather idle, disengaged sort of queen.

Two real political problems began to build from her sloth. One was Mary's standing overseas, where her exercise in Scottish religion attracted rising dismay and disapproval. This was an age where, as part of the sacred mission of monarchy, a sovereign was held answerable to the Most High not merely for the rule of his kingdom but as one responsible for the wellbeing of his subjects' souls; it was an age when, in Catholic realms, kings still trembled at the word of the Pope, and where the Pope's agents could teach: '*Justum necare reges impios*,' 'it is right to kill ungodly rulers.'

Mary's policy in religion might, four centuries on, be erroneously hailed as far-sighted, broad-minded and tolerant. She did not, however, live in an age where these concepts were valued nor, for the most part, even understood. Mary was in any event not a tolerant woman, as far as the souls of Scots went: she was, frankly, not at all interested. So she presided over a tide of drift in matters religious, unable to see that not only was the True Faith losing its hold on Scots but so, remorselessly, was her own authority. It became a matter of bewilderment, to observers overseas, what the Queen of Scots was about.

She attended mass, zealously. But her law prosecuted her subjects when they did likewise. She was loyal to the Church of Rome. But the Scots Kirk was allowed to collect one-third of the old Church's revenues. We have seen the fate of a loyal Roman Catholic magnate when he revolted against the rising Protestant order. We have seen the full might of her wrath against the impertinent lecturing of John Knox: Her Majesty, Queen of Scots, burst into tears. Good professional monarchs, throughout Christendom, had to face the issues of the day and the rising struggle of Reformation. But they saw only two clear paths to take. One was to endeavour, hard, to restore the Roman Catholic order, whether by guile and persuasion, or by force. And the other was to allow a Protestant establishment as long as it remained moderate, amenable to executive control, and stayed firmly in its place. In England, Bloody Mary had tried – badly – to reimpose Romanism; but she had tried. Elizabeth had suffered the establishment of the Church of England, but on her terms, putting the stability of the realm – and the safety of her subjects from riot and bloodshed – above all else. The religious policy of the Queen of Scots was inoperable and, indeed, incredible to the aghast international audience.

The other major political problem arose from Mary's style of life. She removed herself from day-to-day affairs, and as her statesmen sat in council in one part of Holyroodhouse, she amused herself with European pets and courtiers in another, surrounded by twittering women and amorous poets and effeminate men and randy musicians and assorted easy-living, feather-brained dilettantes. There came sensation when a besotted French poet was found concealed in the queen's bedchamber.

Pierre de Châtelard was an elegant, good-looking charmer who had joined the queen's retinue on her return from France. He was a poet of ability, by the standards of the day, and excelled at composing passionate, lyrical, lovelorn balladry in hopeless adoration of the queen; his verses were chaste, chivalrous, and utterly romantic: 'much more to her taste,' writes Fraser, 'to be celebrated in verses, than dragged into a Highland fastness and forcibly married.' De Châtelard duly returned to France; but, in the autumn of 1562 visited again, with covering letters and another book of pretty poems for the queen. Appropriately flattered, Mary was good to him, making a present of a nice horse and some money to buy good apparel. There was nothing improper nor unusual in such royal bounty. But there resulted an evening when, making routine search of her room as the queen conferred with two of her council, her horrified ladies found de Châtelard hiding under her bed.

Mary was told next morning. She immediately ordered de Châtelard to leave the court. Instead, that same day, he followed her to St Andrews, and burst into the royal chamber as the queen made ready for bed, accompanied by only one or two of her ladies: this time his advances were so outrageous that Mary screamed and roared for help. When Moray rushed to her aid, the hysterical Mary demanded that he stab the wretched de Châtelard on the spot. She was persuaded to the wiser course of imprisonment and trial.

To the St Andrews dungeons he went, pleading – implausibly – that he had only sought audience of the queen in her chamber to explain his first appearance there; he had wandered in by mistake, and fallen asleep. By now, of course, de Châtelard's conduct was the scandal of Europe. John Knox – who never ceased to hint that Mary's court was the setting for every debauchery and vice – had been handed a propaganda weapon of the first order. There was no hope of sparing de Châtelard's life, mad or no, and he was duly executed in February 1563. It has been suggested, subsequently, that he had been part of a plot deliberately to blacken Mary's reputation. As he was a Huguenot – a French Protestant –

this cannot be lightly dismissed; the adventure, though, cost him his life.

Days after de Châtelard walked to the gallows, the queen's uncle, Duke Francis of Guise, was assassinated, shot in the back by a gunman. Another Guise uncle died, in France, weeks later, and Mary was racked in sorrow and self-pity. More than ever she longed for support: specifically, the practical friendship of Elizabeth, in England, and a good marriage to a good and strong husband.

Queen Elizabeth was a much abler woman than Mary, no less beautiful – by the standards of the day – and, psychologically, a good deal tougher. Her childhood had been as disordered and frightening as Mary's had been relatively serene. She had no memory of her mother, the wretched Anne Boleyn. Henry VIII held no dislike against his second child, but took little to do with her; and had completed Anne Boleyn's despatch by declaring Elizabeth bastard. She had, too, frightening memories of the fall of Catherine Howard. His final will had given the princess due place in the succession, but in the short reign of Edward VI the Princess Elizabeth had been viciously investigated for treason: it was said she had connived in the plans of Thomas Seymour, Lord Admiral, to marry her without the consent of the Privy Council. Certainly Seymour had tried to abduct the young king and marry him off to his ward, Lady Jane Gray.

Things were even tougher under Mary. Elizabeth was linked to the Wyatt conspiracy of 1554 and held for a time in the Tower of London; at one point she had come within an hour of execution. She was, she always declared, married to England. She never in her long life left its coasts. And Elizabeth never married any man. Perhaps it was cold political logic: marriage, she might have felt, would irrevocably weaken her grip on affairs. Perhaps her perpetual virginity (and there is not the least evidence, for all we might titter, that she ever had any sexual relationship) had deeper, darker causes. From an early age, after all, Elizabeth had seen about her passion and death repeatedly combined: her mother's fate, and the fall of Catherine Howard after spectacular adulteries, and the execution of Seymour, who had flirted with the fourteen-year-old princess at Hatfield House. Seymour's wife, Queen Dowager Catherine Parr, had loved him dearly – and died in childbed.

This formidable woman was now wooed by her cousin, another queen. The initial bargaining chip was the Treaty of Edinburgh, vital to the English: it put the French from Scotland and confirmed a Protestant religious settlement. Maitland, perhaps the cleverest of Mary's men, was sent to London to win concessions for his queen. Specifically, he said there would be no ratification of the treaty until Mary's place in the English succession was acknowledged: that Elizabeth duly recognised the Queen of Scots as heir-presumptive. Maitland was duly received by Elizabeth in the presence of William Cecil, her 'Spirit' and most trusted minister, and of Robert Dudley, the queen's favourite, from whom scandal was never far away.

Scotland's lords, as well as Mary herself, were eager to see her right to England's throne asserted; once Elizabeth grasped this political reality, she dealt with Maitland in terms both reasonable and cunning. She let it be known – in not so many words – that she herself preferred Mary to all other claimants; that there was no one with a stronger claim than Mary's, and probably no one who could deny Mary the throne supposing some unfortunate fate befell herself. But Elizabeth had to consider other pressures. Her father, Henry VIII, still haunted English affairs as a revered if terrifying ghost, and his will specifically excluded Margaret Tudor's descendants from making any claim to the English throne. Mary herself, in France, had insulted Elizabeth when Francis was allowed to quarter England's arms. And Mary was loathed in England. Parliament, dominated by the Puritan party, detested her. Popularly, Mary was perceived as a virtual Frenchwoman; a fanatical Romanist; a conniving, wanton woman capable of every viciousness and intrigue.

Elizabeth extricated herself by refusing to give any concrete title to Mary's hopes. She argued that it would put great strain on their queenly relations. With some reason, she pointed out that an heir-apparent was inevitably the focus of faction, plot, and discontented individuals. In her own sister's reign she herself had been the involuntary figurehead for her sister's enemies, to great peril of her own life. Now, 'The desire is without example to require me in my own life, to set my winding sheet before my eyes. Think you that I could love my own winding sheet? Princes cannot like their own children, those that should succeed unto them.'

Maitland could not budge her. Elizabeth did, however, grant that Mary's claim be not expressly repudiated in the treaty articles; the Queen of Scots was required merely to forgo any claim to England's throne in the lifetime of Elizabeth and of Elizabeth's putative offspring. And she concurred in a plan of continuing discussion and correspondence between Maitland and Cecil. So Mary had yet much for which to hope, especially as the other claimants – descendants from Margaret Tudor's subsequent marriages, and the seed of Mary Tudor – were all, in one way or another, tainted in Elizabeth's eyes by religion, or dubious legitimacy, or complicated marital careers. Indeed, Elizabeth's sensitivity to the conduct of these cousins went beyond dislike of indiscretion to hysteria and spite. She did all in her power to prevent them marrying: one cousin, who married in secret, was clapped in the Tower with his wife, and their offspring pronounced illegitimate.

In the meantime English opinion remained largely anti-Marian. One fierce Puritan spoke against Mary in parliament; that she could never sit on England's throne: 'Our common people and the very stones in the streets should rebel against it.' In the autumn of 1562 London quaked in uncertainty and terror when Elizabeth succumbed to smallpox. For some days the queen was not expected to live. The Spanish ambassador, Bishop de Quadra, wrote of the confusion surrounding the succession. Protestants were split between Lady Catherine Grey, or the Earl of Huntingdon. Romanists wanted Mary; or her Catholic cousin, Margaret Lennox. Elizabeth duly recovered and the atmosphere of crisis receded. But her council redoubled their efforts to persuade her – now in her thirtieth year – to get married to some suitable princeling and beget decent uncontroversial heirs of her own body. And Mary now pinned all her hopes on securing the personal favour of Elizabeth; she therefore bent all her limited abilities and energy to securing a meeting, in the flesh, before all, of the queens.

Now there is abundant evidence that, granted confidence in Mary's capacity and judgement, Elizabeth would in due time have acknowledged her as heir-presumptive. Mary had, after all, indisputably the best title by blood. She was of impeccable royal pedigree: the assorted Tudor and Plantagenet claimants were tainted by common, if aristocratic, lineage. And there was much sense in securing, at last, future union of the crowns, ending any threat to England from north of the Border. Elizabeth would certainly have pegged it to iron-clad conditions. There could have been no Scottish league with France. There would have to be co-operation and friendship with England. Mary would have to marry well, and with Elizabeth's blessing. Probably, too, the Queen of Scots would have been expected to convert to Protestantism.

Mary herself understood that Elizabeth would have to be impressed with her as a woman and a sovereign; hence she pinned all her hopes on securing a meeting. She had charmed Throckmorton. She could certainly then hope to charm Elizabeth.

We know, of course, that they were fated never to meet. There was always a fundamental difference in approach. Elizabeth liked secret negotiations through a third party, by emissary. Mary wanted a showy summit-conference. Elizabeth wanted hard political deals: critically, ratification of the Treaty of Edinburgh. Mary preferred to withhold concrete concessions and write sugary, flattering letters. Both desperately wanted one thing – a treaty; an acknowledgement to succession – and both wanted the other to give ground first. There were difficulties, too, in the road of physical meeting. Mary's legendary charm rather intimidated Elizabeth, who had seen too many hard-eyed diplomats return veritably entranced by the Queen of Scots. Her natural vanity, too, ran against appearing in a common arena with another queen, who might indeed prove more lovely, or gorgeously dressed, or otherwise upstage her. (Elizabeth, in fact, never met any other reigning sovereign.)

On the Scots side, too, Mary's lords were anxious at the prospect of such a meeting: how safe was it for Mary to travel to England, when but a year or two before the English had been threatening to imprison her? And, being Scots, money was a consideration. Royal encounters – banqueting, horse shows, revelry, rich clothing, much wine, grandiloquent presents – were notoriously expensive. There was, too, a real danger that Elizabeth might be so entranced by Mary as, at last, to take her cousin's side against them. The Catholic party in Scotland were for their part fearful of further corruption of their queen by the usurper Elizabeth. So, though Mary herself longed to meet her cousin, there was no body of opinion in Scotland supporting her; and, frankly, no one in Scotland who cared about her aspirations to England's throne, save as a useful bargaining ploy to intimidate the Auld Enemy.

All this conspired to delay matters. And time was not on Mary's side. She was not Elizabeth's equal: no match for the Queen of England in politics, judgement, wisdom or statecraft. Worse: Mary did not realise this. And, the more she cajoled and pleaded and wrote and manoeuvred, the more likely it became that Mary would expose herself as a fool, win only Elizabeth's abiding contempt, and ruin all her prospects.

The very face of Providence seemed against a royal meeting: the summer of 1562 proved inordinately wet, and the roads from Scotland to England almost impassable. England's council, too, argued fearfully about the cost of conference: they reckoned a meeting as elaborate and grand as protocol duly required would demand at least £40,000 to stage. Still, Mary was eager for the meeting, and could override her ministers; Elizabeth was not without curiosity, and seemed prepared to go along with the scheme. Venues were considered: York first, then Nottingham. Party themes were devised: three nights of masques, and the usual stylised compliments to both queens – carefully balanced, of course; as an allegorical theme, the God Jupiter would punish False Report and Discord, hurling them into the Prison of Extreme Oblivion at the behest of Prudence and Temperance . . .

And then, almost at the last moment, turmoil in France wrecked everything. In that land Huguenots were now in open war; a spell of peace had provided an apparent window for the Queens of Scotland and England to meet at Nottingham. Days before Mary was to set forth for Nottingham – Cecil was already drafting her safe-conduct, on 8 July 1562 – the fragile armistice collapsed, and the French were again at each other's throats. England might be forced to intervene. Or the turmoil might cross the Channel. Whatever: the situation made it the height of folly for Elizabeth even to think of a journey away from London to the north of her kingdom. The glorious pageant was cancelled. Word was sent to Scotland. Mary received the news in characteristic fashion. She burst into torrents of tears and spent the rest of that day in bed.

There was kindly talk of rescheduling, of a suitably reconvened summit in the spring or summer of 1563. It was never to be.

The matter of Mary's marriage now assumed urgency. She needed heirs, too; she sought a husband, being of a passionate nature; and she was increasingly distrustful of the Scots about her. (What if Moray decided to bid for the throne in his own right?) But her marriage was also a useful weapon in dealing with Elizabeth. Mary could buy her cousin off, and win the recognition she craved, by consenting meekly to marry whomsoever Elizabeth nominated. Alternatively, the Queen of England could be intimidated. Mary could betroth herself to an ardently Catholic prince, someone hostile to the Reformation and prepared to threaten England. Such a prospect might make Elizabeth most amenable. Yet there were risks. Marriage, once embarked upon, was not an estate from which even a queen might readily break free. What if Elizabeth refused to commit herself to Mary as heir-presumptive until *after* a Protestant wedding? What if Elizabeth took a Catholic wedding as good ground for repudiating Mary altogether? Or, worse, as a declaration of war?

Anyway, the usual Catholic links were newly probed: Archduke Charles of Austria; Don Carlos of Spain. Elizabeth, predictably, let it be known she would regard these matches as highly offensive. Again, Elizabeth hinted at untold benefit if Mary wed appropriately – though the queen had not, to date, indicated any preferred spouse for her Scots sister. Then, in the autumn of 1563, Elizabeth began to drop the plainest hints. The trouble was that her proffered candidate was a figure of such controversy it was hard to take Elizabeth at all seriously.

Lord Robert Dudley was notorious as Elizabeth's favourite. They were childhood friends. In her spell of imprisonment, in Bloody Mary's reign, he had sent flowers to the Tower; or, afterwards, said he had sent flowers. On accession, Elizabeth had made him Master of Horse. He had no royal blood. Worse, he came from a line of traitors: his father, Duke of Northumberland, had actually been beheaded. Worse still, his relationship with Elizabeth was one of such warmth, so great familiarity, that many hinted at scandal. We have already read of this man and of his first wife, Amy Robsart, who had died in mysterious and violent circumstances; of the rumour and excitement that spread through Europe, and shocked Mary herself. It was, on the face of things, almost insulting to offer such a one for the hand of the Queen of Scots.

Maitland's immediate response to the proposal was to laugh it off as decorously as he could. Why, the Queen of Scots would no doubt be much warmed at Her Majesty's great proof of love, in offering for her hand something she herself so dearly prized. But the Queen of Scots could scarcely deprive her sister of one so precious. Could Elizabeth not marry Lord Robert Dudley herself, and bequeath both man and kingdom to Mary when she died?

Elizabeth, though, persisted in the offer. It was again conveyed to Mary that friendship with Elizabeth would cease if she wed either Don Carlos or the archduke. In March 1564 Lord Robert Dudley was formally proposed to Mary as a husband she could take with Elizabeth's blessing. Mary prevaricated. She still longed for imperial alliance. Dudley, quite apart from his dubious reputation, was of no value to her unless he brought Elizabeth's express guarantee of the English succession. It was beginning to dawn, even on Mary, that this was the last thing the Queen of England intended to concede. On the other hand, Scots opinion was hardening against her desired foreign matches. Knox preached ferociously against the Spanish negotiations. The queen unwisely summoned the preacher to another audience at Holyrood, and proceeded to make a complete fool of herself, with tears and temper and bad own-goals. 'What are you within my commonwealth?'

'A subject born within the same, Madam.'

Religious unrest rose about Scotland; militant Protestants even burst into the queen's chapel and disrupted her household mass. Knox then meddled with their trial, whipping up the Lords of Congregation to make their way south and throw a ring of moral Presbyterian steel about the accused. This was insulting to the queen, and perilously close to treason; Knox was duly arraigned. When the queen saw him before the council to explain himself, she burst into wild laughter. 'Yon man gart me greit and grat never tear himself. I will see if I can gar him greit.' ('That man made me cry and wept no tear himself. I'll see if I can make him howl.') It does not sound like the conduct of a normal woman; and the council did not gar Knox greit. It was found that he had committed no treason. Some months later the sturdy old man – he was past his fiftieth birthday – married Margaret Stewart. His second wife was only seventeen; she was a daughter of Lord Ochiltree and, indeed, a distant cousin of the queen.

Bereavement, frustration, hostility, intrigue, humiliation, embarrassment: the queen's health broke, and she spent much time in bed, seeing in the New Year of 1564 quite confined to bed, with vague and mysterious pains in her right abdomen. That year, 1564, passed with further, and increasingly doomed, attempts at a Spanish match: the King of Spain, though few abroad, was now grimly persuaded his son was quite insane. It was on his way to another fruitless bout of Spanish negotiation that James Melville, at the English court, was invited to witness Dudley's investiture to the peerage. The English suitor was elevated to the titles of Earl of Leicester, Baron of Denbigh. This, presumably, was to fit him to consort with the Queen of Scots; the effect, though, was rather spoiled in Melville's report, for in mid-ceremony Elizabeth fondly tickled the new earl's neck.

All the time, though, the harder Elizabeth and her ministers were pressed on the matter of the English succession, the more evasive and slippery they became. In the meantime, Mary had no heir of her own, in Scotland, nearer than the Hamiltons. Some saw a third way through the impasse. The continental, Catholic union was too dangerous. An English union brought no benefit or blessing. But if Mary married some English kinsman, someone of royal blood, whose blood would strengthen the claims of herself and her seed to England's throne, then she might strengthen her position. It was at this juncture, in an abiding mystery, that Henry, Lord Darnley, appeared in Scotland, in February 1565. He was a strong claimant to both the thrones of Scotland and England; and was the right age to be a husband to the Queen of Scots. He had always been mentioned as a minor, but real candidate for Mary's hand and the astonishing thing is that Elizabeth let him leave the country.

Whatever: the tall, lusty youth had reached Scotland. Queen Mary's doom was assured.

4

IN MY END IS MY BEGINNING

Mary: Her Ruin

When Dudley's neck was tickled by his queen, as she raised him to the purple, one shrewd observer saw more to the action than undue and indiscreet familiarity. James Melville saw cunning statecraft: the humiliating reminder, to a proud and tempered man, how utterly he depended on the goodwill of his sovereign and queen. Perhaps Elizabeth sensed this. As Leicester remained on his knees, she turned to the Scots ambassador and asked what he thought of the new earl.

> I answered that as he was a worthy subject, so he was happy who had a princess who could discern and reward good services. 'Yet,' she said, 'you like better of yonder long lad,' pointing toward my Lord Darnley, who, as nearest prince of the blood, did bear the sword of honour that day before her. My answer was that no woman of spirit would make choice of such a man; for he was very lusty, beardless and lady-faced. And I had no will that she should think that I liked him, albeit I had a secret charge to deal with his mother, my Lady Lennox, to procure liberty for him to go to Scotland . . . that he might see the country and convey the Earl his father back again to England.

Elizabeth was quite aware that Melville was on some mission to secure Darnley for the Queen of Scots; Melville knew this, and it amused her to let him know she knew that he knew. She was also – as a cold judge of men – no doubt taken with his apt judgement of Darnley.

Darnley's antecedents were noble. His mother, Lady Margaret Douglas, was a daughter of Margaret Tudor, by her second and turbulent marriage to the Earl of Angus. His father, Matthew Stewart, Earl of Lennox, was descended from James II. So he stood high in the succession to the thrones of England and Scotland. Life had been turbulent for his parents: in the chaotic and strife-torn years following the death of Henry VIII, any trace of royal blood was perilous indeed. The shadow of the Tower was never far away. Travel from England, whether to Scotland or France, aroused great suspicion; permission from court was not granted lightly.

Darnley was an accomplished young man. He was held to be very handsome: fair, with an oval face, regular features, big blue eyes and full lips. His biggest asset, as far as the Queen of Scots was concerned, was his height. He was at least six feet one inch tall; some accounts suggest he was as high as six feet four. Certainly he was described, with admiration, as 'the tallest man in the Kingdom'. He was of well-proportioned build. Portraits of the young Darnley show him in plain, close-fitting black, the better to emphasise his trim, muscled figure.

His education was of the usual order. Darnley was well schooled in French and Latin, and kept through youth at the toil of writing pompous essays and learned squibs. Many years later an old tutor published *Apothegmata Regis*, a collection of Darnley's epigrams and witticisms, in all their heavy self-consciousness. But we also know he was fluent in Scots and English: letters, in both tongues, survive.

He was a good dancer, had a pleasant singing voice, and played the lute extremely well. Darnley was a superb horseman, and his inordinate love of hunting and field sports demonstrated the Stuart blood. All in all, this parfait gentle knight seemed the fittest consort for a queen. The trouble was that Darnley, in character and personality, was an appalling human being, to the end of his days utterly immature in temper and judgement.

There was, too, an air of effeminacy, as Melville hints in his memoir. Shrewd observers looked beyond his accomplishments and saw a well-coached parrot; a less than average man crammed and coached to apparent accomplishments beyond his native ability. One of Mary's Guise uncles described Darnley, succinctly, as a 'pleasant twit'. You had to be very close indeed to the man to sense the viciousness beyond the courtly charm, the learned pretensions. Darnley's short career is that of a man of inordinate vanity, appalling temper, ludicrous ambition, sexual debauchery, and – the evidence is overwhelming – alcoholism: sustained bouts of uncontrolled, addictive, destructive drinking.

None of this, though, was evident to the Queen of Scots. She met Darnley, for the first time in Scotland, at Wemyss Castle in Fife, in February 1565. Darnley was certainly enchanted, like most men, by her physical beauty, her smouldering charm. But she was utterly smitten by him. Excitedly the queen described him as 'the lustiest and best proportioned man I have ever seen'. For the first time in her life, Mary fell in love, and her wits – such as they were – deserted her completely. In April Darnley succumbed to illness – measles, officially – and Mary hastened to nurse him at Stirling, spending hours supervising his needs, staying by his bed till very late at night. By the time he was better, she was quite lost. 'So altered with affection towards the Lord Darnley,' noted a troubled Thomas Randolph, who had quickly come to true judgement of the young fop, 'that she hath brought her honour in question, her estate in hazard, her country to be torn in pieces.'

Which brings us back to a question perhaps born of paranoia: was this a plot? Why had Elizabeth so blandly consented to Darnley's journeying to Scotland? Was it her judgement of him, and Mary, that their marriage was earnestly to be hoped for – because it would encompass Mary's destruction? There is one clue. The Earl and Countess of Lennox had lobbied Elizabeth hard for Darnley's safe-conduct. But so, too, had the Earl of Leicester, who poured out his feelings to Melville, and 'began to purge himself of so proud a pretence as to marry so great a Queen, esteeming himself not worthy to wipe her shoes, declaring that the invention of that proposition of marriage proceeded from Mr Cecil, his secret enemy. "For if I," says he, "should have appeared desirous of that marriage, I should have lost the favour of both the Queens."'

Leicester still, no doubt, harboured the wistful hope he

might yet win the hand of Elizabeth herself. But he may have grasped the game Elizabeth was playing. Elizabeth had no intention of marrying Leicester, but was eager to avoid an outright refusal of him. Further, she had no desire to see Mary marry anyone, and sought to keep her unmarried as long as possible. It is the stuff of fantasy to argue Elizabeth was endowed with such cunning – and foresight – she deliberately let Darnley go to entangle Mary in a ruinous marriage. She probably thought Darnley was firmly on her leash, with his mother at the English court for hostage, and all Lennox's great possessions in England for security. Nevertheless, once Darnley was over the Scottish Border, he was quite beyond her control.

The Earl of Lennox later claimed that Darnley won Mary by his superlative chivalry and charm, the Queen of Scots being 'stricken by the dart of love, by the comeliness of his sweet behaviour, personage, wit and virtuous qualities . . . as also in the art of music, dancing and playing'. Certainly Darnley sent her verses, in a quaint metre of the day:

> Schaw, schedull, to that sweit
> my pairt so permanent
> that no mirth quhill we meit
> sall caus me be content,
> but still my hairt lament
> in sorrowfull siching soir
> till time scho be present
> Fairwell. I say no moir . . .

> *My word, oh tell my sweet*
> *my part so permanent*
> *that no joy till we meet*
> *shall make me be content*
> *but still my heart laments*
> *in woeful sighing sore*
> *till time she is present –*
> *Farewell. I say no more . . .*

But the early stages of courtship were not without setback. Darnley's arrival, and the restoration of his family to favour, threatened the power-jostling games of many at court. The Earl of Moray took strong dislike to Darnley and did his best to prevent the queen's marriage. The two men had got on well at first, but then Darnley caused great offence when their kinsman Lord Robert Stewart showed him a map of Scotland, pointing out the great estates of Moray. 'Too much,' said Darnley sourly; Moray heard, and Mary had to force Darnley to apologise. It solved nothing and thereafter he and Moray were enemies. Wild tales went about of plot and counter-plot.

Moray could be sure of the backing of the Earl of Argyll and Sir William Kirkcaldy of Grange, who had great standing as a soldier. But Moray's star was no longer in the ascendant. A pro-Darnley faction won support from the Douglases, the Earl of Morton, the Lords Lindsay and Ruthven. The division was founded on stronger grounds than personal disliking. Darnley, who had professed Protestantism in England, was now an enthusiastic Roman Catholic. So rumours spread of strong and desperate plans. It was said that Darnley had a plot to murder Moray. Or that Moray was set to kidnap Darnley, and every available Lennox, and ship them back to England. That summer, in a confused episode called the 'Raid of Beith', Mary and Darnley returned from a fast morning gallop insisting they had just escaped an attempted ambush.

Darnley was really his own worst enemy. He pressed his suit too hard at first, Melville reporting that after Darley

> had haunted court some time, he proposed marriage to Her Majesty, which she took in an evil part at first, as that same day she herself told me, and that she had refused a ring which he then offered unto her. I took occasion . . . to speak in his favour, that the marriage would put out of doubt their title to the [English] succession . . . She took ever the longer the better liking of him, and at length determined to marry him.

Darnley's illness was a heart-melting experience for the queen; just before Darnley succumbed, she was also handed a strong political motivation from London. Leicester refused to pursue the cause of marriage to Mary – he 'so uncertainly dealeth that I know not where to find him, nor what to speak or promise,' ranted Randolph – and England's council dithered and dallied. Then Elizabeth spoke decisively. In March she declared that she would never pronounce on the succession until she herself had married or resolved for certain never to marry. Mary had been utterly humiliated. The Queen of Scots wept.

She hastened to Darnley's bedside – not literally to nurse him, of course, for she had her dignity, but to soothe and chat and flirt – and sent word to Elizabeth that she meant now to marry Darnley, and sought the Queen of England's blessing. Elizabeth, in due time, had the message; she stormed and raged. Throckmorton was sent scurrying to Scotland to forbid the match. On their allegiance, Lennox and Darnley were ordered to return instantly to London. In the meantime the Countess of Lennox was escorted to the Tower.

Matters had gone too far by now. Darnley recovered. Mary was tired of playing games with Elizabeth and too overtaken in passion further to delay. In May she made Henry, Lord Darnley, Earl of Ross. On 20 July he was declared Duke of Albany. A week later, without concern for constitutional propriety, she proclaimed him King of Scots; and the following day, around dawn, on 29 July 1565, in the Chapel Royal, they were married. It was a Catholic ceremony. Such was her haste to wed that Mary did not even trouble to obtain a papal dispensation, though she and Darnley were within the 'forbidden decrees' of consanguinity. (We will still refer to him as Darnley, to avoid confusion.)

The reign of Mary, Queen of Scots, now descends to soap opera.

Her marriage put Catholicism in the ascendant and, willingly or no, the queen had appeared to back a new Catholic policy, threatening the brittle peace of her kingdom. There were already many nervous heads about after the years of compromise and vacillation. Now the monarchy, strengthened by a head, seemed to threaten the order of things. What was even more alarming was that it was unclear who, precisely, the monarch was. Proclamations after the wedding had actually given King Henry first place, before his wife, signed by 'Thair Majesties . . . the penult day of July, and of our reignes the first and twenty-third years'. An astonished multitude heard this first declaration, which gave King Henry precedence over the hereditary and lawful queen. There was a fraught silence. Then a lone voice cheered, 'God Save the King!' It was the Earl of Lennox.

Under his spell, and deeply in love, Mary now strove to make this strange position legal. She sought – and Darnley demanded – that he be granted the crown matrimonial. This would make him monarch in his own right; a king regnant, rather than mere king consort. More, it made him heir, should she die without issue. Even if Mary bore him a daughter, and then died, a son to Henry by subsequent marriage would take precedence over that daughter. Her death, then, would lead to a change of dynasty. The prospect shocked her nobles. But there was no reasoning with Mary. 'All honour that may be attributed to any man by a wife, he hath it wholly and fully,' sighed Randolph. 'All dignities that she can endow him with are already given and granted . . . she hath given over unto her whole will, to be ruled and guided as himself best thinketh.' Even Philip of Spain, marrying Mary Tudor, had failed to win the crown matrimonial. But the Dauphin Francis had won it: why not King Henry?

Moray was the first to break, in open revolt. He rose, with the support of Chatelherault. Moray was a man of great guile and statecraft, and this episode is the silliest of his career. He had quite failed to prevent the royal wedding. He had no convincing alternative, no grand rallying cry, with which to overthrow the queen. Mary insisted that her brother 'would set the crown on his own head'; but Moray's illegitimacy was an impenetrable barrier to the throne; anyway, he had tholed Mary, as queen, all his life. He had no visible proof that Mary intended to restore Catholicism by force; no proof that she ruled against the wishes of the mass of her subjects. Nor, unlike 1560, was there a foreign army, hostile to England, camped on Scottish soil. There was never the least prospect of Elizabeth supporting such a rebellion against a legitimate sovereign. It went against her trade-union view of monarchy.

The scheme had but two advantages: Moray had strong support; and Mary's marriage was most unpopular. But for once Mary was given good advice and acted swiftly. When Moray refused to come to court and explain his opposition to her match – he was summoned immediately after the wedding – the queen had him 'put to the horn', and outlawed. His properties were seized. So were lands and houses belonging to such allies as Kirkcaldy of Grange. Moray attempted to muster forces at Ayr. Mary moved quickly to rally her own, pledging her jewels, that the soldiers would be paid. They left Edinburgh on 26 August – Mary and Darnley leaving with them – and for some weeks the two armies scurried about the Lowlands, never meeting in combat; hence we remember this weird affair as the Chaseabout Raid. It failed, and by October Moray knew his resistance was useless. Leaving Mary and her husband triumphant, he fled to England. He was told from London to stay in the north, but would not listen, making instead his way to court, where Elizabeth wiped the floor with him, receiving the errant Stewart before the French ambassador and haranguing him on the baseness and infamy of unlawful rebellion. So Moray had to trudge back to Newcastle, with much to think on.

It was the high point of the royal marriage, which began remorselessly to deteriorate. Darnley continued to huff and push for the crown matrimonial, which the Scots parliament would not allow and which the queen – as her ardour cooled – grew increasingly reluctant to grant. More: Darnley kept asking for money, to spend on apparel and pleasure; Mary could not afford thus to indulge him. Then there was his scheming, unsubtle father. Besides, Darnley was no practical support or help to her. For a man who longed to be king in his own right, he showed no interest in matters of state, no desire for practical administration or patient negotiation. 'As for the King, he past his time in hunting and hawking and such other pleasures as were agreeable to his appetites, having in his company gentlemen willing to satisfy his will and affections.'

Government meetings often had to be held up, or cancelled; the king was out hunting, or hawking. Documents could not be processed, for they required his signature as well as Mary's, but where was the king? Late in November Mary was very ill, lying in bed with the usual acute abdominal pain. Darnley went off to Fife and hunted for nine days. It was then, tired of hold-ups, it was agreed to make an iron stamp of the king's signature and apply this to documents in his absence.

Mary began to weary of her husband, who emerged ever the more each week as irresponsible, loutish, unfaithful – and drunk. He caroused into the small hours with low-life company. He slept with whores. One writer hints at some untold outrage on an island in the Firth of Forth: this may have been a homosexual incident. Whatever, the marriage had accomplished one point of such business: the queen was pregnant. As in former days, she retreated from council and from affairs, and especially from Darnley, into her little huddle of household retainers and familiars. Among these was a small and distinctly ugly Italian, David Rizzio, who was Mary's French secretary, and a sweet player of the guitar. Into this Rizzio's care was entrusted the stamp of Darnley's signature.

Mary could never resist the exercise of feminine charm. And she had, perhaps, a liking for the faint frisson of scandal. She took to sitting up late into the night in the company of this Rizzio. Further, her ear was increasingly bent by James Hepburn, Earl of Bothwell, a leading Protestant magnate of huge ambition who was widely disliked.

But there were other Protestant lords, linked to the Chase-about Raid, and still rather discredited from that episode, eager to ingratiate themselves with their king Darnley. And they had no great difficulty with the silly lad, late at night, moaning in his cups. It was an easy matter to persuade him that the queen was making a fool of him; that the little Rizzio was enjoying who knew what favours from her; and that everyone was laughing at the king and if he was a real man he would do something about it.

By January 1566 Mary may have felt herself distinctly secure. Moray was in exile, with her principal enemies. She knew she was pregnant, hopefully with a healthy male heir. After the triumph of autumn, her resolution was stronger than ever. Her silly husband left her in peace. But signs were in truth ominous. Knox and the Kirk did not trust her; they feared she would take advantage of her present strength to launch persecution. In England, Moray remained in close touch with events. Nearer home, lords such as Morton and Maitland grew increasingly jealous of Rizzio and Bothwell. They spoke of 'base-born' men who had usurped their own rightful position in the nation's affairs, and Rizzio fitted the description perfectly. Darnley was already straining to avenge himself.

The Scots court buzzed with intrigue and bluff. Protestant lords began pleasantly to talk of a coronation for Darnley: a notion they had once violently resisted. He began now ostentatiously to flaunt his Catholicism. Meantime Mary and her close advisers planned moves in parliament to seize the property and riches and estates of the Chaseabout rebels. It seems the increasingly frightened Protestant lords were quite prepared to consider the inadequate and pliable Darnley as a candidate for supreme power. This, of course, necessitated the removal of the queen.

There follow two hugely complicated murders, those of Rizzio and Darnley himself. They are two of the bloodiest, most mysterious episodes in the colourful history of the city of Edinburgh, and to this day there is confusion about their details and about who, precisely, was responsible.

What is certain is that Darnley was involved in Rizzio's murder and that he was utterly convinced Rizzio enjoyed the queen as mistress. In this he was almost certainly wrong. The small, pocky, monkey-like Italian was scarcely the lover of Mary's dreams. They would not have enjoyed the privacy for a sexual relationship – this was the claustrophobic world of a sixteenth-century court – and, as the queen was pregnant by the end of 1565, and in evident love with Darnley until at least the autumn, it is hard to see when undue familiarity could have taken place. Reality mattered less than pretext.

Darnley was sucked into a murder plot and even persuaded to sign a bond, a declaration of united loyalty: the signatories included the lords Morton, Ruthven and Lindsay. Their stated aims were the acquisition of the crown matrimonial for Darnley; the securing of the Protestant faith; and the return of the lords exiled in England. There was no mention of Rizzio, nor of killing anyone, save perhaps for one dark clause: 'So shall they not spare life or limb in setting forward all that may bend to the advancement of his [Darnley's] honour.'

The bill for the attainder of the Earl of Moray was to go before parliament on 12 March 1566. On the evening of 9 March the queen was enjoying a little supper party in a small chamber in her own Holyrood apartments. There were only a handful of intimates: Lord Robert Stewart; Jean, Countess of Argyll; Arthur Erskine, the queen's equerry; her page, Anthony Standen; and wee David Rizzio. According to Randolph – who had a morbid eye for detail – the guitar-playing favourite was wearing a 'night-gown of damask furred, with a satin doublet and a hose of russet velvet'. It was Lent, but the queen was big with child and excused from its proscriptions, so the company supped on meat. We have two eye-witness accounts – one from Mary's own hand; the other from Ruthven – as to what happened next.

To the party's great surprise, Darnley suddenly emerged from the shadows, having appeared by the private staircase. (The room was not at all large, and lit only by one candelabra.) Startled, they made the king welcome; but then Ruthven appeared, who was supposed to be in bed and dying of fever; armour gleamed beneath his gown. (Ruthven was not a nice man at all; many whispered that he practised witchcraft.) 'Let it please Your Majesty,' he roared, 'that yonder man David come forth of your privy-chamber where he hath been overlong!' The queen, bewildered and angry, asked Ruthven if he had taken leave of his senses. She was told that Rizzio had offended against Her Majesty's honour. Mary now turned angrily on Darnley. Ruthven ranted against Rizzio, who by now was trying to hide himself in a window recess; then, as Ruthven lurched in his direction, Mary's attendants belatedly laid hands on him. 'Lay not hands on me, for I will not be handled,' cried Ruthven, grabbing his dagger, and at this signal in rushed the rest: Andrew Ker of Fawdonside, Patrick Bellenden, George Douglas, Thomas Scott and Henry Yair, piling in from the little staircase. Ker pointed his pistol at the queen's stomach. The men wrestled for Rizzio. The table overturned in the confusion; all but one of the candles were knocked out. Rizzio clung to Mary's skirts, screaming for his life; the plotters drew pistols, and more daggers, and so he was torn and dragged, struggling and begging, through her bedroom and through her chamber and to and down her stairs, crying, '*Justizia! Justizia! Sauvez ma vie, Madame! Sauvez ma vie!*'

He was butchered to death; afterwards, between fifty-three and sixty stab wounds were counted on his body. (Mary believed, ever after, that the first blow was struck over her own shoulder.) What is known is that the first knife wound was made by George Douglas, an illegitimate brother of Morton's, and for it he deliberately used Darnley's own dagger. Rizzio's body was stripped, a porter calling, 'This was his destiny . . .' By now, of course, the commotion had aroused the entire palace. So men came running to the queen's aid, armed and frightened and vengeful; meanwhile, assorted Douglases piled up the stairs to assist their kinsman.

David Rizzio routinely had gone about the streets of Edinburgh unarmed and unescorted. His murder could easily have been accomplished in the wider city. The decision to kill him here, so publicly, and before the queen, puts the darkest aspect on this affair. We are forced to the conclusion that more than Rizzio's life was the aim here. The plotters must have hoped, perhaps, to kill Mary in the confusion – or perhaps, at least, to terrify her into miscarrying her unborn child. Mary was convinced of this. Her love for Darnley died at this moment; but, for once, her courage came to the fore rather than fountains of tears, and she conducted herself with near-supernatural calm.

She raged at Darnley, telling him just what she thought of him. Ruthven insolently ordered wine, and continued to miscall her as a wife. 'Is that your sickness, Lord Ruthven?' she asked coldly, and said she had 'that within my belly' which would one day be avenged upon him. Edinburgh was now in uproar: someone had rung the city's alarm bell. Darnley went and spoke to a restless crowd from the window, trying to soothe them. The queen made to join him. Lindsay threatened to 'cut her in collops' if she tried. At length Mary and her ladies were left, alone and terrified, without service of priest or doctor or midwife, to pass the night with the rebels in control of affairs. Word reached the queen, now, that Rizzio was dead. 'No more tears, now,' said Mary. 'I will think upon revenge.' It was soon known that the Protestant exiles were returning to Edinburgh.

The coup had failed in some particulars: Bothwell and Huntly, other targets, had escaped by a rear window. The rebels contented themselves with killing a Dominican priest, Father Adam Black. Meanwhile Mary plotted in her own turn to save herself and her child and her crown. She achieved this by forcing down her revulsion against Darnley. His weakness had imperilled her cause. Now it might imperil that of his new associates. Her survival must have embarrassed them. Had she not wooed Darnley back to her side – as she now did – we would have learned of their plans for Mary. They would probably have confined her to Stirling or Linlithgow, awaiting the birth of her child. Darnley and the new council would have taken charge of the land; Mary would not have emerged from imprisonment, and in due time would have died conveniently of unspecified and mysterious causes.

Next morning Darnley dared to visit the queen. He found her cool, collected and rational. There were no tears and no further recriminations. He himself was terrified; even hysterical. It was she who comforted him. 'Ah, my Mary!' said Darnley, much the weaker and less mature of the two. Mary quietly persuaded him they had – both – to escape. Under this new regime, his long-term prospects were little better than her own. Did he want to end up with her in castle walls?

Sunday passed. Monday came. Mary duly met the assembled conspirators, with all the air of a constitutional monarch meeting cabinet after the passing of some mildly contentious legislation. She was calm, even charming. The queen even drank to their bond. Then Moray appeared. Mary did not know of his part in the recent outrage, and flung her arms about him, crying, 'Oh, my brother, if you had been here they would not have used me thus!' Moray launched an ill-timed lecture, and Mary's temper rose. Cleverly she feigned labour pains, and called for the midwife, who pronounced her most ill indeed. The lords departed. The queen sent word to Erskine, Standen, and the captain of her guard, begging them to assist her as a defenceless woman and mother of their future king. So they joined in aiding the royal escape. That midnight, she and Darnley hastened down the same discreet staircase that had, two nights before, brought up Rizzio's killers. They escaped the palace through the servants' quarters and kitchens, and through a cemetery – by Rizzio's newly dug grave – and there met, whispering and apprehensive, loyal men with horses, including Erskine and Standen.

They galloped to Dunbar Castle, according to plan, pausing at Seton to collect the surviving sympathetic nobles. The ride was headlong and stressed. Darnley was especially frightened: what would his former allies now do to him should he fall into their hands? So he spurred his horse on the more furiously, crying, 'Come on! Come on! By God's blood they will murder both you and me if they catch us.' His queen begged him to remember her delicate condition. Darnley, thoughtful as ever, screamed and swore and declared that if this baby died they could readily have more. Dunbar Castle stands twenty-five miles east of Edinburgh; it was dawn when they reached it, at the end of a fearful journey for a woman in advanced pregnancy. Yet it is recorded that Mary, before retiring to sleep, calmly ordered eggs, and cooked breakfast for the party.

She had escaped. More: she had placated – and gulled –

Darnley. Now she pressed her advantage, writing to London to acquaint Elizabeth of these perils and indignities. Timing was perfect and the momentum of success sustained. Bothwell, critically, had escaped too, and so rallied men to their aid. By 16 March Mary had 4,000 soldiers at her disposal. The *coup d'état* now ignominiously collapsed. On 17 March, apprised of Darnley's defection, his fellow plotters fled from Edinburgh. On 18 March the king and queen returned to the city in triumph. Even Knox, who had played no part in the conspiracy, though tacitly approved of Rizzio's removal, saw it prudent to leave for Ayrshire. Only Moray remained. He had not taken part in the gruesome business at Holyrood. Mary did not know of his role in the conspiracy. So he was pardoned. Other survivors of the Chaseabout Raid were likewise rehabilitated. Mary was back at court and the administration, though shaken and re-formed, seemingly once again in her hands. What had irrevocably gone was any regard for – or trust in – her pitiable husband.

Mary took things quietly, dampened down her Catholic policy, and on 19 June – safely secure in Edinburgh Castle – was delivered of a son, the Prince James. It was a relief to Mary and a tremendous relief to the nation. It also, of course, furnished an alternative monarch, should it seem necessary again to be rid of her. There were only two irritations in the new serenity. Mary had defiantly appointed Joseph Rizzio in place of his dead brother. And the Earl of Bothwell stood higher in her esteem than ever; this she did not trouble to hide.

Meantime, Darnley disintegrated. Perhaps the fiasco of March, his uncovering as conspirator and ignominious betrayal of co-conspirators, sapped what little real sense of self-worth he retained. By day he wallowed in sulking self-pity. By night he drank himself into a stupor. On 17 December the Prince James was to be christened. Darnley ostentatiously refused to go. Perhaps he was jealous of the little mite. Whatever, his conduct fuelled rumours that he was not, in truth, the child's father. Then the king dared to complain to the Pope, and to write to the Catholic monarchs in Europe, saying the queen was not doing nearly enough to restore – or even protect – the old religion in Scotland. By now, too, some unknown plotter from the events of March had taken care to send a copy of the bond to Mary – with Darnley's signature. She read it with horror and disgust. Darnley could not openly be proceeded against; he had it in his power, after all, to repudiate James as his son, and was doubtless daft enough to do it – if pushed.

As the queen's health wavered, and she lay low in repeated aches, fevers and depressions, she doubtless gave much thought to how she might rid herself of her tedious liability of a husband. In turning to Bothwell for support and advice, however, she again proved herself to be a hopeless judge of character. Bothwell was little more than a Borders robber-baron. His history was full of escapes, scandals, and narrow squeaks. He had intrigues in half the courts of Europe: was notorious as an adventurer in Scotland, England, France, Denmark and the Low Countries. He was constantly in debt. He had an unhealthy interest in sorcery and the black arts; more, Bothwell had a vigorous sexual appetite. His instinctive solution to trouble or confrontation was to shed blood. More than once he challenged opponents to a duel.

Bothwell's one redeeming feature was unremitting constancy to the Protestant religion. He was, too, physically courageous, and a gifted soldier; Mary wanted him to have command of her armies, but Darnley and Moray had mightily resisted. Everything else we know of Bothwell confirms him as a rogue and a blackguard. Yet he became Mary's chief adviser: a swarthy, broken-nosed, snake-eyed Lothario of violent personality and unsubtle politics. Now Mary had her baby prince, she had no further need for dramatic and public reconciliation with Darnley. Besides, childbed had broken the balance of her health, and thus what survived of her judgement.

So her relations with Darnley spiralled downwards once more. July saw them violently quarrel at Traquair. In September they rowed again, in front of the French ambassador, Lennox chipping in to declare his son had been so insulted he would be best advised to sail abroad. Darnley made insolent leave of the queen, refusing to kiss her, muttering she would be lucky to see him again. Then, in October, Bothwell was wounded in some Border skirmish, and a few days after hearing the news Mary travelled from Jedburgh to visit him. On her return to Edinburgh she again fell seriously ill. Darnley waited eleven days until, disappointed at her survival, he made his slow way to the city to be at her side. He did not stay long.

By December Mary was in black depression. She wished, aloud, that she was dead; she made plain to all her utter distrust of her husband. She lay in her chamber at Craigmillar and bewailed her lot and deplored her husband at every opportunity; she made abundantly plain she longed to be rid of him. 'The first is,' reported one witness, 'the King will never humble himself as he ought; the other is, the Queen cannot perceive any nobleman speaking with the King, but that she presently suspects some contrivance between them.' There was real talk of divorce. The notion was first raised, it seems, by Moray and Maitland. It gathered support and the chief lords put the idea to the queen. Maitland said she could certainly divorce Darnley, if she would but pardon the Rizzio conspirators, such as the Earl of Morton. The queen liked the idea, but insisted nothing could be allowed to prejudice the future of her son. Maitland spoke darkly of 'other means'. He said he was sure that the Earl of Moray would 'look through his fingers'. The queen said quickly that nothing was to be done against her honour. So Huntly and Argyll recalled, in their 'Protestation' of 1569.

There is abundant evidence, amid competing argument, that by the end of 1566 Mary was desperate to be shot of Darnley and gave little for the means of his removal as long as nothing impugned her reputation and made her son a bastard. She was certainly in acute melancholy; she was also, again, expecting a child. It was probably Darnley's; he was still, if rarely, admitted to her bed. After the fall, of course, many insisted it was Bothwell's.

In New Year 1567, Darnley was laid low with syphilis.

When he caught this disease is not known. He may have had it even before his marriage – and there was that odd attack of measles. Tertiary syphilis would certainly have affected his sanity; venereal disease would have done little to enchant the queen. But she herself went to collect him in Glasgow, and bring the sick king back on a litter. He repaired to Kirk O' Field House, in the city outskirts – it stood where now the Old College buildings of the University of Edinburgh stand – to recuperate. Mary remained charming, sending kind words, promising she would again take him to bed. Meantime, Prince James was brought from Stirling to Holyroodhouse.

The city buzzed with rumours of attempts on the king's life. Darnley had left his allies and kindred in the west of Scotland. He lay in a city surrounded by enemies, not least the Earl of Morton, newly pardoned and restored. Yet he clung pathetically to the belief he was fully reconciled with his queen. On 10 February, his doctors declared, he would be well enough to quit Kirk O'Field; then he could return to court and to public life. In that last week Mary visited him, even spending the odd night under the same roof. She was there on the Sabbath, 9 February, the king's chamber crowded with her entourage, and 'the most part of the nobles then in this town'. Huntly was there. So was Bothwell. Late that night the queen was reminded she had promised to attend a wedding masque at the palace, and so duly left. She decided there was no point in returning to sleep at Kirk O'Field that night; was not her husband to return to Holyrood the following day? And had she not plans to ride early to Seton? Darnley was upset at this change in plan, but the queen lightly chided him for his petulance, and gave him a ring. So she left. At her horse, she started to see an old servant of Bothwell's, French Paris, dirty and black. 'Jesu, Paris,' said Mary, 'how begrimed you are!'

She did not recognise the smell of gunpowder, nor know that Paris and other lackeys had spent the day piling enough casks of gunpowder into the cellars of Kirk O'Field to blow it skyhigh.

What happened next is even more confused and conflicted

a picture than the slaughter of Rizzio. Colourful details have been painted of Darnley's last hours; some suggesting pious prayer; some suggesting more wild drinking. We know only that the queen left late on the Sabbath night; that they parted on friendly terms; and that there was even some music. Darnley retired to his chambering, ordering that his horses be made ready for five in the morning. At two in the morning Edinburgh was shaken by a huge explosion: 'The blast was fearful to all about, and many rose from their beds at the noise.' People rushed into the streets, into a choking stench of smoke and powder, to find Kirk O'Field reduced to smouldering rubble. All knew the king had lodged there. Panic, first; then hope, for one of Darnley's servants was found safe and well. Then, minutes later, the worst was confirmed. In the garden, beyond the town wall, lay the dead bodies of Darnley and his bodyservant Taylor. The king was naked, but for a nightgown. There was no sign of scorch, blast or stabbing. King and servant had been strangled.

Bothwell was heavily implicated. He had been seen at the moment the house exploded; present the night before; and henchmen and servants of Bothwell were all heavily implicated. Certainly he had abundant motive to finish off Darnley. So what finally had happened? We can only conclude that something terrified Darnley so much he had risen in the night. Perhaps he had seen the very match put to a trail of powder, and Bothwell's men amassing. A chair and a rope were found beside the bodies. Darnley and Taylor must have escaped from a window into the alley below, then into the adjoining garden. But, as they dashed off in their nightclothes, they must have been seen, and pursued, and efficiently throttled as the erstwhile lodging-house blew up.

Some women afterwards reported that they had heard Darnley's last beggings for mercy: 'Pity me, kinsmen, for the sake of Jesus Christ, who pitied all the world.' He was twenty years old, but pity found none.

Of all the excitements in Mary's career to date, nothing so astounded Scotland – and England and Europe – as the

appalling death of her husband. William Cecil himself hastened to secure an accurate (and illustrated) report of events
for his queen. All hinged now on what Mary did next. Few
shed tears for her pathetic and foolish husband. Many wise
heads nodded sagely, and said his removal could only be for
the better. There was no threat at all to Mary's position, as
long as she conducted herself with wisdom and stateliness.
There is no doubt that her first reaction was one of genuine
horror, though her immediate response – she wrote at once to
Ambassador Beaton, in Paris – is as much alarm for her own
safety as grief for a murdered husband. It betrays no hint that
she suspected the involvement of any of her noblemen. The
court was ordered into mourning. One hundred and fifty
pounds worth of black cloth was bought, on the queen's
order, for herself, ladies and retinue. Darnley's body was
carried to Holyrood, embalmed, laid in state for some days,
and then buried in the vault of Holyrood. Everything, in
short, most fit: and done by the book. Mary herself mourned
for forty days. She showed no reaction at the sight of
Darnley's body, but she had not been herself at all since
the Jedburgh sojourn. Her doctors worried about her nerves
and were troubled by her unrelenting melancholy. A week
after the murder, Mary was prevailed upon to quit Edinburgh
and all its gloom and gossip for the quiet coastal charm of
Seton. The chief nobles, including Bothwell and Huntly,
remained at Edinburgh to guard Prince James.

After the shock, the truth must have dawned on Mary. This
was not the work of crazed Protestant assassins, or mysterious and unknown fanatics. Her own men had done this, the
men who had raised the question of Darnley's removal with
her at Craigmillar. She must have also realised she herself
stood in no personal danger. Nor did others in the royal trade
union fail to grasp the truth. But her erstwhile mother-in-law,
Catherine de Medicis, and her cousin Elizabeth knew how
bad this business was for the business of queens. They wrote
to Mary at once. They were certain of her innocence, but
pointed out the facts. A king had been murdered. All the
evidence – and talk – pointed to the culprits as some of the

chiefest men of the land. The Queen of Scots must act now, decisively, and with vengeful hand. It did not matter if justice was done. What mattered was that justice was seen to be done.

Had she had the wit or strength to exploit it, Mary was in a strong position. Darnley, bane of her life, had been removed. She stood entirely innocent and had no prior knowledge of the plot. To clear her own reputation, and to assert her authority, she should have moved quickly to roll a few heads. Even if Bothwell was too formidable a proposition, there were ample servants and underlings.

But she did nothing. Tongues wagged and matters began to slide from her grasp. Anonymous placards began to appear in Edinburgh streets. A week after the murder, one declared Bothwell and Balfour the killers, and that Mary had agreed to the foul deed, as a result of witchcraft by one Janet Beaton. Another placard accused the foreigners at Mary's court, including Joseph Rizzio. By night voices cried in hidden closes and wynds that Bothwell had killed the king. By day more placards and handbills appeared to morning onlookers. The most infamous depicted the Queen of Scots as a mermaid, bare-breasted, crowned; below her, a hare crouched in a circle of swords. The libel was plain and deadly. A hare was the crest of the Hepburn family. The mermaid was a contemporary emblem of prostitution.

Yet there were still no arrests. There was still no vigorous enquiry into the Kirk O'Field outrage. Not the placards, nor the letters from foreign courts, nor all the wild talk in the city stirred Mary to action. And the last thing the hard men of her council wanted, of course, was close investigation of the last hours and death of Darnley, King of Scots. So the initiative slid from Mary's grasp. When the period of formal mourning ended, and she was no longer able to withstand a vociferous Lennox, Mary allowed him to petition parliament and put Bothwell on trial for the late king's murder. But, on the stated day, Lennox did not appear, and the case had little hope without the presence of the chief accuser. So Bothwell, after a seven-hour trial, was 'made clean of the said slaughter'. Few believed the verdict. And most understood Lennox's absence. By law, a nobleman was only allowed six followers when he entered the capital. Edinburgh jostled with 4,000 of Bothwell's men.

Parliament could be gulled: but not the multitude. Bothwell himself postered Edinburgh with declarations of innocence. Further posters and placards sprung up in protest, though, denouncing him as the 'chief author of the foul and horrible murder by law of arms'. The queen rode again to parliament, but this time with a heavy guard – a careless admission of her insecurity. Parliament obediently voted grants of good lands and estates to Bothwell and his cronies. On 19 April, after throwing a lavish feast, Bothwell signed up twenty-eight of Scotland's chief men to a sensational bond, declaring that the queen was now 'destitute of a husband, in which solitary state the Commonwealth may not permit her to reign'. If his own 'affectionate and heart service . . . and other good qualities' moved the queen to offer her hand to the Earl of Bothwell, signatories to this bond were to do all in their power to promote such a marriage. This fantastic and impudent declaration – proof of how low Mary's standing had shrunk – was signed by eight bishops, nine earls and seven barons.

Bothwell pocketed the precious paper, and rode after the queen, who had retreated to Seton. He pressed his suit upon her. She had sufficient sense of the scandalous implications to refuse. A few days later she went to Stirling to visit her baby; Mary would never see him again. On Wednesday 23 April she began her journey back to Edinburgh. On the following day she was suddenly seized at Almond Bridge, by Bothwell, backed by a force of 800 men. Mary does not seem to have realised what was happening. She allowed Bothwell to divert her from Edinburgh, and they journeyed instead to Dunbar; she made not the least effort to seek help or assistance as they passed through the countryside. One messenger reached Edinburgh: far from ensuring calm, news of the queen's change of plan raised the alarm. But there was little they could do. That night Mary was fast in Dunbar Castle, this time a prisoner. There Bothwell completed his plan to entrap

COBVS · 4 · D · GRATIA
REX · SCOTORV\

JAMES IV
Perhaps the ablest of all his line: this ruthless King of Scots connived at the
deposition and murder of his own father, and destroyed the mighty Lord of the
Isles. In a first, fatal error of judgement he fell, with the cream of his country,
at Flodden.

MARY, QUEEN OF SCOTS
Queen of Hearts: Mary as wife of the French Dauphin, at perhaps her happiest.

opposite MARY, QUEEN OF SCOTS *(Anamorphosis)*
A morbid curiosity still displayed at Edinburgh: this 'anamorphic' portrait of
mary, painted on corrugated wood, offers two aspects as viewed from one side or
the other – the proud Queen and the head of death.

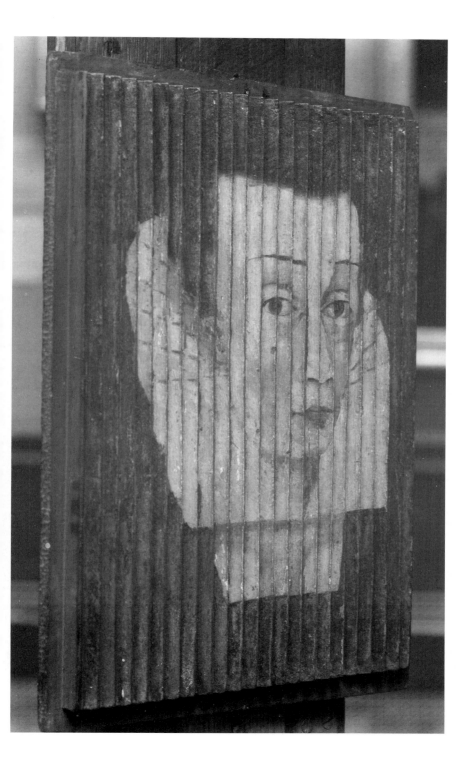

LORD DARNLEY
'Yon strapping lad', fancied by Queens. Certainly the image is of a youth who fair fancies himself.

JAMES VI AND I
The 'wisest fool': or 'God's silly vassal'? One of the rare portraits of this shrewd
monarch which shows him neither gormless nor cocky.

EXECUTION OF CHARLES I
A dramatic portrayal of this rite with the gorier details gleefully highlighted.

CHARLES I AND JAMES VII AND II AS DUKE OF YORK
The vacuity of the future James VII is already apparent; there is a tenderness, though, in his regal father seldom seen in Charles I portraits.

her. He raped the Queen of Scots. As fast as he could encompass it, they were married.

Two versions of events did the rounds. Some believed in the abduction and the rape. But Mary's enemies insisted that she had freely fled with her lover, bypassing the capital and its responsibilities, and there in Dunbar Castle made wanton with her lover. Whatever: Mary's credibility was finished; her personal rule at an end. The political nation now revolted against a queen they were convinced was a liability of the first order. The lords once aligned with Bothwell now rebelled. The city was in their hands. The Lords of Congregation were with them. A body to install a new order was raised, called the Lords of Confederacy. So troops marched out, and met the queen's army at Carberry, on 15 June, and won decisive victory. Bothwell fled the country. Mary was captured, and hauled to Edinburgh, where for the first time she grasped the hatred of the mob. Soldiers cried, 'Burn her. Burn the whore. She is not worthy to live.' So, once again, Mary entered her capital, broken and degraded, her fine clothes dirty and creased, her grimy face streaming with tears, as the people of the city spat and cursed and jeered. Two years before, she had married Darnley. Four weeks ago, she had been wed to Bothwell. The Queen of Scots, confined to the provost's house at Craigmillar, leaned from a high window and cried she had been betrayed. She had no jewels, none of her grand clothes, none of her effects: only the red petticoat in which she had come from Dunbar, filthy and torn open, her breasts exposed.

The rest of Mary's life is long, wretched and meaningless. She spent virtually all of it in prison. Her throne was declared forfeit, and her infant son pronounced King James VI of Scots in July 1567. She was forced to abdicate a few days after she miscarried of twins. The Earl of Moray became regent. She was then confined to an island prison, on Loch Leven, at the border of Fife and Kinross. By a last wild exercise of charm, she effected her escape in May 1568, and enjoyed eleven days of liberty in Scotland. Supporters flocked to her cause; but not enough, and they included no men of substance save the Earl of Argyll, who deserted her cause at the last moment. On 13 May Mary's forces collapsed, without even a fight, at Langside, some miles south of Glasgow. She ignored calls to make a further stand, and fled the country. Mary declared she would make for England and appeal to Elizabeth for aid.

On a fishing boat, crossing the Solway Firth, she changed her mind. She asked the crew to alter course for France. But the boat was too small, ill-equipped. They refused. On the evening of 16 May the sometime Queen of Scots disembarked at Workington. Within two weeks of arrival she was under house arrest as an aghast and furious Elizabeth tried to establish how best to deal with her. The flight to England was probably the most stupid decision of Mary's life.

Her English hosts were in a quandary. She could not be welcomed at court: it threatened the religious stability of the realm and, perhaps, the stability of Elizabeth's own position. Nor could Mary be allowed to go abroad, and thereby hand a trump-card to England's Roman Catholic enemies. Nor was Elizabeth prepared to return Mary to the Scots. There was no guarantee that the Scots would be pleased to have her. It would threaten the improving relations between the two countries; and if in fact the Scots tried and executed Mary themselves that would set a bad precedent for Elizabeth's own future.

Elizabeth instead set up an enquiry, between herself and the Earl of Moray and Mary, to examine the charges against the royal fugitive. It was a delay mechanism; almost a cover-up. Elizabeth had not the least interest in finding out the truth. Mary was not allowed to attend these sessions in person. The Scots produced the notorious Casket Letters: these purported to be love-letters, some most indiscreet and coarse, between Mary and Bothwell. They were probably forged. The originals have not survived. Despite this, the enquiry's findings were inconclusive. The Earl of Moray went home with a loan: the nice sum of £5,000. Mary, sometime Queen of Scots, remained a prisoner.

So she embarked on a long and weary tour of the more obscure castles and stately homes of northern and central England. Mary was never allowed to spend more than two years in the same place. Some lodgings were agreeable enough. Sheffield Castle was pleasant. Chatsworth was comfortable. Tutbury, where she spent most of the last two years of her life, in the charge of Sir Amyas Paulet, was a grim heap, cold, rambling and medieval. She was allowed some dignity. She maintained a sort of court-in-exile, numbering some forty souls. For a time she was allowed to correspond freely, though her letters were always read. She was allowed, at first, Catholic rites. She embroidered, exquisitely. She wrote, including poetry: wistful stuff, some of it very good. But her liberty had gone, and her hopes, and, above all, Mary's health. Though she was given the best medical attention, and allowed to exercise – under guard, of course – her beauty faded and vanished. She put on weight. She began to stoop, as arthritis set in. Her face grew mean, lined and tight. Increasingly she lost touch with reality. She dreamed of deliverance, and restoration. She grew the more fanatical in religious exercises. As her son grew to manhood, and to exercise monarchy in his own right, Mary sent him letters; despatched north presents of clothing and embroidery. He never replied. It is not known if James VI ever read them.

Many in high places in England feared that her presence would destroy them all. Certainly Mary was frequently the focus of plot and conspiracy. In 1569 the northern earls, all Catholic, rose against Elizabeth, with the stated intention of putting Mary on the throne. They were readily crushed. In 1571 there came the Ridolfi Plot; it, too, failed, though Elizabeth was compelled to execute one imprisoned survivor of 1569, the Duke of Norfolk. As international affairs grew worse, with relations between England and France or Spain always fraught, Mary's life was ever more imperilled. She survived the Throckmorton Plot of 1583. But the last straw came in 1586, with the Babington conspiracy. By then the Pope himself had excommunicated Elizabeth: an act which, effectively, vindicated any Catholic bold enough to kill her. Predictably, the Pope's action made the lot of English Catholics quite wretched: the mass was all but extirpated, and travelling priests, if caught, were tortured and killed.

In this climate Sir Anthony Babington appears as an earnest, romantic, empty-headed fool of a noble youth, persuaded by a Jesuit priest, John Ballard, to raise other young Catholic nobles in a plot to liberate Mary and kill Elizabeth. This coincided with the quiet resolve of Elizabeth's advisers – principally, Sir Francis Walsingham, an ardent Puritan – to force Mary's execution. From an early stage Walsingham and his secret service had knowledge of the Babington conspiracy. A double-agent in Walsingham's control, one Gifford, was encouraged to establish secret communication between the imprisoned Mary and her admirer Babington. Letters from Mary, pressed into Gifford's hands, were smuggled in leather bungs, in barrels of beer, to the outside world from Tutbury. These letters reached Babington, as Babington's reached Mary, but Walsingham's agents intercepted – and read – the lot.

On 6 July 1586 Babington, his plans well advanced, helpfully wrote to advise Mary of all; as he put it: 'I writ unto her touching every particular of this plot.' The letter was foolish in the extreme, outlining invasion from abroad; strong and synchronised risings by bands of English Catholics; the rescue of Mary and, fatally, 'the despatch of the usurping Competitor'. This last – Elizabeth's murder – was to be carried out by six noble gentlemen among Babington's circle of friends. Babington himself would head a hundred men, and ten more nobles, to deliver Mary from her bonds at Tutbury.

For days Mary had the sense to stay silent. Walsingham had read the letter and eagerly hung on her response. At length, on 17 July, she replied, cautiously approving the scheme and, of Elizabeth's murder, said: 'Orders must be given that when their design has been carried out I can be *quant et quant* got out of here.' There was more: but that was enough. She had signed her own death-warrant.

Babington and his associates were seized, imprisoned, tortured, and tried, and condemned. So terrified was Elizabeth that she expressly ordered, *pour encourager les autres*, that the executioner be instructed to extract the full extremity of pain. England's law held forth as penalty for high treason hanging, drawing and quartering; a man was hanged, disembowelled alive, then hacked to chunks. Normally, though, for common humanity, the executioner made well sure his victims were throttled and dead before wielding the knife. Such a concession was not extended to Sir Anthony Babington, who died so horribly that the gleeful mob themselves revolted and booed their anger.

A commission, largely of peers, was formed to try Mary. The trial was a farce and the ageing ex-queen made no effort to conciliate the judges. She insisted they had no authority at all over a sovereign princess. With some wit, she pointed out that as a citizen of another realm, and that as Elizabeth did not acknowledge her as true kin and rightful successor to the throne, Elizabeth had not the least lawful authority over her. Mary made no effort to beg for mercy. She had resigned herself to die the glorious death of Catholic martyrdom. Her last days, and hours, were geared to that end. Elizabeth prevaricated; swayed this way and that; was most loth to sign a warrant of execution – but at length did; and soon it was out of her possession and wending its way to the castle of Fotheringhay, where Mary was lodged in her bleakest conditions yet.

On Wednesday, 8 February 1587, Mary met her end. She dressed for the block in deep rusty red, the colour of Catholic martyrdom. She behaved with remarkable serenity and dignity; pardoning her executioner, consoling her ladies, disposing of jewels and effects. Perhaps the eerie spectacle overawed the axeman. At any rate he botched his job. The first blow bit into the back of Mary's head. The second severed her neck, but left one sinew; the executioner had to wield his axe as a saw to cut through this. The head fell; when the executioner lifted it by the hair, the auburn cloud came away in his hands. It was a wig. Mary's real hair was sparse, and grey; the hair of an old woman, her beauty gone.

So deadly was the corpse considered, even now, that it was not embalmed, but wrapped in sheeted lead. None of Mary's blood was allowed to escape Fotheringhay. Handkerchiefs, clothes, and all stained by it were washed or burned. The block was burned. All was purged; even Mary's little dog, a terrier, which had hidden in her skirts as she died, and then came whimpering forth. Spattered with blood, the pet was washed and washed, then washed again. But the creature refused to eat. It pined away, and died some days later.

In my end is my beginning declared Mary in ominous threat. Despite all the efforts of Elizabeth's court, she proved more dangerous in death than in life. The execution shocked Christendom. The following year, Philip of Spain despatched his Armada. In Scotland, James VI made but perfunctory protest.

It was in his birth, perhaps, that Mary enjoyed her one real triumph over Elizabeth, virgin and childless queen. 'The Queen of Scots is lighter of a fair son,' cried Elizabeth, in 1566, 'and I am but a barren stock.' No descendant of Elizabeth survives; nor any seed of Henry VIII, legitimate or otherwise. The progeny of Mary, Queen of Scots, are today without number; they include every man and woman who has ever since sat on our throne. Her remains today lie, encased in lead, in a deep vault below Westminster Abbey, surrounded by the coffins of royal youths, princesses and children. Elizabeth's remains lie in another vault, with only those of her sister for company. The Queen of Scots had always the better in theatricals.

5

GOD'S SILLY VASSAL

James VI and I

King James, VI of Scotland, I of England, is surely the most fascinating of Stuart monarchs. He is still famous, beyond the pages of history books, for his sponsorship of the Authorised Version – widely known, around the world, as the King James Bible – and for his stern opinion on matters such as smoking. A French king's soubriquet for the Scots monarch – the 'wisest fool in Christendom' – has stuck fast to his reputation. Every schoolboy still remembers him as the monarch Guy Fawkes wanted to blow up.

He embodies a mass of contradiction. He was the first King of Britain, the figure in whom cohered the Union of Crowns in 1603. But James was, physically and by upbringing, the most uncouth, ungainly, grubby, physically repulsive man for that moment in the history of these isles. King James was immensely learned, widely read, fluent in tongues, the author of pamphlets and books. Yet, time and again – especially in his English reign, traditionally judged less successful than his government of Scotland – James showed the most elementary lack of regal deportment. He was incurably religious and a genuinely expert theologian; he was, in doctrine, a Calvinist. Yet his court became renowned for drunkenness and debauchery. He married well and begot several children. Yet, all his life, he took homosexual pleasure with a variety of pretty and, latterly, ambitious, male favourites.

James, like many a forebear, could never remember *not* being king. He was born in Edinburgh Castle on the morning of Wednesday 19 June, 1566 after a protracted labour; moreover, there was a caul stretched over the baby's face. Those hazards notwithstanding, he struck observers as a big and healthy infant. He was fast furnished with a wet-nurse, and shortly removed to Stirling Castle, to be raised in safety and at some distance from the tensions of the capital. His birth was the occasion for much rejoicing. Five hundred bonfires were lit to brighten Edinburgh's sky. Every cannon in the castle boomed and roared. The great and good gathered in St Giles to praise the Lord for this gift of an heir. Sir James Melville was despatched within the hour to take the glad tidings to Elizabeth. (We know her personal response; James's birth was also a political threat, for the arrival of a bouncing boy could only strengthen Mary's claim to inherit.)

Darnley, of course, was bumped further down the queue of succession by the birth of his son. Mary, mindful as she was these days of the king's fragile temperament, took good care dramatically to display the infant to him. 'My Lord, God has given you and me a son, begotten by none but you. Here I protest to God as I shall answer to him at the great day of Judgement, that this is your son and no other man's son. I am desirous that all here, with ladies and others bear witness.'

And then, unable to resist a jibe, the queen bitterly added, 'For he is so much your own son that I fear it will be the worse for him thereafter!'

Yet, to this day, rumours persist that the child who became James VI was not Darnley's son at all – and not even Mary's. All his life James would be sensitive to the taunt of 'Davie's boy', the libel that he was the child of Rizzio. That was certainly not true. But, in 1830, the skeleton of an infant was found in the wall of a chamber at Edinburgh Castle, wrapped in good cloth. It gave some life to an old tale that Mary's child had died at birth, and was quickly substituted with the baby son of the Countess of Mar, a child of Erskine blood. That tale gained credence from King James's close resemblance, in adulthood, to the second Earl of Mar who, on this version of history, was his natural brother.

The story is fantastic and absurd. Royal birth chambers, crowded with ladies and doctors and gawping witnesses, did not lend themselves to such games of pass-the-parcel; besides, Mary's *accouchement* included such attendant dignitaries as Archbishop Hamilton, who stood in close line of succession to the Scots throne, and would scarcely have allowed such nonsense. King James was in fact related to the Erskines, who shared Lennox Stewart blood. And childhood portraits of the king show striking resemblance to those of the young Darnley.

On 25 July 1567 the Queen of Scots abdicated, signing the papers under some duress at her jail on Loch Leven. Four days later the Earl of Mar and assorted lords – Morton, Atholl, Hume – assembled for an extraordinary ceremony in the old Church of the Holy Rood in Stirling. The building was still in some chaos from the Reformation. The niches were bare of plaster saints. There was no altar, nor cross. There was but a table, and behind it – where choirboys had once sung anthems and orisons – rose that innovation in Scotland, a pulpit, and before this pulpit stood John Knox. Around him were more earls, more lords, assorted gentlemen, two superintendents of the Kirk and even the Catholic Bishop of Orkney.

The Earl of Atholl carried the sword of state. The Earl of Morton carried the sceptre. And the Earl of Mar carried the king, who was thirteen months and ten days old. Matters were rushed and fraught. Mary's statement of abdication was quickly read aloud. A proclamation was declared, making the Earl of Moray – still absent in England – regent. Another proclamation named the regent's council.

The legalities done, the little king was anointed with oil, the bishop pouring this on his head, shoulders and the palms of his hands. The two Kirk superintendents held the crown over King James's fair head, while Morton and Hume took the coronation oath on his behalf. The armoured men present came, one by one, to touch the crown with the tips of their swords and so swear loyalty. John Knox took the pulpit and preached, with passion and aptness, from the Book of Kings, of the anointing and coronation of young king Jehoash, while the vile Queen Athaliah had ranted in her palace. And so the captains of Israel and the priests of the Lord had gone forth to kill Athaliah, flatten the temples of Baal, and restore the land to true religion . . . So was a revolution, of doubtful legality, given credibility and vision.

They proceeded forth to govern Scotland. Their king was

carried back by Mar to Stirling Castle, where the Countess of Mar, a wet-nurse, four nursemaids or 'rockers', two musicians and three Gentlemen of the Bedchamber were to attend on his needs and comforts and upbringing. That night, and for years afterwards, King James slept in the gloomy comfort of a 'bed of black damask, the ruff, headpieces and pillows being fringed with black'. The room was cheered by a huge portrait of his grandfather, James V. So James was launched in renewal of that noble Stewart tradition, a wretched and unhappy childhood.

For twenty years James had to await his own personal rule. He was five before he made any public appearance: that was the opening of the Scots parliament, when the council thought the little king's presence would lend the gathering of the estates further legitimacy. James managed a little speech, and commented that there was a hole in the roof, 'an observation shortly afterwards interpreted as oracular profundity,' comments one writer. Such outings were rare and the boy was kept, most of the time, well away from court and hard at his studies, under the tutelage of two mighty Protestants. George Buchanan was a noted scholar and propagandist; he had done much to blacken and besmirch the reputation of James's mother. He was an old man. Peter Young was milder. James's management set an interesting new precedent, perhaps a sign of Scotland's new political maturity. For the first time personal control of the monarch was quite divorced from the running of the country. The Erskines played no part in Scotland's affairs.

The king's day was dreich. It began with prayers, followed by stern studies in Greek. Then he was allowed breakfast: meat, washed down with ale or wine. Latin study was followed by ancient or Scottish history. He dined at midday. Subsequent hours were devoted to composition, arithmetic, astronomy, rhetoric, geography. He was taught to produce quite respectable verse. Supper was late. His quarters were spartan and the atmosphere at once one of grim discipline and chill, feudal respect.

The course of education was rigorous in the extreme. James grew to be surely the best taught and learned of all the Stuarts. In manhood he declared – and it was probably true – that he had learned 'Latin before Scotis'. He had an astonishing knowledge of the classics: there seems to have been no author, Greek or Roman, with whose work James was not familiar. The boy also developed remarkable facility in language. His mother, too, had shown this skill – something of a necessity in children born to monarchy – but not to James's degree: he could simultaneously translate from Greek, Latin, French and English. Scripture was not neglected. The king could recite most of the Bible by heart. He knew the scope and detail of the history of Christendom. No King of Scots knew so much of the history, and past intrigues, of his own country.

Impressive as such achievement was, though, it compensated little for a childhood never far removed from danger or violence. James's earliest memory – he described it, later in years, as the start of his 'conscious life' – was the sight of the bloody, bulleted remains of his grandfather, Earl of Lennox, being carried through the gates of Stirling Castle. Nor did he know much of love and tenderness. One did not look for gentle comfort to George Buchanan, author of *The Detection of the Doings of Mary, Queen of Scots, touching the Murder of her Husband, and her Conspiracy, Adultery and Pretended Marriage with the Earl Bothwell.* Buchanan believed in schoolroom discipline. One day the little king was bored, having spent hours in study with his classmate on the contorted political games of Archibald Bell-the-Cat. Their noise at play bothered Buchanan, who snapped at the lads to be quiet. So James asked, out loud, who might bell the schoolroom cat? Buchanan lost his temper and beat the king mightily for cheek. The Countess of Mar heard the wailing and tears and burst in to complain. 'I have skelpt his airse,' roared Buchanan. 'You may kiss it if you like!'

It was a dark, dull household dominated by men and misogyny. Worse: it was a household dominated by old men who, if learned, were of low birth and crude background. It was not only a hopeless environment for emotional security and healthy male development; it was the worst schooling, as far as courtly etiquette was concerned, for a king. James grew up in an atmosphere without love. It left him with a lifelong emptiness, a lack of personal security, and a pathetic craving for affection and intimacy; specifically, a longing for tender male companionship. He grew up highly nervous, morbidly afraid of assassination; from the age of seventeen, finding it dulled his anxiety, James drank heavily to the end of his life.

His nerviness – and, no doubt, dread of the violent and unpredictable nature of his tutors – also drove him into patterns of deceit and dissembling. King James attained manhood as a first-rate liar; even the great Elizabeth, one of the smartest double-dealers of all, found him a formidable match, and once spat scorn at King James, that 'false Scots urchin'. The combination of learning, anxiety, drink and religiosity lent him intense interest in the unseen future. So James grew fascinated by the supernatural; probed the mysteries of soothsaying, divining and witchcraft.

Unlike his mother, he was an ungainly and strange figure; some details we know of James's appearance and gait suggest a degree of physical deformity, perhaps the result of inbreeding. In manhood he cut a grotesque and chilling figure, all the worse for his dreadful table manners and rough behaviour. An embittered London courtier, Sir Anthony Weldon, has left this memorable 'codpiece portrait' of James VI:

> He was of a middle stature, more corpulent though in his clothes than in his body, yet fat enough, his cloathes being ever made large and easie, the doublets quilted for stiletto proofe, his breeches in great pleites and full stuffed. He was naturally of a timorous disposition, which was the reason of his quilted doublets: his eyes large were rowling after any stranger come into his presence, insomuch as many for shame have left the room, as being out of countenance. His beard was very thin. His tongue too large for his mouth, which ever made him speak full in the mouth, and made him drink very uncomely, as if eating his drink, which came out into the cup at each side of his mouth. His skin was as soft

as Taffeta Sarsenet, which felt so, because he never washt his hands, only rubbed his fingers, and slightly with the wet end of a napkin. It is true, he drank very often, which was rather out of a custom than any delight, and his drink was of that kind of strength as Frontinack, Canary, High Country wine, Tent wine and Scottish ale, which had he not a very strong brain, might have daily been overtaken, though he seldom drank at one time, above four spoonfuls, many times not above one or two . . . His walk was ever circular, his fingers ever in that walk fiddling with that codpiece; he was very temperate in his exercise and in his diet, and not intemperate in his drinking . . . he would never change his clothes until worn out to very rags.

It is a savage portrait. There is no reason to doubt the shabbiness of James in person and court; yet, these gross habits apart, he was an effective king.

It must be borne in mind, noting his lifelong 'timorous disposition', how haunted James was by that sight of the dead Lennox. The Earl of Moray, too, was shot to death. The Earl of Mar died violently, on the executioner's block; in all, three of the four ambitious regents met violent ends. He would have been well aware of his father's fate, and the brutal end of many further forebears. More: his predecessor remained very much alive; it was always possible she might effect escape, and try to recover by violence her crown. To James – who had not, of course, the least memory of other – Mary was not his mother, but the foul Jezebel of Buchanan's tract. And, by the time she was dead and he was governing in his own right, the young James had survived no fewer than nine kidnap attempts. It seems a little unfair when Sir John Oglander writes: 'King James was the most cowardly man that I ever knew. He could not endure a soldier; to hear of war was death to him and how he tormented himself with fear of some sudden mischief may be proved by his great doublets, pistol-proof; as also his strange eying of strangers.' James may have been paranoid, but it served him well enough: he lived to his fifty-eighth year, which by family tradition was a ripe old age and, indeed, an age reached by none of his successors on the throne, save a grandson, who by his death was long deposed.

James's language was dreadful. It abounded in blasphemy, sex jokes, and toilet humour. At hunting, which he loved, he had one ghastly custom. Once the stag was felled and gralloched, the king would plunge his bandy legs into the creature's bowels, so that Weldon could recall, nauseated: 'The manners made me devise the beasts were pursuing the sober creation.' The ambassador of France could sneer, in London: 'When he wishes to assume the language of a King, his tone is that of a tyrant, and when he condescends he is vulgar.' Yet the king disliked spectacle, hated crowds, and resented the gawping of the people when he ventured into the streets. He was assured they only wanted to see their sovereign's face. 'God's wounds!' swore King James. 'I will pull down my breeches and they shall see my arse.'

And yet you have this precocious intellect. 'He speaketh the French tongue marvellous well,' recorded Sir Henry Killigrew, 'and that which seemed strange to me, he was able extempore to read a chapter of the Bible out of Latin into French, and out of French after into English, so well as few men could have added anything to his translation.' Sir Henry had just met the king for the first time. James was then eight years old.

George Buchanan, greatest of the Scots humanists, was more than a rough pamphleteer. He had studied in Paris, and wrote magnificent Latin poems and dramas. He also had radical new views of monarchy, which he determined to drum into his charge. The king might be anointed in God's name, he insisted, and ultimately answerable to the Most High for his discharge of the royal trust. But Buchanan formulated a Calvinist understanding of kingship: that the sovereign also derived authority from the people, and could in certain circumstances be forcibly removed if he failed them. 'He must believe,' wrote the old man, 'that as King he exists for his subjects and not for himself.'

The trouble was that as the boy-king huddled over his texts at Stirling, Scotland seemed permanently to teeter on the brink of civil war. The deposition of Mary had plunged the land, already divided by Catholic and Protestant faiths, and between churchmen and nobles, and between some factions of nobles against others, into unprecedented and uncharted waters. In 1567 the lords had agreed to make the Earl of Moray regent. But in January 1570 he was shot as he rode through Linlithgow. The assassin had fired from a house belonging to Archbishop Hamilton; so, in 1571, the old cleric was hanged at Stirling. Time was not wasted on a trial.

Elizabeth had lobbied hard to make the Earl of Lennox regent, and was obeyed. Yet the nobles rallied back to the cause of Mary, leaving only the king's party – and the mass of Lowland Scotland – supporting Lennox, who in turn was shot, in the back, in September 1571, after a botched raid on the king's lodgings which followed bewildering months where Scots nobles fought for control from two competing parliaments. The Earl of Mar became regent in turn. He lasted twelve months, and then died rather oddly, being 'nobly treated and banqueted by the Lord of Morton; shortly after which he took a vehement sickness which caused him to ride suddenly to Stirling where he died.' The Earl of Morton, rather conveniently, became regent instead. And that November, as if to mark the passing of an epoch, John Knox died quietly in Edinburgh.

Morton was at least competent. His regime lasted a full six years. He fought hard to restore order. Edinburgh Castle, held by the Marian party, was battered, subdued and rebuilt. His great achievement was to solve the problem that had defied the land for years: the financing of the new Protestant Kirk. He set up a quasi-episcopal system: bishops would be nominated by the crown, but 'chapters' of ministers had the right of veto, and only Kirk superintendents could consecrate them. There was a strong Kirk reaction against this, though, especially as most of the bishops' revenues vanished into private hands rather than to the stipending of ministers. Radical minds, like that of Andrew Melville – who had spent years at the heart of the Reformation, in Calvin's Geneva, and had a mighty impact on Scots education – devised the new ecclesiastical order of Presbyterianism. It was put forth in the work of thirty ministers, with Melville at their head, in *The Second Book of Discipline* of 1574. At some levels this remarkable piece of scholarship merits parody. It majors in the minor, specifying such matters as clerical dress; the permitted adornment of ministers' wives; the precise observation of the Sabbath; and somewhat barbarous punishments for gossip, nagging wives, fornication and witchcraft. (These penalties ranged from the 'brank', a kind of iron muzzle to shut the shrew up, to the extremity of being burned at the stake.)

Yet, at a time when the crown sought once more to force its executive control on the Kirk, the *Second Book* reaffirmed principles dear to the Reformation: the concept of 'twa kingdoms'; the rejection of royal supremacy; and the autonomy of the Kirk's General Assembly. Morton angrily told Melville, 'there will never be quietness in this country till half a dozen of you be hanged or banished,' but in time Melville himself would insist firmly to the face of James VI, at Falkland Palace in 1584: 'There is twa Kings and twa kingdoms in Scotland. There is Christ Jesus and His Kingdom the Kirk, Whose subject King James the Sixth is, and of Whose Kingdom not a King, nor a head, nor a lord, but a member!'

This James could never accept. But, as a confined and controlled lad at Stirling, there was little he could do to influence affairs. He was so strapped for cash he was often unable to pay his bills. If he was lucky, surrounding nobles approved his choice of advisers. Usually they did not. Then, in 1579, James found the most wonderful adviser; more, lonely and starved of esteem and comfort, the king found love – and sex.

Esmé Stuart, Seigneur d'Aubigny, reached Scotland from France in 1579. He was James's cousin, thirty years old, extremely handsome and no doubt exuded every air of grace and sophistication. He first met the king in the Great Hall of Stirling Castle, on 15 September. James fell instantly in love with him. He might have known that Esmé had been Gentleman of the Bedchamber to Henry III of France, whom even a secular historian describes bluntly as 'the most perverted of all

French monarchs'. He would not have deduced that Esmé, accordingly, would be mightily versed in every homosexual art. What is certain is that, very quickly, Esmé rapidly extended the king's education. Details of their relationship are mercifully hidden from the prurient eyes of posterity. It was certainly sexual, and it inspires revulsion not for its physicality but for the grotesque exploitation: a lonely child being used for the gratification – and vaunting ambition – of a nobleman seventeen years his senior.

There is no doubt that James adored his Esmé, being 'in such love with him as in the open sight of the people, oftentimes he will clasp him about the neck with his arms and kiss him'. The king showed no discretion, either, with honours. In 1571 Esmé became Duke of Lennox, and attained the Privy Council. Rumour spread that the Frenchman was a Catholic agent. James was forced, two years later, to issue a proclamation denouncing every dogma and tenet of popery. The 'Negative Confession' was so blistering that, many years later, it was lifted for the preface of the National Covenant. Still, many Scots nobles remained unconvinced. They were further shaken when, in December 1581, the Regent Morton was suddenly denounced – at the Privy Council, in James's presence – for his part in the murder of Darnley. This was the doing of the Duke of Lennox. Morton was at once arrested and, despite the desperate attempts of Elizabeth to secure his liberation, was tried and beheaded in Edinburgh, on an early guillotine called the Maiden – which he had devised himself.

Two months on, in 1582, the lords resolved to rid themselves of Lennox. Hunting in Atholl, James was invited to lodge with the Earl of Gowrie, and found himself imprisoned at Ruthven, where he was compelled to sign an order declaring himself a free king and commanding Lennox to quit Scotland. James burst into tears; his jailers laughed. 'Better bairns greet than bearded men!' said the Master of Glamis. As he left, Lennox sent sad word to James: 'I desire rather to die than to live, fearing that in your disdain you have found a cause for loving me no more.' They never met again: Lennox died in France in May 1583, bequeathing James his embalmed heart. It was the following month that James escaped Gowrie's clutches; it was May 1584 before he completed his triumph with Gowrie's execution.

But the Raid of Ruthven had permanently diverted Scots policy: back to vigorous Protestantism, a distancing from France and a steady wooing of England. This James grasped as the one political reality and, free of Lennox, he made no future effort to reverse it. Harsh anti-Roman laws were passed. He was determinedly nice to cousin Elizabeth. In July 1586 – as Walsingham laboured to ensnare Mary at Tutbury – James and Elizabeth agreed a pact. She paid him a small, but much appreciated, pension of £4,000 a year, and thereafter he was careful not to offend the great queen and risk the inheritance for which he longed. When his mother's head at last rolled, the following February, he confined himself to very correct but muted complaint. He felt no shred of emotion whatever.

In October 1589 his finances were further improved by a lavish dowry: James VI married the Princess Anne of Denmark, who bore him several children. James may have had an essentially homosexual orientation, by our modern understanding; the sixteenth century knew no such concept, and many a nobleman was *capable pour tout*. He did not, in fact, demonstrate the inordinate sexual appetite of his grandfather or other Stewarts. Before the royal wedding, indeed, it was said of King James that he was 'very chaste and desirous of marriage'. Whatever the detail and scope of his sexual activities, he certainly had no difficulty begetting heirs.

Marriage brought James VI the only windfall of his Scottish reign: £150,000. His 'little wiffe-waffe' was blonde and petite and of gentle disposition; when she was stormbound in Norway, James abandoned plans for a Scots wedding and sailed out himself – in violent seas – to marry her in Oslo. He stayed in Scandinavia for a honeymoon of a full five months; and Queen Anne was grandly crowned when they returned home. She was pretty, vivacious, but not academic, and distinctly scatter-brained. Over the years the marriage cooled. James turned to pretty young men. Anne took solace in the arts, and in Roman Catholicism: she converted in the 1590s, and James, oddly, did nothing about it. Three of their children survived into adulthood: Henry (1594), Charles (1600) and Elizabeth (1596). Henry, gifted, handsome, and gracious – he seems to have been an earnest Christian, and a youth of great ability – died of typhoid in 1612. The family tragedy was to prove a national disaster. Queen Anne died in 1619.

The king was, by 1590, established in command of his kingdom, and James in fact proceeded to govern Scotland with brio and competence. He showed guile, resolve, and shrewd judgement of character; he could also be extremely vicious. The whole is leavened by his most likeable feature: a keen and genuine sense of humour.

James pursued a 'Middle Way' in affairs. The Black Acts of 1584 curbed radical Presbyterianism and impressed Elizabeth. The Kirk was persuaded to accept some limitation of its religious authority; in return, the crown recognised a Presbyterian structure and the spiritual authority of the General Assembly. He rejected the last pleas of his mother for an association and strengthened ties with England. He built up a machinery of professional administrators, like Sir John Maitland of Thirlestane. He also moved fast, when he had to, to stamp out revolt. There was trouble in the Highlands. Three Catholic earls – Angus, Huntly and Errol – schemed with the Spanish court to launch an invasion of England from Scotland. James was highly embarrassed when Elizabeth's ambassador furnished proof that these 'Northern earls' had formerly written to the King of Spain to express condolence over the Armada's failure. He stripped Huntly of office – he was commander of the guard – and imprisoned him for a time.

Later, Huntly warred with the new Earl of Moray; James tried to effect a reconciliation, but in 1592 Moray's house was fired and the young lord slain. James handled this outrage with what appeared to be astonishing leniency. Huntly was merely confined to his house for a week. Huntly was, by the way, young and very handsome; he was married, moreover, to Esmé Stuart's daughter. Perhaps the king fancied him. The corpse of poor Moray lay unburied for six years.

Then, at year's end, these Catholic barons played into the king's hands. One George Kerr was detained, *en route* for Spain, and searched. Blank papers signed by the chief Catholic nobles were found. Kerr was tortured, and spilled details of an elaborate Catholic plot. James gathered his forces and marched north where, cornering the Catholic earls, he gave them two choices: exile or conversion. By 1597 all had obediently embraced Protestantism. It was a triumph that astonished Europe.

At the same time he treated Catholicism with distinct tolerance. The Catholic Archbishop of Glasgow was in exile. James restored him to favour and made him ambassador to Paris.

This gentle approach made enemies. Francis Stewart, Earl of Bothwell – a nephew of Mary's last husband, who had died in horrible Danish incarceration; and who himself was rabidly anti-Catholic and quite mad – began to pursue James. Bothwell was scholarly, clever, dissipated and rumbustious. He seemed able to overawe James in any confrontation. Attempts to try him for witchcraft were delayed by Bothwell's repeated escapes, raids and threats. He made four separate attacks on the king, until forced into exile after the Battle of Glenlivet, to James's profound relief.

Weary of these great peers, James quietly transferred reliance – and gradual power – upon a new class of lesser nobles, drawn largely from the mass of minor lairds. Properties of the old Church, in the king's hands, were made heritable lordships, and new 'Lords of Erection' raised to counter the dangerous magnates of the country, in the 'feckless and arrogant conceit of their greatness and power'. Here Maitland – who was not of noble birth, and an experienced survivor of the Arran administration – joined the king in waging hard tactics against the insolent and destabilising threat of the aristocracy. Maitland was a shrewd if blunt operator. He also had the handy function of attracting the criticism which might otherwise have been flung at the king. Crazy Bothwell dismissed Maitland as nothing but a 'puddock-stool of a knight'; but Maitland saw him off, and others.

So a new class in Scotland's governance grew up, largely petty lairds and smart lawyers. They were rewarded the more for loyal service: moreover, as James VI observed, he could ruin them as easily as he had made them.

He considered, and studied, the nature of kingly power and authority. In 1598, addressing his son in one of his most significant works – *The True Lawe of Free Monarchies*; it was later expanded into the notorious, and less theoretical, *Basilikon Doron* – James exhorted: 'First of all things, learn to know and to love that God, who to ye have a double obligation; first, for that he made you a man; and, next, for that he made you a little God to sit on his throne, and rule over other men.' God alone judged kings: but James was genuinely scared of God, and did not care to think about the Last Judgement. He distrusted the nobles mightily, for they had a 'feckless, arrogant conceit of their own power'; as for the merchants of the kingdom, they only saw their sovereign as a handy source of profit. He had airy contempt for the mass of his predecessors, speaking of years of inept rule 'by women, little children, and traitorous and avaricious regents'.

He was not a big man – 'of the middle size, more tall than low, well set and somewhat plump, of a ruddy complexion, his hair of a light brown' – but as James increased in confidence so he grew ever more sly. He could show terrifying force. In August 1600, riding from Falkland Palace, the king was accosted by Alexander Ruthven, brother of the second Earl of Gowrie, who told James he had just caught some fellow trying to bury a hoard of gold coin. Ever on the quest to replenish his coffers, James was lured into Gowrie House to meet the miscreant and, by his version, the door was slammed and locked behind him. What happened next was certainly in character: the king appeared howling at a high window, screeching, 'I am murdered! Treason! My Lord Mar! Help, help!' So noblemen dashed to his aid; they burst in to find the king struggling with the Master of Ruthven, whom swiftly they stabbed to death. The Earl of Gowrie was also killed. At August's end their dead bodies were produced in Edinburgh for a grotesque diet of parliament, and solemnly found guilty of treason. Their 'name, memory and dignity' was formally extirpated; all their property devolved to the king. Suitably chastised, the corpses were hanged, drawn and quartered, and rotting portions nailed up for public execration in Edinburgh, Perth, Stirling and Dundee.

It is a bewildering episode. Some see it as a failed homosexual tryst: perhaps the king was trying to seduce Ruthven. But why in a grim tower and not in his own palace? Maybe James feared an ultra-Protestant coup. More to the point, we know that he owed them some £80,000; and, of course, there were old scores, from his kidnap in 1582 to the grandfather Ruthven's part in the killing of David Rizzio. Perhaps it was all a dreadful misunderstanding. Whatever, the Ruthvens paid dearly for it. James continued to persecute them for twenty years. 'It is known very well that I was never bloodthirsty,' he complained. 'If I would have taken their lives, I had causes enough: I needed not to hazard myself so.' The clergy of Edinburgh were commanded to put up prayers in thanks to God for his deliverance; only one refused.

Yet the same king, sorely provoked by Andrew Melville in 1596 – the formidable divine angrily wrenched his sovereign's sleeve and told him he was 'but God's silly vassal' – laughed the incident off, and did nothing. James thrived in ecclesiastical debate and perhaps would have missed verbal jousting with such a stern opponent. He was, by *Basilikon Doron*, 'ever for the medium in every thing'. God's lieutenants, as he described kings, were to temper might with tolerance.

In affairs he grew more duplicitous, more cat-and-mouse. He took Elizabeth's money, and corresponded in grovelling terms. But King James also flirted with assorted Catholic crowns and plots, trying to scare the queen into nominating him as heir. The Spanish Armada was sent to avenge his mother and, when the 'enterprise of England' so catastrophically failed, hundreds of wretched Spaniards were forced ashore on the British Isles. Those washed up on England died, for the most part, unpleasantly. James insisted on the humane treatment of those making landfall in Scotland: they were fed, clothed, and helped to go home. He even corresponded with the Earl of Essex, Elizabeth's spoiled and unstable favourite, who in 1601 actually tried to raise London in rebellion against her. Essex paid for the tomfoolery with his head. James enjoyed nice notes from Sir Robert Cecil, now the queen's secretary, who assured him: 'Your ship shall be steered into the right harbour, without cross of wave or tide that shall be able to turn over a cockboat.'

He worked hard and, preferring co-operation to coercion, won widespread trust throughout the ruling orders. It was a new tack, which his forebears would have despised; but bore fruit, and the achievements of James's reign in Scotland proved enduring. Unlike his mother, James regularly attended meetings of council, and appeared genuinely to enjoy them, and played an important role in discussions. Sir Henry Wotton reported to London that the king was 'patient in the work of government . . . makes no decision without obtaining good counsel'. The king issued a plethora of exhortations, declarations, proclamations, urging Scots to uphold the law and pay due regard to his authority. He failed only in one matter: he did nothing to overhaul and simplify Scotland's eccentric and creaking legal system.

Elsewhere, with patience and wit, he triumphed. In the north-east of his realm King James had tamed the Catholic earls. Now he dealt with the Borders, enjoying a measure of peace in the new accord with England, but still torn internally by its merry culture of feud, vendetta, raid and cattle-reiving. Lord Maxwell despised the king, until James in 1588 sent to borrow artillery from Carlisle, and overawed him into proper respect. The agencies of law enforcement were upheld and funded. Peace broke out on England's edge.

In the Highlands, especially in the Gaelic west, James's endeavours are more controversial: much of his most decisive activity took place in the London years. He feared the Gaelic culture, and sought to anglicise the clan chiefs. If the views of his court poet, Alexander Montgomerie, were the king's, James indeed held Highlanders in low esteem:

> *How the first Helandmen*
> *Of God was maid*
> *Of a horse-turd in Argyll*
> *It is said . . .*

And in that map to his own psychology, *Basilikon Doron*, James observed of the Highlanders that some 'dwelleth in our mainland, that are barbarous for the most part, and yet mixed with some show of civility; the other, that dwelleth in the Isles, and are utterly barbarous, without any sort of show of civility.' For a spell he tried traditional Stewart tactics. He granted lieutenancies to the Earls of Argyll and Huntly, who engaged in assorted posse-politics. James considered making expeditions to the north-west himself, but never did. He finally devised a curious new scheme of Plantation. As England was colonising the Americas, and settling tracts of verdant land with decent white God-fearing people and extirpating the heathen, so the good sons of Lowland Scotland should take over the Hebrides. So the government of King James VI devised appropriate situational ethics. Nothing was barred, be it blackmail, torture, massacre, scorched earth or extortion.

He had romantic views of the islands' wealth. Lewis, said the king solemnly, was 'inrychit with ane incredibill fertilitie of cornis and store of fischeings and utheris necesaris, surpassing far the plenty of any pairt of the inland'. To colonise this Atlantis, James drew up an Act of Parliament. The island was declared beyond the bounds of civilisation; its people pronounced 'voyd of any knawledge of God or His religioun . . . gavin thameselfis over to all kynd of barbaritie and inhumanitiee'. The coming 'Adventurers' were granted every right necessary for 'ruiting out the barbarous inhabitantis'. There was not even lip-service paid to a mission of Christian conversion. All understood that the barbarians of Lewis were to be put to the sword; moreover, as was now so would be in the rest of the region, where no lands were henceforth to be 'disponit in feu, tak or utterways bot to Lowland men'.

The 'Fife Adventurers' set forth on expedition under the Duke of Lennox, James's cousin, authorised for 'slaughter, mutilation fyre-raising or utheris inconvenieties' necessary to subdue Lewis. In 1598 they made landfall. To their great surprise the barbarous inhabitants were less than overjoyed to see them. The settlers tried to build a little town at Stornoway. But they had not expected such a wet wild climate. They had not brought enough stores. And the people of Lewis attacked them with vigour, venom and courage, under the leadership of Neil MacLeod. The Adventurers sent word south for help. The messenger was captured at sea. Another was despatched. The camp was meantime sacked again by 'two hundred barbarous, bluidie and wiket Hielandmen'. The folk of Lewis pirated their ships in the Minch; twice seized and held Stornoway Castle; and at length slaughtered the garrison. So the project quite collapsed. James would find rather more success with plantation tactics in the counties of Ulster.

He successfully outlawed the Clan Gregor, after the MacGregors massacred dozens of Colquhouns at Glen Fruin; as the MacGregors were generally loathed in the Highlands, none was prepared to assist them, and the clan's power and wealth were destroyed. James resorted to more conciliatory tactics for the Hebrides. Counselled by Andrew Knox, Bishop of the Isles, he lured the principal clan chiefs aboard a ship of his navy, and so they were brought to Edinburgh, where they were graciously treated and released on condition that they attend a conference on Iona and accept certain terms of Bishop Knox and His Majesty.

These Statutes of Iona, duly homologated by the chiefs, bound them to uphold the Kirk and its ministers. They were commanded to keep inns for the benefit of travellers. Chiefs were to live more modestly, within their means, and not by exploitation of their people. No one should be suffered to live in the Isles without a trade or income. Thievery – the islands had a nasty culture of forced hospitality, known as 'sorning' – was outlawed. No wine was to be imported into the Hebrides: they were to make their own ale. (King James resented the lost duty in smuggled claret.) Any who owned more than sixty head of cattle must send his sons to a Lowland school. Firearms were forbidden. Bards were not to glorify war.

These were anti-cultural tactics: James wanted the 'Inglishe tongue . . . universallie plantit and the Irish language, whilk is one of the cheif and principall causis of the continewance of barbaritie and incivilitie amongis the inhabitantis of the Ilis and the Helandis . . . abolisheit and removit'. It is a little unfair to accuse him of condoning savagery towards High-landers: the Gaels, at this time, were violent enough towards each other. But, in the long term, his measures did not work. It would be decades before chiefs even began to take them seriously. The Highlands would remain sufficiently lawless and unpoliced to, in time, be a source of succour to James's hapless heirs – and pay the price.

There is one good story of James's attempts to deal with a specific and embarrassing Highland problem: piracy. The people of Barra were notorious for it, and their chief, Mac-Neil, made a good living from the business. No ship passing their shores was safe, Scots nor Spanish nor English. So vigorous were MacNeil's depredations that James began to receive furious letters of complaint from Elizabeth herself. She he could not afford to offend, and decisive action was called for. MacKenzie of Kintail was commissioned to capture MacNeil and bring him to Edinburgh for trial. James VI no doubt expected to confront a villainous, battle-scarred old ruffian. He was startled when MacNeil appeared, a placid old fellow with flowing white beard and much charm. So the king laid into him for his wicked attacks on English shipping. MacNeil was his match. The 'piracies', said he sweetly, were but just vengeance on the queen who had beheaded His Majesty's mother. James had to set him free. MacNeil's estates were formally forfeit, but he returned to Barra never-theless, took them, held them, and in good time died serenely in his bed.

Yet the mass of Scotland now enjoyed peace and prosperity on a scale unknown for years. Even the Kirk was brought to heel. James shouldered more responsibility on to the bishops. He tightened management of the General Assembly, calling it to meet at short notice; once refusing to meet its Moderator because the fellow was not appropriately dressed. (Ever since, the Moderator of the Kirk, with the exception of 1986, has worn court attire: buckled shoes, black breeches and stockings.) He was careful not to convene the General Assembly in areas of great Protestant fanaticism. He appeared a lot in person; he paid the costs of moderate members, to ensure their attendance. By 1603 the Kirk was no longer a source of trouble to James VI.

His abiding problem was insolvency. James could not live in the state of other European monarchs. The grants of parliamentary taxation were not enough; Elizabeth's pension was most welcome, but fell short of his desires, and, bearing her goodwill in mind, he could not look to France for the handouts his mother and grandmother had enjoyed. His annual revenue, at £15,000, was less in real terms than that enjoyed by James V. A wicked king would have scoured funds by foul means. A prudent king would have controlled expenditure. James was not a robber-baron but, alas, rather a spendthrift. So he borrowed money. He tried to persuade courtiers to carry their own expenses. He debased the coinage. He tried the occasional sacrifice, like doing without the afternoon quart of wine. Above all, he badgered Elizabeth.

'Right excellent, right high and mighty princess, our dearest sister and cousin, in our heartiest manner we recommend us to you,' he would launch a typical epistle. The request usually failed. Sometimes he lectured. Sometimes, unwisely, he would scold; then, perceiving Tudor displeasure, he would grovel: 'I perceive sparks of love to shine through the midst of the thickest clouds of passion that are there set down.' One can imagine his frustration. To win her favour he had offended powers in Europe; significant blocs of opinion in his own kingdom; pursued a fearfully delicate middle ground in matters of religion. Yet Elizabeth never publicly acknowledged him as heir-presumptive; never even acknowledged her own mortality. She enjoyed keeping James on tenterhooks and was not above playing games with his pension to achieve it.

Sir Robert Cecil, though, had the smooth transference of power to think of; a transference surely inevitable. As the seventeenth century grew through infancy, he and King James corresponded by code. James was '30'; the secretary '10'; the failing Elizabeth '24'.

On Saturday, 26 March 1603, a bedraggled and weary rider, Sir Robert Carey, appeared, late, at the gates of Holyroodhouse, and told a delighted James Elizabeth was dead and he was king of three kingdoms: Scotland, England and Ireland. He left Edinburgh shortly afterwards, and only once saw Scotland again.

James assumed a multiple monarchy in a Europe still rent by religion and over three realms with distinct and competing tensions. He had two advantages: ample confidence – he had governed Scotland well, and knew it; and great popularity in his new realm. There was, at her death, no cult of Queen Bess, no great extreme of mourning. People had wearied of her and of her increasingly unpopular policies. It took the disasters of the next few decades to create the myth of sweet Elizabeth, beloved by all subjects, sadly missed.

James's reputation has not weathered well in history. He had, of course, the colossal strain of that hardy perennial: Anglo-Scottish animosity. There came also, as he mouldered in the grave, the catastrophic reign of his son and the turmoil of the Civil War and the Cromwellian epoch. Naturally history has blamed James for the 'Great Rebellion', which followed but seventeen years upon his death. This was most unfair. The biggest problem of seventeenth-century monarchy was money, and it was in the reign of Elizabeth that the great damage was done. Few sovereigns have suffered as viciously at the hands of biographers as King James, essentially a competent and genial man. His feline predecessor is extolled as Gloriana; his preposterous and incompetent mother has been enshrined in romance.

The fact is that it was only in the very last years of his reign, when he was tiring, and largely in the grip of unscrupulous catamites, that James became at all unpopular in England. As late as 1619, recovering from serious illness, the king's survival excited spontaneous and genuine rejoicing. The new king accomplished rapidly aims dear to the hearts of England's people. He ended the weary war with Spain, brokering a satisfactory peace in 1604. He parleyed with the Puritans, whom Elizabeth had long detested; and they found in him a clever man who enjoyed religious discourse and dispute and was fully their equal in wit and scholarship. A highly successful conference was held at Hampton Court, where the most offensive aspects of the Anglican compromise were adjusted to fit their requirements. More famous an outcome was the new translation of the Scriptures which James commissioned. Completed in 1611, the Authorised Version is still the most read and venerated translation of the Bible in existence: more – strange for a Scotsman's achievement – it is rightly treasured as the glory of English literature.

James also survived plots. Two, in 1603, were trivial; one Lennox cousin, Arbella Stuart, paid for her part by lifelong incarceration in the Tower. In 1605 came the celebrated Gunpowder Plot. It was a most frightening episode for James, always quivering at the thought of daggers, pistols and explosions; moreover, his intended fate had unpleasant echoes of Darnley's end. The plot, too, compelled James to sanction new, fierce anti-Catholic measures, which he intensely disliked. Yet it was all a propaganda gift of the first order. A popish plot to blow up parliament! And the Commons! And the Lords! And the king! More, this was no paranoid fantasy, but a real conspiracy, which could be proved. The Stuarts were never as lucky again.

He also survived parliament. It must have been a thorn in his side. It was farcical in procedure, unrepresentative of the country, peopled largely by mediocrities, and seldom rose above the haggling, hectoring and nit-picking that had generally marked its dealings with Elizabeth. Lords and Commons fought jealously to defend their mysterious privileges – if they felt them threatened – but refused ever quite to vote enough money to the king to govern the land as it needed to be governed. Most short-sighted of all, the English parliament repudiated the carefully thought-through terms James had devised for full union with Scotland. His scheme was a measured scheme and, incredibly, most Scots supported it.

The trouble was that James seriously overestimated the wealth of the English crown. Elizabeth had scrimped and saved her way to living, in fair state, on some £220,000 a year. In 1607 alone King James spent over half a million. So he – and his son Charles extended the habit – increasingly called parliament to demand money. So parliament met more and more often, and began to appear – and feel – very important. Parliament began to enact distinctly Scotophobic measures. Scots born before James's accession to the English throne were forbidden to hold public office, forbidden to sit in the English parliament. And the reputation of James VI itself suffered from this bigotry.

Take Sir Anthony Weldon's 'codpiece portrait', repeated above. But this was no moderate man of letters. Weldon had an irrational hatred for Scots, Scotland and all things Scottish. Accompanying James on a visit home in 1617, he wrote of the land that Scotland was 'too good for those that possess it, and too bad for others to be at the charge to conquer it. The air might be wholesome but for the stinking people that inhabit it . . . I do wonder,' continues Weldon thoughtfully, 'that so brave a prince as King James should be born in so stinking a town as Edenburg in lousy Scotland.' When James discovered this book he was beside himself with rage, and Weldon was promptly sacked from office in the royal household. It was then he wrote his *Court and Character of James I*, with its 'codpiece portrait' and all its pique and bile; for too long historians have taken it too seriously.

James's standing did suffer, though, from all the jollification at court. For him, inheriting Elizabeth's estate and Treasury must have aroused feelings akin to those of a small boy let loose in a sweetie-shop. For London, too, after years of Elizabeth's parsimony, of tightly rationed balls and masques and still more tightly rationed honours, the bounty of the new regime came as great relief – for a time. But there were soon so many Scots that resentment was aroused. Honours, presents and pensions flowed forth, depleting the Treasury and lowering the worth of the titles. Denied work and usefulness, frustated, drinking, partying Scots cluttered the palace and gave their native land a bad name.

King James lacked the courtly graces that the English admired, and now fully exposed his deficiencies to a hostile, critical audience. They were shocked by his heavy drinking, his ghastly manners at table, his blue jokes and bad language. They were shocked by his homosexuality. By the end of his life he was kissing Villiers and other favourites full on the lips, fingering their bodies, writing them silly letters with such endearments as 'my sweet child and wife', signed by 'your dear old dad and gossip'. He even dared to defend this from Scripture: 'You may be sure that I love the Earl of Buckingham more than anyone else, and more than you who are here assembled. I wish to speak on my own behalf, and not to have it thought to be a defect, for Jesus Christ did the same, and therefore I cannot be blamed. Christ had his John, and I have my George.'

The ambassador of France had seen much at his own court, but even he was taken aback by what he witnessed in London. King James

> has made a journey to Newmarket, as a certain other sovereign once did to Capri [the Emperor Tiberius]. He takes his beloved Buckingham with him, wishes rather to be his friend than King, and to associate his name to the heroes of friendship in antiquity. Under such specious titles he endeavours to conceal scandalous doings, and because his strength deserts him for these, he feeds his eyes where he can no longer content his other sense. The end of all is ever the bottle.

Francis Osborne was quite shocked. 'The King's kissing them after so lascivious a mode in public and upon the theatre, as it were, of the world, prompted many to imagine some things done in the retiring-house, that exceed my expressions no less than they do my experience.'

James had a nasty misogynist streak which grew worse with age. There are reports of him delighting in making the most beautiful women drunk, till they fell about vomiting in the court; he would laugh aloud at the sight, and finger his genitals – that childish and horrible habit which many observers noticed. Standards certainly slipped at his court: old measures of decency, sobriety, language and decorum. What is more disturbing is his treatment of able and loyal men, including some of great service in the past to Elizabeth. Sir Walter Raleigh was, in 1603, widely disliked at court and popularly detested as a monopolist. King James treated him so badly that he died a veritable martyr. There is good evidence that, having ordered Raleigh on a last expedition, James deliberately connived with the Spaniards to ensure its failure. His execution of Raleigh made the old warrior a national hero.

James got along well with Puritans and scholastics. He fared less successfully with men of wider and more sophisticated ability; and there were many such in London. He himself loved history, the classics, and in general the study of antiquities. He had not the least interest in science. 'His Majesty rather asked counsel of the time past than of the time to come,' noted Francis Bacon. James retreated from Bacon's company. It was much more fun to act as sage and counsel, Paul Johnson sharply remarks, to 'ignorant young Philistines like Carr and Villiers'. He did enjoy the company of the Spanish ambassador, one Gondomar, who had the same sort of 'schoolman' education: he and James would sport themselves (and bore observers to tears) by arguing in learned Latin syllogisms.

James even censored. Elizabeth had now and again banned books explicitly subversive of herself and the order of the realm: never, though, had she forbade the publication of a text in learned themes. Under her successor it was hard to publish anything. Works by Raleigh, Bacon and Coke – all *bêtes noires* to the king – only saw the public press many years after James was dead.

Scotland inevitably suffered from the absence of its king, who sat some 400 miles distant. Burgesses in the cities complained that trade was suffering. The king controlled the Scots Privy Council and the Lords of the Articles, key instruments of power; he had no need to fear the Scots parliament. From 1609 he began to encourage Scots to embark on the Plantation of Ulster. Already, on the coasts of Antrim and Down, several hundred Scots had settled. They were joined by more than seventy nobles, lairds, merchants and burgesses, who took up large holdings and settled new Scots tenants. Not all were Protestants – there was at least one Catholic planter, George Hamilton of Greenlaw – but James delighted in this 'settling of religion, the introducing civility, order and government amongst a barbarous and unsubdued people, to be acts of piety and glory, and worthy always of a Christian prince to endeavour'. From our perspective we see the history of Ulster somewhat differently.

Denied a court at home, or much chance of advancement in England, many able Scots simply emigrated elsewhere. From 1605 hundreds joined foreign armies, like those of the Swedish king, Gustavus Adolphus. Others made their way to Holland, or France, to study, or to buy and sell, or to find work as mercenaries. By 1616 William Lithgow reckoned at least 30,000 Scots had settled in Poland. By 1621 Scots were looking to Nova Scotia.

From the perspective of England, James grew determined to break the grip of Presbyterianism further in Scotland. He was charmed by the ordered, hierarchical, compliant nature of the Church of England. When eight leading Scots ministers accepted his invitation to London, in 1606, they were startled to find themselves harangued before the English court. Andrew Melville never set foot in Scotland again: after three years chilling in the Tower, he fled abroad. 'A Scottish Presbytery,' cried James, 'agreeth as well with a monarch as God and the Devil.' To another delegation from the Kirk, he roared: 'I give not a turd for your preaching.' By 1610 he had made eleven bishoprics in Scotland. He added two archbishops. Two Courts of High Commission were created to enforce Scots religious life on the obedient English model. Some of his bishops, like gentle Forbes of Aberdeen, won real respect. Nor, unlike his successor, was James daft enough to meddle with the actual congregational worship, at this stage. By 1665 Scots would look back wistfully on such a moderate religious settlement.

Yet, in 1617, when he returned for a Scottish visit, James installed an organ and choir at the Royal Chapel of Holyrood, and this caused huge offence in Edinburgh. Further, James made it known he wanted four changes in worship. He thought Scots, like the English, should receive the Sacrament on their knees. He wanted them to celebrate Christmas and Easter. He wanted episcopal confirmation of new communicants; he thought private baptism and private communion should be allowed. In 1618 the General Assembly was bullied and cowed into adopting these 'Five Articles of Perth', though many ministers refused to put them into practice. Angrily, James banned the General Assembly. It did not meet again for twenty years.

Abroad, he did his best to build continental peace. James underestimated the well-ingrained hatred of England for Spain. He achieved a fine Protestant marriage for the Princess Elizabeth, to Frederick, Elector Palatine in Germany. But when the Spanish invaded the Palatine principality, he was still hopefully wooing the Catholic powers, and looked silly. At the very end of his reign there was a last humiliation. Charles, his heir, returned in humiliation from a supposedly incognito trip to woo the Spanish infanta; unconvincingly disguised with false beards and assumed identities, and with such indiscretion that by the time they reached Paris everyone in Madrid knew they were coming. Worse, in the process Charles and Buckingham had – as part of their unsuccessful mission – given away chunks of England's crown jewels, including a great ruby which Henry VIII had seized from the shrine of Thomas à Becket. James kept his kingdoms from war: for that he deserves some praise.

In these last years one favourite, George Villiers, Marquess of Buckingham, began to exercise serious power. James dealt with increasing eccentricity. He was old, overweight, and toothless. He suffered dreadfully from piles and gout, and arthritis made it difficult for him to move around. Physically and emotionally he was quite dependent upon Buckingham, who was undeniably able, but of fundamentally nasty character. It is of these years that we are told the worst of the king's excesses: it is worth noting that the most vicious accounts are not contemporary. (Weldon's book was not, indeed, published until 1649, when another monarch had much to think on.) But James's decrepitude can be exaggerated. Till the last weeks of his life, old as he was, he rose often at dawn to go hunting. He might be silly, too, in his letters to Buckingham: 'My only sweet and dear child, Blessing, blessing, blessing on thy heartroots and all thine,' wrote James in 1624. 'This Tuesday morning here is a great store of game, as they say, especially partridges and stone curlews. I know who shall get their part of them!' But the letter is lucid, detailed and not in the least senile.

King James never lost his shrewdness; but by the end of his life he had shed some dignity. The old man endured a series of convulsions in the spring of 1625. Near the end of March he took a massive stroke. On 27 March he died squalidly and pitiably, half choking in his own phlegm, awash in his own excrement. Thus passed King James, multifaceted and most intriguing of monarchs, to the Great Judgement he had always – and sincerely – dreaded.

6

CLEAN DIFFERENT THINGS

Charles I: Moron

The seeds of the Great Rebellion had some root in the reign of James, and Elizabeth. And, too, there were wider social forces at work. But scholars no longer hold James as the great villain who set the crown on its doomed collision course with parliament. The disaster was very much of the personal making of his son and heir, Charles I. He was a deeply religious man, almost certainly a virgin when he married; a king who, in his personal dealings, showed deep paternal kindness and judgement. Yet he proved, in the judgement of historians, the most inept monarch of England since Henry VI; as for Scotland (and he was the last king to be born north of the Border) Charles I's pig-headed incompetence spread disaster and turmoil on a scale that would have appalled his grandmother. Like her, the blundering cost him his throne and his life: the first monarch in Christendom to be overthrown, tried and executed, by due judicial process, at the hands and will of his own subjects.

Charles was born on 19 November 1600 in Dunfermline Castle in Fife, north of the Firth of Forth. He was the third child of James VI and his queen and the last to survive infancy. So he was very much the baby of the family, cast firmly into the shadow of his precocious and talented big brother, and not taken too seriously by his family or anyone else.

For one, no one expected the prince to survive. He was so sickly at birth that he was baptised almost immediately. At two, he was considered far too delicate to join his parents on the triumphant journey to London. It was August 1604 before the prince was brought to England. More: he was slow, deformed and backward. He probably had rickets. Certainly he was very late to walk and talk. There was a weakness in the joints of his legs and, even at four years old, he could not walk or stand unsupported. The child also had a bad speech impediment and, while Charles did manage to conquer his weakness in limb – though he would always be short – he never quite overcame his stammer. It made him a man of few words, awkward and withdrawn, and the enforced shyness was a great disadvantage in his reign.

He saw little of his father, or of the Prince of Wales, who seems to have teased his little brother dreadfully, mocking 'till he made him weep, telling him that he should be a bishop, a gown being fittest to hide his legs'. Charles spent his earliest years in the charge of Lord and Lady Fyvie at Dunfermline. The royal palace enjoyed fine views over the Firth to Edinburgh, the capital strung on a distant ridge between Holyrood and the castle. King James liked to travel about Scotland, attending to affairs and fitting in much hunting and hawking. The queen liked Dunfermline – she preferred it to Edinburgh – and spent much time there. Reports of Charles's tutors survive. When he was nearly four, it was optimistically related that 'although yet weak in body, he is beginning to speak some words. He is far better as yet with his mind, than with his body and feet.'

Reaching London at length, Charles was put in the care of Sir Robert and Lady Cary. (It took time to find a willing couple of suitable background; so fragile was the prince known to be, and so widely expected was he to die, that most approached were frightened off by the responsibility.) The Carys' task was further complicated by the nasty atmosphere at court and the dying marriage of the king and queen, who were not long in London when they began to live apart. Lady Cary was, however, instrumental in defending Charles from doctors, the king being

> very desirous that the string under his tongue should be cut, for he was so long in beginning to speak as he thought he never would have spoke. Then he would have put him in iron boots, to strengthen his sinews and joints, but my wife protested so much against them both, as she got the victory,

and the King was fain to yield. My wife had charge of him
from a little past four till he was almost eleven years old, in
all which time he grew more and more in health.

Despite Henry's scorn, Charles grew up in veneration of the
older prince and determined to model himself on him. Henry
was a fine horseman, so Charles set himself likewise to master
equestrian skills; with obstinate determination, he succeeded,
and greatly strengthened his legs in the process. He was good
at tennis, too, and other sports. His education was conventional, rather dull: it majored in Latin and theology. He seems
to have had great difficulty in writing. We are told he was 'as
slow as pen as of speech', and preferred to dictate documents,
or even sign 'ghosted' declarations, than write things out
himself. Certainly he never attained the heights in scholarship
of his father; indeed, Charles was a striking contrast to his
father in almost every regard.

He stood no more than about five feet one in height. His
legs were always feebly thin. In features he most resembled his
great-grandfather, James V, with the long nose and petty
mouth and auburn hair, beard and moustaches. His portraits
do not show the authority we see in his father's face. There is,
in them all, that aloof and remote quality. Charles I is still, in
many ways, the most unfathomable of the Stuarts: a king
whom nobody knew. Yet he was capable of deep affection.
He always had a warm relationship with his father; they had a
long and intimate talk just before King James died. (Charles
laid on the most lavish funeral London had ever seen, and
accompanied the coffin on foot, from Denmark House to
Westminster Abbey: a long tramp for weak legs.)

Strangely, too, he was extremely fond of Buckingham, and
the two were bosom friends, though Charles was entirely
correct in sexual things, and must have been fully aware of the
favours Buckingham enjoyed from his father – or was believed to enjoy. Charles's marriage to Princess Henrietta
Maria, in 1625, started badly: for several years things were
cold, and they quarrelled over her household, and at times
would go days without speaking. But in troublous times he

found in her a tough and unflinching depth of support, and the marriage grew into one of deep love.

He was always close to his mother. From her Charles inherited a love for the arts and an appreciation of great music and, especially, fine paintings. He was perhaps the most acute patron of the arts ever to sit on the throne, and though his support of such genius as that of Van Dyke and Inigo Jones made him enemies – there were plenty of parliamentary Philistines about to mock the king's heavy spending on 'old rotten pictures and broken-nosed marbles' – Charles I had a significant cultural impact, both on the fashions of his day and the tastes of the country's gentlemen.

Nearest his heart, perhaps, was religion. It is worth remembering that he was the first monarch to be raised, virtually from birth, in the Anglican tradition. He was devoutly loyal to the Church of England, and was determinedly 'High' in his views; that is, he delighted in a fixed, chanted or sung liturgy, and preferred the Eucharist to the sermon, and in general was inclined to the more Roman side of Anglican worship and practice. His mother had embraced Roman Catholicism and his wife never abandoned it. Charles I had begun the dynasty's flirtation with a religion the mass of Stuart subjects feared and loathed.

Anglicanism, too, underpinned his politics. Even more, perhaps, than his brother Henry, he adopted ardently his father's philosophy of the divine right of kings. The trouble was that, unlike his father, he was no pragmatist; further, he was as determined to exert the royal writ over the Church in his three kingdoms as in any branch of civil life. His zealous bid to bestow utter uniformity in worship, from Shetland to the Scillies, did him appalling harm in the political sphere. Of his personal piety there can be no doubt. He was probably, as they say in evangelical circles today, a born-again Christian. Of all the Stuarts none was more chaste, and the court of Charles I was a haven of decorum and sobriety in disconcerting contrast to that of his father. But his godliness showed sad lack of acquaintance with common sense. In statecraft he lacked fundamental ethics: from the earliest days of his reign

Charles gives abundant example both of the most artless arrogance in rhetoric – 'Take not this as threatening,' King Charles kindly told his third parliament, after a long and imperious harangue, 'for I scorn to threaten any but my equals!' – and of dreadful, demeaning duplicity. He never meant to lie: but he had pathological difficulty in telling the truth and keeping his word. Certainly the court of Charles was serene and respectable. But it was also badly divorced from real life and the people who mattered. Charles I was not long king when he grew dangerously out of touch.

As prince, there are two important events in his life. One, of course, was the removal of Henry, an athletic, energetic, extrovert young man of considerable ability. In 1612 the Prince of Wales fell ill. For the next three months he steadily faded; it was an intestinal trouble, probably typhoid. But for his doctors, Henry might have survived. They vied in applying the most grotesque treatments and mixing the most disgusting medications. Henry was poulticed with the flesh and blood of fresh-killed cocks and pigeons; the last straw, perhaps, was the administration of a mighty purgative, combined with a formula invented by Sir Walter Raleigh: a wholesome mix of pearl, musk, hartshorn, bezoarstone, mint, borage, gentian, mace, sugar, aloes and brandy. The Prince of Wales died on 12 November. As chief mourner at the funeral, Charles – by now Duke of York – performed his first public duty. King James did not attend, hating as ever reminders of disease and death. Queen Anne was too heartbroken to appear. Some weeks later the Princess Elizabeth left to marry her German spouse, Prince Frederick, the Elector Palatine.

It was near the end of 1616 before Charles himself was elevated to Prince of Wales. But his marital future figured high in King James's plans. King James was well aware how little his British kingdom mattered in Europe's order. Compared to empires of Spain, France or the Hapsburgs, his realm was poor, scattered and weak. But he had dreams of playing the peace-broker of Christendom. The British Isles could play a balancing game, keeping Europe from war and thus gaining significance beyond its actual importance or that of its ruling house. Marriage was James's strategy. He had tied himself to the Protestant cause by wedding Elizabeth to Frederick. Now he schemed to win credibility in the Catholic camp by winning a Catholic princess for Charles, and the princess he sought was the Spanish infanta. Apart from placating Spain, still the most mighty and dangerous of England's rivals, the match would bolster James's position of studied neutrality.

It was not a good idea. So powerful was Spain that, had it consented to such nuptials, it would have been on terms practically reducing England to a Spanish satellite. In England itself the match would be most unpopular. After 'Bloody Mary' and her Philip; after the Armada, anti-Spanish and anti-Catholic feelings rode deep and high in the English psyche. More: James's timing was poor. Far from Protestant and Catholic tensions in Europe ebbing away, the Continent exploded in the Thirty Years' War from 1618. At the centre of this war was Frederick, the Elector Palatine, who had just accepted the crown of Bohemia and so disturbed the fragile balance of peace. The Catholic Hapsburgs made war, and with much success; Frederick lost not only Bohemia, but most of his German possessions. Restoration of Frederick's territory and standing in Europe obsessed James – and Charles – for years to come, though it had little to do with the national interests of their own kingdom.

Still, and oddly, James could not grasp that such a goal of policy necessitated a breach with Spain. So the last years of his life were dominated by an increasingly silly effort to win the hand of the infanta, an effort the Spanish were happy to encourage. They had not the least intention of marrying away their princess to England, but they could waste much of England's time and energy in protracted negotiations.

In the meantime Charles – who took little part in affairs – grew into close friendship with Buckingham, sometime George Villiers: he had been progressively made a knight, a viscount, an earl, a marquess, and finally a duke. (The early Stuart kings were so liberal with such honours, often selling them for large sums, that, by 1640, no man who valued his dignity wanted a title.) The rise of this Villiers is a key element in the developing Stuart calamity. Buckingham was the penniless son of a noble family, whose great assets were his pretty looks and very long legs. He was superficially bright and with a tongue to charm the birds out of the proverbial trees. Around him were relatives and hangers-on on whom he strove to bestow wealth and position. He was vain, incompetent, and of the poorest judgement in statecraft, whether in England or abroad. Yet from 1618 he enchanted James, enthralled Charles, and over the next decade steadily poisoned good relations between the monarch and the gentry of the shires who dominated parliament. By the end of 1619 – Queen Anne died that March, removing an important obstacle to Charles's favour – Buckingham had as strong a personal hold on the prince as he had a sexual grip on the king.

James was absent from Anne's deathbed too. Charles attended on his mother's last days. As he emerged into manhood, he won good reports. The Venetian ambassador recorded, in 1621, that he was 'dignified in manner and active in habits. He rode well and distinguished himself at tennis and at the tilting yard. He had good taste in music and painting. His moral conduct was irreproachable and he used to blush at an immodest word.' The Prince of Wales played a bigger part in politics. He was set before the House of Lords to plead for Francis Bacon, then Chief Justice and under impeachment. Parliament had been recalled, always a risk, but James needed money to wage the war that could restore his son-in-law to lands and power – or to threaten the Spanish king with such a war.

Instead, the parliament of 1621 enthusiastically embarked upon an examination of felt grievances. Resentment of the Buckingham family and their new power and influence was the motive; continued and determined challenge to royal authority was the means. Impeachment of men like Bacon was the chosen weapon. Impeachment – unlike Acts of Attainder, which the Tudors had used to remove discarded or threatening statesmen – did not require the royal assent. So, though it could not deal with Buckingham, parliament triumphantly removed Bacon and another king's man, Giles Mompesson. As for James's Spanish endeavour, they voted for only two inadequate subsidies, insisted on debating foreign policy subjects, though James insisted such were for the king alone, and limited any military action to a naval war.

The death of the old king, in March 1625, could have brought in a new era of administration. Charles might have taken advantage of the honeymoon spell, and the much more attractive figure he cut in court than his father, to ordain new men and new policies. He did nothing of the kind. Instead, the same quarrels and tensions were renewed, with all the more bitterness, and the removal of James VI and I proved no more than an administrative blip. Buckingham was given higher place than ever, far beyond his wisdom as a statesman or his value as a human being.

The population of the British Isles in 1625 stood at less than 5 million. Apart from the wild places of the Celtic fringe, however, it was spread much more evenly than it is today. Virtually all workable land was occupied and tilled. Only four towns held more than 10,000 people and only London, with a quarter of a million, would rate as a city today. Because of this even spread of people, communications were good. There was a better network of roads and bridges than anywhere else in Europe. England was also a remarkably centralised country, compared to the assorted federations and empires of the Continent. Power was concentrated on London, which from early medieval days had been the commanding apex for taxation, the administration of justice, and the making of law. Out of this had grown England's parliament, a body again without its like in Europe. The king in parliament, then, commanded England. It was one of Charles's many grievous misjudgements that he assumed his writ could run with the same authority – and effect – in the very different environments of Scotland and Ireland.

Only parliament could raise funds by taxation, and as the crown revenues dwindled parliament had grown the much more important; as we have seen, without its consent (and loosened purse-strings) a king could not make war. When Charles I took the throne the country was in economic recession; the woollen trade had declined in the last years of James VI. There were some immensely wealthy aristocrats, and a comfortable if small middle class. Had England been a solidly agricultural economy the troubled wool market would have mattered less. But there were stronger commercial and industrial elements here than elsewhere; England was already advancing faster towards the Industrial Revolution than any other nation. So merchants and millers and weavers and those who made money from money in England's many little towns were under pressure.

Still, most of England's people were poor – very poor. The great mass had but a subsistence living. Yet, because there was no population pressure, England was not liable to catastrophic famine. There were times of hardship and shortage but they did not lead to massive loss of life. The great fear, from high to low, was the plague.

England had few aristocrats. In countries such as France you had a large class of noblemen who, despotic each in his local sphere, bolstered the monarch on whom his fortunes depended. Even in 1625 – and James had showered forth many honours and titles, to the point where there were complaints that the purple was now debased – there were still only 122 peers, and some 2,000 knights. What was significant in political terms was that, under the law, the class of knights and gentlemen enjoyed no special privileges. England's subjects were much more equal, under the crown, than in any other nation of that day. The knights and gentlemen had money, of course, and owned land, and could vote for the Commons; and they had, perhaps, the right to bear a coat of arms. But they were almost as far from the crown as their farm-hands, and had no consciousness of their estate surviving solely by the will and grace of the king's majesty.

The King of England, too, was in a curious position compared to his own peers abroad. He presided over no mighty administration, which for other monarchs acted both as a civil service and a sinister security force. The routine government of the land lay, to a remarkable extent, in the hands of the gentry, who did most of the tax-collecting and, as justices of the peace, enforced the law. Worse, from the point of view of Charles I, the king enjoyed no standing army. In England, perhaps, there was less need of it. Armed revolt was rare and the few rebellions of the preceding hundred years were tiny, half-cocked affairs, never seriously threatening the crown.

So the king's weal depended on good relations with the landowning gentry; which meant that good order and happiness in the land demanded a good relationship with parliament. It was because Elizabeth had managed parliament so well – calling it as little as she had to, but always treating it with respect, knowing when to give and when to take – that England had weathered the years of religious turmoil so well; there had never been the all-out civil war between Catholic and Protestant factions as had ravaged France and other lands in Europe. The Elizabethan Settlement had created, in the Church of England, a body sufficiently wide – and ill-defined in specifics – to encompass every shade of orthodox Christian taste, from the High and Catholic to the most plain and earnest Calvinist.

A rising problem for the Stuarts was that this religious consensus was under rising strain; the settlement was in bad need of adjustment. This was a time, too, when religious conviction and polemic was the warp and woof of politics. Political struggle was expressed in religious terms; radical new ideas were clothed in the discourse of theology. The great party in this was that most maligned and misunderstood group in Britain's history: the Puritans. Most know the Puritans only as caricature: dour men and pudding-like women in funny hats and black garb, who went about with mighty Bibles, determined to stamp out every sort of joy and diversion in life. When not having a cheery time enforcing the Sabbath or burning witches, Puritans listened to sermons of inordinate length or, by chaste and darkening night, begot huge families of children with names like Jabez, Ahithophel and Chosen-By-God. They are recalled, if at all, by images from inaccurate movies about the Salem witch trials, or in Lord Macaulay's damning quote about the Puritans' opposition to bear-baiting: 'not because it gave pain to the bear, but because it gave pleasure to the spectators'.

This is defamation. The Puritan movement came to England with the accession of Elizabeth, in 1558, when exiled leaders of England's Reformation could head home from Geneva. It was, in a sense, an alien movement, heavily influenced by the thought of such continental churchmen as Calvin, Bucer and Zwingli. The key tenet of Puritan thought was the absolute authority of the Bible (which, they demanded, should be cheaply available to all, in accurate translation) and in systematic theology: that an entire worldview, for Church and state, for the order of public worship and the duties of daily life, for the betterment of souls and wider society, could be established from the pages of Scripture.

The main principles of their theology were Calvinist and Protestant. They were Calvinist because they believed in the absolute sovereignty of God, even in the salvation of the individual soul; fallen, heart-darkened man could not seek God in his own strength – did not want to seek God – so God's work in salvation consisted of unconditional election; whereby a vast multitude (by such means as the free offer of the Gospel from faithful pulpits) were awakened from their sins. This 'predestination' is today a widely derided concept, much misunderstood. But Calvinist teaching had further implications. It carried the 'regulative principle'; Puritans came to teach that nothing should be done in public worship but what the Bible expressly taught: the plain elements of prayer; praise (in inspired Psalms, translated in metre); the reading of Scriptures; and preaching from the same by called, devout and trained ministers. So an early battle for the Puritans in England was one of liturgy. The Elizabethan Settlement fell short of their biblical convictions; they were especially opposed to vestments, instrumental music, choirs and candles. More: Calvinism taught the sovereignty of God in every sphere. From music, to painting, to agriculture, to medicine, all had to be done to the glory of God: all explored in systematic and faithful fashion, faith in an orderly God commanding faith in an orderly world full of truths to be discovered.

But there was also the Protestant ethic: and the essence of Protestantism was its stress on the individual soul and his right of private judgement. One did not believe something in a blind or fearful spirit, because Pope or vicar or king said so; one went to the Bible, and judged for oneself. So Puritanism was essentially democratic. The brethren in the Church were equal before God; and even the clergy, to them, were teaching elders, different from but equal in ecclesiastic weight to godly laymen – ruling elders. In Scotland this found satisfactory expression in the order of the reformed Kirk. In England, it might seem inevitable that Puritanism was on a collision course with the hierarchical structure of its Church. In truth, hardly any Puritans opposed episcopacy when Charles took the throne. Most were reconciled to the hybrid character of the English Church. We can find little support for Presbyterianism in England until about 1640. There were virtually no independent Protestant Churches, save for Henry Jacob's movement in London. It has been calculated that the handful of independent Churches, before 1640, totalled a bare 1,000 members at most.

'The Puritans,' writes Paul Johnson as a hostile witness,

> like the Roman Catholic extremists, believed that religion was the only important thing in life, whereas most Englishmen thought it was something you did on Sundays. They were influential out of all proportion to their numbers because, like the Communists in our own age, they were highly organised, disciplined, and adept at getting each other into positions of power. They were strong in the universities, at a time when a growing proportion of university figures were being elected to Parliament.

It is important not to whitewash Puritanism. At its worst it was, as Johnson rightly argues, a mirror-image of the

Counter-Reformation; some Puritans were as evil and intolerant as the most vicious Jesuits. Nor, though the process was already beginning, had they yet thought and argued their way to such concepts as liberty of conscience or toleration in religion. The mass of Puritans did not want liberty of conscience for anyone except Puritans – *The Free Disputation Against Pretended Liberty of Conscience* would appear from the pen of Scotland's Samuel Rutherford in 1649 – and would have persecuted Catholics and Anabaptists with sorrowful zeal. They waged war against the English stage, which they would have happily banned, thus denying the world the genius of Shakespeare, Jonson and Webster.

They were not without wit. Their founding father, Jean Calvin, had great fun with the superstition of popery when he solemnly discussed the sacred relics of St Sebastian.

> The consequence has been that his body has been multiplied into four bodies, one of which is at Rome, in the church of St Lawrence; a second at Soissons; a third at Pilignum, in Brittany; and a fourth near Narbonne, the place of his birth. He has, moreover, two heads – one at Rome, in the church of St Peter; and another at Toulouse, in the possession of the Dominicans. Both heads, however, are empty, if credit is to be given to the Franciscans of Angers, who gave out that they have his brain. Nay, these Dominicans also have an arm. There is also another at Toulouse, in the church of Saturninus; another at Casede, in Auvergne; another at Brissac, in Germany, besides minute fragments which exist in various churches. When all these things have been well considered, let anyone guess where the body of Sebastian really is.

The Puritans fought against such tomfoolery; unfortunately, they had superstitions of their own. Their most notorious was their enthusiasm for witch-hunting, which was a source of great turmoil in Jacobean England, and even more so in Scotland. There had always been witch-hunting: the Puritans, rather too apt to see the Wicked One's hand in everything, accelerated it. The most ardent of Protestant apologists cannot defend the business. In England alone over 1,000 women were put to death in the sixteenth and seventeenth centuries and the great mass of them must have been innocent. Yet it is going too far to agree with Johnson when he argues that the Puritans did not believe in reason, but in the Bible. From Puritanism sprang the first great English novel, Bunyan's *Pilgrim's Progress*; from the Puritan culture arose Sir William Harvey, who discovered the circulation of the blood, and Sir Isaac Newton, father of modern physics. He quit science in middle age, and devoted the last four decades of his life to the study of theology. (Like many of the later Puritans his veneration of Scripture over creeds led him, at length, to Unitarian views.)

The Puritans were united by a hatred and fear of Catholicism. The old faith was scarcely a force in England now; it survived in pockets of remoter England, under the protection of surviving Roman Catholic squires, and Catholics no longer intrigued against the crown or ruling order. But anti-popery was now an embedded force in English culture. Memories of the Marian persecution, of the Spanish Armada, of the Gunpowder Plot enforced it. John Foxe's mighty *Book of Martyrs*, published in Elizabeth's reign, was a terrible record of the atrocities under Mary, and a book of incalculable influence. Though it was large, and expensive, more copies were sold than of any other book save the Bible. By the end of Elizabeth's reign more than 10,000 copies had been printed, more than enough for every parish church in the land. Everyone who could read read it. The illiterate had it read to them. It was England's first work of popular history, fiercely Protestant, ardently nationalist, and a pillar of the Elizabethan order: a broad Church, with some tolerance; an anti-papal foreign policy; and a new vision of literacy, science and learning, in English, and not in the Latin of the hocus-pocus schoolmen.

The turmoil of Europe as Charles took the throne excited the millenarian, nationalistic Protestantism of the Puritans. The Counter-Reformation seemed to be overpowering the

Continent as the popish states prospered in the Thirty Years' War. In France, Germany and elsewhere, Protestantism was being battered to extinction. Many Puritans saw this as the Last Battle, an Armageddon, where soon the godly would be rallied to war against the papal Antichrist. They saw England as an 'elect nation'; they, like the mass of the English, seriously believed their race to be God's chosen people. There was yet work of reformation to be done at home – the Church was but 'half reformed' – and, to be sure, they did their best to eliminate Romish features from English worship, and to engineer a 'reformation of manners' through the land, battling against sexual licence, drunkenness and Sabbath-breaking. But they had this wider vision of an England, under God, against the nations.

The Puritan movement had no discernible class base. There were Puritan nobles and Puritan peasants, though there was an unmistakable regional base: they were strongest in southeast England. Their religion, in practice, is best described as one of 'experimental predestinarianism'; it survives today in the Strict and Particular Baptists, or the fellowship of the Free Presbyterian Church of Scotland. The godly spent their days at high spiritual intensity, reading their Bibles, praying in secret, immersed in self-examination for signs of the new life, of spiritual regeneration, of election. They often kept diaries, recording their hopes and agonies. They spent much time in fellowship with others, or corresponded with godly divines, like Richard Baxter. They saw the Lord's hand in all events that befell them, personally and nationally: this 'Providential view of history' is of great importance in understanding the popular reaction to events.

They loved family life, and domesticity. There was family worship morning and evening. Godly mothers taught children – and servants – scriptural truth; godly fathers catechised them. On Sabbath nothing was done save works of necessity (like preparing food) or mercy (caring for animals); the day was spent in still more intense exercises of private and public worship. The Puritans worked hard, lived soberly, and saved money. They delighted in literacy and did their best to promote education. Everyone should be able to read; the clergy should be as highly trained as possible; and an intelligent, close-argued, thoroughly biblical sermon should be the central act in public worship.

In short, the Puritans wanted the land reformed and renewed before God and to act as God's people for the truth; in particular, to wage war for the extirpation of popery and the extension of the Gospel. At the same time they prized order. Most Puritans were conservatives, happy enough with the political status quo. They sought to change men's hearts, not to overthrow institutions. They dreaded upheaval and feared diversity. They were no killjoys – in proper times and places, they delighted in merriment – but they genuinely feared that, should their work of reformation falter and fail, God would at last cast off England from His purposes, and leave it to ruin and perdition.

Beyond religion there was a further force in this England of 1625: the rise of learning, and the idea of progress. Until the Reformation every science had been gagged and bound by the Roman Church and the dead hold of tradition. Thought, observation and experiment were stamped upon. Ancient texts and scholars were revered as revealed and eternal truth. Galen, Ptolemy and Aristotle were still the supreme intellectual standards. All illness stemmed from four humours; the best remedies were bleeding and purging. Galen's anatomy was ludicrously inaccurate and, under popery, dissection was forbidden. The world was made of but four elements: earth, fire, wind and water. The earth was the centre of the universe: sun, moon, stars and planets all revolved around it. From this inherited baloney stemmed all medieval science. No one dared to think for himself, or to experiment. It was believed, seriously, that all truth was known and that there was nothing left to discover. Change was positively dreaded. Clever men read their Galen and Ptolemy and Aristotle and, by deduction, created weighty new theories founded entirely on error.

The Reformation and the Renaissance blew this up. In 1543 two important books appeared. Vesalius published a mighty volume of anatomy, drawn not from Galen but from his dissection of cadavers. Copernicus issued a book of astronomy, founded not on Ptolemy but on his own studies of the night sky with an early telescope. Kepler, Brahe and Galileo in turn watched, studied and published works supporting Copernicus in his revolutionary statement that, in fact, the earth revolved around the sun.

The great discoveries, at this point, were in Europe. But serious advance – both in the philosophy of science, and in the reordering of university life – soon swept England. The great practical achievements, by the Jacobean era, in British thought were in the fields of mathematics and medicine. In Scotland, John Napier invented logarithms. William Oughtred, a clergyman, invented trigonometry – this of huge importance in navigation and map-making. William Harvey discovered and outlined the human circulation. Sir Francis Bacon is the father of modern scientific method; more than anyone else, he led the challenge against the 'ancients', and urged experiments, observation and induction. So the concept of progress took hold: the understanding that man, by thought and discipline, can constantly change his conditions and world for the better.

This was the inheritance of Charles I and, with remarkable and near-wilful ineptness, within fifteen years he managed to cross, offend, and finally alienate every section of the political nation that mattered, while disaster and mishap befell his regime at every turn.

He inherited a country in looming economic crisis. To its woes he now added open war. Parliament had granted some funds, grudgingly, in 1624 for the liberation of the Palatinate. In the spring of 1625 England's force – an army of 12,000 conscripts – was crushed at Breda, being pounded to only 3,000 men a few days after crossing the Channel. In the meantime, Charles had concluded marriage negotiations with France; the stern deal exacted by the French included the suspension of anti-Catholic 'recusant' laws in England and the withdrawal of all English aid for the Protestant Huguenot forces at La Rochelle. So, apart from dramatically reversing the Protestant policy England had pursued for many years, he had hugely complicated his war position, roping in the Danish, among others, and pledging them £20,000 a month in support, which was money the king did not have. In 1624 Charles and Buckingham had won parliamentary grants by promising a short war at sea. They had not even formally declared war; but they had now wasted much life, were incurring more expense assembling new forces at Plymouth, and were plainly committed to an expensive land campaign in Europe of doubtful outcome.

Naturally, the first parliament Charles I called, in June 1625, did not go well. The king refused to explain his position to parliament; far from asking for a specific subsidy for a stated war goal, he demanded guaranteed revenue, for unspecified military purposes, for the rest of his reign. Parliament had been sufficiently alarmed by the losses of the first few months; the waste of its grants in 1624; and the Roman Catholic entanglement of the French alliance. So Charles won nothing but two paltry subsidies and promise of military supplies for one year only. The year ended with further military humiliation at Cadiz. Buckingham was in charge and it was Buckingham's calamity: more English troops died of drunkenness, or starvation, than by gunfire. Cadiz, a poorly defended town, successfully withstood English attack; and the Spanish treasure fleet easily evaded capture.

By 1627, far from being in alliance, England was embroiled in war with France; there were further military reverses, thanks to Buckingham's incompetence, and his bid to relieve the Huguenots at La Rochelle utterly failed. Parliament had in these three routs a powerful target for discontent and a particular, personal target in Buckingham.

The trouble was that Elizabeth – even James – had been careful never to favour one faction at court. The perks, pensions and honours available for aspiring men of affairs were rationed around. By elevating Buckingham to such unprecedented responsibility and honour, Charles had created what one member angrily called a 'gilded bottleneck of patronage'. Only Buckingham's cronies and intimates won any of the baubles, positions and commissions available. Worse: with all advancement at court denied them by Buckingham, many men of ability now tried to make a name for themselves in parliament.

In the meantime, as if deliberately, Charles had gone far to offend the godly. He honoured one Richard Montague, a divine who in 1624 published a book called *A New Gag for an Old Goose*. Montague's text was an utter rejection of the Calvinist, predestinarian doctrines accepted as the central teaching of the English Church since the Elizabethan Settlement. Besides this 'Arminianism', as we call it, Montague had a strong Romanising bent, prizing vestments and liturgical flim-flam of the type the Puritans detested. In sum, Montague was at the extreme edge of the Church and held views loathed by the great mass of Charles's subjects. So the king made Montague his personal chaplain. Another churchman was also made welcome at court, one William Laud: Charles shortly made him Bishop of London. He later became Archbishop of Canterbury, and his hated Convocation tried to impose the most prelatical and elaborate church order throughout England and even Scotland. Laud fell with his king and was beheaded in 1645.

Prominent parliamentarians spoke angrily against this religious policy. Criticism was not something Charles could understand or accept. He reacted with anger, and extreme measures; his vague, petulant philosophy of government is best captured in his remarks to Bishop Juxon.

> As for the people, truly I desire their liberty and freedom as much as anybody whatsoever; but I must tell you their liberty and freedom consists in having government, those laws by which their lives and goods may be most their own. It is not their having a share in the Government, that is nothing appertaining to them. A subject and a sovereign are clean different things.

But they were not. Government was by consensus: by king, parliament and people united in common purpose. Elizabeth,

all her days, in speech after speech, had reminded the nation –
and herself – that 'I reign with your loves.' The machinery of
government was ever more threatened by Charles as he
blundered abroad, offended at home, and forced confrontation and division with every important institution. He made
promises he did not mean; he made threats he did not keep; he
would take a high and firm stand, then abandon it; he made
speeches oozing contempt for his hearers; he resorted, in
pique, to mean and vicious measures.

So complicated are these years that it is hard to disentangle
the skein of men, events and affairs without much detailed
and weary explanation. To save Buckingham – as members
clamoured for his removal – Charles dissolved parliament in
1626; after further and acrimonious sessions, he dissolved a
second, and then a third, and from 1629 – for eleven years –
governed without a parliament at all, embarking on this
period of direct rule by making hasty, and costly, peace with
Spain and France. In the meantime he dealt with dissent by
draconian means. Opponents – or gentlemen who merely
refused to lend the regime money; it was almost impossible to
collect taxes without parliament – were gaoled without trial.
Judges who refused to endorse the legality of Charles's forced
loan fund-raising policy were removed from office. An archbishop was suspended; he had refused to license a sermon by
some creature-vicar defending the loan.

Meantime there was great and alarmed debate about what
the king was about, running the land without parliament. Was
parliament in truth an integral part of England's government, or
was it, as Charles argued, merely a support to the king in office,
handy to rubber-stamp laws and raise money at the king's mere
bidding? Charles's opponents – and they were more numerous
than he cared to admit – argued that the very existence of a
representative body was at stake; that the king was determined
to reduce the British Isles to an absolute monarchy. The king
argued, in turn, that it was parliament who had crossed the line
and parliament who threatened the stability of a well-ordered
realm. For a decade he tried to run the land without it and
imprisoned the noisiest and most recalcitrant members.

At the personal level, these were serene and easy times for the king; his supporters, even today, argue that it was a prosperous, peaceful time for England. Between 1629 and 1638 all went most smooth. Charles and Henrietta grew close in marriage. His health was good – he suffered only a light attack of smallpox – and he took pleasure in his growing family. Six children of the marriage survived to adulthood: Charles, Mary, James, Elizabeth, Henry and Henrietta Anne. The king and queen spent more time with their offspring than had hitherto been royal practice. They walked in palace grounds with the children; they spent musical evenings together.

He collected magnificent paintings. Portraits of his late brother were commissioned from such masters as Mytens and Van Dyck. Under Buckingham's tutelage, in his last years as Prince of Wales, Charles had cultivated a taste for the Venetian school: Titian and Tintoretto. But he also collected works by Van der Goes, Holbein, Rubens. Rubens, seeking the prince's patronage, sent him one work as a present; but Charles recognised it as something from the back of the Rubens shop, with much finishing by studio-hands, and sent it back, requesting instead a self-portrait. The magnificent result is still in the royal collection today. The Spanish wooing brought more Titians, including the priceless *Venus of Pardo*, which now hangs in the Louvre. Then word went to Genoa, where the prince had word that the great Raphael cartoons were for sale.

The ritualistic High Anglicanism of Charles I found architectural expression. He commissioned Inigo Jones to design the Queen's Chapel, in the Italian Palladian fashion, at St James, where, for the first time anywhere in England since the reign of Mary, mass was daily said, by priests; Henrietta Maria never forsook Romanism. The impact at home can be imagined; abroad, it awakened Catholic monarchs to the possibility of wooing the English king by art. Even the pope sent beautiful things. The nephew of His Holiness, Cardinal Barberini, commissioned Bernini – master of sculpture – to make a bust of the king. The cast was lost in a fire in 1698, but a copy still survives at Windsor; and more famous still is the triple portrait of Charles I commissioned from Van Dyke, the better to aid Bernini's work. It shows the king full face, half face and profile; it remained with the Barberinis until George IV bought it in 1822.

There was no end to the work of Charles I as aesthete. In 1627 he bought the incredible collection of the Duke of Mantua, a veritable treasury of Renaissance art: there was modern and ancient sculpture, and pictures by Titian, Raphael, Caravaggio, Correggio, del Sarto, and the wonderful cartoons of Mantegna, *The Triumph of Caesar*. Meantime the Protestant Dutch chipped in a gift of five paintings, including Mabuse's *Adam and Eve*. The German princes made gifts too; the king acquired engravings by Dürer. It is Van Dyck, though, and his great portraits of Charles I – on horseback; standing with his groom; and so on – which are the most compelling images of well-meant, wistful, and doomed Stuart monarchy. 'When it comes to fine pictures,' said Rubens, 'I have never seen such a large number in one place as in the royal palace.' To him, Charles I was the 'greatest amateur of painting amongst the princes of the world'.

But the extravagance of the king's spending on art at a time of faltering economy and rising inflation caused great anger; Puritans like William Prynne saw veritable conspiracy in these attempts to 'seduce the King himself with pictures, antiquities, images and other vanities brought from Rome.' The overt Catholicism, the warm relations between the king and the pontiff, were politically foolish. Prynne later denounced the queen for loving the theatre so; the outburst cost him his ears, sliced off in the ever nastier punishments under Charles's regime.

Henrietta Maria is not an attractive figure. As child-queen she seems at first forlorn and at times Charles treated her with near-cruelty. Later, as the marriage deepened, she became a bad influence. She was the most intolerant of Roman Catholics and had the most vengeful concepts of monarchy. She egged the king on to ever greater extremes of arrogance and obstinacy. She promulgated the seeds of Romanism in her children: most became Catholic in later life, and in the case of James it would destroy his reign.

Once Buckingham was removed from the scene, at least Charles I no longer put his affairs in the hands of one over-trusted favourite. He surrounded himself with a small group of clever men, who shared his views on religion and monarchy, and seemed for a while to govern efficiently. Laud was elevated to the See of Canterbury. Richard Weston served as Lord Treasurer; Thomas Wentworth – later Earl of Stafford – was President of the Council of the North and Lord Deputy in Ireland. Ireland for a time seemed subdued; and, though such means as 'ship money' were most unpopular, the country was ruthlessly farmed and levied, till by 1637 the crown's revenues exceeded a million pounds a year.

If the disaster ahead had two clear roots, it was the king's policy in religion – he sought determinedly to impose his doctrine and liturgy on the Church of England, all the time protesting he meant merely to enforce uniformity according to the Elizabethan Settlement – and, explosively, his extension of that policy to Scotland. But, at home and abroad, beyond the serenity of the palace, there were mounting grounds for concern. The foreign policy of the administration continued from blunder to embarrassment; the enforcement of law under Charles I began to frighten the rural gentry, and the political nation everywhere; and, slowly, the fabric of the Stuart state broke down.

Take the Church. At Charles's behest, the Anglican communion moved further and further to the prelatical right, further from Geneva and scriptural preaching, ever nearer Arminianism, salvation by works, and Rome. The great mass of Englishmen stayed where they had always been: at the sensible centre. As the Church moved away from them, they found themselves dubbed Puritans, or Presbyterians; which they were forced to become, with the Romanising of the episcopate. Laud's vision of the Church was Hildebrandian: a despotic episcopacy, meddling in every level of learning and life, and amounted to an entire reversal of the Reformation. The distrusted Montague became Bishop of Chichester. In the meantime, the king was heard rebuking his queen – for missing mass.

As in Rome, so England now saw religious censorship. As Charles I took the throne a new law was barely dry on the statute book, forbidding the printing or import of any book dealing with religion, or the government of the Church, or matters of state, without the express approval of the crown. By 1637 Laud had raised this to a Star Chamber decree (the Star Chamber was the court for trying high treason) prohibiting the issue of any book without his personal imprimatur. Dissenters, like Prynne with his illicit pamphlets, were mutilated. Disobedient printers were jailed, pilloried, whipped. Laud banned even the reprint of Foxe's *Book of Martyrs*, the most popular work in England. In 1637 Charles declined permission to a poet who wanted only to reissue verses he had penned on the Gunpowder Plot. 'We are not so angry with the Papists now as we were twenty years ago,' said the king.

There was, desperately as they strove, continuing worry about money. For all the sums extorted by ship money and forced loans from gentlemen, the crown was all but bankrupt. Johnson records that in the previous century royal revenues had tripled; prices had quadrupled. Stuart extravagance – a seeming inability to understand the value of money – made things worse. Crown lands were sold cheap. Presents and favours worth millions of pounds were bestowed on pet peers. Even in the last years of Elizabeth, monopolies were unpopular, and causing concern. Under successors, they became a national scandal. They were not even dispensed competently, making the king serious money. Parliament learned, for instance, that the monopoly on wine had raised £360,000, but King Charles had got less than £30,000. Charles tried to raise money from London syndicates: he drove them to bankruptcy. Because he would not allow parliament to join in government, he could not raise legal taxes. And his extortion of illegal ones met mounting difficulty; he needed the gentlemen of parliament to collect taxes, after all, and they were proscribed. Ship money caused great resentment; in the end, it raised less than the cost of election.

So the king went begging abroad. Even Spain gave him a little money. The Pope was courted, to no avail. Meanwhile, England's legal system was in disarray. The courts of law were downgraded under the king, or terrorised, or bypassed altogether. As we have seen, judges were made to suffer, should they cross the royal will. And the prerogative courts, like the Star Chamber, meant to monopolise violence, and preserve the nation, became instruments of judicial terrorism. The king's will – or the will of the king's ministers – became the law; the courts operated more and more without regard for statute. Sir Thomas Wiseman was accused, and convicted, of slandering the Star Chamber; though there was scant proof and in event the crime was unknown in English law, common or statute. But convicted he was. He was fined £10,000, and an additional £7,000 in punitive damages. He was stripped of his baronetcy. He was degraded from knighthood. His ears were cut off. Then he was pilloried, and condemned to imprisonment during His Majesty's pleasure. 'When the law not merely fails to guarantee the safety of life and property,' writes Johnson of this time, 'but directly threatens both, the subject is absolved from obedience to it, and civil society collapses.'

Abroad, England became a laughing stock. After La Rochelle, the administration of Charles I took no more to do with the defence of Protestantism in France. The high seas were abandoned; even the narrows about England's coast. When the popish nations complained, the king ordered his navy to cease sailing in the Mediterranean. Piracy abounded. In 1631 Turkish pirates landed with impunity on far coasts – Cornwall, Ireland – and took away hundreds of Charles's subjects to slavery. In return for Spanish money, Charles agreed to ferry the wages of Spanish troops through England, to bypass Dutch shipping; these Spanish troops were fighting to suppress Protestantism in the Netherlands. Once, though, the Dutch bested the Spanish at sea, and drove them ashore on England; more Dutch troops landed and pursued them, without interference by the civil authorities. This caused widespread outrage.

It was beyond England, though, that the worst blows befell the regime. Charles had been born in Scotland, never quite lost the hint of Scots in his voice, and of all his possessions should have found a secure political base in his northern land. But such was the man that he had no great difficulty in dispelling centuries of loyalty and provoking armed revolt. By 1625, of course, the few Scots still in London were long absent from their native land and badly out of touch. Charles himself made little effort to familiarise himself with Scottish concerns. It was 1633 before he even visited the land – for a highly belated coronation as King of Scots – and until then tried to run the country by remote control. He made foolish appointments to the Scottish Privy Council. He treated the Scots parliament with even greater contempt than he treated England's. High new taxes were imposed, and taken south; the coronation, too, was a costly extravaganza.

The real blunder was the determination of Charles I to hammer the Scots Kirk into full uniformity with the Church of England and his own prejudiced Church order. He personally used the English liturgy whenever he was in Scotland; not least at his coronation. St Giles was enlivened by full Anglican rites; but the Scots were not impressed by the pomp of anthem, choirs and surplices, as one observer darkly noted:

> There was a four-cornered table in the manner of an altar standing within the kirk having thereupon two books, with two waxed chandeliers and two wax candles which were unlighted, and a basin wherein there was nothing. At the back of this altar there was a rich tapestry wherein the crucifix was wrought; and as these bishops who were in service passed by this crucifix, they were seen to bow their knee and beck, which bred great fears on in-bringing of popery!

Most outrageous was the king's use of Laud, whose legal writ by no order or justice or common sense was extended to Scotland. According to the 'beauty of holiness', Laud commanded Scottish clergy to wear gowns or surplices. In 1634 nine bishops were appointed to the Scottish Privy Council. James VI had introduced two High Commission courts; these were amended into one, and this new court was given sweeping powers.

Charles determined to make the Church the principal instrument of his will in Scotland. So he appointed, as Lord Chancellor of the land, Archbishop Spottiswoode of St Andrews. Presbyteries were abolished. The General Assembly was prohibited. Further, the king imposed a new liturgy. He was sensible enough to grasp that Cranmer's *Book of Common Prayer* would not be popular north of the Border, and so set up a commission to produce a *Revised Prayer Book*. For none of this was there any authority of parliament or Assembly and this, above all, infuriated the Scots.

The new liturgy was read for the first time, on 23 July 1637, at St Giles, and the service had scarcely begun when the congregation exploded in uproar. Amid cries and execrations, someone flung a stool at Dr Hanna, the presiding minister; tradition records this was a woman, one Jenny Geddes, who is supposed to have howled: 'What! Dost thou say Mass at my lug?' The church seethed with rioters; armed guards had to be called to restore order. But in the streets of Edinburgh, and other towns, there continued demonstrations of the most impassioned violence. The Scottish Privy Council, fearing for their lives, locked themselves in the palace at Holyrood. A minister at Kilwinning, Ayrshire, wrote grimly in his journal: 'almost all our nobility and gentry of both sexes counts that Book little better than the Mass.'

Opposition to the king's ecclesiastical will was not long organising. A committee, called the Tables, was set up in Edinburgh under the leadership of John Leslie, Earl of Rothes, and James Graham, Earl of Montrose. Charles refused to discuss the matter. In February 1638 he sent north a proclamation demanding that all Scots nobles who continued to resist the prayer book now submit to the king's will. It was the last straw and, on 28 February, a large body gathered at Greyfriars Kirk, in Edinburgh, to sign a bond, a National Covenant. It was written by a clever minister, Alexander Henderson, and a minor gentleman, Johnston of Warriston, whom a contemporary describes as a 'lynx-eyed lawyer full of fire and energy and gloom'. The National Covenant was more than a bond to uphold the Reformation order of the Church in Scotland. It was a declaration of national resistance, by leading men of the realm who felt reduced to political impotence by an absent and despotic monarch. It incorporated the Confession of Faith of 1581, and all the Acts of the Scottish parliament anent true religion and the Kirk. Those who signed the Covenant – they included Montrose; he was first to sign – bound themselves 'to labour by all means lawful to recover the purity and liberty of the Gospel as it was established and professed', fearing that the ecclesiastical policies of the king 'do sensibly tend to the re-establishing of the Popish religion and tyranny, and to the subversion and ruin of the true reformed religion, and of our liberties, laws and estates.'

It was signed by 150 nobles; and further copies signed around Edinburgh over successive days by other nobles, assorted clergymen and the entire Edinburgh congregation. Johnston of Warriston declared the National Covenant 'the great marriage day of this nation with God'.

Charles, in London, had managed to engineer the one crisis guaranteed to unite his own people against him. But, calling for support from his council in England, he demanded force to subdue 'this small cloud in the north'. The king's men knew that his standing was now so low in England there would be widespread opposition to the raising of an army against Scotland. But the situation in Scotland was fast advancing towards revolution. Around the Kirk the assorted innovations of Charles and his father were fast withdrawn. In November the General Assembly met, at Glasgow, and proved far more radical than the regime had anticipated; in vain, the king's men tried to dissolve it. The General Assembly continued to meet, and abolished the entire hierarchy of bishops, in utter defiance of the king.

The king determined to fight, and so rallied forces in England to launch the king's war.

7

THAT MAN OF BLOOD

Charles I : Martyr?

After all the threats and bluster of Charles had failed to quell the National Covenant movement, or to prevent the bold decisions of the Glasgow Assembly, the king first played for time. He had no standing army, after all, and raising a force in England tested his limited political skills to the uttermost. So he tried, as so often in his career, conciliatory tactics, far too late to do any good. His officials even drew up a covenant of their own for Scots to sign in pledged allegiance to the crown. Hardly anyone, though, cared to sign this 'King's Covenant'. Far from bringing the Scots to parley, such measures only excited them to bolder resistance. 'Charles acted at this conjuncture,' writes Macaulay, 'as he acted at every important conjuncture throughout his life. After oppressing, threatening, and blustering, he hesitated and failed. He was bold in the wrong place, and timid in the wrong place.'

But he had now to fight. Scotland was out of control and if the king could not bring this little land to heel – the land, after all, of his own birth – even Charles understood his prestige would sustain a smashing blow. So the creaking machinery of administration ground away, cajoling and squeezing and begging and pressing, and at length a good number of reluctant English gentlemen marched on Scotland at the head of a good number of reluctant English conscripts. At the end of May 1639 Charles and his army approached Berwick-upon-Tweed. The difficulties of raising the expedition increased the king's embarrassment. Quite apart from the turbulent Scots, he had exposed to the world the considerable, if as yet passive, resistance to his writ in England too.

The Covenanters, meanwhile, had raised a formidable and much more enthusiastic army of their own; it included many of the Scots nobles and gentry, and, critically, a large body of enthusiastic volunteers, especially from Ayrshire and the south-west of Scotland, where the Covenanting movement was strongest. The Scots could also number a large body of trained and highly experienced men in their midst: officers who had fought in the German wars; and Highlanders who had served under Gustavus Adolphus; and hardened mercenaries who had honed the arts of Mars all over Europe. At their head was a tough, experienced general, Alexander Leslie, an 'old, little, crooked soldier' with abundant experience of warfare.

On 5 June the two armies took their ground. The Scots made their camp at Duns Law, some twelve miles from Berwick, in neat billets: canvas tents for the officers, turf-covered huts for the men, and these tents decorated with blue banners declaring, in gold letters: FOR CHRIST AND COVENANT. The Royalist force took its station at the Birks, on the south bank of the Tweed and some three miles west of Berwick.

But there was no battle. The stakes were high and both sides knew it. Messages went back and forth, and at length it was agreed to talk terms, and an agreement of sorts was hammered out at Berwick. The king refused to acknowledge that the decisions of the Glasgow Assembly were legitimate. But he granted the Scots power to meet in a further, free assembly and a free parliament. So ended the first Bishops' War, in the Peace of Berwick. The real loser, of course – and he knew it – was King Charles. His weakness, in both kingdoms, had been made plain, and already his opponents, either side of the Border, were in discussion with each other, united against the king they had grown to despise.

Peace did not long hold. In August, according to the terms of Berwick, the Scots met at Edinburgh in General Assembly and parliament. Both were dominated by the Covenanters. And both homologated the decisions of the Glasgow Assembly a year before, repudiating all the ecclesiastical innovations of the Stuart monarchy and overthrowing episcopacy. According to the Peace of Berwick, these were free deliberations and the king, by any logic of honour and wise policy, should have accepted reality and agreed to honour the wishes of the Scottish people. He refused to grant the royal assent, ordered the estates to adjourn until June 1640, and began the tedious job of raising another army. So the peace evaporated, and now men marched to war for real.

By this time Charles had been rejoined by Thomas Wentworth, newly created Earl of Strafford. Strafford was undoubtedly the ablest of the king's ministers and, like Charles, was an enthusiastic believer in absolute monarchy, with little regard for parliament or the niceties of the common law. Unlike Charles, Strafford was clever and utterly ruthless. He was cunning, cynical and unscrupulous. But he was not infallible. It was Strafford who persuaded Charles to a step disastrous for them both: the recall of parliament in England. Rule by royal *fiat* had proved unequal to this crisis. The crown needed money for a sustained military campaign; much more important, only with the co-operation of the gentry – the 'political nation' – could a large and effective army be raised.

Strafford's mistake was to misjudge the mood of the political nation and grossly overestimate the support Charles could hope for in parliament. As in 1629, he expected a minority of extremists so to discredit themselves that the mass of moderate opinion would swing to the king. Not only would parliament then co-operate but it could swiftly be dissolved, the royal purpose accomplished, and the king's direct rule resumed. So parliament was called to meet on 13 April. In the meantime Strafford dashed back to Ireland and persuaded the Dublin parliament to grant four subsidies, for the crushing of rebellion in 'this kingdom'. He meant, of course, the defiance in Scotland.

As soon as parliament met in London it became apparent that Strafford had utterly misjudged the mood. The opposition was large – in the majority – and in touch with the Covenanting Scots: both parties now knew they would stand or fall together. Parliament was not interested in granting vast subsidies to the king to deal with Scotland, even if as a *quid pro quo* King Charles would abandon ship money. Parliament instead began a lengthy recitation of grievances against the king, and a natural leader emerged, John Pym, who appeared to command a majority of the Commons and was a master in debate and political tactics. It became obvious that he was in communication with the Scots. When it became plain, too, that Pym was organising a petition against the Scottish war – and had all the votes necessary to carry it – the 'Short Parliament' was hastily dissolved. Charles had failed entirely to persuade the Commons to support the heavy costs of war with Scotland. What little support the king had retained was damaged still further when he arrested some of the most vexatious lords – Warwick, Brooke, Saye and Sele – and tried to restrain the noisiest opponents in the Commons, like John Pym. Worse: he continued the Convocation, the ecclesiastical body devising further and detested Romanising forms, at Laud's orders, for the Church of England.

The Scots had never disbanded their army, and in May 1640 Leslie remustered his forces at Kelso and Dunbar. In June – breaking his word again – Charles refused to recall the Scots parliament. They met again regardless, defiant and righteous, and again re-enacted the legislation that so outraged their sovereign. Further, they were determined to enforce their will against the king's, and to preclude any attempt by Charles and his London government to invade and occupy Scotland. Besides, there were encouraging signs that the king was losing control. He had got nowhere with the Short Parliament. He had dared to arrest but three of its members. Riots in London were briefly quelled, but disorder broke forth elsewhere. Great difficulty was encountered in raising funds by a variety of forced, doubtful means. Constables so ordered refused, declaring 'they would rather fall into the hands of His Majesty, than into the hands of resolute men.' As law and order began rapidly to fail, gentlemen everywhere sourly refused to accept office as justices of the peace. Nothing the Scots heard suggested they would meet serious resistance.

So, on 29 August 1640, Montrose led the Scots forces in an invasion of England. Leslie's army waded the Tweed at

Coldstream and stomped in triumph to take Newcastle, easily scattering a feeble force of Royalists. The king's reluctant, mutinous, indisciplined forces ran precipitately back to York, leaving the garrison at Newcastle no option but to surrender. So the Scots now occupied Durham and Northumberland.

By now the political authority of Charles I had entirely collapsed, his countries demoralised, strife-torn and bankrupt. He called a Council of Peers at York, to meet in September. Hardly any bothered to turn up; those who did insisted on the summons of a new parliament. In one of the silliest acts of his career – and certainly the most vicious – Charles here at York tried to curry Protestant favour by seizing and hanging two Catholic priests: one was a feeble old fellow of ninety. It only served to cause further revulsion against him. York itself was in disarray, with English troops billeted on the townsfolk against their wishes, soiling homes and devouring produce and ravishing women.

The Scots were in bold defiance; Ireland was racked in bloodshed and disorder. The king's ecclesiastical policies were as unpopular now in England as in Scotland; Laud was hated (a remarkable achievement) by his fellow countrymen as much as by the Scots. Leading English peers – such as William Fiennes, Viscount Saye and Sele, who was an ardent Puritan – plotted with the Scots, with whom they shared a 'godly commitment'. Charles's efforts to raise an army from assorted local militia had brought a clamour of complaints; gentlemen and corporations hated paying for them and disputed their legality. The king had not the money for sustained warfare. He appealed to city financiers, but none was prepared to grant the crown a loan. Even the detested ship money had dwindled: in 1639 only a fifth of the expected receipts had reached the Treasury, and men now openly threatened and assaulted the ship money collectors. Charles I had no choice but to make peace with the Scots, and on their terms. Worst of all, he had to recall parliament. The decision to dissolve the Short Parliament had shown the world he would only govern by parliamentary norms, and under the common law, if he were under coercion. And the disaster in the north finished his credibility as an absolute monarch.

So the king issued writs for a new parliament and swallowed the stern demands of the Scots. At Ripon, on 21 October, the king's commissioners accepted terms that the Scots army be paid £850 a day as long as they occupied any English land. The king had to grant all the concessions the Covenanters had sought, and more; further, the cas-bond sought by the Scots would come to some £300,000. The king, of course, did not have that sort of money. When Strafford returned from Ireland he told Charles, bluntly, that there was no hope of raising such a sum from London loans and tax farmers. The king could only raise such money from the English parliament; and in the most humiliating of circumstances. And only if parliament was recalled would city financiers consider lending him a penny.

The Long Parliament assembled in December 1640. Few of any standing seriously believed in the possibility of civil war: that there might be open and armed battle between the king and his 'political nation'. It was not because the king was not unpopular, distrusted and detested. That he was. Civil war seemed unlikely because Charles I had no support to speak of. It was only when the growing radicalism of the king's parliamentary opponents alarmed enough people of substance that the 'Cavalier' movement began to build. But the radicalism, and angry oratory of the Commons, only itself built as the king behaved yet more outrageously. He had learned nothing. He seemed incapable of learning anything.

What was more, parliament fast stripped King Charles of his most trusted ministers. 'Their achievements during the last eleven years may not have been brilliant,' writes Watson, 'but Charles soon showed that without them he was as helpless as a dismasted ship, drifting in a storm-tossed sea.' Within days of its opening, the Earl of Strafford was impeached. No man had served Charles more loyally. Strafford had been entrusted with Ireland; he had sailed gladly to aid his king in the Scottish crisis, and won Charles's praise as 'one of the fairest flowers of his garland'. Now Strafford lodged in the Tower. A month later he was joined by Laud. Other ministers, like the Secretary, Sir Francis Windebank, fled abroad: he had been accused of harbouring Roman Catholics.

Strafford's fall is one of the great betrayals in royal history. His trial began at length in May 1641, in Westminster Hall, before a great audience: he faced the vague but damning charge of 'endeavouring to subvert the fundamental laws and government . . . and to introduce an arbitrary and tyrannical government against law'. The worst evidence against him was regarding the Irish parliamentary business the year before, when Strafford sought troops to reduce 'this kingdom'. He had meant Scotland; his foes took the remark, which Sir Henry Vane's son had leaked – Vane was Strafford's secretary – to mean England. With the Irish popularly perceived as barbarous, popish, drunken, bloodthirsty Protestant-slaughtering bandits, it was easy to arouse the mob against the minister. But a man cannot be convicted of treason on the words of one witness alone. Strafford himself thought the charges derisory. If mere advice to the sovereign could later be construed as treason, what man of wit or judgement would dare risk all and join a royal council?

'Do not, my lords, put such difficulties upon ministers of state that men of wisdom, of honour, of fortune, may not with cheerfulness and safety be employed for the public. If you weigh and measure them by grains and scruples, the public affairs of the kingdom will be waste. No man will meddle with them that hath anything to lose.'

Strafford was already a dead man; his enemies – and the king's enemies – were determined he should not escape. As their legal position was parlous, they changed tactics, and moved from process of impeachment to process of attainder. Impeachment made the House of Lords a court and due legal process had to be observed. An Act of Attainder was but an Act of Parliament, whereby a simple majority vote of Commons and Peers could condemn a man to death without the tiresome need for grounds or proof. The trouble was that impeachment did not involve the king. An Act of Attainder, however, required the royal assent.

On 21 April the Act against Strafford passed its third

reading in the Commons. Charles at once gave him his word of honour that he would not sign the warrant; would not allow his execution. The word of honour of a Stuart king, though, was a light thing against political pressure. Charles plotted and planned and toyed with one scheme or another, teetering as always between conciliation and oppression. In the meantime vast and angry mobs terrorised the city, calling for Strafford's blood. Pym exposed some of Charles's wilder military plots to the Commons, to deadly effect. The mob grew worse. It frightened the Lords, and frightened the king, who was sincerely concerned for his queen and his children. So, reluctantly, he did not veto the Act. He declared his conscience would, none the less, not let him sign the royal assent. On this basis the fearful Lords rushed to pass the measure. Ten days later Strafford himself nobly released the king from his promise; the Bishop of Lincoln persuaded Charles that his conscience as king could – and on this occasion should – override his conscience as an individual. So Strafford was beheaded. Archbishop Laud wrote in his diary, that night, in his cell in the Tower, that Charles was a monarch who 'knew not how to be, or to be made great'.

There is no doubt that Strafford's removal was, in law, quite illegal and unjust. It has been argued by historians that it can be justified as a political act, notwithstanding its legal dubiety; as killing in warfare could be justified for the safety of a nation. 'The attainder,' writes Macaulay, 'was a revolutionary measure. It was part of a system of resistance which oppression had rendered necessary.' In true Whig fashion, then, Macaulay deemed it expedient that one man should die for the people. Yet posterity has never forgiven Charles I for abandoning Strafford; and, in all fairness, Charles never forgave himself.

So he was bereft of advisers who, for their failings, had been men of such gifts and always loyal to him. Only Henrietta Maria remained, and Charles relied all the more on her counsel and judgement, with fateful results. He was as noisy, aloof, obstinate and duplicitous as ever. Charles had agreed to all the demands of the Scots. Yet he continued openly to intrigue against the Earl of Argyll, his own cousin, Lord Hamilton – who had allied himself now with the Scots cause – and other Covenanting leaders. He remained obdurate with regard to the Church of England; he refused utterly to abandon Laud and the policies Laud was pursuing. It was not just the Convocation, the imposition of frocks, bells and altars on the English Church. Laud had hauled the nation back to the Dark Ages.

Not merely did he censor all books; he had enforced a clerical control on every aspect of learning. Scientists were frightened into silence, or fled into exile. In control of Oxford and Cambridge, and backed by elderly doctors and professors threatened by the new learning – backed, indeed, by the College of Physicians, who still stubbornly clung to the ludicrous notions of Galen and Hippocrates – Laud throttled light and progress everywhere. He and the bishops alone could issue licences, for instance, to doctors, surgeons and midwives. He also controlled university appointments; so none of the new men of genius, in maths and science, could win jobs. This was the man who had presided, with the blessing of King Charles, over England's Church. But Stuart appointments were ever bizarre: in December 1641, a convicted felon was by the king appointed as Lieutenant of the Tower of London, where Laud still lodged.

Another fatal blow to the monarchy came from Ireland, where in 1641 the Catholic majority rose in revolt, attacking Plantation settlements, butchering Protestants. Tales of this reached London: more, tales that these infidels were quite out of control, that there was no power in Ireland able to hold them down, and that shortly the vicious mob would be in England. So there was widespread panic, and the panic triggered the gathering recession into a full-blown slump. Trade, especially in wool, collapsed; inflation spiralled beyond anyone's worst dreams. The south-east of England, the most advanced and prosperous part of the realm, was hit worst. Vast deputations of people, great marches of demonstration, advanced into London with wild cries for help, redress, responsible government; someone, somehow, to take charge of their utterly ruined and abandoned country.

> What men found difficult to believe [writes Johnson], was that the calamities affecting England were a pure conjunction of chance: no conceivable degree of ineptitude on the part of Charles and his ministers, they felt, could have brought about such national ruin in every department of State. It must be a conspiracy. The impression was formed – and on the face of it there was plenty of evidence – that Charles, Strafford and Laud were engaged in a deliberate operation to destroy English liberties and the Protestant religion and install instead a Catholic absolutist monarchy of a Continental type.

But Charles, as we have seen, had sacrificed Strafford to save his own neck. Thus ridding himself of the only effective servant he possessed, he further encouraged his opponents to press in upon him.

Parliament did not overthrow the Stuart regime. It collapsed of its own incompetence and haplessness, with every department of state grinding to a halt. Ministers had run away after Strafford's fall. Braver ones ignored the king and went to parliament, asking quietly for orders and authority. The king had no Treasury, no army, no civil service, no judiciary. The farce at York had pitiably exposed his moral and political bankruptcy. Yet he refused, to the last, to co-operate with parliament, who remained as reasonable as they could; they repeatedly, and with courtesy, summoned the king – as he had once summoned them – to come and consult with them about the management of the country. Charles would not.

In January 1642, at the taunting behest of Henrietta Maria, 'Go, you coward! And pull these rogues out by the ears, or never see my face more,' the king even dared to send troops into the Commons, to the chamber itself, to arrest more opponents. They failed, and the king panicked. Charles fled London and effectively quit the responsibility of government. Parliament pressed on, trying to restore order, trying still to make meaningful contact with the king. Charles ignored them. On 22 August 1642 he raised the royal standard at Nottingham and launched war on his enemies. It is important to grasp what he was doing. Charles was not deposed by a rebellion against his government. He himself was that rebellion against the only competent authority left in the land. In a sense, too, he was not in revolt merely against the nation but against the crown itself.

The tragedy of England's Civil War is that it was an accident, born to an extent from the king's perfidy but also from cumulative misunderstanding. Parliament had raised an army only as a precaution. The king, after all, seemed to have no meaningful support. It had been generally assumed that, vastly outnumbered, overwhelmed by events, he would reasonably submit to the politicians and accept their demands. In fact, his weakness and isolation had an entirely opposite effect. It left a political vacuum that frightened a significant section of noble, propertied and landed opinion, alarmed by the rising disorder in the realm and fearful for their houses and estates. Such began to rally to the king's side. They had no intention of supporting a rebellion. But they wanted a conservative force of sufficient weight to balance matters out; to ensure order, the renewed rule of law, and above all protection from the forces of the left. We can, even in 1642, use that word; for radical thought and speech was now most vocal, with the 'Levellers' pressing such astonishing ideas as universal manhood suffrage in parliamentary elections.

Charles I sensed this support, rallied it at Nottingham, and turned it into a military instrument against parliament and the great majority of his own people. So the standard was raised. Two days later it blew down in a gale.

Charles remained at liberty until May 1646 and survived until January 1649, when his countrymen cut off his head because there was simply nothing else that could be done with him.

He cut a decent figure as a soldier, and it is the third sphere of his life – apart from his sexual continence, and his aesthetic talent – where he merits a degree of admiration. Charles faced huge odds. His enemies were more numerous, and in control of the capital, and in control of the sea. They were far better funded than he. Further, especially near the end of the war, they had strong and well-organised support from Scotland. The parliamentary forces enjoyed a stronger logistical position and much strategic advantage. Most of all, they had popular support. It was never probable that Charles could recapture the reins of government, but he did his best. He proved himself physically strong, very brave, and with a competent grasp of battlefield tactics.

What he had to do – it was his only hope – was quickly to win a succession of battles, ending with the capture of London. This he failed to do. He lacked a decent general, for one thing; the best he had was his nephew, Prince Rupert of the Rhine, who was more dashing than brilliant. Nor had he significant support from abroad. His best general, Montrose – and thereby hangs a tale – was cut off in distant Scotland, fighting the Covenanting forces in the Highlands. His own forces were a disparate mix of volunteer gentlemen, foreign mercenaries, Irish freebooters, and yet more unhappy conscripts, booted to battle by feudal squires. There was an archaic, old-fashioned quality about the Royalist forces. Worse: they had no one in their ranks, and certainly not the king, who could compare in ability or authority with the leader of the parliamentary army, Oliver Cromwell.

Cromwell has a claim to be one of the greatest men in the history of England: up there with Alfred, Edward I, Elizabeth, Pitt the Younger and Churchill. But he is, too, one of the most controversial. It is remarkably difficult to study Cromwell with objectivity. It is also very hard to ascertain the inner man. He rarely made his own motives, his personal aims and hopes, clear, though he has left us a mass of papers and recorded speeches, and is abundantly described in contemporary memoir. He has been widely accused of disguising selfish ambitions under the cloak of pious professions. Cromwell is a contradictory personality. He is recorded – and they are all true – as a firebrand soldier; a meticulous organiser; a devout man of God; a ruthless pragmatist; a patient, calculating politician; a man of implacable goals; a man of tormented indecision.

Oliver Cromwell was born in Huntingdon in 1599. He was a gentleman, of land and substance, and a Puritan. Essentially a country squire, there were two powerful emotional springs that explain much of the conflict – the repeated paradoxes – in his life and career. One was a love of order, stability and peace. He craved domesticity, privacy, and pleasant pastoral things and edifying entertainments. Throughout the Civil War it was one of his most powerful wishes simply to restore order. He called it 'settlement' or 'healing and settling', and it explains much of his pragmatic behaviour. He was no less a radical. He believed in massive and essential change in the fabric of the state. But he yearned for 'settlement' as the best means of reconciling an aghast gentry, the clergy of the established Church, and in general the mass of conservative opinion both to the abiding reforms in the order of England and to peace with the violent events of the recent past. So, constantly, Cromwell strove to restore an atmosphere of normality.

But this love of 'settlement' was resisted by an opposing strand in the man: religious zeal. Cromwell had a high regard for Providence – he spoke of it incessantly – and strove, at all times, for 'godly reformation'. One historian has neatly dubbed Cromwell a sufferer of 'ideological schizophrenia'. Certainly the man was a militant Protestant. Like the bulk of Puritans, he longed to see massive, universal, individual reformation as well as reformation of the state. Piety mattered to him. But so did social justice, as we would call it today, and on that Cromwell had clear views. He thought all, rich and poor, had responsibilities towards the 'Commonwealth', as he called his England. He wanted restraint on private greed; he wanted equal access to the law, to education; he wanted equitable local and national government. He also believed in toleration, though – as a man of his age – he would not have used the word in the sense we would use it today. Oliver Cromwell would certainly not have extended toleration to Catholics and High Anglicans; nor to extreme Protestant sects such as the Unitarians or the Quakers.

He dreaded religious diversity and deplored the proliferation of denominations which, in seventeenth-century England, was already under way.

This belief in the vital nature of ongoing reformation strengthened throughout Cromwell's life and career. He often compared England to the children of Israel, delivered from Egyptian bondage. If the nation backslid, into sin, licence and idolatry; if it forsook its God; then it would once again return to the yoke of the Stuarts and of ungodly archbishops like Laud. In this Cromwell was a man of principle. When reformation came into conflict with normality, he always chose reformation, often ignoring the temptation of great political advantage, or easy compromise for an easy life. It brought Cromwell an untold amount of trouble. It haunted his reputation, then and now. Once and again, before he died, they offered to make him king. Within a year of the Restoration they had disinterred his remains and set his skull on a spike for execration.

Cromwell had an adoration for the memory of 'Good Queen Bess', and the enduring cult of the great Tudor queen owes much to Cromwell. His mother, his wife, and his favourite daughter were all called Elizabeth. He often spoke of 'Elizabeth of famous memory'. One of the first acts of the Long Parliament – with his approval – was to appoint the anniversary of Elizabeth's accession as a day of solemn fasting, humiliation and prayer. Much of his political philosophy, such as his love of order, and his belief in one broad national Church, he derived from her. He could trace a long lineage himself, back to days before the Norman Conquest; an unusual claim, even then, but true. His whole family were part and parcel of the political nation. When Cromwell was first elected to the Commons, in 1628, nine of his cousins were also MPs. Six had been gaoled for resisting the enforced loan of 1627. Cromwell was utterly English; utterly confident in England's destiny and his right to shape it; utterly contemptuous of the Stuarts. He saw the king as no more than a blundering, foreign adventurer, whose cruel pride now drenched the land in blood.

Yet Cromwell was a moderniser too. He embraced the new science and embraced merit and had little regard for the constricting, feudal bands of tradition, superstition, blood and class.

There was, then, no comparison between the forces of Charles I and the New Model Army marshalled by Oliver Cromwell. Cromwell's was a democratic force: not in terms of its internal order, but in terms of its composition. It effectively enfranchised the people of England; brought in whole new classes and sections to its political community. The army, its officers and commanders, came from a vast variety of backgrounds and trades – generally, humble ones. Grocers, butchers, labourers, squires of tiny estates who did not even have the vote, shoemakers, sailors, clerks, tanners, goldsmiths: all were officers in Cromwell's army. Some were regimental commanders. The force encompassed a huge variety of religious opinions, some eccentric and extreme. But, as Cromwell said, 'the State takes no notice of their opinion: if they be willing faithfully to serve it, that satisfies.'

It was an intelligent army. The great mass of them were educated men, able to read, and ardently committed to the cause of parliament and to the building of an entire new order of things in England. They were disciplined, firmly; trained, ferociously; marched, arduously. But they were treated with respect and encouraged to play full part in the unfolding political drama; to contribute to debate. Its efficiency made the New Model Army dangerous to Charles, but it was the absolute commitment of all its soldiers – as a matter of fixed principle – to his overthrow and ruin that made it lethal:

> that we are not a meer mercenary Army hired to serve any Arbitrary power of a State, but called forth and conjured by the severall Declarations of Parliament to the defence of our owne and the people's just Rights and Liberties; and so we took up Armes in judgment and conscience to those ends, and have so continued in them, and are resolved according to your first just desires in your Declaration . . . and our own common sense concerning those our fundamental

rights and liberties, to assert and vindicate the just power
and rights of this Kingdome in Parliament for those common ends promised against all arbitrary power, violence,
and oppression, and against all particular parties or interests whatsoever.

It was in 1647 that Cromwell's son-in-law drew up this
declaration for the New Model Army, seeking to unite it in
common purpose with parliament; there was always the
danger of the army disintegrating in religious and political
factions. On the extreme left were the Clubmen (revolutionary anarchists); the spectrum proceeds through Diggers (early
proto-Communists): Levellers (social democrats); Independents (radical gentlemen officers); the Presbyterians (who at
this time, as the biggest force of the centre, commanded the
Commons) and so on. There were even a few puzzled Royalists. The declaration – founded on grand-sounding concepts
like 'the Law of Nature and of Nations' – served to bind the
army to parliament. Critically, as in every democracy, the
army was brought under civilian, executive control; for its
part, parliament agreed to be 'rightly constituted': fairly
elected, for limited terms, and frequently summoned.

It was by no means the end of strife. One of Cromwell's
incessant headaches was trying to control the radical demands
of army factions, and especially those who sought vast ex-
pansion of the suffrage. Cromwell insisted on a property
qualification for entitlement to vote; he carried the day in
the end, and it remained a central constitutional doctrine until
the Reform Bill of 1832. And it was 1948 before one demand
of a Cromwellian judge, John Cooke – for free medical
treatment for the poor – would be met in Britain. Cromwell
would placate his radicals by abolishing the Lords and
beheading the king.

So he went forth with his New Model Army, with their
arguments and learning and ideas, with all their books that
now began to pour from a liberated press, with all their faith
in the future, their excitement with progress. It was modern at
every level. It had, for instance, highly organised medical

support, staffed by the apothecaries and surgeons of the new medicine, whom Laud had so despised. 'The antique doctors of the College of Physicians,' remarks Johnson drily, 'had mostly joined the Royalists, whose wounded they despatched by the thousand.'

The Civil War is a succession of battles in two theatres, England and Scotland, interrupted by periodic truce and spells of negotiation, the odd devilment with the Irish, the tedious negotiations of Cromwell in establishing his Commonwealth, and the bewildering machinations of the king. Battle was first joined at Edgehill, near Warwick, on 23 October 1642. It was an inconclusive fight. Taking Oxford, the Royalists advanced on London, where Prince Rupert managed to seize a parliamentary outpost at Brentwood. But the parliamentary forces holding London itself were too strong. Charles thought better of waging battle against bands outnumbering his men some two to one. He and his generals retired to Oxford for the winter, where they bought time by chewing over peace proposals as they planned the next stage of campaign. The negotiations came to nothing. Meantime Charles made a foolish agreement with the Irish Catholics. It was foolish because it brought him no help whatsoever – they were not in the least position to grant him military support – while yet again confirming to the mass of his subjects that he could not be trusted, least of all as a defender of Protestant liberties.

The following year, 1643, went rather better, with some satisfying Royalist victories in the north and west, but these were of no strategic value and control of England remained far beyond the king's grasp, especially after 1644, when Cromwell was entrusted with the reorganisation of the parliamentary army. In Scotland things seemed much brighter. The Covenanters had begun to fall out. A camp formed under the Earl of Argyll: godly, zealous, fiercely nationalistic. He said it was the prime duty of the nobles to protect the Scottish people, and that King Charles should be deposed. A moderate party formed, however, under Montrose. He and eighteen other nobles signed the Cumbernauld Bond. While professing equal religious ardour with Argyll and the others, they repudiated their political position. So the Covenanters split.

Argyll and his allies made the majority, and held the reins of governance in Scotland for eleven years. It was probably the nearest the land ever came to a theocracy. The Kirk held more power than ever before. Its presbyteries, and its General Assemblies, became a good deal more important than parliament; the Committee of Estates did what the godly told them. Church attendance was made compulsory. Merchants were forbidden to trade with Roman Catholic countries, for fear of 'religious contagion'. There was much good accomplished. A serious push was made to establish a school in every parish. Poor laws were passed. There was also darkness. A frenzy of witch-hunting and witch-burning seized the land, at the behest of the General Assembly. In 1643, in one Scottish county alone – Fife – thirty witches were burned.

Under Argyll, open cause was made with parliament in England. In 1643 the Scots and English combined in the Solemn League and Covenant. It was a treaty both military and religious. The Scots agreed to attack Royalist positions from the north. The English agreed to pay for this: about £30,000 a year. The 'solemn' part of the agreement was the commitment, on the part of the English, to bring their worship and ecclesiastical order into entire harmony with that of the Scots: in other words, to create a single Presbyterian Church across the island of Great Britain. Further, a great assembly would meet at Westminster to debate and decide on the finer details of this new common Church of Scotland and England, and its proposals adopted by parliament.

Montrose – one of the most honourable and thoughtful figures of this era; it is too crass to call him a traitor – saw the goings-on with England and smelled a rat. He grasped, correctly, that the English intended to use Presbyterian zeal for their own ends. They had not the least intention of a Presbyterian settlement for the Church of England. What they were determined to win was Scots military support in their Civil War. Montrose, too, was what we would now call a Tory. Like Cromwell, he valued order and godliness. Unlike

Cromwell, he drew the line at a 'godly reformation' that threatened the overthrow of rank and title, and especially the removal of a crowned, anointed king.

That king was now in great difficulty. The Royalist forces had failed to seize, or even threaten, parliamentary strongholds in the south-east. Following the Solemn League and Covenant, his enemies won vastly stronger forces in northern England, and on 2 July 1644 Prince Rupert and his army were put to flight on Marston Moor. In the summer of 1645 Charles did something he had not done before: he ventured his principal army in battle. It was his first, and last, tactical mistake in the arts of war, and a ruinous one. The New Model Army met the Royalist force at Naseby, in June, and overwhelmed it. 'I must say there is no probability but my ruin,' wrote Charles in July 1645, wallowing in melancholy in the old Stuart tradition.

This was most unfair to the Marquis of Montrose (as he had been newly upgraded) who was waging battle in Scotland with a skill and brilliance still studied in awe by students of war. The king's Lieutenant-General in Scotland had smashed his way back through Covenanting lines and harried the Scots administration from the north as they themselves pressed on Charles I. Montrose had an able, if ferocious, deputy in one Alasdair MacDonald, Alasdair mac Colla Ciotach, son of the chieftain MacDonald of Colonsay. MacDonald's career had been spent largely in Ireland, and he had acquired all the skills of hill warfare and the ragged but shocking tactics of the Highland charge: ambush, surprise attack, always from higher ground, with bloodcurdling battle-cries and ferocious weaponry. For men fighting a doomed cause, against huge odds, the leadership of Montrose and MacDonald was inspirational. It also led them to dreadful atrocities: Aberdeen was sacked, and everywhere they went property was looted, women raped, and surrendered prisoners put to death by the men of Montrose.

In February 1644 Montrose took Dumfries. With six cannon acquired from the Duke of Newcastle's arsenal, in May the Lieutenant-General liberated Morpeth, in Northumberland. His army was small – a little over 2,000 men – but they were tough, experienced soldiers and supremely led. Montrose beefed his strength with bowmen, and at Tippermuir, near Perth, on 1 September he led them against a huge Covenanting force. Lord Elcho commanded 7,000 men: more, he had cannon, and 700 cavalry. Yet this vast army was utterly routed, with much loss of life. Montrose made triumphant entry to Perth. Despite building desertion – by the end of September he had but 1,500 men – he took Aberdeen, again defeating a superior Covenanting force. There Montrose gathered reinforcements and decided to strike deep into Argyll, in the West Highlands. It was the base of his enemy, the Earl of Argyll – Campbell country.

In coldest winter, Montrose marched his men through the mountains to attack the earl's army at Inveraray. Argyll assembled his host there, convinced Montrose and a ragged, hypothermic, hungry rabble of Royalists would never reach him through the frost and snow. But they did. The earl, scared for his life, fled by sea. Hundreds of his clansmen were slaughtered by Montrose's army; homes burned, farms wasted, goods and cattle driven off. Through the winter the campaign continued. At one point Montrose was trapped in the Great Glen, with the Covenanting Earl of Seaforth at Inverness and Argyll's army at Inverlochy blocking both points of escape. So he did what they least expected. He led his force on another forced march over mountains, by night, and fell suddenly on Argyll at Inverlochy. Again the earl fled by sea. This time the slaughter was nauseous. There was no mercy and no quarter. It is recorded that the shallows of Loch Eil lapped red with the blood of desperate Campbells fleeing for their lives. It was both an astounding military triumph and perhaps the most shameful slaughter in the history of the Highlands. At least 1,500 Campbells and Covenanters were killed; Montrose lost about two dozen men – and some put his casualties as low as ten.

As the Covenanters appealed to England for help, Montrose moved on Elgin in the north-east Highlands; then to Aberdeen again, on to take Dundee (burning Brechin in the process) and then back to the north, to the little county of Nairn, where he won another battle at Auldearn, on 9 May 1645; it was the first time he and MacDonald used cavalry, and another defeat of superior numbers. They won another battle at Alford, east of Aberdeen, on 2 July. So Montrose was master of the Highlands. There were more astonishing feats of arms, with Argyll again fleeing from battlefield disaster at Kilsyth, Stirlingshire, in August. There was no one left to stop the Lieutenant-General and Montrose took Edinburgh.

The trouble was that he could not stem the constant desertions, especially when his army crossed back over the Highland Line. His unruly army, too, won a bad name for atrocities and looting, and only the Irish gave it much backbone, and only MacDonald could control the Irish. He and Montrose had, in any event, different aims. MacDonald was fighting for the fortunes of Clan Donald, largest of the Highland clans, against their most detested enemy, Clan Campbell. Montrose was fighting for Charles I. Having killed enough Campbells for his immediate appetite, MacDonald went to Ireland, and never returned. He died there in 1647.

As the Covenanting forces rallied again, Montrose pinned his hopes in breaking through them to join up his tough little army with the main Royalist force and the king himself. Then, on 13 September, at Philiphaugh in the Borders, they were themselves the victim of a surprise attack. The Covenanting force, under Lord Newark – a veteran of Marston Moor and a friend of Cromwell – fell upon Montrose. It was the end of the *annus mirabilis* for Scottish Royalists and it was a fearful bloodbath. Montrose himself now quit the field and ran for his own safety. As his men had won a foul name for bloodthirstiness, so the Covenanters disgraced themselves in triumph. Officers and lords and other eminent Royalist captives were hanged, or beheaded. There were many executions, including three eighteen-year-old boys. It is said that as the last of these lads died, a minister, standing by, rubbed his hands and declared: 'The work goes bonnily on.' All who had supported Montrose paid dear. The 300 men he had left to garrison Dunaverty Fort were smoked out. They came out to surrender and were swiftly butchered. Other Royalist troops were pressed into service in France, and did not see Scotland again. The Lamonts of Argyll, loyal to the king and Montrose, were massacred by the Campbells in June 1646. Their castles were besieged and battered down. Two hundred prisoners were sailed to Dunoon, where the mass were executed, or buried alive; it is recorded that thirty-six were hanged from a single tree.

One prisoner was treated a little more delicately. In the nine months succeeding Naseby, Charles had known nothing but bad news. The Royalist war effort had fallen apart, outgunned and outmanoeuvred. Castle upon fortress upon town upon port fell into the hands of the king's enemies. His commanders sailed abroad, or gave themselves up. Soon the king himself was in serious danger at his headquarters in Oxford. His family had been despatched to safety as best they could be; his heir was already out of the country. His three other children were prisoners of state, but treated humanely. Henrietta Maria was safe in the palace of St Germain-en-Laye, near Paris. She would never see Charles again. On 27 April 1646, heavily disguised, Charles managed to escape from Oxford. Eight days later, to their astonishment, he threw himself on the mercy of his family's oldest subjects, appearing before the Scots army where they were encamped at Newark.

He was, perhaps, now set only to salvage the institution of monarchy, to judge by his letter to Henrietta Maria, as he prepared to surrender:

> I conjure you, by your unspotted faithfulness, by all that you love, by all that is good, that no threatenings, no apprehensions of danger to my person, make you stir one jot from any foundation in relation to that authority which the Prince of Wales is born to. I have already cast up what I am like to suffer, which I shall meet (with the grace of God) with that constancy that befits me. Only I desire that consolation, that assurance from you, as I may justly hope that my cause may not end with my misfortunes, by assur-

ing you that misplaced pity to me do not prejudice my son's rights.

It is hard to see what he was now about. Perhaps he bargained on the old loyalty of Scots to their dynasty. Perhaps he remembered that, at her worst, his grandmother Mary had been able to command a formidable following in 1568. Perhaps he gambled on the ancient hatred of the Scots for the English. And, too, if he was wise he now feared Cromwell. Parliament was no longer in control of the New Model Army; only Cromwell and a few other key figures who, like him, were both officers of the army and sat in the Commons, commanded meaningful authority in England now. Charles may well have looked on the rubble of his realm and, confident as ever in his own abilities, felt he could play a useful mediating role between the assorted factions and parties.

The Scots held the king until 1647. Even at this juncture, with all lost and his very life in danger, Charles I stubbornly refused to homologate the Covenant. Nor, as the English requested, would he homologate the Solemn League, and agree to a Presbyterian order in the Church. They wanted his agreement, too, to their other demands. The king must surrender control of the militia to parliament for twenty years. He must further acknowledge the new constitutional ascendancy of parliament. In sum, Charles I was being asked – with remarkable meekness, in the light of all the ruin he had wrought – to co-operate in the creation of a limited constitutional monarchy. It was anathema to the man. He spun out the debate; he delayed and prevaricated. He assumed, as Watson suggests, that the more time he wasted the more his enemies would begin to quarrel with each other. He began to cheer up. He asked if he could go to London, no doubt the better to intrigue. Meantime he harped on about trifles: choirs, surplices and prayer books. 'It has been the King's constant unhappiness to give nothing in time,' wrote a Scots observer, Robert Baillie, 'all things have been given at last: but he has ever lost the thanks, and his gifts have been counted constrained and extorted.' Baillie further wrote, to a friend, in final exasperation: 'if that man now goe to tinckle on Bishops and delinquents, and such foolish toyes, it seems he is mad.'

Meantime the English were slow to pay the Scots their dues under the terms agreed in the Solemn League. At length they brightly offered part-payment, in exchange for the person of the king. They got Charles and the Scots got a million pounds. It was the last thing Charles had expected could happen: they had made agreement without him, and he was now firmly a prisoner. He was cheered a little as his new captors took him down to grand lodgings in Northamptonshire, and the common people flocked out to hail him: at times the prisoner's journey had the air of a triumphant tour. But shallow popularity with northern peasantry – who would have cheered King Herod, such being the novelty of seeing any king at all – weighed little against the power of the New Model Army and the formidably schooled politicians with whom Charles must now deal.

In June 1648 soldiers escorted the king from his lodgings at Holdenby House to Newmarket. By the autumn the army had brought him to London. He managed briefly to escape – he was being held at Hampton Court – and reached as far as Carisbrooke Castle on the Isle of Wight. Charles had been sure of sympathy and support from the governor, Colonel Robert Hammond. He was sharply disabused. Hammond locked him up. There was not much more to be done with Charles until other and more urgent crises in England had been resolved. The New Model Army was on the brink of mutiny; their pay was badly in arrears. There was ecclesiastical crisis, with a Presbyterian settlement all the more elusive, despite the Westminster Assembly's completion of a Confession of Faith. (Parliament insisted on each point being accompanied by a proof-text of Scripture.) Worse: the Scots had invaded.

The calm exchange of their king for English gold had shocked many north of the Border. The Earl of Lauderdale had managed to visit Charles and together they concluded a sly engagement. The Scots would grant the king full military support if he would make England Presbyterian for a trial time: three years. By this point Charles was happy to sign anything that offered him short-term comfort or advantage. It is hard to believe he meant a word of the engagement, concluded in December 1647. Nor can he have seriously expected the Scots to liberate him from southern fastness and Cromwell's army. In any event it all depended on the military outcome, which was further affected by the continued division in Scotland. The 'Engagers' were led to battle by the Duke of Hamilton, and met crushing defeat at Preston, Lancashire, in August 1648. What remained of this last Royalist effort was scattered north in a series of running skirmishes.

By now the king was on trial for his life and radical republicanism hung heavy in the air. Men in the street, soldiers in the New Model Army, dismissed him contemptuously as 'Charles Stuart, that man of blood'. All of any substance had given up on him. He made deals, and broke them; he puffed on about liturgies and vanities. Sometimes he would seem to see sense, and give ground. And then Charles would be huffing away again. 'You cannot do without me,' he insisted, 'you will to ruin if I do not sustain you.' He was additionally distracted by Henrietta Maria, who now pled in her correspondence that he do all he could, promise anything, to secure his liberty. By now only one thing seemed to matter to the king: his High Anglicanism. For the Church of England – episcopacy, ritualism, sacerdotalism, the peculiar ideal for it that he cherished against the great majority of his fellow countrymen – he would happily die.

No one saw any point in talking to Charles I any more. Even at his trial, a brisk affair in January 1649, in the Great Hall of Westminster, he thought himself indispensable, ranting about his plans for lasting peace. Charles I had abundant opportunities to save his life and even his crown, to leave affairs of state to clever men and enjoy being royal. He could have kept even his 'broken-nosed marbles and rotten paintings'. He talked himself to the scaffold like lemming heading for the cliff. He had refused even to take advantage of credible plans for his escape. Yet he had botched personal, cack-handed efforts to arrange his own escape. He could not even see how monstrously cynical he sounded when he admitted, at trial, in defence of a bargain he had briefly struck with the Presbyterian party in parliament: 'The great concession I made this day – the Church, Militia and Ireland – was made merely in order to my escape, of which if I had not hope, I would not have done.'

He would not recognise the authority of the court with power over his life. He refused to answer the charges he faced. He insisted, absurdly, that 'the freedom and liberty of the people of England' were on trial with him. He was at length condemned as a 'traitor and murderer' who had tried to introduce 'an arbitrary and tyrannical government', and so must die 'by the severing of his head from his body'. Charles was not allowed to speak. He was bundled away, calling, 'I am not suffered for to speak. Expect what justice others will have.' His son, Charles, Prince of Wales, a youth of eighteen, is popularly remembered for sending to the parliamentary authorities a sheet of paper bearing nothing but his own signature, Charles P: on this they could write whatever terms they wanted if his father's life was spared. This is a myth. There is such a blank sheet, still existing, in the great archives of Oxford, signed in the name of some Charles or other: it survives from some bizarre, and entirely theoretical, military exercise of the Irish.

The New Model Army ran England now and they were determined the king would die. Parliament was of little account and Henrietta Maria of such irrelevance that the letter she at the last hour despatched, begging for the life of her husband and king, remained unopened for thirty-three years.

On the eve of death, in 1649, Charles declared that the execution he faced was the judgement of God he deserved for betraying the Earl of Strafford. Like his grandmother, he lapsed into stoical saintliness, and groomed himself for episcopal martyrdom. His last days were spent in prayer, meditation, assorted religious exercises, and rambling discussions with his spiritual friend, Bishop Juxon. In an affecting scene –

even his gaolers wept – he received his youngest children, including Henry, Duke of Gloucester. He pressed the boy never, whatever came to pass, to be manipulated into any compromise; even if it brought him the throne – anything that might cost the lives or rights of his older brothers. The child said solemnly that he should rather he were torn in pieces.

The morning of the king's death, 30 January, was extremely cold. There was frost and ice. Charles, mindful now of his image, was afraid he might be seen shivering from the chill and be judged trembling from fear, so that day he donned an extra shirt. He was taken from St James and spent his last hours at the Palace of Whitehall, where he had spent perhaps the happiest hours of his life. Parliament and army had used it in recent years. It was dirty and dilapidated. The royal art collection was already being dispersed. Shortly the crown of England itself would be melted down for coin.

The scaffold was built before the Banqueting House, an extension designed by Inigo Jones to Charles's orders: it featured a ceiling painted by Rubens. This Banqueting House still survives today, a beautiful and splendid place, but in 1649 likewise grubby, its windows boarded up. Through this room Charles walked and out on to the scaffold, through a window. Around was a vast, hushed crowd, kept well away by mounted soldiers. Perhaps it was feared the crowd might rush the stage, and bear Charles away to liberty. More likely the authorities were determined to make it difficult for them to hear the deposed sovereign's speech: 'I never did begin the war with the two Houses of Parliament, and I call on God to witness (to whom I must shortly make an account) that I never did intend to incroach upon their privileges. They began upon me. It is the militia they began upon, they confest that the Militia was mine, but they thought it fit to have it from me . . .'

And so on. It was a long, dull oration, full of excuses and pieties. Charles conceded he was a sinner. He alluded to the betrayal of Strafford. He insisted that sovereign and subject were 'clean different things'. Nevertheless God was punishing him. For all that the sentence passed upon him was unjust, he forgave his opponents. He preached of liberty. He said, 'I am the Martyr of the People.' He said he died 'a Christian according to the profession of the Church of England as I found it left me by my father', which was rather stretching a point.

So he stopped talking, and readied for death. He removed his cloak, his jewels, his hat and his doublet, and donned a cap, stuffing his hair under it to escape the blade. So Charles gave the signal, and died, his head struck clean off with one blow. A terrible groan came from the crowd, 'such as I hope never to hear again', wrote someone afterwards. Those nearest attempted to dip handkerchiefs in royal blood. The troopers quickly cleared the streets.

Wretchedly as he lived, and badly as he had ruled, and longwinded and confused as were his last words, the dignity and courage of this last act in the life of Charles I moved even hardened opponents. It was a Puritan poet, Andrew Marvell, who included in a mighty work of panegyric for Oliver Cromwell, *An Horatian Ode for Cromwell's Return from Ireland*, some lines recording the final moments of 'that man of blood':

> He nothing common did, or mean
> Upon that memorable scene:
> But, with his keener eye
> The Axe's edge did try:
>
> Nor call'd the Gods with vulgar spite
> To vindicate his helpless Right
> But bow'd his comely head
> Down, as upon a bed.

He had taken many a poor, and noble, head with him.

8

'ODDS FISH!'

The Young Charles II

The clergy, in all times, seems to attract a few men who take delight in pronouncing bad news. Such a man, perhaps, was Dr Stephen Goffe, a royal chaplain to the court in exile, and who was now attached to the Prince of Wales at The Hague, in the Low Countries. When Dr Goffe saw the newspaper report, in January 1649, he spared no time on reflection. He joined a frantic huddle of advisers, arguing how the news should best be broken; at length he strode through the palace, into a crowded room, and up to a tall, dark, swarthy young man, and addressed him simply as, 'Your Majesty . . .' The new king, shocked and overwhelmed, burst into tears. He could say nothing, nothing at all. At length he signalled Dr Goffe to leave. The king, inheriting 'nothing but the name', retired to a chamber and brooded for hours, quite alone. He never again let his emotional control slip so completely in public. Compared with others, in fact, his reaction to news of the execution at Whitehall was moderate. That gallant Lieutenant-General, the Marquis of Montrose, who had seen much mutilation, bloodshed and horror, fainted dead away when he was told.

Charles II was in his nineteenth year. His effective reign was not to start until the restoration of Stuart fortunes in 1660. The last years of his childhood had been lost in the Civil War. In the spring of 1646 the prince had managed to escape the tightening parliamentary net, reaching first the West Country and then obtaining ship for the Scilly Isles. After assorted ploys and adventures, and a hugely enjoyable time on Jersey (where he seems to have discovered sex, an activity which he took up with great enthusiasm for the rest of his life) the young Charles at length obeyed the imperious wheedling of his mother and joined her in Paris at the Palace of St Germain-en-Laye.

There followed two dull and wretched years, bored stiff by the fantastic formality and protocol of French court life, half bullied by his mother and half ignored, his inheritance ever uncertain and his father's fate perilous in the extreme. Henrietta Maria, convinced of her mastery in statecraft and high in status as queen, troubled not her son for his views or opinions on policy, and kept him out of affairs, engaging in intrigue herself with the Royalists or the French court, or bombarding her hapless husband with a stream of well-meant letters, warm and ardent and full of advice that was no less well meant for their author's general ignorance of what was really going on. By the end she was ranting at the king to concede anything, anything at all, if it might recover him his thrones and spare his life.

She had only one thought for her eldest son, when he came to her mind at all, and that was marriage. Henrietta Maria was determined to match Charles with her niece, an icy princess dubbed 'La Grand Mademoiselle', daughter of her brother Gaston, Duke of Orléans. For Charles this was a consummation devoutly not to be wished. In the summer of 1648 he was glad to escape the claustrophobic household of his mother for The Hague. Here he stayed with his sister, Mary, and her husband William, Stadtholder of the Calvinist United Provinces. In the Low Countries he found himself in greater measure his own man. The trouble, the prince found, was the turmoil among his own support. As in all forlorn hopes, the surviving band of supporters and allies was split in factions and division.

He had his brother, James, Duke of York, who was hot-headed, libidinous, and slow-witted, but an exuberant soldier. (James had managed to escape England earlier in the year, disguised as a girl.) There was their cousin, Prince Rupert, an experienced general, more flamboyant than successful. There was Henrietta Maria, of course, and such support as she had won to their cause in France. Beyond the family circle was a weird ragbag host of unlikely comrades. There were the prosaic and very Calvinist Dutch. There were the ardent and very Catholic Irish. There were English parliamentarians, spurned by the building power of Cromwell. There were assorted Royalist survivors from all the lost battles. There were, too, assorted parties of Scots, from the whole-heartedly Royalist, like Montrose, to the more cynical of Covenanters – the Engagement faction – to the most fanatical, like Archibald, Earl of Argyll, with his squint and his holy zeal. All this was scarcely the making of an effective coalition. Those who, as part of their world-view, thought it might be a good thing to effect Stuart restoration had, as other parts of their world-view, hopes and dreams of many a competing variety. Many, too, had lost much, and looked only for money, of Stuart sponsorships in careers abroad. Solomon himself could have made little of all this. It was quite beyond the abilities of a teenage prince, who had played his own exciting, but largely impotent, part in the last years of the war.

Nevertheless Charles was desperate to save his father, and knew it was important to be seen to be doing something. In the summer of 1648 he relieved James of the command of what remained of the Royalist navy, the ships that had recently mutinied against parliament and sailed to France. James was Lord High Admiral. The office had hardly been awarded for experience and merit: he had acquired it when he was four. Charles passed out 1648 directing this fleet in a rather pointless patrol of England's south-east coast. He was further diverted by a dose of smallpox, and by first love. Lucy Walter is described by a contemporary as 'brown, beautiful, bold but insipid'. She was not, though, of low birth: her mother was the niece of an earl, and her father of Welsh gentlefolk. The boy Charles was infatuated by her and in April 1649 she bore him a son, James Crofts. His surname was that of his first guardian; his paternity would haunt Charles for the rest of his days. The king could never shake off rumours that he had secretly married his Lucy and that the boy was the true and right heir to his throne.

Now, as fatherhood impended, he was King Charles II, grief-stricken by events, weighed down by responsibility and badgered and exhorted at every turn.

*   *   *

Charles II is a compelling mix of charm, pragmatism and evil. He is popularly remembered – and with surprising affection – as a libertine, a womaniser, a hearty drinker, the 'Old Rowley' who roamed incognito the pubs and stews of London. Then there are the dramatic disasters during his reign, such as the Great Plague, stopped only in the capital by the Great Fire of London. There are the mighty works of Sir Christopher Wren, and the jolly, risqué plays of Restoration comedy, which are supposed to have delivered England from a pall of Puritan gloom. Historians soberly judge him as a cool, cynical fellow who finally recovered his thrones, against all expectation and without doing anything much himself; and thereafter devoted all his energies 'not to go a-travelling again'. He muddled through the strains and plots of his reign without doing anything very well. He died in his bed, still Charles II, still enthroned, having enmeshed his land in a web of secret treaties with its ancient enemies.

In Scotland he should be remembered with loathing. Charles came to hate the land and its religion with a passion. He had a mean streak, and in Scotland and elsewhere his return in 1660 was marked by a burst of executions and score-settling. In Scotland his regime launched the most vicious persecution in religion the land had ever seen, going far beyond the infamies of Stuart predecessors. Charles is scarcely remembered in Ireland, which his government ran, by viceroy, with the usual English incompetence. He himself never bothered to visit the place.

Oliver Cromwell regarded him with contempt. All the pretender wanted in life, he snorted, was a 'leg of mutton and a whore'. In England the vast majority of the people shared Cromwell's opinion. It was hard for them to regard this distant youth as English at all. He was, by his grandparents, a quarter Scots, a quarter Danish, a quarter French and a quarter Italian. The Tudor blood, to which he owed any claim to the English throne, was essentially Welsh. He had heroic ancestors, of course. One whom especially he had later occasion to curse was Henri IV of France, his grandfather, who had blithely abandoned the Huguenot cause for Romanism, with the crack, '*Paris vaut bien une Messe.*' This was too frequently quoted against Charles II for comfort; and, because of this blood, cynicism was read into all he did. Nevertheless the early years of his childhood had been most happy – happier than those of his father or grandfather – and he proved himself throughly English in his pleasures.

Charles II was a king of striking appearance. He was extremely dark; abnormally dusky of skin and eye and hair. His mother had been half mortified, writing after her confinement that the child was so dark she was ashamed of him; she would send a portrait 'as soon as he is a little fairer'. Dark her son would remain. He was quickly dubbed the 'Black Boy'. The name is still found on English pub signs. Enemies, of course, would traduce this to the 'black bastard' and, when they wanted to appeal to England's worst prejudices, they would make out some unknown and popish 'black Scotsman' had begot Charles on Henrietta Maria.

Darkness was then unfashionable, even sinister. The word 'saturnine' was often used and it was universally assumed that saturnine appearance invariably went with saturnine character: something of the night. Dark people were expected to be morose, lugubrious, suspicious, irreligious, and perhaps given to witchcraft and all the black arts. Lord Mulgrave, who served in the court of Charles II, thought it remarkable to record that the king was both dark and cheerful.

Charles grew to be extremely tall. When he was on the run in 1650 the posters put in circulation for his capture described him as 'above two yards high'. He was at least six feet two, perhaps six feet three; and in the seventeenth century this was a prodigious, commanding height, well becoming a king. It was a liability in a fugitive. 'The problems of tall men today in aeroplanes, cars and beds were as nothing compared to the problem which faced Charles . . . compelled to try and disguise the one physical attribute which no make-up can conceal,' writes Antonia Fraser. His parents were small, but Anne of Denmark had been a big woman; Mary and Darnley had both been of striking height.

He had a big Roman nose – his enemies seized on this to

make sly allusions to ancient despots, like Tiberius – and a full, thick-lipped, rubbery, sensual mouth, which in our time would be thought most attractive and in his age was deemed hideous. Once the king, sitting for a portrait by Peter Lely, took a break to eye the work in progress. 'Odd's fish, I *am* an ugly fellow,' he said cheerfully. As a young man, though, he was very handsome, and at twenty Sir Samuel Tuke remembered the king had been 'very lovely'. By the time of the Restoration, age, adventure and frustration had much marked the king. His face was much leaner; the nose seemed even larger. Deep lines carved their way from nostrils to chin. His hair did not go grey till quite late in life; before then his thick black locks attracted much admiration. Once he was 'mighty grey', Charles II donned a mighty periwig. He never grew a beard, but had always a thin moustache.

His best feature, perhaps, was his eyes, which were vivid and sparkling, if always watchful; the mind beyond entirely veiled. The king had long muscled legs – he enjoyed, daily, long and rapid walks, and so kept trim – and fine hands. If never handsome, he was majestical. He moved with dignity and his mighty, well-proportioned figure fitted his state. Contrary to his abiding reputation, he conducted himself – all the sexual activity apart, which was of course privily conducted – with moderation and dignity. Like his father, Charles II ate and drank sparingly. He dressed plainly. Sir Samuel confirms the report of contemporaries that the king was never heard to swear. He had gravitas, perhaps even a touch of sorrow; but Charles II seems to have been spared the incapacitating melancholia that cursed all the other late Stuart monarchs.

His most winsome feature is his wit. No other Stuart dropped so many laconic, often acidulous one-liners, generally prefaced by the curious oath that marked his every other sentence, and made do for the profanities he forswore: 'Odds fish!'

Now, in January 1649, the young king looked to his kingdoms, where Montrose had shut himself away for two days in secret mourning, emerging in black armour ranting that he would sing for Charles I 'obsequies with trumpet sounds'; that he would engrave his epitaph 'in blood and wounds'. Scotland – where the king's beheading had awakened passionate anger: how dare the English execute their monarch without permission? – was the obvious theatre for Charles II to seek restoration. But Scotland was still torn between the policies of Argyll and Montrose.

Argyll sent deputation to The Hague, offering the king the throne of Scotland; all he need do, of course, was to sign the Covenant. Montrose sent conflicting advice: Charles II should sign no treaty. If the king left it to him, Montrose would seize Scotland by conquest. Charles II quickly proved himself, like his father, a double-dealer; but, unlike his father, he was good at it. He blithely sent Montrose back to Scotland – to his death – and continued to negotiate with Argyll.

Montrose issued elaborate appeal to the Scots.

> All those who have any duty left them to God, their King, Country, Friends, Homes, Wives and Children, or who would change, now at the last, the tyranny, violence and oppression of these rebels with the mild and innocent government of the just prince; or revenge the horrid and execrable murder of their sacred King, redeem their nation from infamy, themselves from slavery, restore the present and oblige the ages to come, let them as Christians, subjects, patriots, friends, husbands and fathers join themselves forth with us. Dead or alive, the world will give them thanks.

He had 500 mercenaries, Germans and Danes, and with them Montrose sailed to Orkney to launch his last campaign. He more than doubled his force with Orcadian recruits. So he crossed the Pentland Firth, before hitting slamming defeat in the wild county of Sutherland, at Carbisdale on the River Oykell, on 27 April 1650. Montrose managed to escape, and eluded capture for two days in the hills and moors, until he was caught at Ardvreck Castle, where he had found shelter from Neil MacLeod of Assynt, who now handed Montrose over to his enemies for the blood-money of £25,000. It is one of those low betrayals of the Highland code of honour, still remembered in Gaelic execration. It is recorded that Neil MacLeod never, in the end, got any money: just a quantity of sour meal. And one of the great curses in Gaelic poetry, by Iain Lom MacDonald, of Keppoch, in the West Highlands. Iain Lom had been bard with Montrose's force at Inverlochy, and lived to become the first – and only – Gaelic Poet Laureate:

> Neilson from dreary Assynt
> if I caught you in my net
> I'd give evidence to encompass your doom
> nor would I save you from the gallows
> The shroud of death be about you
> despicable one
> for sinfully you have sold the truth
> for Leith meal and the most of it sour . . .

Montrose had been attainted as a traitor in 1644, so there was no necessity for a trial. He went to his execution in Edinburgh, on 21 May, 'like a bridegroom', with a brave little speech. 'I do not follow the light of my own conscience, which is kindled to the working of the good spirit of God that is within me . . . I leave my soul to God, my service to my prince, my good will to my friends, and my name and charity to you all.' As they thrust him off the scaffold he cried to God to have mercy on Scotland. He never saw the letter from Charles, breaking the news he could do nothing to save him; but he died knowing that, at Breda, Charles II a month before had agreed to swear the Solemn Oath of the Covenant; had conceded the establishment of the Presbyterian Kirk; and the ratification of the Scottish parliament and all its Acts. It must have shocked Montrose; it certainly shocked the bulk of English Royalists, and Charles lost a deal of support in his largest kingdom.

Montrose was hanged, like a common criminal, on gallows thirty feet high, and three hours later cut down, disembowelled and quartered. His head was spiked at the Tolbooth; a limb each went to Perth, Glasgow, Stirling and Aberdeen. It was a despicable fate for an honourable man. All his officers, at least, died by the axe, or by the Maiden. The hapless Orcadians survived to slavery: they were put to black labour in the coalmines of Fife. Eleven years later what was left of Montrose was collected at last for a state funeral. He lies today in the High Kirk of St Giles, under a marble statue, recumbent; a framed copy of the National Covenant stands by his bones. Romance, not dishonour, was the ruin of Montrose.

Neatly keeping his name out of the *démarche* at Carbisdale, Charles II had taken the one alternative remaining and accepted the terms of Argyll, whom the previous year he had raised to the title of marquis. The name of Montrose haunts the reputation of Charles II as that of Strafford haunts that of his father. The defenders of Charles II argue that he was gambling for his thrones and for a full restoration; Montrose had freely volunteered his services, and provided an insurance – for a spell – against Argyll. It was only reasonable, once Montrose's gallant folly had failed, for the king to accept the best terms open to him. Such logic is, perhaps, an instance of the ethical distinctions we are apt to draw between kings and mere men.

Charles quit France on 24 June, with the general approval of Europe and the disdain only of the Anglicans. 'They must needs go where their Fates drive,' said a Commonwealth spy cheerfully of this latest Stuart plot. He had a horrible voyage – there were contrary winds, and the crossing took twenty days – and only escaped Commonwealth capture by the providential descent of a great bank of good Scottish fog. He had an equally unpleasant arrival, for he was confronted with new and still more stringent demands by the Covenanters, who now insisted he extend his ardent embrace of Presbyterian order to encompass his rule of England. Not the neatest argument Charles could muster got him out of this bind. He agreed. It was expedient, of course, the fruit of *Realpolitik*. Montrose had failed. Cromwell had ruthlessly crushed all his support in Ireland. Even the Dutch wanted rid of him; the Covenanters were the sole hope of Charles II. But by no logic of morals or law had the Scots the right to demand that he commit another of his realms to their form of Church government. The wiser, and truly godly sort of the Covenanters, admitted this. 'We did both sinfully entangle and engage the nation ourselves,' wrote Alexander Jaffray in his diary, 'and that poor, young Prince to whom we were sent, making him sign and swear a Covenant which we knew from clear and demonstrable reasons that he hated in his heart.'

So Charles landed, on the Moray coast, and embarked on what Tom Steel cuttingly describes as the 'farcical role of a Covenanted King'. He was treated coldly and with little courtesy. The Scots kept him out of their deliberations and consulted him as little as possible. Nor does the king seem to have been impressed by vital religion. 'Nothing,' snapped Charles II in later years, 'could have confirmed me more to the Church of England than their hypocrisy.' At the back of his mind, of course, was always one memory: only five years before, his father had trusted the Scots with his person and life.

He was harangued by assorted divines, compelled to denounce his parents, forced to repudiate the policies of his father. He found Scotland cold, grubby and uncomfortable, with 'women so dirty and ill-favoured that they resembled those witches the Scots were so fond of burning'. In Aberdeen, King Charles was thoughtfully lodged in a house overlooking the Tolbooth, where he would have a good view of Montrose's putrefying hand, nailed to its wall. It is unlikely Charles II enjoyed the 'day of humiliation and prayer' ordained by the Kirk for the nation to bewail, before God, the sins of the late king and all the royal house. In all, his Scottish sojourn was an unpleasant mix of 'ardent religiosity and mean, disagreeable living.'

The Scots could not even grant Charles II that most elementary thing for sovereigns: security and safety. The New Model Army came charging north, Cromwell resolved to flatten Scotland and catch – or frighten away – its king. On 3 September 1650 came the critical Battle of Dunbar. It was one of those ridiculous Scottish defeats, where the doughty little land threw away its tactical advantage. Cromwell and his exhausted soldiers were trapped between East Lothian cliffs and a vastly superior army of Scots, under Leslie, occupying a fine position on high ground. Then Leslie, nagged and beset by meddling clergymen, foolishly led his troops down to the level playing field of their enemy. 'The Lord hath delivered them into our hands,' exulted Cromwell. After weeks when guerrilla forces had harried his army, and the men of the Commonwealth were still greatly outnumbered, he utterly routed Leslie and his men: 22,000 Scots were put to flight by about 11,000 English; 3,000 Scots were killed or wounded.

It is said that Charles II actually threw his cap in the air for joy when he heard the news. The story is certainly false but by this time there can be no doubt he detested the Scots. A few days later he was deeply upset to learn of the death of Princess Elizabeth, his favourite sister, in imprisonment at Carisbrooke Castle. (It was nastily said, by High Anglicans, that she died of a broken heart on learning that the king, her brother, had embraced the Covenant.)

There is an unfortunate kind of false religion that sees readily, in every Providence, an unmistakable and infallible message from the Most High. Robert Douglas, of the General Assembly, assured his king that the disaster at Dunbar was due to the 'guiltiness' of the royal family. Perhaps a new day of humiliation and prayer should be held, against the 'controversy that God hath against you and your family, for which His wrath seems not yet to be turned away . . . If self-interest and the gaining of a crown have been more in your eye than the advancing of religion and righteousness, it is an iniquity to be repented of and for which Your Majesty ought to be humbled.' So Charles, yet again, was told he must repent, to which he replied, with droll stoicism, 'I think I must repent me ever being born.'

Early in October he tried to escape, using the pretext of a hawking outing to gallop from Perth; he was caught north of Dundee, 'overwearied and very fearful in a nasty room on an old bolster above a mat of sedge and rushes'. He was hauled home to more lectures, sermons, and recrimination. He was at the end of his tether and beside himself with the arrogance of men who thought they could beat off Cromwell's forces without the defiling aid of non-Covenanting Royalists, not least in the Highlands: they called them the 'Malignants'. Even worse were the stupid 'Classing Acts', born of pure fanaticism, and a terrible example of the dangers of devout men being granted authority beyond their abilities. Under these Acts the Covenanting forces were purged, as the army of Gideon had been cleansed in the Book of Judges: only the most faithful and unspotted sons of the Kirk, as endorsed by faithful ministers, were allowed to bear arms for Charles II – the same ministers who had meddled, calamitously, with Leslie's dispositions at Dunbar.

As Cromwell advanced, they now sought to boost their king in esteem, both in himself and abroad. So Argyll and the Covenanters planned a coronation. It was held at Scone, on 1 January 1651, and was almost certainly the last held in Scotland. (There is some evidence that Charles's nephew, the Old Pretender, had a Scots coronation in 1715.) This wintry show at Scone, however, was of unique character. It was a Covenanting coronation and more akin in many respects to the ordination of a Free Presbyterian minister. This sat absurdly, to modern eyes, with the more lavish and sacerdotal elements long associated with coronation rites: but, as an early biographer of Charles remarks, 'a fresh farce was now necessary and His Majesty had a principal part to play in it.'

It was not without pomp. The king was allowed to wear a plush robe of expensive cloth. The sons of noblemen – sound Covenanting noblemen, of course – were appointed to bear his train. There was a canopy of state, of red velvet, above his throne. But there was no anointing with oil. He received the crown from Argyll and the sceptre from the Earl of Crawford and Balcarres. A leading Malignant was then admitted to the Covenanting fold, in a bizarre ceremony; this John Middleton was garbed in sackcloth. Among other things, Charles had to homologate the Longer and Shorter Catechisms and, of course, the Covenant:

> I, Charles, King of Great Britain, France and Ireland, do assure and declare by my solemn oath, in the presence of Almighty God, the searcher of all hearts, my allowance and approbation of the National Covenant and Solemn League and Covenant above written . . . and I shall observe these in my own practice and family, and shall never make opposition to any of these, nor endeavour any alteration therein.

There followed a sermon of inordinate length by Robert Douglas. 'The sins of former kings have made this a tottering crown . . . A King, when he getteth his Crown on his head, should think at the best, it is but a fading crown.' Afterwards, there was a lavish and no doubt much-appreciated feed. Charles and party partook of meat, partridges, ten calves' heads, and twenty-two salmon. In the days following, as further chunks of Scotland fell to Cromwell's efficient forces, the king made hasty progress about those parts of his realm it was still safe to enter: Pittenweem, St Andrews, Stirling, Perth, Dundee, Aberdeen. He still found time to relax though, and, like his forebears, including Mary – and many a Scots tourist since – he enjoyed some time playing golf.

More: he enjoyed new authority. He helped to rehabilitate Middleton, who had sufficiently purged himself of abetting Montrose. He persuaded the Scottish parliament to sanction recruitment in the Highlands. The Engagers were allowed back, to play their part in affairs. He also had a delicate problem with Argyll, who was determined to wed the king to his daughter, Lady Anne Campbell. She must have been of plain appearance: when Argyll, in 1649, met Charles on the Continent with a gift of six Flanders mares, a wag suggested he intended in due time to bestow the Lady Anne as a seventh. Whatever her appearance – and, in deportment and manners, we are told the maiden was as well behaved as anyone at court – Charles knew the marriage would be political suicide. The Lady Anne was not royal; more, she was Scots, and, worse, the daughter of the arch-Presbyterian Argyll. The match would all but finish the king's standing in England. Yet Argyll could not be offended; and the king was indubitably a bachelor.

Incredibly, Charles was delivered by the wisdom of his mother. Time had lent Henrietta Maria new capacities of tact and judgement. She judged the Lady Anne well-born and quite fit to be a queen, she wrote with discreet cunning, but ought he not to consult his English subjects first? So Charles managed to play for time. In the meantime the monarchy's standing in Scotland was ebbing fast in the face of Cromwell, who had survived a dreich winter in Edinburgh. Almost daily the lands under the control of Charles and his regime were reduced. By the summer virtually all of Scotland was under Cromwell's yoke, save for the Highlands. So Charles at last ran for it, but, in a daring move, not north but south, to England, with a small but valiant army. The last straw was the triumph of Cromwell at Inverkeithing, granting him the Fife peninsula, which hitherto had guaranteed the security of Charles and his government in all the north-east Lowlands. It was a gory triumph with horrendous Scots casualties. The only hope lay south.

Nothing seemed to go right for Charles II. The Royalists safely left Scotland, crossing the Border on 5 August; but the important castle-city of Carlisle refused to admit them, or to surrender. It was at Penrith that Charles II was first declared King of England. And, the further they tramped from Scotland, the more reluctant Scots were to march. Many, especially the Highlanders, deserted, and slunk back home. Cromwellian generals began to harass the Royalists from the rear. Meanwhile the Commonwealth government was moving with a speed and efficiency unknown in Jacobean days to quell alarm and maintain order. All public meetings, for instance, were cancelled. Any sign of new support for the king was decisively met. The Earl of Derby, great baron of Lancashire, rose for the Royalist cause. But as soon as he landed at Wigan to rally his tenantry, he was at once defeated in battle. The many Catholics of Lancashire refused to rise for themselves. Why should they follow a king at the head of a bunch of Presbyterians?

There were spies everywhere in the Royalist organisation. The further Charles marched, the more English resentment against his Scots force seemed to increase. Once-loyal monarchists, especially the Highest of Anglicans, refused to rally to the cause, meet their king, or even respond to his letters. 'I confess I cannot tell you,' wrote the tired Duke of Hamilton, 'whether our hopes or fears are greatest, but we have one stout argument – despair; for we must shortly fight or die.' It was a dispirited and exhausted force, numbering at most 16,000 men, which on 22 August arrived with their king at the city of Worcester. They were outnumbered and quickly surrounded. Twelve days later the Commonwealth army attacked, with 30,000 men. Victory for the Royalists would not have meant much; there would have been battle upon battle to follow. In the event, despite many brave deeds, much courage, and some clever tactics, the Royalists were crushed. The Duke of Hamilton was among the fatalities, in a desperate charge which for a brief moment gave the Royalists a genuine advantage. Leslie could have ordered a decisive cavalry charge, but failed to do so. (After the Restoration, when he was created Baron of Newark, bitter veterans of Worcester declared what he deserved was a hanging.)

Charles himself fought, with remarkable courage. He charged into the heat of the battle, again and again, till men marvelled that he lived, and unwounded. But the day was lost and he could not turn it. As he fled back into the city to try and rally retreating officers, he could not even persuade them to shut the gates. It seemed for a time he wanted only to die; he had, after all, two brothers safe on the Continent. He was persuaded at length to escape. Meantime, having destroyed the Royalist cause, the men of Cromwell had nothing more to do than catch its runaway king.

There are many good stories of Charles II's escape after Worcester. He himself loved telling them in later years, to the point of becoming a bore. It is said he quit his lodgings by the back as a parliamentary officer began to search the house at the front. With a few friends, and especially with the help of the Roman Catholic underground, he stayed at liberty for six weeks until finally winning a ship to Europe. First came a long, grim, sleepless tramp, through fields and forest, from Worcester to Whiteladies: by the time the king reached a safe house, he had gone without sleep for over twenty-four hours. He gobbled bread and cheese and had the presence of mind at once to get rid of his clothing, which was rich and distinctive and already being publicised by his enemies. The tallest lad of his house supplied replacements: a green jerkin, grey breeches, a leather doublet, a grubby hat. The king kept his socks but ripped off their embroidered tops. The only thing he could not find to fit were shoes, for he had mighty feet; and of all the torments and perils Charles remembered of this time it was the agonised chafing of too-small boots. His thick curls were shorn. His grand apparel was flung into a privy. Thus was King Charles II disguised as an honest woodcutter.

Having divested himself of royal garb, he now insisted on sending away all his royal entourage. He knew he would survive best alone. And, instead of doing the obvious – fleeing to the ports of Wales, or Scotland – Charles did the unexpected, and headed towards London. He left Whitechapel by the back door and hid in a wood nearby. By happy chance his host, John Penderel, bumped into a passing Roman priest, Father John Huddleston, and arrangements were swiftly put in hand to find the king lodging in the house of a Roman Catholic gentleman. Meantime Charles had a worried day in the forest. He was hungry, thirsty, and scared by the sight of troops passing by. Only a heavy shower of rain, he said afterwards, shortened their search and kept him from certain discovery. He decided not to make for London. When Penderel returned the king said he would try for the Welsh ports.

So that night they grabbed some bread and cheese and headed towards the River Severn. (They were chased at one point by a local miller, who shouted, 'Rogues! Rogues!'; this man was actually harbouring some Royalist soldiers.) The land was in disorder, with soldiers and fugitives everywhere, and still indeed some confusion about the outcome of the battle. And no one, of course, had news of the king. Six days after the battle, proclamation was put out for his capture. The lieges were offered the great sum of £1,000 for the person of this 'malicious and dangerous traitor'. It was a fortune beyond the dreams of avarice. Yet, of the sixty and more who at one time or another sheltered Charles in these weeks, and knew where he was, not one answered the government's call and claimed the reward for 'Charles Stuart, son of the late Tyrant . . . a tall black man, over two yards high'.

He spent the night of 5 September in a barn. No boats could be had to cross the heavily guarded Severn. His hosts, a Catholic family, the Wolfes, disguised the king with walnut juice. He and Penderel had to retreat to Boscobel, fording a river on the way. (Charles was an excellent swimmer.) But there was no refuge at Mosely Old Hall, where the friendly priest had secured them lodging; it was shortly to be searched by soldiers, now combing the area. So, famously, Charles II spent a night with Major Carlis, another fugitive, hiding in a mighty oak tree. Soldiers passed so close that it is said the king could hear them discussing their fine plans for Charles Stuart, once they caught him. At length they could return to Boscobel House; Charles was so relieved that he asked if there was mutton for dinner. Meat had not been tasted for weeks in the household, but the gallant major hurried out with a dagger and killed a sheep, which he and the king helped to cook.

(The oak tree was not forgotten. At the Restoration, there was much oak tree imagery; the Royal Oak became rather a symbol of renewed Stuart fortune, and later the name of English pubs and English warships.)

They spent that night in a 'priest's hole', a secret cubby-space high in the house. Charles moved on, after a more relaxing day – it was the Sabbath, and military activity quietened – to Mosely Old Hall. So he parted with the faithful Penderels. He stayed there for two days – the house narrowly escaped another search – and then moved on to another great hall, this time pretending to be a servant, one William Jackson, escorting a young lady Jane Lane to the confinement of her married sister. So he donned new disguise. On the way, the maiden's horse shed a shoe, Charles had to oversee its replacement and chatted gaily with the blacksmith. What news? 'There is no news, except the good news of beating those rogues the Scots.' And had that rogue Charles Stuart been captured, who deserved to be hanged more than all the Scots for bringing them in? 'Spoken like an honest man!'

At another house, Long Marten, he was put to kitchen duty, operating a roasting-jack, which he did very clumsily. (He explained to the cook that, as a poor tenant's son, he had rarely tasted meat and never used a jack.) On the way to Stratford the little party had to evade a troop of horse. They had to cross to Bristol to reach Abbot's Leigh. There 'Will Jackson' greatly enjoyed hearing himself eagerly described by others; he was told that Charles Stuart was very tall, about three fingers higher than himself. Then he had a real fright, when one of the chattering company said he had actually been in Stuart's regiment of guards. Charles made his excuses and retired upstairs, 'infinitely more afraid of the fellow', writes Fraser, 'now he knew him to be one of his own men, than when he had believed him to be an enemy'. (His instincts proved correct, for the house's butler recognised him, but swore to Jane Lane he would not betray his king.)

Government troops, in fact, now blocked the approach to the Welsh ports and all efforts to charter a suitable boat at Bristol failed. So Charles and his little band thought of making for Dorset, or Devon. Unknown to them that area too would shortly be full of military activity, as the Commonwealth prepared to recapture the island of Jersey. But the days remained full of incident. Hiding in the manor of the village of Trent, north of Sherborne, they heard the bells of the parish church in joyous peal. Charles was sent to investigate. He came back with the news that the village had heard joyous rumour: the king was dead. 'Alas, poor people!' said Charles, trying to find it funny. His conditions remained uncomfortable. The nights he passed in another priest's hole. Meanwhile they planned, and decided on the sleepy, isolated, but not too small harbour-village of Lyme as the best place for escape by sea. Charles said goodbye to Jane Lane and transferred abode to Charmouth, by Lyme Bay, riding double with another young lady. This time the cover story was an elopement.

Arrangements had been made with a local captain to take him and party to France, for the sum of sixty pounds. But night came, the tide ebbed, and there was no sign of boat or skipper. Things had gone farcically wrong. The seaman's wife, suspecting he was up to no good, had locked him in his bedroom.

This, of course, Charles did not know. He at length persuaded everyone to head to a much bigger town, Bridport, which was so crowded with troops and fellow travellers they had a fair chance of going about unnoticed. Charles even made his way to the largest and busiest pub. An ostler remarked that his face seemed strangely familiar. 'Friend,' said the king easily, 'you must certainly have seen me then at Mr Potter's, for I served him above a year.' But rumours began to spread, and wisely they all hurried out of town. That night the local magistrate roused the troops. Soldiers chased out towards Dorchester. Charles, fortunately, was heading north. In fact he and his companion, Wilmot, were quite lost. They reached the hamlet of Broadwindsor and booked lodgings in an inn under false names. Over forty soldiers were staying in and around the same inn, and an accompanying whore gave birth during the night. A lively row broke out – villagers were determined the infant should not be left behind to be raised on the parish relief – and the king escaped all discovery in the confusion.

Next night he was back at Trent Manor and here he stayed for two more weeks; a romantic Royalist wife would in later days celebrate the house as 'the Ark in which God shut him up when the floods of rebellion covered the face of his dominions'. Friends went back and forth, trying to find a boat that would rescue the king from the Sussex coast. On Tuesday, 6 October, Charles set out yet again, double-horse, with one Juliana Coningsby. He stayed five days at Heale House, by Amesbury, where the widowed lady of the house knew who he was and made everyone very tense by flirting shamelessly.

The king, though, was not without diversion: he managed to visit Stonehenge. Nights were passed in another cramped hidey-hole. (In his later years, understandably, the king developed a degree of claustrophobia.)

On 13 October he crept on to Hambledown, staying with friendly Royalists. Not all knew who he was; one worried husband told his wife that the fellow's short hair suggested he was a 'Roundhead rogue'. The next day he made Brighton: or, as it was then called, Brighthelmstone. There he stayed at the George Inn. A local merchant, plied with drink and bribed with sixty pounds, had arranged a boat. The ship's master came to meet the party and recognised the king at once. He fell on his knees to kiss his hand. It was given out that the ship was heading to sea with a party of duellists, duelling being illegal. They were to sail from Shoreham. Charles spent his last night at nearby Bramber, again just evading capture when some soldiers unexpectedly ambled by. But he made harbour at the right time. In the small hours of Wednesday, 14 October 1651 the king sailed away from England after six weary, tense, cramped and uncomfortable weeks. Before dawn another ship appeared at Shoreham, searching everywhere for a 'tall black man, six foot two inches high'.

The *Surprise* sailed first towards Wight, then out to the French coast, and after the odd false alarm the king was landed at Fécamp, near Rouen, going ashore piggy-back on the shoulders of a Quaker called Carver. Few now believed, in the last weeks of 1651, that the Stuarts would ever be restored.

It is not fashionable to admire the government of Britain under Oliver Cromwell. By warfare he united the kingdom and by force he established his authority. He declined the title of king but accepted that of Lord Protector, and lived in state at Hampton House. He went about in some fear of assassination, and often wore armour beneath his clothes. (Charles II, in exile, offered a pension of £500 a year 'to any man whosoever, within any of our three kingdoms, by pistol, sword or poison, or by any other ways or means whatsoever, to destroy the life of the said Oliver Cromwell'.)

It is most unfair to traduce the Lord Protector as a man who presided over Philistine gloom. More plays were actually published, in the Cromwellian era, than ever before. Great poets were commissioned to public works, and well honoured. Cromwell put abrupt stop to the continued sale of national treasures, such as the royal art collection, and Hampton Court was a serene, dignified, and exquisitely furnished place to receive the envoys of Europe. He made one reform to the English: for the first time, women were allowed to act – perhaps a practical measure to reduce cross-dressing and the rampant homosexuality for which the stage was then notorious. Cromwell loved music. It was he who sponsored the first performance of an English opera. At Hampton Court he installed two fine organs. There were often musical evenings, if business permitted. Fine tapestries hung in his own bedroom. When there were no foreign visitors – the Lord Protector liked to give the impression of solemn decorum – the palace rang with chatter, songs and laughter. He also had a disagreeable penchant for slapstick practical jokes. Occasionally he sat with his servants, composed funny verses, drank ale with them, and smoked a pipe.

It is popularly believed that Cromwell's administration sanctioned the wholesale destruction of church ornaments, statues, stained-glass windows and so on. There is not a single proven instance of he or his men deliberately despoiling a church. The damage often attributed to the Cromwellians, when investigated, has been traced back to the Reformation. In fact it was Cavalier troops, largely elegant and well-born, who were remembered with detestation, especially in Oxford, where Charles I had long made his headquarters. 'To give a further character of the court,' wrote Anthony Wood angrily of his unwanted Royalist guests, 'though they were neat and gay in their apparell, yet they were very nasty and beastly, leaving at their departures their excrements in every corner, in chimneys, studies, coal-houses and cellars. Rude, rough, whoremongers; vaine, empty, careless.'

In the time of Cromwell England recovered much self-respect and, by the time of his death, was the most powerful country in Europe, regarded abroad with respect and dread. The New Model Army finished off two long-abiding threats to England: the lion in the north – the Scots; and the constant murmuring rebellion of Ireland, though, as Johnson writes, he had the British Isles united in perfect tranquillity, but not justice. So strong was his position by 1651 that the Royalist invasion from Scotland was swept aside almost with contempt; a rebellion near a century later, in 1745, would stretch the London government to its limits of military ability and cause panic in the streets. In Europe the Cromwellian regime was regarded at first with disdain. By 1655 the new administration was recognised by every country that mattered, and its exploits attracted increasing awe.

Between 1649 and 1651 alone, forty huge warships were built in England, with mighty cannon, and put to sea. A huge army of men, gifted and talented, many of low birth, served their country on the seas and abroad: officers and captains, civil servants and diplomats, engineers and doctors and scientists. Meantime parliament raised huge, unprecedented sums in taxation. So, wherever the exiled Stuarts seemed to be on the point of winning aid and comfort, the British navy would appear, or English troops be landed. God's Chosen People prospered everywhere. The colonies in America were at last supported with full strength. Portugal was battered into alliance with Britain, and has remained in alliance ever since. The Dutch were repeatedly bested at sea, for the first time, and demoted in the international pecking-order. A vast merchant navy developed, and British business won and exploited great new markets abroad. Spain's West Indian empire was broken, and Jamaica seized for England. English ships patrolled the Channel and probed the Baltic and policed the Mediterranean and won fear and respect from the Arabs. Thus Cromwell ushered in the age of gunboat diplomacy.

In the meantime the last restrictions of popery on learning and science were swept away. Charles I had banned machines that threatened the interests of some petty crafts guild or trade. Now they came into use. All monopolies were abolished; critically, those in minerals, like coal and iron. Oxford and Cambridge surrendered to science. A university was demanded for Manchester, and then by York; plans were drawn up for more universities in Wales, Norwich, Durham. It was wonderful that Britain, wrote Charleston proudly in 1657, 'which was but yesterday the theatre of war and desolation, should today be the school of arts and learning'.

It was a strong government. It was also, by the standards of its time, a government of remarkable tolerance. Under Cromwell, Roman Catholics – at least in England – were protected from prosecution. He did his best to stamp out the absurd wickedness of witch-hunting, and for the most part succeeded. In 1656 Jews were again allowed in England; they had been banished since the reign of Edward I. (It is worth remarking that they were never, and never have been, persecuted in Scotland.) Cromwell told the Speaker of the Commons, after his siege of Bristol, that

> Presbyterians, Independents, all had here the same spirit of faith and prayer . . . They agree here, know no names of difference; pity it should be otherwise anywhere. All that believe have the real unity, which is most glorious because inward and spiritual . . . As for being united in forms, commonly called uniformity, every Christian will for peace sake study and do as far as conscience will permit; and from brethren, in things of the mind, we look for no compulsion but that of light and reason.

And by 1650 he was saying: 'I had rather that Mahometanism were permitted amongst us than that one of God's children should be persecuted.' Yet Cromwell had not the strength, or perhaps even the will, to extend this tolerance to Ireland. He treated that land and its people with studied harshness and the atrocities of his era left deep scars in Irish history. Nor did he get on very well with parliament. He entertained grand schemes for his 'godly reformation'; he wanted, especially, sweeping reforms of the legal code. He could not find any parliament to rise to his vision. 'He recognised, grimly, that Parliament is the custodian not so much of liberty, as of the existing division of property, as indeed it still is today,' observes Paul Johnson. Cromwell's only weapon was a radical extension of the franchise. From that he hung back. 'If the common vote of the giddy multitude must rule the whole,' he said, like any Tory, 'how quickly would their own interest, peace and safety be dashed and broken!' So instead he devoted himself to developing new tactics in parliamentary management, and strove to create political stability. You could call Cromwell the first Whig.

He admired Elizabeth to the end, abolished the monarchy with great reluctance, and himself refused the crown. He probably would have accepted it in time, and established his own dynasty; then, perhaps, the Cromwellian vision would have endured. It faded, and the rush of development and innovation and progress slowed; though, despite the Restoration, it proved impossible to put back the clock. Absolute monarchy had vanished from the British Isles for ever. New institutions were entrenched; infant liberties were permanent, and growing into bigger liberties. The most damaging legacy of his reign, though he did all he could to prevent it, was the disintegration of the Church. Puritans of every stripe hived off into a host of sects, denominations and assorted 'Independencies', leaving the Church largely to the gentry. It never recovered its place in national life, nor anything like the hold on the people the Kirk had in Scotland. In the short term the exclusion of Non-Conformists from the political life of Britain – after the Restoration – was a serious brake on progress. Today the Church of England is the Church 'to which nobody goes'.

In Scotland we have less reason to remember Cromwell with affection. He imposed full union on England's northern neighbour. The Scots parliament was abolished, and thirty suitably loyal Scots selected to sit in parliament at Westminster. Seven commissioners – four English, three Scots – oversaw justice in Scotland. All the Scottish counties were given new sheriffs. But the cost of this occupation was considerable and the Scots were savagely taxed to pay for it. The hapless General Monck had to raise the sum of £10,000 every month. The regime was hugely unpopular. 'For all that,' writes Tom Steel, 'Cromwell was responsible for the most efficient and just government Scotland had witnessed in centuries.'

Charles II was so thin and dirty when he reached the French court, in October 1651, that most of his acquaintance quite failed to recognise him. In Rouen people had taken one look and dismissed him as a tramp. It was a difficult time for him and, after some days of forced cheeriness, he lapsed into a depression. He could not even tell in detail the full adventure of his escape, for fear of endangering all who had helped him.

France was still in civil war itself, between the monarchy and a noble faction under Cardinal Mazarin. It was a tense time at court. Charles lived off his mother and Henrietta Maria lived off the goodness of the French king, Louis XIV, who had still not attained his majority. From the first night Charles supped with her she kept a meticulous bill of all that he ate, so that when at length Charles won a grant of his own, he found he owed most of it to the queen dowager.

The years went by. Abroad, Charles II kicked his heels, travelling with his much-reduced, impecunious court 'like a shabby circus in search of a sponsor', as Stuart Ross puts it.

He was twenty-two when he fled Shoreham and he had gone through ten times as much adventure as most men see in a lifetime. By the end of 1653 there was nowhere on earth, not even in furthest Scotland or in America, where he was owned as king. The Cromwellian regime had become a trusted if feared part of the European scene. It had even concluded an alliance with France in 1655. That, of course, provoked a Stuart flight to Germany, then – when Charles was so short of money he would settle gladly for a Spanish pension – to the Spanish Netherlands.

Meantime James, his brother, gave up on attempts to secure a lucrative marriage and signed a commission in the French army. He had a brave time as a cavalry officer and deeply resented the end of his French career when Charles concluded his Spanish alliance. It was not the first row between the brothers, nor was it the last.

There were strokes of bad luck. One of the best friends the brothers had was their brother-in-law, Stadtholder William II. He had died in November 1650, only twenty-four. Six days later their sister Mary produced his heir, another William, a pale and sickly little thing whom few expected to live. There was a prolonged squabble over his guardianship – though the office of Stadtholder had vanished with his father – and Charles ended up on the losing side. The Dutch were not greatly interested in such assistance as he could provide against the Commonwealth. In any event, Charles had suffered much, as he felt, from one rabble of rude, fanatical Calvinists and had no yearning to pitch his tent with another.

From 1654 the Commonwealth was the Protectorate and such a force at home and abroad that no one dared to grant the Stuarts any aid beyond basic pensions, jobs in their armies and arms-length hospitality. As conditions eased in England, exiled Royalists trickled back, and found themselves readily rehabilitated and very much more comfortable under the new order. All about Charles came shrill complaints, begging demands for money from his dwindling band. In July 1655 it is recorded the king was so hard up he had no meat for ten days. Some well-meant admirer from England sent a gift of hounds. It was a huge embarrassment. They cost a fortune to feed and it was impossible to send them back. By 1656 it was becoming a problem to afford even the costs of laundry. By September 1657 Edward Hyde – still faithful in exile; a sometime parliamentarian who had rallied to Charles I in 1642; later, Earl of Clarendon – recorded in wonder that everything the king had lately acquired, literally everything, 'every bit of meat, every drop of drink, all the fire and all the candles', had been bought on credit. It is said that Charles II had sunk so low he had to manage with only one dish for his meals. This was serious in political terms: the formal dining of royalty, in public, was an important part of contemporary kingship. By 1659 Hyde bewailed 'insupportable debts'.

There were women, for all that. Once he had embarked on

the last years of exile, at Bruges in the Low Countries, Charles found pleasant dalliance. By the time of the Restoration he had begotten three more illegitimate children by two different women, Elizabeth Killgrew – sister of James's chaplain! – and Catharine Pegge. In Paris there had been a mistress, Eleanor, the twice-widowed Lady Byron, who did remarkably well: she even squeezed money out of him. There were common whores and amiable, consenting one-night stands. It was certainly immoral conduct. It was not, by the standards of an unmarried prince for that time, unusual. It is unlikely if Charles II, in exile, slept with any more woman than, today, a healthy student of indiscriminating sexual appetite might bed during four years' urban study.

Lucy Walter was now a loose cannon, lost in drink and foolishness, dragging her little boy everywhere and even to England, where she was at one point described as the 'wife of Charles Stuart'. She escaped back to the Continent. Tales of horror surrounded her. It was said that she had procured the abortion of two more infants, of confused paternity; that she had murdered a maid. She kept demanding money, kept drinking, and kept talking. She was a liability and any passion Charles had entertained for her was long dead. By 1658, in an unpleasant business, little James was successfully kidnapped, and put under the care of Henrietta Maria. It was undoubtedly for the child's good. In 1659 Lucy Walter died of venereal disease.

Other Stuarts – Charles I, Mary – had found, in extremity, consolation in religion. There are only two things that can with certainty be said. Charles was born a member of the Church of England. (Antonia Fraser incorrectly says this was like his father: Charles I was born a member of the Scots Kirk.) He died, fifty-five years later, a member of the Roman Catholic Church. No one knows when, precisely, he converted, though we know he took the Roman rites on his deathbed. It was probably well after the Restoration and as part of one of his pernicious secret treaties. In exile he deeply resented his mother's rampant Roman Catholicism and denounced it with public fervour. He was aghast when she tried to pervert his brother, Henry, Duke of Gloucester, to the Roman faith. Privately, he wrote to her in stern terms: 'And remember the last words of my dead father (whose memory I doubt not will work upon you) which were to charge him – Harry – never to change his religion, whatsoever mischief shall fall either on me or my affairs, hereafter.' Whatever his spirituality, it seems to have had no ethical weight in his life. Like his grand-nephew Charles Edward, Charles II was to all intents and purposes an agnostic who would take his chances.

Meantime the Almighty had ushered another into eternity. Charles II was playing tennis, at Hoogstraeten, when on 10 September 1658, news was brought from England. On 3 September, as Hyde ruefully remarked, 'it had pleased God out of His infinite goodness to do that which He would not allow any man the honour of doing.' Oliver Cromwell died on the seventh anniversary of Worcester and the eighth of Dunbar.

His son, Richard, inherited the Lord Protectorate. Richard had not the skills nor standing of his father. More and more rumours began to grow of restoration. Envoys went back and forth. There was much plotting.

In January 1660 General George Monck crossed the Border from Scotland into England, with a big, well-ordered army, and set the events of restoration in motion. Charles was allowed back to the United Providences as it grew ever more apparent he was the man of the hour. On 4 April he issued the Declaration of Breda. He would accept restoration on these terms: a general amnesty, liberty of conscience, fair terms of pay and land settlement for the army. Parliament would see to the details. All was promised and nothing guaranteed. On 25 May 1660 King Charles II stepped ashore at Dover, to a wild and frenzied welcome. 'As it was,' says Paul Johnson sourly, 'the Restoration put the clock back, in a thoroughly English spirit of muddled compromise.'

9

BY PUDDING LANE

King Charles II

So Charles II had his shoulder of mutton and his whore. The Restoration was a bonanza of feasting, music, dancing, ordnance, boozing, bells, balls, bonfires, loyal addresses, sermons, pomp, circumstance and bad poetry. Samuel Pepys saw people drink the king's health on their knees in the streets; this, thought the diarist, was 'a little too much'. As Charles's fortunes so quickly reversed, so – before he left The Hague – the envoys of France and Spain hastened to throw rival dinner parties. The *Royal Charles* sailed towards England laden with plate, wine, and a hundred pounds of roast beef.

> Thus from the Belgick states delicious seat
> Triumphantly departed Charles the Great!

The king paced restlessly, as was his habit, up and down the deck. He rambled to Samuel Pepys, taking notes, of his perils after Worcester. There was much to grant him amusement in this hour of unwonted triumph. That same day the royal ships had been hastily renamed, before sailing: the *Richard* (as in Cromwell) became the *James* (as in Duke of York) the *Dunbar* (as in 1650) became the *Henry* (as in Duke of Gloucester.) The royal brothers had breakfasted on pork, boiled beef and peas. At three o'clock in the afternoon, the voyage over, the king was rowed ashore to Dover. Ever master of the occasion, he knelt at once on dry land and praised God. The Mayor of Dover made the first of the very many speeches of welcome, and presented Charles II with a richly bound and mighty Bible. This, said the king solemnly, receiving the gift, was 'the thing he loved above all others in the world'.

His head rang with guns, fireworks, vast and cheering

crowds. From Dover he went to Canterbury, and from Canterbury to Rochester; the roads strewn with flowers, or sweet-smelling herbs, and everywhere lined by adoring throngs. At Canterbury he took in Sabbath worship, the first meeting of his Privy Council, and a reward for George Monck: he was presented with the Order of the Garter. At Blackheath, on the outskirts of his capital, he saw the army. Riding on horseback, he must have been diverted by the ever-risible performance of morris dancers. It was May, after all; the next day was Charles's birthday, and the king was come into his own again. There was much richness and spectacle, of a kind seldom seen in the days of Commonwealth and Protectorate: much gorgeous garb – silks and velvets and ornate robes; cloth of silver, cloth of gold. The streets flowed with wine. That is no figure of speech. Fountains were piped with it. The ambassador of Venice had a tap of it, constantly flowing, outside his house.

On an evening the king reached Whitehall and was addressed by the Speakers of both Houses of Parliament. The Earl of Manchester spoke for the peers of the realm: 'Dread Sovereign! I offer no flattering titles, but speak the words of Truth: you are the desire of three Kingdoms, the strength and stay of the Tribes of the People, for the moderating of Extremities, the reconciling of Differences, the satisfying of all interests.' We should be glad, perhaps, he refrained from flattering titles. By the end of hours of salute and oratory the king was utterly exhausted. He declined to attend a thanksgiving service at Westminster Abbey. He could not avoid a ceremonial dinner, in public, where he pecked at his food before gawping crowds, as monarchs of England had always done.

That night, or very near it, it seems he entertained his present mistress, Mrs Barbara Palmer, for nine months later she was delivered of a daughter, Anne, for whom the king made provision. She grew up to resemble her father closely and, with a younger sister, became a valued part of his inner circle. These girls were made countesses when they became of age.

The wry wit had not deserted Charles II. As the exuberance and flattery and partying and congratulations continued, he turned to those about him and chuckled. It was plainly his own fault that he had been away for so long, said the king; he had yet to speak to anyone 'who did not protest that he ever wished for his return'.

Though the institution of monarchy had been restored, the disorder of the last two decades had transformed the political universe. The advances and institutions made in the days of Commonwealth and Protectorate could be stemmed, reversed a little, but in no way abolished. In Scotland and Ireland Charles could do more or less as he pleased; his writ was essentially military. In England he had three new realities to face. There was a fierce new nationalism, which found its highest passion in a Protestant identity. Anti-popery was a powerful force and the least Romanising trend detected, in policy ecclesiastical or civil – or in the habits of the king's own family – excited uproar and threatened confrontation and crisis. Parliament, too, was now a permanent partner of the king in government, and could not be dismissed by his *fiat* nor threatened by his wrath. The survival of kings depended on their co-operation with parliament. The Commons could not, now nor at any time in the future, be set aside.

At the same time the Commonwealth and Protectorate experience had provided some vindication of monarchy. The people wanted a king. They liked majesty and glamour and they were moved at the deepest level by the continuity and mystery of a hereditary kingship and a royal family. More, monarchy was still the norm of government every- where else, and in the peculiar new politics of the British Isles, with its competing nations and parliaments and Churches and factions and commercial interests and landed interests and a good many striving, ambitious, distrustful men, a king – a good king – could be both just and generous. By virtue of his majesty, his primitive authority of kingship, he could chair the whole clamour; ease the paths of agreement; legitimise the law. In the name of the king was effective and stable govern- ment.

He was not the merry youth of the Civil War; nor even the gallant captain of Worcester. Charles was thirty, well into middle age by the life-expectancy of his time, his face already creased with experience. He was no stranger to humiliation and helplessness. He had known what it was to fear for his life. He had seen abundant evidence of the fickleness of crowds; the vagaries of Providence. His quips, as we have seen, indicate a profound scepticism; even a tinge of melancholy. The times were terrible and full of rumour and, as the bonfires of Restoration died down, and the wind dispersed their ashes, plots and talk of plots continued to haunt his realms. His overwhelming goal in life was simple: to survive as king *de facto* as well as *de jure*, for he believed utterly in the institution of monarchy; and never to be forced abroad again. Charles, from the day he landed at Dover, never left his kingdoms. He had two immediate goals, both hard fully to accomplish, and to a degree antithetical: he had to make peace with the Cromwellians, and due rewards to the Royalists.

He had a long memory, and be it fairly recorded that Charles II rapidly set to rewarding and honouring all who had helped him in the desperate days after Worcester. With his own hand the king drew up lists of them all, everyone he could remember. Carver, who had carried him ashore at Fécamp, got a pension. So did the master of the *Surprise*; she herself, surviving, became a yacht, the *Royal Escape*. All his hosts won gifts, titles, incomes. Jane Lane received a gold watch; a jewel worth £1,000; an annual pension of £1,000. The Penderel family were received at court. The brothers were awarded pensions, and their children, in perpetuity. So the king paid his debts.

But there was also vengeance, and Charles's capacity to bear a grudge was considerable and unedifying. The dead were slighted first. Three corpses were dug up: Oliver Cromwell; and his son-in-law Henry Ireton; and John Bradshaw, who had led the prosecution of Charles I. The bones were hung for execration at Tyburn. As passionately as he located and rewarded his hosts and helpers from 1650, so the king at first pursued the 'regicides', the forty-one men surviving who, in some way or another, could be held responsible for the death of Charles I: prosecutors; those who had signed the warrant; the death-guard; and so on. The executioners were fortunate: so intensely had their identities been covered up in 1649, for fear of the mob, that to this day we do not know who they were. In the end, thirteen regicides were executed. Nineteen others, hopeless, gave themselves up. These, however, the king spared. He told Hyde he was 'sick of hanging', though he refused to pardon them. Sir Henry Vane, who had been instrumental in the fall of Strafford, was put to death, but for treason against the present king and not the last one.

Archibald Campbell, Marquis of Argyll, was the most tragic casualty. He had refused to follow Charles into England, in 1650, but it was the death of Montrose that provided pretext. Charles hated Argyll with a passion and needed little excuse. Argyll sped to London, after the Restoration, to ingratiate himself with the king. Charles refused to have anything to do with him; refused even to see him. His ministers bundled the wretched man home to Scotland and fixed up his arraignment for treason. He was prosecuted by General Monck, and defended by George MacKenzie, who managed to secure his client's acquittal as a regicide. Monck, however, had the effrontery to produce in evidence letters to himself from Argyll, arguing that he had worked alongside the Commonwealth administration; that he was thus a traitor to Scotland. The marquis pointed out, quite properly, that to condemn him for this was to condemn him for the 'epidemical fault of the whole nation'. It was to no avail. 'This cold-blooded treason,' says Rev Thomas McCrie, 'sealed the doom of the Marquis. Monck, who had been the active agent of Cromwell, was made Duke of Albemarle; and Argyll, who had only yielded to the usurper after resistance was vain, was sentenced to be beheaded!'

Unlike Montrose, he was granted the merciful end of beheading, by the Maiden. On the appointed day in 1661, the marquis took a good dinner and then a long nap, sleeping until two hours before his execution. He paid full attention to arrangements on the scaffold. The block was not level; he produced a ruler to check it, and demanded – and was granted – a carpenter to correct it. He made a last passionate speech for the Covenant. 'I had the honour to set the Crown on the King's head,' he had said after sentence, 'and now he hastens me to a better crown than his own.'

Argyll's severed head was impaled on a spike on the Edinburgh Tolbooth, recently vacated by the skull of Montrose. His remains lie today in the High Kirk of St Giles, in a tomb across the aisle from that of Montrose. Both typify the agonies of Scotland in the days of the Covenant, for both Argyll and Montrose were truly good men, of high principle and, in their respective ends, lousy timing.

In the administration of Scotland Charles II is seen at his worst. He was hardly restored when there began a series of decrees and measures that should echo in infamy, for their betrayal of the most solemn trusts and the bloody tyranny they unleashed. There was no effective resistance to his will. He had the brains of three cunning and wicked men at his disposal. Monck, of course, was one; an ambitious general who judged times deftly and was ever out for the main chance. Still more repellent was John Sharp. Sharp, born in Banff in 1618, was minister at Crail and had stood eminent in Covenanting councils. He was experienced in academe: he had been professor of philosophy at St Andrews. Many distrusted him. He was nakedly ambitious, for a start; there were also well-founded rumours of private debauchery. But, in 1657, as the men of the Kirk began to fear for the safety of the new ecclesiastical order, James Sharp was sent to London to represent the interests of the Scottish Church and keep the General Assembly accurately informed on political developments. He came and went from Scotland, until the Restoration, and covertly plotted the revival of episcopacy and the winning of a high place for himself. Once the king was returned, Sharp sold his brethren down the river. In an age not short of rascals and traitors, it is hard to convey the depravity of this man of God. Oliver Cromwell interviewed Sharp once, and concluded he was an atheist; Charles himself both used him and loathed him, describing the creature as 'one of the worst of men'. The atheist became Archbishop of St Andrews.

And there was Lauderdale. He was a London Scot, who seldom bothered to take the Great North Road. Charles II appointed him soon after the Restoration to oversee the Scottish Privy Council and ensure the thorough execution of the king's will. Lauderdale had suffered for the Stuart cause: after the Battle of Worcester he served time in the Tower of London. He was a strange, uncouth figure who 'made a very ill appearance; he was very big; his hair was red, hanging loosely about him; his tongue was too big for his mouth, which made him bedew all that he talked to; and his whole manner was rough and boisterous, and very unfit for court.' Certainly he drank too much.

Lauderdale presided over what amounted to a *coup d'état* in Scotland and what was certainly a constitutional outrage. First, in January 1661, he recalled the Scots parliament, suitably packed with Royalists, and chaired by the Earl Middleton, who had come a long way since he had posed in sackcloth at Scone. Middleton was a profligate and a drunkard. At his behest the estates first reasserted the royal prerogative; this made the king, personally, without regard for estates or General Assembly, supreme judge in all matters civil and ecclesiastical. (Later, the estates attached this to an oath of allegiance, which bound every subject invited to take the oath – as a good many eventually were, on pain of death – to acknowledge this same supreme power of King Charles II in matters civil or ecclesiastical.)

What really takes the contemporary breath away is the Act Recissory. This astonishing measure abolished every single piece of legislation passed by the Scots parliament since 1633. It made all the steps of reformation in the Kirk between 1638 and 1650 rebellious and treasonable. It made the National Covenant and the Solemn League and Covenant unlawful oaths. It repudiated the Glasgow Assembly of 1638 as an unlawful and seditious meeting. 'In short,' writes McCrie, 'all that had been done for religion and the reformation of the Church during the second Reformation was completely annulled.'

Bishop Gilbert Burnet, in England, was well aware of what was going on in Scotland, and as an essentially decent man was revolted; he wrote later that this was a maddening time in that little kingdom, 'when the men of affairs were perpetually drunk'. Middleton seldom came to the estates sober. The Act Recissory – which, by the way, has never been repealed, and still sits on our statute books – was first proposed by the 'miserable junta', as McCrie calls them, at a drunken banquet. By these Acts, 'the servile parliament laid the civil liberties of the nation at the feet of a despot.'

Charles II knew what was going on in Scotland, naturally, but never troubled to visit the kingdom. The Kirk, of course, was turned upside down; by the king's will, Lauderdale insisted that all ministers settled over congregations since 1649 should seek out lay patrons to be formally presented to their charges, and then ordained by the new bishops. (The Kirk had abolished the system of patronage, granting congregations the right to elect their own ministers. Patronage still survives in England today and the constant determination of an English-dominated government to impose it on Scotland – it was not finally abolished until 1874 – caused untold trouble and denominational division.)

But the Scottish ministry were a key class in the land: educated men, highly trained, articulate, and very much the political nation. Over a third refused to comply, and were forced to quit their churches and manses, and were followed by the mass of their people. They continued to hold services of worship – on the hills, in the woods, in barns, in private homes – and these 'conventicles', of course, were illegal. Government troops were sent to disband them and arrest all present. So, within months, the king had created a formidable and increasingly organised opposition in Scotland. The government tried all the harder to crush the conventicles, and soon Scotland was in a state bordering on civil war.

More warriors of the Covenant were executed, such as Thomas Guthrie and Lord Warriston. The new Covenanters organised themselves into incursion and pitched battle, such as the disastrous rout at Rullion Green, outside Edinburgh, on

28 November 1666. Nine hundred Covenanters were easily beaten by General Tam Dalyell, of the Binns, in West Lothian. Fifteen of their leaders were hanged in Edinburgh; more in Ayr and Glasgow. Many were jailed and even tortured.

The thumbscrews mashed digits. Even more ghastly was the 'boot', a devilish device of cruelty, 'which had not been used in Scotland for upwards of forty years before,' writes McCrie,

> and the very appearance of which the people had forgotten; but the bishops had taken care that a new pair should be made for the occasion, and they were brought into frequent use during the subsequent years. This instrument was made of four pieces of narrow boards nailed together, of a competent size for the leg. Into this case after the criminal's leg was inclosed wedges were driven down with a hammer, which caused intolerable pain, and frequently mangled the limb in shocking manner, compressing the flesh and even forcing the marrow from the bone.

Two early victims were John Neilson of Corsack, who had fought at Rullion Green, and a minister attendant on the Covenanter force, Rev Hugh MacKail. They were put to the boot 'to ascertain the secret causes and agents of this rebellion'. Neilson 'was so cruelly tormented that he shrieked enough to move a heart of stone'. The wretched men had no information to give.

Thirty women and children were among the prisoners taken at Rullion Green. Dalyell had promised them quarter. Instead the regime had them put to the sword. Posterity remembers this general as 'Bluidy Tam'; be it recorded that he was so disgusted by this crime he resigned his commission.

The second generation of Covenanters included wild men, some fanatics, some adventurers; and there was atrocity on their side too. But the great mass of them only sought the liberty to worship their God in the order and manner they believed, in deepest conscience, to be that of Holy Scripture. The king himself had sworn fearful oaths, in 1650 and 1651, of loyalty to this order. Their parliament and assemblies had legislated fully on these matters in the Kirk in lawful fashion. Now the government was wicked, its king an infidel; and they were hunted like dogs. One could list hundreds of executions, shootings, torments and outrages. Victims included women by the score and children by the dozen.

In one of the very worst episodes, two women in Wigtownshire were drowned at the stake in 1685, the last year of Charles's reign. Margaret McLauchlan was sixty-three; Margaret Wilson a girl of eighteen. Their crime? They refused, point-blank, to attend episcopal worship in the parish church, and were eventually caught at a conventicle on the moor. So they were tied fast to stakes on the Solway sands and drowned by the incoming tide, refusing to the end to take the 'abjuration oath'. 'What possible danger the government could apprehend from old women of sixty-three and girls of eighteen, it is hard to say,' records McCrie. Many efforts have been made over the years to prove this particular crime against humanity never happened. All have failed. The spot on the Solway shore is marked to this day.

By the end of Charles's reign the persecution was at its height. His own brother declared that 'there would never be peace in Scotland until the whole of the country south of the Forth was turned into a hunting-field.' Everywhere soldiers roamed looking for fugitive Presbyterians, or anyone who looked like a fugitive Presbyterian. People were shot for carrying Bibles; shot for stammering over the oath of abjuration; shot for failing to produce documents and pass-papers; shot for running across the road or walking too hastily over a field.

Renewed and desperate efforts were made by the government to impose the king's will. Lauderdale came north in 1669 with revised terms for pastoral settlement, determined to press 'indulgences' on the 'outed' ministers and restore them to lawful parishes. But the Episcopalian order, and Anglican liturgy, remained. So only a hundred ministers accepted. The rest continued to be chased like dogs. The regime was further alarmed when, on 3 May 1679, Archbishop Sharp was assassinated. Nine Covenanters jumped his coach on Magus Muir, and hacked the prelate to death. On 1 June a government force was badly beaten at Drumclog; the losing general was John Graham of Claverhouse, a relative of the late Montrose.

But the Covenanting victory did not last long. Twelve hundred troops defeated at Bothwell Brig, later in 1679 – the government army was led this time by the Duke of Monmouth, sometime James Croft – were jailed in cages, open to the air and to the night, unroofed, in the Kirkyard of Greyfriars in Edinburgh. This state might have been envied, though, by their clergy, many of whom were now confined in the fetid squalor of special new prisons; there was one built on the Bass Rock, in the Firth of Forth. Alexander Peden, one of the most memorable characters of the Covenant, wrote that he and his brethren were 'close shut up in our chambers, not permitted to converse, diet, worship together, but conducted out by two at once in the day to breathe in the open air, envying with reverence the birds their freedom. Again we are close shut up, day and night, to hear only the sighs and moans of our fellow prisoners.'

After a week or two of the cages, all but 340 of the prisoners had signed a bond not to take up arms against the king, and sworn the oath of abjuration. The rest were sentenced to slavery in the West Indies. One ship left Scotland in November, bearing 210 Covenanters to forced labour in the sugar fields. The vessel sank in a storm off the Orkneys, and all were drowned. By the 1680s, Scotland was launched into what we remember as the 'Killing Time'; the land drenched in blood so that Charles II might have ecclesiastical conformity.

In England, the king was much weaker than his predecessors and, ironically, frustrated in his own vision for the Church of England. Many Royalist supporters, who had lost much in the Civil War, clamoured for rewards Charles could not afford to give them. He did his best, but he could not do enough, and there was much ill-feeling. Nor did he find his parliament in London as compliant as that in Edinburgh. In the Great

Rebellion the prerogative institutions of the monarchy had been abolished. They were not reinstated. A Triennial Act was passed in 1663, against the king's wishes: he was now compelled to have a parliament at least once every three years. Nor, it turned out, did the terms of Restoration grant him as much money as he had expected. As for the Church of England, he wanted a broad-based Church, broader even than that of the Elizabethan Settlement. Parliament settled for something a good deal narrower; more, they entrenched the Church of England in a privileged position in national life, with what is erroneously remembered as the 'Clarendon Code'. From 1665 no one outwith the Church of England – no Roman Catholics, no Independents or other Non-Conformists, no Quakers, and certainly no Jews – could hold a parliamentary seat or serve as a justice of the peace or sit on a parish council or in a municipal corporation. So the Church was bound up nicely in the ruling order: the Tory partnership of parson and squire, which would run rural England well into modern times.

Charles was now rather unpopular. He made matters worse when, in March 1665, he led England to war against the Dutch. It was largely a naval conflict and soon the Dutch were having much the better of it. In 1667 the country was humiliated when a Dutch fleet with impunity sailed up the Medway, burned three capital ships, and sailed gaily away with the king's flagship in tow. The Treaty of Breda granted peace on poor terms for England, and finished the career of Edward Hyde, Earl of Clarendon, who had to scuttle abroad to avoid impeachment by the Commons.

It was a bad time in England, a time men now began to contrast darkly with the glories of Cromwell. By late 1666 the honeymoon of Charles II was plainly over. His standing was hit by two calamities and only a little improved by a third. First came the Great Plague, in the summer of 1665; there was a bad heatwave, and the pneumonic plague – highly infectious, incurable, and deadly – took its first London life in May 1665, in the parish of St Giles in the Fields. In the sticky heat of summer the epidemic took fast hold. In one week at the end of June a hundred deaths were recorded. Soon each night was busy with burial. There were dozens – hundreds – of sad, near-anonymous deaths recorded: a child from such-and-such an alley, a girl from such-and-such an inn. On 10 August Samuel Pepys drew up his will, for 'a man cannot depende upon living two days to an end.' Soon the pressure of death was so heavy the consecrated burial-grounds could not cope. They began to dig communal plague-pits in London.

By August king and court had fled the capital. It struck men as odd, with the Dutch War at its height; it is hard, though, to blame Charles for leaving London. He would have done not the slightest good by staying and would certainly have endangered his life. (The President of the Royal College of Physicians also fled, which was a true disgrace.) Nevertheless, in the king's absence, central authority in the capital quite broke down. Until nine justices of the peace were marshalled to support the Lord Mayor – who stayed in the city; but his writ did not extend to the outlying parishes – nothing effective was done. The Anti-Plague Laws of 1648, another antiquity from the College of Physicians, were cruel and crude. A plague-ridden building was shuttered, the inhabitants immured inside, dead or dying or alive, until the pestilence was spent. So tenement stair upon tenement stair became a gaol, and a half-dozen families at once left to swelter, survive or die. Sanitation was non-existent, clean water virtually unobtainable, the burial of the victims increasingly impossible. And at this time only the haziest notions of hygiene and the transfer of infection were understood. Chewing tobacco became popular: it was said to be a sure prophylactic. People carried posies of aromatic herbs in their pockets; the red hives that first indicated infection were said to resemble rings of roses, and so the plague gave us a nursery rhyme. People began to say, in nervous concern, 'Bless you,' when you sneezed.

'Piety and Profaneness', as one observer noted, marked the city at this time. Some immersed themselves in religious exercises. Others took to drink, or sex. People wrote 'Lord Have Mercy On Us,' on the imprisoning doors and shutters.

Doctors went about in eerie beak-like masks and voluminous gowns; the masks were filtered with herbs. There were funny stories and tragic stories. (Fraser records one of a drunken piper, taken for dead, and so hauled away on a cartload of corpses. When he awoke he began playing his pipes again and folk dashed away in terror, thinking he was the Devil.) There was looting; even the corpses were stripped of clothing and jewellery, or the sick robbed as they wallowed in bed. The poor suffered enormously. The wealthy, even if they too were condemned inside shuttered houses, bribed their way to escape to the country.

By September London was so desolate of crowds and traffic that grass grew on Whitehall streets. In September the plague peaked: 7,000 died in one horrific week. Thereafter the malady dwindled. It is hard to obtain accurate figures; most were compiled by parish, and restricted to Anglican households. Probably 100,000 died, in London, during the Great Plague. It was February 1666 before the king returned to his capital.

On 11 June came another calamity: a dreadful English defeat in the Four Days' Battle. It was a huge naval engagement which the Dutch, with far superior artillery, won easily and with the shedding of much English blood: 5,000 men died, mostly in exploding or blazing ships. There was much grief and much recrimination against the king and his government. The English fought back, winning a petty counter-skirmish or two, but all sides, English and Dutch and French, moved reluctantly towards the negotiating table, weary of a war that seemed without purpose or end. Parliament was no longer prepared to grant money for its prosecution and Charles was in no position to fight further.

In the small hours of the Sabbath, 2 September a fire started in Pudding Lane, quite near London Bridge. There was a brisk, dry east wind and the fire made its steady way along the Thames and through the city. By Monday the flames fanned a half-mile front. Soon the glow of the fire, by night, could be seen from the palace windows. Already the people had begun to shout for help, to their king, and to the Most High. Fires

CHARLES II
A miniature portrait of 'Old Rowley'; there is wit about the mouth, but
melancholy hangs heavy on the features.

JAMES VII AND II
The spirit is willing, but the flesh is weak: this exquisitely cynical portrait captures all of James VII – the sanctimonious demeanour; the empty head; the hint of carnal appetite in his full mouth and heavy eyes.

WILLIAM III AND II
The Prince of Orange: the Calvinist King. The painting suggests virtue was its
own punishment. The enduring libel of hypocritical homosexuality may be
discounted: but this pious King deserves no excuse for Glencoe.

PRINCES JAMES FRANCIS, EDWARD STUART AND PRINCESS MARIA CLEMENTINA
A royal wedding, by the Pope himself. The marriage collapsed amidst wild
allegations of infidelity; the bride's mental breakdown, and ensuing suicide

attempts, paranoid outbursts and eating disorders. It all sounds depressingly
familiar.

QUEEN ANNE
The last of the Stuarts to sit on a throne: painted before her looks deserted her entirely. (The Queen was so fat at her death in 1714 her coffin was almost square.)

PRINCE CHARLES EDWARD STUART
Charles Edward's unfortunate pretty-boy features belie reality: he was a tough, honed and highly skilled man of field, sword and gun, fluent in several languages and a keen musician.

PRINCE CHARLES EDWARD STUART
The 'Bonnie Prince', late in life. He had lost the '45, and discovered drink.

were not at all uncommon in London, even extensive ones; there were still many wooden buildings, with gables and abutments that leaned to each other across high and very narrow city streets. It was late on Monday before the scale of this conflagration was grasped. Efforts were quickly organised to direct operations against it. The Duke of York took charge of an emergency committee of the Privy Council. Fire posts were established; funds issued for rations of bread and beer and cheese for the fighters.

Charles himself played a full part. He sent his own guards at once to fight the flames. He sailed down the Thames on Monday afternoon, exhorting the people to tear down combustible sheds and wharves and markets – anything to stop the fire spreading. But by Tuesday it had moved into Blackfriars and the entire parish of St Bride's. New buildings at Scotland Yard were hastily stripped, on the king's order, of roofs and wooden panelling, lest the fire take hold of Whitehall itself. The king and the Duke of York spent all Tuesday patrolling the city on horseback, helping to distribute water, trying to encourage the efforts of all. He bore on his back a pouch stuffed with gold, which he pressed on the most industrious men at demolition. If a wide enough area could be cleared, the king shouted, the fire would at length be unable to leap on. At times he grabbed a bucket himself, or a spade, or an axe. During the course of the blaze he is said to have spent over thirty hours on horseback. Certainly, by Tuesday's end, he was soaked and scorched and sooty.

His efforts continued. Food was organised for the homeless. He ordered a day of humiliation and prayer. The king also ordained a collection to be uplifted for the poor and suffering. One legacy, perhaps, of his sufferings after Worcester was an ability to identify with the dispossessed and wretched: a rare quality in a monarch.

And still the Great Fire marched on. The court was again evacuated. Queen Henrietta Maria hastily removed herself from Somerset House (unsafe) to Hampstead Court (safe). Her Chapel Royal, though, survived the holocaust. The

Anglican St Paul's did not. It was utterly destroyed, like another 140 'heretic churches', reported a gleeful priest. Churches, prisons, graveyards, warehouses . . . all burned. At night the glow in the sky could be seen from forty miles' distance. Soot fell softly in distant, rural Kensington. As far as Windsor Great Park, light, scorched, wispy stuff fell gently to the ground. After four days of fierce blazing, the Great Fire declined, and rains on Sunday damped it down finally, though smoke and smouldering continued for weeks, until a mighty cloudburst in October. The flames had obliterated a large oblong of central London, about one and a half miles long and half a mile across.

The Dutch, of course, attributed it to the judgement of God. There were rumours of deliberate arson; years later, poor James himself, who had fought so valiantly against the heat, was widely rumoured to have started the conflagration. We must agree with the Privy Council's own considered conclusion, that 'Nothing had been found to argue the Fire in London to have been caused by other than the hand of God, a great wind and a very dry season.' Charles himself exhorted the people, on 6 September – addressing a large crowd of the dispossessed – to assure them there had been no plot; it was but that same and mighty and inscrutable hand of God. It availed little. From the first, almost everyone blamed the Roman Catholics. Remarkably, though there was massive homelessness and great suffering, deaths were but in single figures.

So, the Dutch War ended, and eager to start afresh and restore popular standing, and quit of Clarendon, Charles assembled a new administration, led by five peers: Clifford, Arlington, Buckingham, Ashley Cooper, and Lauderdale. The acronym, C-A-B-A-L, has entered the English language. Arlington was the most important and the king himself took a bigger part in affairs, especially with intrigues abroad. He allied himself with Protestant powers first, in a Triple Alliance with Sweden and the United Provinces. But, by 1670, eager for money, Charles broke the pact and allied himself with Louis XIV. His Most Christian Majesty was now king in his own right, more than a match for the British sovereigns he faced during his very long reign. Mystery still surrounds the full detail of his deals with Charles II. He certainly wrung a commitment from Charles to fight the Dutch; and to endeavour to restore his realms to Roman Catholicism. It seems likely that at this time Charles secretly converted to the Roman faith. (He has often been accused of perverting during his exile, but there is no proof.) It was secret because his brother James, Duke of York, had tacitly embraced Roman Catholicism; this was widely rumoured, and as a result the duke was hugely unpopular.

Further to his deal, Charles tried to amend the force of the Clarendon Code. In 1672 he issued a Declaration of Indulgence, trying to restore place in public life to Catholics and other religious dissenters. Parliament forced him to withdraw it. More: parliament pushed through a Test Act – the 'test' was another oath of abjuration – which banned all Roman Catholics from public office. So the Duke of York had to own up to his faith, and resign at last as Lord High Admiral. Only that year he had further compromised himself by his second marriage, to a Catholic princess of fifteen, Mary of Modena; only two daughters survived from the Duke of York's first and Protestant marriage, to the late Anne Hyde, Clarendon's daughter.

The succession was now a source of deep Protestant anxiety, for the king himself had no legitimate issue, despite all the women (as early as 1660 he was said to be on his nineteenth mistress) and a host of acknowledged bastards. In 1662, after long negotiations and as part of a complicated arrangement to distance England from Spain, Charles had married the Infanta Catherine of Braganza. Marriage had new urgency, for his brother James had made a most unsuitable and much-mocked match, and smallpox had borne away two others in the succession, the Dowager Princess Mary, his sister; and his brother Henry, Duke of Gloucester.

Catherine was prim, plain, devoutly Roman Catholic, and arrived in England with a household of Portuguese ladies memorably described as 'for the most part old and ugly and proud'. She made one important contribution to our culture. The first thing she asked for, on landing, was a cup of tea. Tea-drinking was hardly heard of in England; the queen did much to make it fashionable. (On that occasion, though, tea was not available. She was offered ale instead, which she declined.)

Charles found little in his queen to delight his sophisticated palate; it is recorded that, in his dry way, he commented that there was 'not anything in her face that can in the least shock one'. At twenty-three, too, Catherine was old for a royal bride. But she was gentle, witty, possessed of a beautiful speaking voice; only her tensions with Barbara Palmer – who ranted and nagged the king until he made her Lady of the Bedchamber, a dreadful insult to his young queen – caused any concern. After a year or three had passed another difficulty became evident: Queen Catherine was barren.

Some have argued Charles himself was sterile, as the result of syphilis. (But he begot children, without difficulty, on other ladies.) It has even been said that Clarendon engineered the match deliberately of his king to a woman suffering a 'bloody flux', unlikely ever to bear children, the better to advance the hopes of his grandchildren of York. This is fantastic and absurd; with such a problem, the king's marriage could readily have been annulled. What is remarkable is how well he treated his queen, even as political pressure mounted over the succession. Charles treated Catherine with every courtesy and civility. He dismissed any suggestion – and there were many of them as the years went by – that he get a divorce. She won his regard, too, by great dignity of bearing, and by her tolerance of his endless philandering. (It is said that she once surprised him with Nell Gwyn; the orange-seller was hiding behind a curtain, but had carelessly left her slipper on the bedchamber floor. The queen sighed and withdrew, remarking it would be a shame if the slipper's owner caught a chill.)

If there seemed no hope of the king siring a litter of legitimate Stuart princes and princesses, there might be another way of avoiding the Duke of York's succession. Was it possible that – as his mother had so ardently insisted – James

Crofts, Duke of Monmouth and Buccleuch, was in fact legitimate; that at some point in 1648 Charles had married his mother? This was seriously rumoured, and came to be widely believed, no doubt because many fearful Protestants wanted to believe it. There is even a modern tale that, last century, one of Monmouth's heirs – a Duke of Buccleuch – found the marriage certificate in the forgotten drawer of an ancient bureau. 'That could cause a lot of trouble,' this duke is said to have said, and then 'very sensibly burned it'.

Is it possible? There is no doubt that Monmouth was Charles's natural son. Any who saw him at court, in the company of his father, was convinced beyond doubt. The resemblance was unmistakable. Portraits of Monmouth as a child show strong likeness to Charles at the same age. Charles himself never questioned the boy's paternity. He had gone to great trouble, even before the Restoration, when he himself was desperately hard up, to care for the child's welfare. He had supplied his material needs and moved swiftly to remove him from Lucy Walters, once she was patently unfit to continue as his mother.

But any notion that Charles was married to Lucy Walters can be dismissed. Antonia Fraser argues a compelling case. Monmouth must have been conceived in July 1648, when the details of Charles's whereabouts and activity are well recorded; the prince was desperately busy, trying to squash a mutiny on the Royalist ships and make some new agreement with the Scots. It is hard to identify the time he would have needed to sneak away and conduct a most unsuitable marriage. Princes did not marry ladies, even ones of gentlefolk and good blood; they married princesses, and the Duke of York was to be widely sneered at for making a 'low' match to Anne Hyde. Besides, in 1648, at a desperately low point in Stuart fortunes, Charles would have been well aware – and his mother would have constantly reminded him – how important his marriageability was; how a match to some foreign princess might prove a vital card, the only hope of Stuart restoration. We know how seriously he approached marriage to Catherine of Braganza. Appeal and love had nothing to do with it: it was a betrothal by cold-blooded statecraft and calculating diplomacy.

Nor did the conduct of either Charles or Lucy, which is well recorded too, resemble the norms of marriage even in our day. Both had lovers. Lucy had a daughter in 1651, which was certainly not that of Charles; and no one thought for a moment that it was. Besides, the lady strove hard to marry someone else, Sir Henry de Vic, who was England's ambassador at Brussels. She asked Charles to help her courtship. It is impossible to believe he was ever her husband. James, Duke of Monmouth, was no more than senior bastard of Charles II. It need not necessarily have kept him from the throne. There were good grounds, by the laws of her time, for querying the legitimacy of Elizabeth I, who was conceived long before her parents' marriage and born while Catherine of Aragon was still very much alive and livid. Charles II, though, did not help Monmouth's ambition in the least; and Monmouth himself was a foolish, strutting, popinjay of a fellow, raised largely by Henrietta Maria, and so shamelessly spoiled it was a wonder the boy did not turn out a good deal worse than he did.

The Second Dutch war, launched in cahoots with Louis XIV, cost England a good deal in men and armour and was largely unsuccessful. Peace was eventually brokered in 1674 with the Treaty of Westminster. Louis XIV continued to provide Charles with generous sums for political expenses, and the king played the usual Stuart double game. Thomas Osborne, Earl of Danby, a very dull but hard-working Yorkshireman, managed parliament with a degree of skill and restored some order to the government finances. The bribes of Louis XIV were a great help. At the same time the king advanced, or seemed to advance, the Protestant interest. English troops were sent to the United Provinces to help the Dutch against the French. And the blood-link the Stuarts enjoyed with the House of Orange was again tightened. In 1677 another Princess Mary, of the house of Stuart, was married to her cousin, another Prince William, of the house of Orange. This match of the Duke of York's elder daughter – she was fiercely Protestant – to Europe's most Protestant prince seemed to secure both abiding alliance, at last, between the English and the Dutch, and a respectable Protestant succession should Charles remain childless and his brother James stay sonless.

The king's lifestyle attracted much disapproving comment. Bastards were publicly owned and honoured, several with peerages. Charles flaunted his mistresses, too, making no attempt to disguise the nature of his relationship with the lady of the day. Lady Castlemaine, sometime Barbara Palmer, was early favourite. Women like Nell Gwyn were more for the bed than for display. The only one of any importance politically was a French Catholic, Louise de Keroualle. He had her portrait painted, by Philippe Vignon, which still hangs in the royal collection; more, he made her Duchess of Portsmouth. She was clever as well as beautiful and he shared state secrets with her; she did all she could to encourage a pro-French, pro-Catholic policy. There was another French Catholic mistress, too: Hortense de Mancini, Duchesse de Mazarin and a niece of the wily and notorious cardinal.

The godly were affronted by this. Neither were they pleased by the king's fondness for the theatre, nor for his love of the racecourse. Charles built himself a small palace at Newmarket, of which only the cellar now survives, and even got Nell Gwyn a little house there; the Devil's Dyke, on Newmarket Heath, is still called 'the Rowley Mile'. Charles endowed the Royal Gold Plate races at Newmarket, as his niece Queen Anne would one day sponsor Ascot.

There was much of the depraved about his court. His circle of friends included libertines and rakes. Bisexuality was for the last time fashionable at court; it caused no surprise – seemed even to be expected – if lusty, adventurous men chased pretty boys as well as attractive women. Samuel Pepys wrote, vexed, that 'buggery is now almost grown as common among our gallants as in Italy, and that the very pages of the town begin to complain of their masters for it.' No one could accuse Charles, at least, of that sin – he was interested in nothing but women – but, according to the historian of homosexuality,

Colin Spencer, the court of Charles II 'was rife with bisexual intrigue and assignations'. The notorious John Wilmot, Earl of Rochester, wrote poems in praise of pederasty, of incredible obscenity. Even worse was his drama, *Sodom, Or, The Quintessence of Debauchery*, which was performed at court; the work, in the crudest terms, extolled alternative sexual practices. Eventually Rochester went too far, and wrote a filthy skit about King Charles himself. He was then banished from court.

The great art collection of Charles I had been largely dispersed. His successor tried to recover as much as he could. Weeks before the Restoration, he encouraged parliament to set up a committee in charge of searching for the treasures of Charles I. Some of the most famous paintings and bronzes and so on were quickly recovered. Sycophants who had bought them in the Cromwellian auction now hastened to make present of their prizes to the new monarch. Francis Tryon, a London merchant, had deliberately acquired royal artwork in the hope, in due time, of presenting them all to Charles II. His gifts included 'one raerre peese of the present King, the Princes Royall, the Duek of Yarcke, the Princes Elizabett holding haer Suster the Prinsesse Anna upan haer lap, al in one peese, of Sir Antonio V'Dike'. The painting was not long kept by the later Stuarts. King James seems to have given it to a mistress, the Countess of Dorchester, and it would cost George III 500 guineas to recover it.

But other Van Dycks turned up, from the collections of Emmanuel de Critz, and the new royal painter, Peter Lely. Statues and embroidery turned up here and there. Much, of course, was irrevocably lost: gone without trace, or abroad, or kept in the hands of some less willing to curry royal favour. For all that, Charles obtained many presents of his own. All the old royal plate had gone, smelted for coin, but in the frenzy of the Restoration corporations and merchantmen vied to give him lovely things. The great companies of London gave Charles II magnificent silver plate. Exeter Corporation sent a huge salt; Plymouth, a huge combined water fountain and perfume burner. (Salts were popular: the king was given a dozen of them.) Another guild, whose name is lost, donated gold communion plate for the Chapel Royal.

Paintings came from abroad. Charles landed at Dover with a collection he had built up himself, in the Netherlands, of seventy-two fine works. The United Provinces, eager for his favour, made him a grand present of twenty-seven Old Masters: they included a fine Lorenzo Lotto, and Titian's *Man in Black Holding a Book*; and, besides, eight oriental lacquer cabinets, from Dutch possessions in the Far East.

An immediate working requisite for a king was regalia. When the Cromwellian administration had needed £30,000 in a hurry all the old symbols of sovereignty had been melted down, their jewels wrenched from settings and sold. So new regalia were made: a St Edward's crown; an orb; a sceptre; assorted swords of state. They cost the government £31,978. 9s. 6d. Most of it is still used. There was no regalia made for a queen consort until 1685, when James succeeded the throne. At the time of the coronation of Charles II the king was unmarried; and, later, Queen Catherine was never crowned.

The king's residences were in poor order. Court was at Whitehall, which alone had been kept in good repair during the interregnum. Because of its Cromwellian associations neither Charles II, nor his brother, used Hampton Court. Windsor was most dilapidated. For a country retreat Charles first bought Audley End, a vast palace built by the Earls of Suffolk, near Saffron Walden. It stayed in royal hands for the rest of the century, but was not in the end much used; it was too far from London and not that convenient for Newmarket, and before railway and telegraph it was difficult for a king to be much away from the capital when his decisions and views were sought almost daily.

Sir Christopher Wren produced a design for a palace at Winchester. It was never built. Tiring of Audley End, Charles decided instead to make Windsor truly habitable. Hugh May was commissioned to build a suite of suitable apartments for the king and queen, from the old suite of Edward III. George IV later remodelled the rooms himself, but one or two were deliberately spared, giving us today something of the flavour of Charles's taste in furnishing and decor. The queen's presence chamber has a grand ceiling painted by Verrio. There are carvings by Grinling Gibbons. Two other Verrio ceilings survive, in the queen's audience chamber and the king's dining room; the linking theme is a banquet of the gods, and the carvings in the dining room strengthen the gastronomic note, with assorted flagons of wine, bunches of grapes, fowl and flesh and fruit of every variety. Here, of an evening, dined King Charles II, and anybody suitably dressed, and passed by the guards, could come in and gape at the monarch. The custom went back to the Dark Ages. Only in private could king or queen eat with other people. At each of their palaces they had to practise this public ritual of dining, alone, before gawping view, like monkeys in a zoo.

Charles liked fine furniture and bronzes; not very much survives. He continued, though, to expand the royal art collection. By far his most important acquisition was a collection of 779 drawings by Leonardo da Vinci, acquired for the king through the offices of Peter Lely, and now kept in the Royal Library at Windsor. They cover most of da Vinci's career and show his bewildering variety of interests: figure drawing, anatomy, caricatures, the way water flowed and the way cannon were cast; every aspect and art of man seem to appear.

It was a reign where, more than before, the monarch posed as the benevolent uncle of progress. Under Charles II the Royal Society was established: a veritable synagogue of science, devoted to the exploration of nature through experiment and observation. He and his brother pursued one science of their own: naval architecture. Both had a fascination with yachts; Charles and James were keen sailors, and eager to experiment with sails and tackle. Soon England was producing the best yachts in Europe, and yacht-racing was established as a sport. Charles was a fine sailor and, indeed, a fine horseman; he had that Stuart love of rapid, sweaty physical activity. King Charles even sent a pair of yachts to King Louis as a present; the Sun King was thrilled. The interest in navigation, as a science, also led Charles to found the Royal Observatory, at Greenwich. The new institution studied trigonometry and cartography, as well as exploring the night sky with ever-improving telescopes.

King Charles II is also associated with dogs. The pug-nosed spaniels that bear his name he made most fashionable, and the lugubrious little things adorned every other lap at court. The bigger Cavalier strain was developed in our own century. Even his Bedchamber was full of spaniels, and spaniel puppies, and spaniel bitches about to have puppies; we are told the air was rather unwholesome.

The Treaty of Westminster ushered in a time of calm after 1674. The calm, though, belied the doubts and concerns under the surface of court frivolity and indolence. Scotland continued to boil away. The king's lifestyle gave continuing offence to the godly. Besides, his tastes in art, furnishing, dress, horses, entertainments – not to mention the bounty he bestowed upon women and illegitimate offspring – were extremely expensive. There was also his duplicity in politics. No one quite knew now where England stood with France and the Netherlands, or where Charles stood with Louis, and how much he was truly in obligation to that prince. Charles II had an army in the Low Countries: but why? He had begot many children, but not a one by his queen: why? His brother, his wife, his surviving sister were as Roman Catholic as Louis: why?

It was good ground for mad conspiracy theory, and in the autumn of 1678 the hysteria of the 'Popish Plot' seized London and its mob. It had its McCarthy, Titus Oates, a big uncouth fellow, voraciously homosexual, of wild mien and big heavy jaw and a remarkable gift in plausible but monstrous lies. And Oates had his Cohn; the slimy Israel Tonge. International politics, royal religious tastes, and assorted happenstance discoveries and incidents lent, to a frightened people, credibility to Oates's repeated claim: that a dark papal plot was well advanced to kill the king, overthrow the government and establish Roman Catholic despotism under the Duke of York. What set everything off was a sudden death. Oates and Tonge had recently made sworn deposition of the 'conspiracy' to a magistrate, Sir Edward Berry Godfrey. On 22 October he was found dead in a Primrose Hill ditch. Then a former secretary of the Duke of York was found to be holding treasonable letters. A former ambassador to the French court let it be known that Danby, who had been a-begging parliament for funds to make war on France, had at the same time been negotiating with Louis XIV.

Such incidents in themselves were embarrassing enough to the king, who was now ailing and fast growing old. Nor, perhaps, did he quickly appreciate how dangerous this pattern of events could be in the popular mind. But, by the end of 1679, his entire government and regime were in crisis. Reason deserted the city. Treason and conspiracy and popery were everywhere detected. On 21 November the first, and entirely innocent, Roman Catholic was executed. Parliament rammed through a new and far tighter Test Act: it barred every single Roman Catholic, save the Duke of York, from sitting in either House of Parliament. The 'Cavalier Parliament' was so determined to impeach Danby – and to displace the Duke of York from the succession – that Charles lost patience and hastily dissolved it. But the succeeding 'Exclusion Parliament' proved even worse.

By May 1680 Danby languished in the Tower of London. The Duke of York had seen fit to take an extended holiday on the Continent. Men began to discuss the position – and loyalties – of Queen Catherine, that gentlest of creatures. An Exclusion Bill was now seriously discussed, to prevent the Roman Catholic James from ever becoming king. There was much speculation about the Duke of Monmouth, who was silly enough to encourage it. He now quite wickedly revived the old canard that his uncle had lit the match for the Great Fire. A faction now formed around Monmouth, led by Ashley Cooper, Earl of Shaftesbury, a brilliant but frustrated man who had years since been removed from the government. Charles called him, sourly, 'Little Sincerity', but these Exclusionists – or 'Whigs', as men began to call them – made a powerful opposition. There was nothing the king could do, either, to shut up Monmouth, who told everyone his parents had secretly married and that he was the true and Protestant heir.

The ordeal endured until the summer of 1681. Two more parliaments met. Two more Exclusion Bills narrowly failed. Many more wretched Roman Catholics were executed, ending in July with the unlucky head of the Archbishop of Armagh. Charles played for time and Monmouth appealed everywhere for sympathy and support and Shaftesbury strove to attain his ends. Then, as these bursts of public hysteria do, it all deflated as suddenly as it had begun. However scared people might be by a Roman Catholic sovereign – and even the loyal 'Tories' about the king blanched at the prospect – few men of standing or property were prepared to meddle with the laws of succession. Such interference threatened everything they believed in; it threatened themselves. So the fight died away, but left the king badly damaged. He had been torn between the concerns to truth and fear of the mob; between love of son and loyalty to brother; he had failed at any point to give a firm and decisive lead. Charles had accomplished his principal aim, as usual, which was simply to survive. But he was now as distrusted, if still popular enough, a man in England as he was abominated in Scotland.

The third Exclusion Parliament adjourned in April 1681. It was the last of Charles's reign. For once he did not need parliament. He had plenty of money: Louis XIV doled out subsidies, and the economy was on rather a boom. James skulked back from Scotland in 1682, after a long, tactful absence; he had tired of hunting Covenanters. That November Shaftesbury fled to Holland. Monmouth, once things were calm, was easily repudiated by Charles as a 'beast and a blockhead'; he too hid abroad. Oates was at last seen for what he was, a hateful and malicious liar. He was convicted of perjury, fined £100,000, and, unable to pay this fortune, was confined to prison. (In happier times for Protestant thugs, he would be entertained at court by William III.) More Tories took their place in the government and more

Whigs were dropped. If Charles II now pursued any policy at all it was to stay alive and avoid war, any war, at home or abroad. The economy continued to prosper and by 1685 the Stuart monarchy at last looked rather secure.

On 2 February Charles took a turn while shaving – perhaps a slight stroke – and was soon rather ill, with great pain in his kidneys. The royal doctors came, to bleed and purge and cup and clyster their monarch, and dose him with cantharides and other horrific medicines, and soon the king was extremely ill. Three days later, with the end to be seen in his face, a priest was summoned; this was Father Huddleston, who had many years before organised his comfort and accommodation as the king had run from Worcester. So Charles II was openly received into the Catholic faith, in mysterious circumstances; perhaps at the behest of Louis XIV; or his brother's; or the haunting shade of Henrietta Maria; or the superstitious fear and hedge-betting of a bad man at the gates of death.

He was quite delirious. He asked James, now present, to look after the Duchess of Portsmouth, and, too, 'let not poor Nellie starve.' By dawn on 6 February he was gasping for breath, and called for the curtains to be drawn, the windows to be opened. Two hours later he was unconscious; gangrene and decay marked his extremities even before, at a quarter to midday, Charles II died. He was in the fifty-fifth year of his life and the twenty-fifth of his active reign in England. The funeral was a dull, matter-of-fact affair that contrasted forlornly – oddly, indeed – with the jubilant rejoicing at his Restoration.

'A secularist,' wrote Gilbert Burnet, 'he shook off Presbyterianism as a viper, utilised Episcopacy as the readiest political tool, and finally put on Popery as a comfortable shroud to die in.'

10

DISMAL JIMMIE

James, Duke of York

Charles II fathered fourteen bastards; at least, in the course of his life, he acknowledged fourteen. Yet he was the first Stuart monarch to die without an heir of his body. The throne passed, amid much disquiet, to his brother James, Duke of York and Albany.

James VII was our last Roman Catholic monarch. He reigned for three years before fleeing to France, as his subjects revolted from fear of Catholic despotism, and his Protestant nephew landed on the English coast with 10,000 men, whom – rather unconvincingly – William of Orange insisted were his bodyguard. James fought for a year or two to regain his crowns, without success. He died in 1701 and his son, and grandsons, never recovered the Stuart inheritance.

James was a dull fellow, quite humourless, distinctly hard to like. He was quite unable to relate to the people he ruled and never understood them. They, in turn, never understood him. It is unjust to view him as a popish tyrant, set on establishing the Church of Rome as the sole and permitted faith of these islands, to be enforced at the point of the sword and the flame of the faggots. In an intolerant age James seems to have had a genuine vision of toleration. But he could not understand – and was quite unable to address – the very real fears of the land. He had all the weaknesses of his brother and few of his strengths. Like Charles, James could from carelessness walk into implacable political barriers. Unlike Charles, he refused ever to retreat. Like Charles, he appointed wicked men to government. Unlike Charles, he trusted them.

To the Scots, who knew him well as Duke of York, he

was 'Dismal Jimmie'. To the French, in exile, James was a crashing bore: pompous, tiresome, incapable of listening, quite incapable of realising how tedious and insufferable he was.

James was born at St James's Palace in London on 14 October 1633, the third child and second surviving son of Charles I and his queen. He was named after his grandfather, and quickly awarded the premier dukedoms of Scotland and England, Albany and York. (There have been many Dukes of York, and the title has by tradition been conferred on the second-born to the heir-apparent but all, oddly, have inherited the throne, or died before they could inherit, without issue; we seem to have established a house of Gloucester, but never a house of York; the present Duke of York has no male heir.) At four, as we have seen, the child became Lord High Admiral. Within the fantastic world of court, where Charles I enacted his masques and pageantry of true monarchy while the realms of which he was real monarch were going to pot, James played his demure and elegant part. With his siblings he was painted, big-eyed and silk-clad, by Van Dyck. We know they played a lot of hide and seek. We do not know much of the education of the children of Charles I. It seems to have been amateurish and bad. They gained the necessary accomplishments for royalty: James could dance very well, and was an excellent guitar player. He spoke fluent French, but this he probably acquired during his exile, before the Restoration of 1660. He had some Italian and could read Spanish. Later he developed an interest in navigation and astronomy. He was a founder member of the Royal Society. We know of only one contribution James made to its corpus of knowledge: he vouchsafed that the herb, star of the earth, was just the thing to cure the bite of a mad dog.

Religion dominated James's life and reign, though it is hard to judge how much his implacable Catholicism was heart-faith and how much impersonal, theological hobby. 'The last Stuart Kings were not Catholics in a meaningful sense,' writes Paul Johnson, himself of the Roman persuasion. 'It is hard to accept they even believed in God (though James was a Mariolater).' He was baptised by William Laud and schooled in holy things by assorted High Churchmen; as a newborn, his mother had insisted on a Roman Catholic wet-nurse, which caused some excitement; it was then believed, even by educated folk, that opinion and doctrine could be literally imbibed with a mother's milk. It was after the Restoration before James grew seriously interested in religion, and began obsessively to immerse himself in books of devotion and Church history and Roman Catholic theology. He was really a self-taught man, since the excitement and pressure of the Civil War were not conducive to a calm classroom environment. His father was aware of the problem. In 1647 Charles I – with much to think upon at other levels – sent sharp word to his second son that the king wanted him 'to ply his book more and his gun less'.

Like his brother Charles, James brimmed with physical energy, and burned much of it off on great, very fast walks. Unlike Charles he had a passion for guns, war, combat, soldiering. Even in 1647 his martial streak was evident to his father. As an adult the happiest days James spent were in the thick of battle. He seems to have enjoyed the brutal discipline, the arduous marches and rides and voyages, the clouds of gunsmoke and the smell of blood. He was certainly immensely brave: entirely free of the cowardice of his grandfather, and so courageous in war that he had more than once to be ordered to quit situations where he plainly endangered his life.

James was very fond of his father; he looked up to him, absorbed his words and philosophy, admired his devotion, and detested his enemies. There is no doubt that his father's fate scarred James very deeply and badly addled what was never going to be an acute political judgement. By contrast he seems to have been less fond of his mother, who is often blamed for his latter Catholicism. He and Charles had enough sense to detect her serious role in their father's downfall; they knew how badly the king had been affected by her ceaseless and ignorant advice. No doubt they held this against her. They also resented her petty power games in exile and her determined efforts to control their affairs and direct their lives.

James was eight years old when the Strafford crisis reached its height and the London mob howled for blood around Whitehall. He remembered this drama vividly and maintained that his father's capitulation to parliament and people, in signing the death-warrant, was a fatal error. When the Civil War broke in earnest, in 1642, the younger royal children, including James, were moved from Whitehall to St James's Palace, which was felt rather safer for them; the Prince of Wales went with his father, and the queen went to France. Later that spring James joined Charles and the king, and had a nasty experience when he was briefly held hostage by the governor of Hull. The princes had view of the action at Edgehill, and were nearly captured by the enemy at dusk, when they mistook a party of parliamentary horse for the king's. Then, for the next three years, James was settled in Oxford, the Royalist headquarters. In this citadel of Stuart absolutism and High Anglicanism the young Duke of York practised arms enthusiastically and studied his books dutifully. Most of the time he was the senior of the family present, with the king and Charles absent, and the lad had to do his best to uphold morale in a decidedly divided, place-seeking, faction-ridden court which was also, monthly, more and more short of money.

By the end of 1645 only the most fanatical Royalists believed in their hearts that victory was coming. The king's game was up. The Prince of Wales slipped to the Scilly Isles in March, and in short time escaped to France. In April Charles I surrendered to the Scots. By the end of June Oxford had surrendered to a parliamentarian army and James was a prisoner. He was taken to London in late July to join the younger royal children – they had never left the city – and he; Prince Henry, Duke of Gloucester; the Princess Elizabeth and the Princess Henrietta were entrusted to the care of the Earl of Northumberland, who reported regularly to parliament on their comfort and security. All James's servants were dismissed, which upset him very much.

The Northumberlands were kindly custodians. The royal hostages were treated politely and with respect, and parliament voted a generous allowance for their maintenance: James himself was granted £7,580 a year. But prisoners they were, closely watched and guarded. James was in an especially critical position. The Prince of Wales was abroad; his father was with the Scots. He was the most senior Stuart in parliamentary hands and in the late summer of 1646 there was serious talk of raising him as king in place of a deposed Charles I. He had letters from his father, ordering him to escape; these were discovered, and James was in bad trouble. Two servants were sacked by his guardians. The boy fell ill and spent February and March 1647 shivering with the ague. By the time James was well again the Scots had given up on Charles I and handed him over to the English. In the meantime the English themselves divided, with parliament and the New Model Army vying for control of affairs. The army kidnapped the king to force parliament's hand. The royal children were moved back to St James from the Northumberland residence. That summer they were allowed to meet their father. They were painful encounters. King Charles feared the worst and spoke in terms of dark pessimism. He gave detailed instructions to James about how, in the event he himself should be slain, he was to escape. Charles banged on, in his tedious fashion, about the Church of England; he exhorted them all to obey their eldest brother; he forced James and Henry to swear they would never take the crown while the Prince of Wales lived.

When James heard of his father's escape to Wight, and how he had then been fast locked up in Carisbrooke Castle, he was devastated. He ranted and wept – 'How durst any rogues to use his father like that?' – and menaced a servant who threatened to report his outburst. Then he wrote to his father, in code. The letter was intercepted, and James was in trouble again. He refused to divulge the cipher until he was threatened with confinement in the Tower. He gave in, then, and provided the code, and begged to be allowed to stay with Northumberland, which he was. But the Duke of York was now more close-confined than ever.

It is all the more remarkable, then, that James eventually escaped. By April 1648 there was more talk of an army coup and increasing rumour that James might be forcibly enthroned. So James, with the aid of a friendly guard, one Colonel Bampfield, a Presbyterian who was in touch with the king, practised the final getaway by lots of games of hide-and-seek with his siblings – an easy sport in a vast Jacobean palace; he became so good at it that it took the younger children half an hour to find him. On the night of 21 April – after a false start, when he blundered into a door and made such a mighty noise he scurried back to his chamber in alarm – he escaped through his sisters' bedroom and down a back staircase, absconding through the grounds. He met up with Bampfield and, after James disguised himself in women's clothing, they slipped down the Thames by barge. (James was hopeless in drag; he behaved so clumsily that the bargemaster grew suspicious and had to be taken into their confidence.) At Gravesend they met a Dutch ship, lying in wait, and on the morning of 23 April James disembarked at Flushing. His brother-in-law, Stadtholder William, met him at Maeslandsluys the next day, and at The Hague James had a tearful reunion with his closest sister, Mary, 'the affectionateness of which meeting I cannot express'. 'It was a daring escapade,' writes John Miller, 'in which

James had shown considerable resourcefulness and courage for a boy of fourteen.'

James spent much of his life in the uncomfortable position
of the younger brother, heir-presumptive but not heir-
apparent, with much obligation and no certainty of
apotheosis. Like Charles he too endured poverty, and much
contumely from the great courts of Europe, and the petty
ploys and pressure of Henrietta Maria, and the endless
striving and bickering of the exiled Stuart court. At first
there seemed every reason to hope for rapid restoration of
fortune. There were riots in London, risings in Kent, building war between England and Scotland. It came to nothing.
The disorder was quelled, the Scots defeated. The army
purged parliament and the 'Rump Parliament' arraigned the
king and their 'High Court of Justice' convicted him and, on
a day in January 1649, they cut off his head. It appalled
Europe; but emotion would not restore the Stuart throne.
Nor was it a good time for family friends in high places.
Stadtholder William died suddenly, in 1650, and the power
of the house of Orange seemed to die with him. The
Dowager Princess Mary could give her brothers money;
she could even entertain them on occasion – if they visited
the United Provinces incognito – but the Dutch would offer
them no help whatsoever.

In France, Louis XIV was a child of twelve and the French
court as full of intrigue and faction as the exiled party
around the Stuarts. Worse: France was at war with Spain.
While that war raged the French policy, under Cardinal
Mazarin, was one of entrenching the regime at home and
avoiding complication abroad; especially, confrontation
with England. By 1657 Mazarin had wrought an alliance
with England. Nor could Spain offer the Stuarts much help.
That great land's best days were behind it. Its economy was
in decline and its might on land and sea steadily diminishing.
It was all the Spanish could do to maintain control of the
Southern Netherlands. The Spanish were friendly to Charles

and James, especially as Cromwell grew the friendlier with France; eventually, Charles and James could make military careers in the Spanish service. But Spanish arms were not pledged to their restoration.

None the less the Stuarts and those about them tried. The rulers of Europe were courted. Most sent them away with mocking laughter; or developed pressing business elsewhere when the Cromwellian navy sailed over the horizon. There was talk, from England, of a rising here, a rebellion there, a conspiracy somewhere else; these came to nothing. At the fringes of the Stuart faction men made mad plots to involve the Pope, or some weird London sect, or a political faction like the radical Levellers. Such plans were little more than fantasy; when exposed, they reduced Stuart credibility still further.

James eased slowly away, over the years, from the struggle to win back England for the family to the more pressing concern of making ends meet. As Lord High Admiral he was entitled to a tenth of 'prizes', the profits made on English shipping captured by Royalist privateers. Much of the money never reached James and the value of the prizes always seemed to be in dispute. Cardinal Mazarin granted him a small pension, but this was paid through the servants of Henrietta Maria, and here expenses were deducted first. Things eased for a time, until James moved to Flanders in the Spanish service in 1656. Then, like his brother, he became desperately strapped for cash. Nevertheless he coped. Everyone likes to entertain a prince, and James had a full social life, with much banqueting and partying. Tradesmen granted credit readily enough. There was jewellery to pawn or sell. There was soldiering, which James much enjoyed.

He was judged a better-looking man than Charles. James was of fair colouring, and he had rich chestnut hair, which he grew to his shoulders, and kept much of its colour till late in life. He had a strong chin – cartoonists of the day tend to exaggerate it – and the thick pendulous mouth of one much tempted in his carnal appetites. His eyes were brown, and his nose large, rather hooked. His features were not at all so different from those of his brother; no doubt it was the more English colouring that lent him relative appeal. What is striking in the portraits of James, as Duke of York and later as king, is the expression. Charles always seems self-possessed, confident, well aware of the world around him and happy with his place in it. That healthy self-esteem is absent in the iconography of James VII. There is always a look of mulish suspicion; there is, too, a hint of disdain; not the hauteur of pride, but the vanity that is born of vacuity.

The biggest difficulty was the constant faction-fighting and especially the determined efforts made to set him against Charles or Charles against him. Charles could pull rank, of course, and on occasion did; and James more than once was bitterly disappointed by his brother's expedient wish. In general his household and advisers were a sillier, rougher bunch of men than those who surrounded the king. He was probably a little closer to the pro-Catholic, anti-Anglican party around Henrietta Maria; they included men of such cynicism they were prepared to make great concessions to English Presbyterians, the better to advance the Roman interest and a Stuart restoration. It was not the last time that James would flirt with Presbyterians to promote popery; it was not, unfortunately, the last time he would show his poor judgement of character. Yet he found the queen most trying. Henrietta Maria skimmed his income, subjected him to many a petty slight, meddled constantly in his business, and in strong terms compared James disfavourably to Charles and even more to Lord Jermyn, who was the leader in her circle, and probably her lover.

From those years of exile – most dull and tortuous to describe in detail – James took home two legacies, both of which were bad. One was his essential political philosophy, cobbled together from the worst rhetoric of the exiled

Royalists and his own violent emotional response to his father's execution. Simply, James could not learn from his father's mistakes, nor accept in any way that Charles I had contributed to his downfall and death. He formed the view that the mass of Englishmen were rabid republicans; he could not grasp that his father had not been beheaded because they hated kings and the institution of monarchy, but rather because they had found Charles I impossible; he had been a very bad king. Critically, James adopted the Royalist paranoia, that parliament and the political nation had been out to kill the king and abolish the monarchy from the start.

It would give him lifelong difficulty in coping with any degree of criticism or opposition. To King James, anything short of instant and unquestioning obedience was rebellion, republicanism and rank insubordination. Bishop Burnet wrote wearily that he 'was for subjects' submitting in all things to the King's notions and thought that all who opposed him or his ministers in Parliament were rebels in their hearts'. James saw republicanism in everything and reacted with fear and loathing. He never understood that most of his subjects wanted monarchy and believed in monarchy; what they did not want was a monarch who threatened their religion.

Worse: James was terrified of concession. To concede anything – as his father had abandoned Strafford to the whim of the mob – was at length to concede everything, and in the end have your head cut off. So James would never, in any crisis, take steps of conciliation; never back down in the face of the most disagreeable political reality; never placate the concerns and anxieties of the many and so detach them from the fanatical and irreconcilable few. This was all heightened, of course, by James's general lack of ability. There is no doubt he was a dim, stupid man, much less clever than Charles II, and indeed one of the dullest in the dynasty, lacking the quality of empathy, lacking imagination, lacking wit (he could not understand, and never himself told, jokes), and quite unable to see the world in terms other than starkest black and white. In affairs he was good at minutiae, poring for hours over accounts, or the finer details of troop dispositions. James had not the capacity, though, for grasping an issue in the round. He could but dimly form tactics and had no mind at all for strategy.

He 'knew the English people,' insisted the Duke of York, 'and they could not be held to their duty by fair treatment'. He himself later, as king, defined that duty: they were 'to follow his wishes blindly, and to own an attachment to his interests that was without any qualification or reserve whatsoever'. But who would take that from any prince? And who from such a prince as this?

Like all stupid men, James was narrow: his interests and pursuits were limited, his reading was confined almost entirely to Latin pieties, and he had nothing of the scientific curiosity, or aesthetic spirit, of his elder brother. His devotion to Charles – from which he never wavered, and whom he loved very deeply – is his most attractive quality. Insofar as he had other horizons beyond lust, battle and Romanism, it was in following his brother. When Charles died something of James died with him, and the blinkered, blundering body that remained was thrust into a capacity beyond his abilities, in times beyond his comprehension. Like most stupid men, he was stubborn: thrawn beyond reason, and thrawn far beyond the patience of men or the fluidity of his times. In his last years, like his father before him, he lapsed into the final refuge of the religious bigot: profound, sanctimonious fatalism.

Stupidity does not make a man useless. James, like many a Colonel Blimp, loved order. He liked things tidy, timetabled, listed. Throughout his career he showed himself a competent administrator. He had a keen eye for a balance sheet, and kept every penny to account, and disapproved of extravagance and waste, and was good at eliminating it. This was one virtue Charles II conspicuously lacked and which did him much damage as king. Nor could James be called lazy. Charles has long suffered a reputation for indolence, though we need not be persuaded by Pepys's tale that, at the moment the Dutch were firing English ships on the Medway, King Charles was chasing a moth round a mistress's chamber. (No one else tells the story and it is probably apocryphal.) James, in contrast, disapproved noisily of 'private ease'. He exulted in the sillier aspects of military life: elaborate drills, inspection of troops, field punishments, hours of bullshine. He led men well in battle. The Duke of Wellington admired the military writings of King James.

He had, too, a strange integrity. Charles II was an expert and accomplished liar. James had a kind of heroic, almost petulant honesty. When his religion became a matter of controversy, and determined efforts were under way to remove him from the succession, James refused to show his face at Anglican worship in the Chapel Royal, though the concession was much in his interests. He refused, unlike Charles II, to accept any subsidy from France. When he was trapped by events into marriage, with a woman's reputation at stake, he insisted on the match – against much opposition, from both families – and won her full recognition as Duchess of York.

So why was James so disliked? Agnes Mure MacKenzie captures it best, observing that:

> as with so many converts, his fervour had in it something of priggishness: he shows the touch of the arbitrary peasant that is in both his father and his grandfather, and like his father lacked humour to leaven it. Though he cared more for the welfare of his kingdoms than his brother had done, he held what was by now the old-fashioned conception of a patriarchal or paternal kingship: and the paternity, with real devotion, had what our age would call a Victorian colour, that prevented its good intentions from being endearing.

A perk of that sort of royal existence, of course, was sex. James was as libidinous as his brother, if less discriminating. He was married twice, with issue of both marriages – we will come to his first match shortly – and besides begot a good litter of natural children, some of whom he acknowledged; the Duke of Berwick, his best-known bastard, had a distinguished military career on the Continent, and lived to play his part in Jacobite intrigue. Even after his embrace of Romanism became public knowledge, James continued to keep mistresses, of such striking ugliness and lack of evident charm that Bishop Burnet wickedly wondered if the duke's priests had prescribed them as a penance. Unlike his brother, though, James's sexuality was laden with morbid guilt. He took to the more masochistic rites of Romanism with something bordering on glee. It was the second Duke of Buckingham, perhaps, who most neatly caught the gulf of intellect, the chasm of guile that lay between the royal brothers. 'The King,' he sighed, 'could see things if he would, and the Duke would see things if he could.'

Such was the emerging character of the man who marched and muddled through the long years abroad, to 1660 and the Restoration; and by the time James saw England again he was in big trouble. Woman trouble.

Anne Hyde was the dark and mildly voluptuous daughter of Edward Hyde, whom Charles elevated to Earl of Clarendon, and who had a long and complicated career in Stuart service. This Clarendon, as we have seen, emerged on the stage of politics as an ardent parliamentarian; but, when the Civil War broke, he cast in his lot with Charles I, and duly joined the surviving court in exile. Faithful service brought him high office under Charles II. When Clarendon's policies failed, and the king abandoned him, he was forced abroad, and devoted his last years to writing his important history of the Civil War. It might be thought, then, that in 1660 Clarendon would have been delighted to see his daughter wed to the king's brother. In fact he was mortified, and did all he could to stop it.

Anne Hyde was in 1655 taken into the service of Princess Mary, James's sister, in the United Provinces. (This much annoyed Henrietta Maria, who hated all the Hyde family.) Early the next year James met Anne for the first time, when Princess Mary visited Paris. It was not long before he began to visit his sister much more regularly; not long before he and Anne were in love. In 1659, when James fell very ill, he signed a document pledging to marry her. Then he got better and destroyed it. By now, though, the relationship was sexual; and, in the spring of 1660, Anne Hyde found she was pregnant. Charles at first denied permission for a marriage, and it was on that fraught basis they all returned to England in May. James, who seems genuinely alarmed for Anne's honour, begged and pestered his brother, and at last wrung the king's reluctant blessing, by which time Anne was well gone with child. Edward Hyde was violently against the marriage. He told the king to send Anne to the Tower; even, in one desperate moment, that he should cut off her head.

On 3 September, nevertheless, she and James were married, in secret, by one of the Duke of York's chaplains. Still the cover-up continued, and renewed attempts to destroy or annul the match. Hyde was fearful for his own reputation. He knew his enemies – and there were many of them – would put about that he had contrived the whole thing; that he presumed to unite himself by blood to the royal family. It was then unheard of for royalty to marry anyone other than royalty; it would be 1923, in fact, before a commoner – if Lady Elizabeth Bowes-Lyon can be so dismissed – again married a prince of the blood. Poor Anne was surrounded by intrigue and James was pounded by pressure and more pressure. For a time he seriously thought of abandoning her. Some argued that the disparity of their status invalidated the marriage. Others questioned Anne's virtue; some even invented claims that they, too, had enjoyed her sexual favours. This sort of talk, of course, swung Edward Hyde round to defending the marriage valiantly. James threatened him angrily that if he kept now insisting the match was valid, he would see to it that Hyde would be driven out of England.

It was Charles, in the end, who put his foot down and preserved this ill-starred union, ignoring the arguments and bluster of Princess Mary and assorted ministers. Charles owed Hyde, and knew it; besides, James had made his bed, and ought to lie in it. Gossips said afterwards the king had insisted on the match because it would make James look stupid in the eyes of their mother; Charles always believed James was Henrietta Maria's favourite. Still the drama continued. On 22 October 1660 Anne was delivered of a son, gasping throughout her pains that she was married to the Duke of York and that he was her child's father. James now accepted the marriage, but more letters streamed in, and more voices were raised in question of Anne's character, and then – no show without Punch – on 2 November the queen descended on London from France, fully armed to break the marriage and, more important to her, break the power of that disagreeable fellow Edward Hyde. Then she and her people might have charge of the affairs of Charles II which, no doubt, she would dominate as calamitously as she dominated those of Charles I.

So James dithered again. Pressed by his mother, of whom he lived in evident terror, he decided to deny again he was married. In the meantime Charles and Henrietta Maria fought. Further tales were invented of Anne's debauchery; yet more insistence that she was a whore and that heaven alone knew whose pup she had just whelped. Again Charles kept his cool. He felt sorry for Anne. He was also determined to face down his mother and set that precedent for the rest of her life and his reign. The king coolly declared that, unless valid legal reasons were found otherwise, the marriage must stand. Only an Act of Parliament could annul it and he would not allow parliament to legislate in any matter bearing on the succession. In vain Henrietta Maria stormed and wept. She threatened to return to France. Charles made pleasantly plain he would not try too hard to detain her.

When one of James's circle, Charles Berkeley, beheld the duke's distress – he was now quite broken, and weeping over the soiled reputation of his beloved – Berkeley's heart melted, and he withdrew an allegation of intimacy between himself and Anne; he had invented it, he explained, because he had thought it best in James's service. So James cheered up and dismissed all the other tales and sent word to Anne to look after the child. He began to visit her; subtly, the climate around her changed. Meantime Henrietta Maria was getting nowhere with Charles. He refused to discuss affairs of state with her; when she probed and pried, the king whistled a tune, or turned his back on her. He wanted her back in France. She refused, tough old thing, to leave until she had a decent pension.

On 20 December the Duke of York publicly acknowledged Anne Hyde as his lawful wife. On New Year's Day 1661, with the matter now causing serious strain on Anglo-French relations, Henrietta Maria was forced to give her blessing. She received Hyde and Anne; even kissed her new daughter-in-law. Then a bitter and fuming Henrietta Maria returned across the Channel.

So James settled into England and the new mysteries of married life. Assorted courtiers crawled to make their peace with the Duchess of York. She was not an outstanding beauty and, by the standards of our day, distinctly voluptuous; later, eating for comfort, Anne grew very fat indeed. But in these early days of marriage she was of good figure and pleasing shape. She was English; she was Protestant; most of all, she was clever, far keener of mind than her husband, and generally a good influence. She was determined of will. She also had a certain gutsiness: she impressed one gentleman by picking up and dandling his pet and very lively snake. In the early days the Yorks marriage was strong. When James went to sea, in 1664, Anne closeted herself away to pray for him. The duchess, too, was fecund, bearing in all seven children in their eleven years of marriage. Their first son, Charles, died in 1661; his parents exhibited little grief. His legitimacy, after all, was distinctly clouded. Nor was the nation much stirred. The king himself had yet to marry and was confidently expected to sire a litter of princes. Three more sons died in infancy, and another daughter also failed to reach her fourth birthday. In the end only the Princess Mary, born in 1662, and the Princess Anne, born in 1665, lived to grow up and play their fateful part in James's career.

Such child mortality was unremarkable for the time, though his enemies spread a nasty rumour that the duke had syphilis, and infected both his wives and their ensuing issue, so that few of his loins lived beyond early childhood. There is no reason to believe this. Royal children had the much greater hazard of royal doctors, too quick to prescribe bizarre and often toxic medicines for trivial ailments; and it was an age when serious infections were rife and medicine for the most part ineffectual. Nevertheless, the marriage of James and Anne deteriorated. He lapsed back into his old ways. He had an unattractive habit of staring hungrily at women, especially new ones in his company, so that James was remembered as the 'most unguarded ogler of his time'. Servants provided obliging tarts for his bed at night. There were mistresses – chosen more for their wit than their faces – and there were quite serious affairs. So Anne turned wearily to sweets and cakes, and turned her energies to administering James's money and directing his political career. She inclined him, naturally, to her father's party; James did not like the Earl of Clarendon, whom he found pompous and apt to be bossy; but in this he obeyed Anne. By 1668 someone could tell Pepys that 'The Duke of York, in all things but his codpiece, is led by the nose by his wife.'

Clarendon fell in 1668; his removal ushered in the most

bewildering period of the reign of Charles II and the first determined attacks on his brother. James, of course, had been associated with Clarendon by marriage. It was widely expected he would try and avenge himself. Men noted he had kept himself well distant from the concerted effort to remove the earl from affairs. Besides, having the charge of the Royal Navy, with much money and many lucrative positions, James could readily be accused of harbouring assorted 'Clarendonians'. As Lord High Admiral James held a high place, and much political influence, men were quick to covet. There was also rising concern about the succession. In June 1669 Queen Catherine miscarried. It was her third failed pregnancy and it was now thought unlikely she would ever give Charles II an heir.

So James found himself under great pressure. Men sought to create bad blood between him and the king. Others tried to make Charles II divorce and marry again and more fruitfully. Still others tried to oust James as Lord High Admiral. They did not succeed in any of these endeavours. Tense as their relations were at times, there was an abiding affection between king and duke. Charles refused, in 1669 and ever, to rid himself of the queen, of whom he was sincerely fond. (Catherine outlived almost all others in these dramas; she attained a good age and died in 1707.) As for the Royal Navy, James worked arduously to rid the service of every variety of mismanagement, disorder and corruption. His foes could find no grounds to demand his removal. They were mostly at court, anyway, and not in parliament, and divided among themselves; James had powerful allies, too, in Queen Catherine and Lady Castlemaine. Yet, amid this difficult time, which by the summer of 1670 had markedly eased, James had achieved something else: he had converted to Roman Catholicism.

Paul Johnson argues that the ideology of the divine right of kings – and the Continental policy which Charles pursued with special vigour after 1668 and which James tried clumsily to continue – inevitably drove the last Stuarts to Catholicism. They might not have believed in God, but 'they needed Catholicism as the only dependable political under-pinning of a regal State. Sooner or later they were bound to seek to restore it, to bind England to a Continental system so closely that a revolt against the throne would evoke a response from the entire European community.' It is hard, though, to believe this was a conscious motivation for James, who probably lacked the sophistication to grasp it. More critical factors were his upbringing, and especially the ex-ample of his father.

He had been raised in High Anglicanism, taught to value elaborate, ordered worship with the emphasis on the Euchar-ist. His early tutors had encouraged him to believe in some sense in the 'Real Presence'; that the elements of communion, bread and wine, were mystically changed. James could see little difference between this and the Roman Catholic doctrine of the mass. Besides, these tutors had not exhorted him against popery. They owned the Church of Rome as a true Church, in the Apostolic Succession, even if faulty and in some ways corrupt. They reserved their venom for Protestant dissenters and especially for Presbyterians. These, the sons of Charles I were taught, were no true Church, but a rabble, without divine authority, and without respect for persons and especially for kings.

James absorbed this and, advancing in years, concluded that if by mere separation from the Church of England the dissenting Protestants must be consigned to outer darkness – unless converted by force – then, taking that logic to its end, the Church of England itself was wrongly estranged from Rome. His slow black-and-white mind, which so prized authority and order, brought him to embrace the claims of the Catholic Church, which 'could not be denied without overturning the very foundations of Christianity. And once I was satisfied on that point (which is the principal point to consider) all the rest fell into place,' as he put it himself in his worthy and very boring autobio-graphy. His historical readings, too, persuaded him that in

Protestantism lay the roots of dissent, disorder, every kind of rebellion, and especially the sort of men who went about cutting kings' heads off.

So James became a Roman Catholic. At first he wanted to have his popish cake and eat it. Early in 1669 he approached a Jesuit, Father Simons, and told him of his desire to be reconciled; but could His Holiness grant a dispensation that would still allow James to attend Anglican service? Simons said he doubted it very much; the Pope confirmed this when James wrote to Rome. Charles, too, was ready to embrace the Roman faith, but not publicly. James wanted the odium of conversion shared. At least Anne was with him, and she ceased to take Anglican communion later that year. It was early in 1672 before the Duke of York was received into the Roman Catholic Church and he still went to Anglican service until 1676, by which time his Catholicism was the worst-kept secret in England.

He had turned his wife. He could not turn his daughters; Charles – who intended to hide his own Romanist convictions as long as he could – forbade James to put pressure on the princesses, and insisted both Mary and Anne had Protestant tutors. James, too, soon had sexual conflict; it was whispered that 'his devotion has withdrawn him entirely from the pleasures of women.' His lust was too strong to be restrained for long, but it went underground; he put away mistresses, and his assignations grew more secret and seedier. When Bishop Burnet tackled the duke – how did he reconcile Catholic zeal with Anglican conformity, not to mention carnal lasciviousness? – James argued, in his usual worthy and foggy fashion, that 'a man might have a persuasion of his duty to God so as to restrain him from dissembling with God and man and professing him to be of another religion than that which he believed was true, though it did not yet restrain all his appetites.'

On 31 March 1671 Anne, Duchess of York, died. At thirty-three she was not an old woman, but her father's fall had affected her deeply – she had been so reduced in social standing that she had started to cultivate one or two of the king's influential mistresses – and her embrace of Catholicism further narrowed her social circle. She ate far too much, and grew immensely, obscenely fat. Repeated pregnancies had broken her health and she had a cancer of the breast. Her end was horrible. She collapsed the evening before, on return from dinner with the Burlingtons at Piccadilly, and sank rapidly and in the most excruciating pain, managing gamely to fight off the attentions of an Anglican cleric with tactful moans of 'truth, truth', and to tell James that 'death is very terrible.' For some reason, her great bloated remains began to putrefy with ghastly speed. Her body could not be put on public display, and the indignities inflicted on her 'stately carcase' attracted pity and revulsion. The funeral was a shabby affair. James, and Princess Mary, did not attend. Almost at once, of course, everyone began to ask whom the Duke of York would now marry.

By 1673 the atmosphere at court, and in parliament, was much altered. The foreign policies of Charles II aroused great suspicion, and it was now plain his queen was barren, and that he had no intention of putting her away. He was in alliance with a Roman Catholic king and at war with the Protestant Dutch. He had just issued a Declaration of Indulgence, which at his own prerogative granted new freedom to papists. And in James, Duke of York, he had what was now plainly a Roman Catholic heir; worse – for James had failed to keep the secret – the king stood very near to joining the papist communion himself.

Overseas, England faced two formidable men. One was Charles and James's own nephew, William of Orange, who was already proving fast to be his father's equal; when the French overran most of the Dutch Republic in 1672, William led the desperate military effort that hurled them back. And in France there was their ally, Louis XIV, but Louis was an absolute monarch, in a powerful country of very different character and social order, and in any event Louis had more brains and guile than Charles and James put together. Whatever: the Stuarts were in trouble. The war with the Dutch had run out of cash and the king needed to recall parliament. He would find that parliament hostile, even mutinous, and for the rest of his reign the politics of England were dominated by the same general fear, of 'popery and arbitrary government'. Typically, trying to dampen the building hysteria, Charles II begged the Duke of York to take Anglican communion at Christmas 1672. Typically, and proudly, James refused.

So parliament met, exercised abroad by one concern: that the French might conquer all the Netherlands, thus destroying at once English and Dutch trade; and, at home, that King Charles had a popish successor. This welded into a prevalent nightmare: that, come the day the popish king succeeded, he would have all the might and armies of Louis XIV at his back, to flatten utterly his enemies and convert all the British Isles to Roman Catholicism. the ordeal of the Huguenots under Bourbon monarchy, the Massacre of St Bartholomew's Eve, the atrocities listed in morbid detail in Foxe's *Book of Martyrs* – these were real and powerful memories in Protestant heads. A popish king meant popish execution. It meant the Inquisition and torture and slaughter and fires of martyrdom. This was something up with which Parliament would not put.

So Charles II could not carry his Indulgence; he had to sacrifice it as a price for continuing subsidies for the Dutch War. Yet he had to abandon his war in 1674 and, after much foot-dragging, by 1678 he was forced to join the Dutch in war against France. Abiding deference, and the general reverence with which the gentry beheld the principle of hereditary succession, muffled their fear of James for the time being. Paradoxically, James's vision of kingship was rather sharper than his brother's. He thought Charles's job was simple: to find out what his loyal old Cavaliers in parliament wanted; to do it; and to reward them with honours and gifts for loyalty. The king should rule firmly and consistently.

The trouble with James was that many of the same Cavaliers, like Danby, believed in the vigorous suppression of Romanism, so he could not throw his weight behind them; he could never understand how such men, loyal to his house and person, could so hate his religion. Charles, strapped for cash as usual and kept afloat only by the pocket money of Louis XIV, could not pursue any consistent policy on anything very much. His administration moved from one expediency and muddle to the next. So the monarchy as an institution lost ground. And James clung stubbornly to a vain hope: that, by reason and force of personality, given the chance, he could turn that huge Protestant opposition into ardent Catholicism. His opponents were but misled and prejudiced against the true faith. He could not accept, as Miller writes, 'anti-Catholicism for what it was: such a dominant feature of the English political scene that James's dreams of a Catholic England were doomed to failure from the start'.

Meanwhile parliament had brought in the Test Act. It was the chief weapon of a concerted policy to drive Roman Catholics from public office; anyone who held such office now had to swear the 'test': specifically, disowning the Roman Catholic doctrine of transubstantiation. James tried to preserve members of his household, and assorted Catholic officers in the army, from the test, but failed. More urgent was his own position. He could not in conscience take the test. So there was nothing but for James, Duke of York, heir-presumptive, to do but to resign all his offices, including the one he had held with much distinction: Lord High Admiral. Thus he sacrificed much influence and income, and made his Catholicism plain to the world. Once again it was open season on the Duke of York. It was only the Catholicism of his brother, Charles was assured, that led to all these troubles. There was renewed argument for a divorce (attended by dark hopes: early in 1673, the queen was very ill.) And James's new marriage, to a

Catholic princess, gave yet more ammunition to his opponents; it was widely believed the latest Duchess of York was the Pope's daughter.

Mary of Modena was only fifteen and James acquired her after some months of farcical matchmaking diplomacy. He had only two requirements for his new bride: that she be Catholic, and beautiful. Charles was in charge of the operation, determined to marry his brother to a foreign princess and that the maximum diplomatic advantage be extracted from it. There was no suitable French princess on the market. There was a very attractive Austrian one, the Archduchess of Innsbruck, of the smaller, Austrian branch of the Habsburgs. Things were going well when the empress conveniently died, and the emperor rather hastily let it be known he wanted to marry the archduchess himself. For some months James's harried envoy, the Earl of Peterborough, scurried all over Europe 'like a demented chessman', as the Duke of York happily bombarded him with word of this princess and that princess. In the end they enlisted the help of Louis XIV, whose courtiers networked on James's behalf. In July 1673 Louis suggested two princesses of Modena, a rather irrelevant principality of Italy. There was the thirty-year-old sister of the duchess, and her fifteen-year-old daughter. James could pick either of them; the dowry on offer was £90,000.

His other options fast diminishing, James chose Mary Beatrice. They were wed by proxy in September and married for real in November, when Mary reached England. The marriage was decidedly irregular in Catholic terms, because James rushed into it without securing the Pope's goodwill on two points: that he himself was a true Catholic; and that his new duchess would be allowed to practise her faith in England. Technically, as he still on occasion went to Anglican service, James was a Protestant and Mary's marriage therefore required a dispensation. He pooh-poohed all these complaints and treated the senior clergy, and indeed the Pope himself, with some rudeness. His personal relations with the Holy See never really recovered and it was 1676 before Rome legally acknowledged the marriage. It was typical of James that, having embraced a religion calculated to offend most of his subjects, he could then offend a good many of its senior clergy, whose support he might one day need very badly.

Mary Beatrice had a tough time. Parliament savaged the union; the Commons drew up a loyal and dutiful address to the king, demanding that the marriage of the Duke of York be not consummated. When they met they expressed new and hysterical fears of popery, and about the Duke of York being granted any place or position at all in the armed services, and declared they would grant no more money till their fears of Romish tricks were allayed. The king had to prorogue parliament, so bad had matters become. His council were divided and irreconcilable. There was even talk of renewed civil war. Charles was paralysed by indecision and no one about him dared to speak their open mind. 'The King calls a cabinet council for the purpose of not listening to it,' said someone sarcastically, 'and the ministers hold forth in it so as not to be understood.' James demanded, with some reason, that his brother restore authority and throw his full support behind him. But nothing had been resolved when Mary Beatrice landed at Dover.

Few dared to accompany James when he travelled down to meet her. An effigy of the Pope was pleasantly burned at Suffolk. Crowds were sullen, sometimes hostile. At court, Mary Beatrice encountered difficulties of protocol. The queen showed her great kindness; Mary was allowed to sit down in her presence. But then Catherine's ladies-in-waiting threw a huff and walked out. The Duchess of York was not allowed a private chapel. It was, of course, politically impossible; but her mother was mightily offended, and soon left the country. Mary cried for days. She was very young; her husband was forty, worn and tall and very thin, and evidently most unpopular. She was also horrified by sex, and James was probably not the gentlest of lovers. The poor duchess wrote that she saw the state of marriage as her personal Cross.

It proved, in the end, to be a very happy marriage. Mary was exceedingly beautiful – lovely features, fine dark eyes and lustrous skin – and never lost her figure. Her sweet, childlike nature won general affection, once people troubled to acquaint themselves with her, and she applied herself to the study of English and learned to speak it fluently. Mary took nothing to do with politics. She lacked some of the usual courtly accompaniments, having been raised by nuns in a convent; her walk, for instance, was deemed most inelegant. But she applied herself to acquire regal deportment too. She was only four years older than Mary, James's elder daughter, and they soon became good friends. There is a happy account of the Yorks tobogganing in winter, throwing snowballs at one another. In the early years of marriage she was almost constantly pregnant, bearing five children, but they all died in infancy. She also had several miscarriages. It was too much to expect James to stay faithful; but he now regarded adultery with guilt, and kept his dalliance discreet. He was good to her, always, and Mary proved a loyal and loving support to him.

In 1677 there was a family wedding, with great bearing on the succession: Princess Mary of York was united in nuptial bliss with her cousin, William of Orange. The union was against the background of tortured international affairs, and signalled the end of the Stuart honeymoon with France. By sanctioning the match, Charles II was moving to war against the French, and everyone knew it. There had been talk of this betrothal since 1674. James at first opposed it; he had optimistic notions of marrying his daughter to the Dauphin. Nor did William himself – a devout, worthy, clever, distinctly priggish character – enthuse. He did not yet feel secure as a head of state. He was also wary of his uncles, who still patronised him, still hoped that under their guidance the

United Provinces might be reduced to an obedient English satellite. So, in 1674, William had said politely that Mary must be too young for marriage and, in any event, he knew nothing about her.

Now he needed to bolster his authority all the more over the Dutch, who increasingly resented the war with France and were not impressed by a recent succession of defeats in the field. William, too, hoped for worthwhile support from England. So Orange went a-courting. His close aide and servant, William Bentinck, served as intermediary, winning a sweet letter from James and permission from King Charles to visit England, as long as William did not come when parliament was sitting. So William made court, at Newmarket, in October, and paid much courteous, studied attention to the Duke of York before settling down for hard negotiation with the king. Charles wanted a peace deal first and marriage terms later. William insisted on the betrothal first and made nice noises about peace with the French afterwards. William won. So Charles granted the Princess Mary in marriage, quite forgetting first to secure the permission of James.

'The King's will be done,' said the Duke of York stoically, when word was brought to him. That was nothing to the reaction of Mary, still only fifteen. When she was told she cried for a day and a half. Cousin William was twelve years her senior, small – he stood four inches shorter than the princess – and a martyr to asthma; he coughed constantly, and he had the hunched build of the chronic asthmatic, and a painful croaking voice. Nor was William otherwise pleasing. He had a hooked nose and a pinched pale face. He was a man of few words and was passionate only in warfare and theology. He had forgotten most of his English. William's general mien was lugubrious: the sort of fellow of whom virtue is its own punishment. Mary herself was big, buxom and pretty; her education had been limited, and her time spent mostly in innocent pleasures like music, embroidery and backgammon. She was not close to her father – they had lived apart for some years – and was already embarrassed by, and hostile to, his Catholicism.

But Mary did as she was bid. The wedding was a hasty affair, on 4 November. The Princess Anne could not be present. She had smallpox. The Duchess of York was not there either: she was big with child (and did, some days later, produce a boy, who did not long live). The king came and joked crudely when the couple were put to bed.

Abroad, the marriage was greeted with suspicion and cynicism; William's enemies saw it as further proof of monarchical ambition. In England, too, he was unpopular: a rumour spread that he was a secret papist, and in London the mob burned an effigy of the Pope, with a string of oranges around its neck. William, already fearful for his standing in the United Provinces, hastened across the Channel with his tearful bride, to a land where she knew no one and could not speak a word of their language. It has been said – and seems to be widely believed – that William was a homosexual or, more cleverly, a 'latent' homosexual, putting the charge in a form to accommodate lack of proof. Certainly he had been raised in an atmosphere that might well have formed a homosexual identity; he had no memory of his father, and had been surrounded by formidable women. And William enjoyed male company, playing cards and talking war; he cherished various close friends, particularly Bentinck, who was devoted to him. His marriage would prove childless; though Mary had at least one miscarriage. But there is no proof, no evidence at all, of homosexual activity. It is a Jacobite smear. William himself said, wounded and vexed: 'It seems to me a most extraordinary thing that one may not feel regard and affection for a young man without it being criminal.'

As with James and his second bride, what began as a match of convenience became one of love. Mary worked hard at the marriage, supping with William each night and diverting him from affairs of state by merry conversation. His reserve slowly thawed. She brightened his life and widened his interests; he impressed her with his practical kindness, his brains and his integrity. Mary became devoted to her prince, and when she died he was inconsolable. But by that time, of course, he was King of Scotland, England and Ireland.

11

A POPE, A POPE

James VII and II

In 1678 France made peace with the Dutch, convinced at last that England was about to intervene on William's side. The Duke of York was prominent in belligerent councils. He enjoyed battles and, no doubt, thought a 'good war' would greatly restore his popularity. He was also eager to raise a large standing army in England, and foolish enough to believe he was the natural man to command it. James, who saw incipient rebellion everywhere, was also of the mind that the king should naturally be supported by a mighty armed force, to keep the peace and deter any designs against the ruling order.

His enemies did not understand this, and jumped to the worst possible conclusion: that the Duke of York wanted command of a big army to secure his succession – perhaps even to hasten it – and, with its power, to put England under popery. To the political nation, standing armies were a pillar of despotism; only a tyrant would want one. Fearful of Catholicism, parliamentarians and others continued to oppose the creation of an army; continued to protest at the turns of foreign policy; continued to worry, aloud, about the succession. James could not grasp this Protestant fear at all. He detested such meddling in fields he deemed solely a matter of the royal prerogative – foreign affairs, warfare, religion – and deemed all the critics republicans, incipient traitors. They would have been highly offended.

The war in the Netherlands ended; such of an army as James had managed to raise was paid off, and late that summer Titus Oates and Israel Tonge unveiled the Popish Plot. By the spring of 1679 London was in hysterics and the Duke of York besieged on all sides.

Anti-Catholicism was, from 1670 onwards, the principal

dynamic in English politics. James never understood this – he probably lacked the capacity to understand it – and his blindness cost him the throne. The intensity of this Protestant feeling is not easy to fathom. An intellectual case was well advanced for toleration by this stage in British history. Besides, there were very few Roman Catholics in England. John Miller has calculated that in 1676 there were perhaps 66,000 of the Roman Catholic faith: about 1 per cent of the population. They were certainly, at the very most, less than 5 per cent. Nor, despite the anxieties of Reformed propaganda, were they aggressively active in politics. There is no evidence that Catholic priests played the same subversive role in the 1670s that they had pursued in the 1580s. There were not, in any event, very many of them. In 1669 a papal agent, Claudius Agrette, recorded 230 secular clergy and 255 regular clergy in the whole realm. The fantasy that thousands of fanatical black-hearted Jesuit intriguers toiled in England to achieve popish revolution is but fantasy.

Such conspiracy would have had no direction, nor practical support, from the Vatican. The curia, then as now, did not understand the English. Nor had they any great concern for England's Roman Catholic population. From 1655 there was not even a Catholic bishop in the country; the Pope could not be bothered to appoint one, and his foolish advisers had taken a dim view of the efforts of such Catholic leadership as there was in England to co-operate with Cromwell. The Reformed myth of the period is that the Pope was counselled, and England targeted, by devious popish agents of skill, guile and ruthlessness. The truth is that the Vatican, in English affairs, was ignorant, ill-informed, indecisive and generally incompetent. We know, for instance how James's marriage to Mary of Modena was hampered by the Pope's dithering; how curial ineptitude over assorted points of canon law nearly prevented the match from happening at all. Yet, to true Englishmen of the day, the marriage was self-evidently part of a foul papist plot; and when it had engineered its goal of a Catholic England good Protestant men would be

forced to fly destitute of bread and harbour, your wives
prostituted to the lust of every savage bog-trotter, your
daughters ravished by goatish monks, your smaller children
tossed upon pikes, or torn limb from limb, whilst you have
your own bowels ripped up . . . or else murdered with some
other exquisite tortures and holy candles made of your
grease (which was done within our memory in Ireland),
your dearest friends flaming in Smithfield, foreigners ren-
dering your poor babes that can escape everlasting slaves,
never more to see a Bible, nor hear again the joyful sounds
of Liberty and Property . . .

as Henry Care luridly put it, in a popular tract of the times. In
the reign of Elizabeth I his fears would have had much
validity. By the late 1670s they were already an anachronism.
The reference to Smithfield, though, where so many had died
under Mary Tudor, is reminder of the enduring potency of
Foxe; note, too, the sour racism of 'savage bog-trotter' and
'Ireland'. The spirit of anti-popery was essentially one of
English nationalism; the increasing dependence of Stuart
kings – and, later, Stuart pretenders – on the Celtic fringes
of the British Isles further alienated the dynasty from the great
mass of their subjects.

There was theology in it too. For over a century preachers,
doctors and ecclesiastics had drummed into an English audience that Catholicism was the most abhorrent of faiths, worse
than any heresy: a defiled, debased parody of the work and
teaching of Jesus Christ. A whole eschatology was shaped, the
Church of Rome being readily discerned in New Testament
prophecy. The Westminster divines, in 1647, had readily
agreed that the Pope was no head of the Church, but that
Antichrist, the 'Man of Sin and Son of Perdition'. The Roman
Catholic institution was the 'Whore of Babylon', on her seven
hills, red with the blood of the saints. Against her stood the
forces of light; the true Church of the Reformed and Protestant order; and principal among Protestant realms – and all
the more secure as an island nation – were the English. Secure
in this view of a struggle between Christ and Antichrist, they

held themselves to be an 'Elect Nation'. And they faced this monstrous popery, which, as a Commons petition declared in 1621: 'hath a restless spirit, and will strive by these gradations: if it once get but a connivancy, it will press for a toleration: if that should be obtained, they must have an equality: from thence they will aspire to superiority, and will never rest till they get a subversion of the true religion.'

What makes the view odd to us is that, in day-to-day English living, and too in Scotland, the Roman Catholic minority got along perfectly well with their neighbours. There was little tension between the religions, and the amity is seen most strikingly in the upper orders: there was still a tiny, but well-esteemed, Roman Catholic nobility. Protestant and Catholic earls dined together, hunted together, partied together; sometimes even developed ties of marriage. Odder still is the proven loyalty of the great mass of Catholics to monarchy and order, seen most strikingly at the time of the Armada in 1588. Only a crazed few had sought to overthrow Elizabeth for Mary, or to blow up James VI and his parliament. Hardly any Catholics, in 1660, involved themselves in politics at all; the Test Acts, of course, had removed the very few who had dared.

The times, though, were not tolerant, and ambitious and unscrupulous men like Titus Oates had a ready mob for their conspiracy rhetoric. Oates could point to the plots and schemes of the past, be it poor Babington's endeavours to free Mary or the 'gunpowder treason' of November 1605. Many Catholics, in conscience, had felt unable to swear the oath of allegiance in 1606; after all, apart from binding them to King James, parliament and the ruling order of things, it required them to own their own faith to be 'impious', a 'damnable doctrine', 'heretical'. But by such pious courage they could readily be held seditious. It was not easy to dismiss a faith as marginal and unthreatening when its few adherents yet included eminent houses such as the Norfolks and the Arundels. And then there was the oldest conspiracy-theory fib of all, the belief that there were thousands of invisible Catholics. They were cleverly disguised, and up to no good, but they were there by the legion, slyly conforming to the Church of England, only awaiting their hour to spring forth and declare their true faith. Even the Duke of York believed this; it would take his accession to prove him wrong.

To the modern, generally secular mind, this vigorous Protestantism may seem extreme; even shameful. There is no doubt that its fervour was excited by many wicked men; and that, then and in some parts of the British Isles even till today, law-abiding and decent Roman Catholics have been terrorised, sometimes murdered, at the hands of neighbours Protestant rather than Christian. But this was an age when, in Europe, the English heard many a tale of repression and cruelty. The regime of Louis XIV savagely persecuted the French Protestants; when, in October 1685, he revoked the Edict of Nantes – the only charter of such liberties as the Huguenots ever possessed – there was widespread pogrom in France, and hundreds of dispossessed Huguenots fled to England, with dire consequences for the Catholic policy of its new king. All could see the human consequences of Roman Catholic terror abroad.

Protestantism remained a force in British politics till very recently. It was only in 1829 that Roman Catholics were granted the vote, and only in the 1970s that legal barriers to them holding certain high offices of state were removed. Two living members of the present royal family have had to renounce their place in succession to the throne in order to marry Roman Catholic wives. As recently as 1994 a parliamentary by-election in Scotland was sullied by fierce sectarian debate; in the last months of the twentieth century, the possibility that the Labour Prime Minister might convert to the Catholic faith still arouses a *frisson* in the newspapers.

In 1854 the Vatican of Pius IX proclaimed the *Syllabus of Errors*; in this, and its accompanying encyclical, the Church denounced such errors as freedom of speech, freedom of the press, and liberty of conscience. The same Pope lived to declare his own *ex cathedra* infallibility in 1870 – at that time he had locked all the Jews in Rome into a squalid ghetto – and sought imprisonment for itinerant Protestant preachers in Tuscany. Subsequent Popes signed concordats with Hitler and Mussolini, and turned a deaf ear – and utter silence – to the plight of European Jews in the Holocaust. Protestants have been persecuted in Spain, Austria and Quebec, and continue to be persecuted in some realms of Latin America. Most recently the Church has been shaken by a succession of dreadful sexual and paedophiliac scandals, involving hundreds of clergy and thousands of women and children. There are still many, in our own day, who view Roman Catholicism with disquiet. In the England of the late seventeenth century, hardline Protestantism was the dominant, and implacable, political reality. It was obvious to Louis XIV. It is obvious to us. It seems incredible it was not obvious to the Stuarts.

James, father-in-law to the brave William or no, was principal target in the Popish Plot hysteria and the ensuing Exclusion Crisis. Oates had forged letters to one of James's past priests. Worse: in the frenzy real ones were found, from assorted Catholic friends to each other, and to the emissaries of Louis XIV, and to cardinals and nuncios overseas. James was mentioned a good deal in this correspondence, and much of his thought was described; one hapless acquaintance had written that the Duke of York was to Catholicism 'converted to such a degree of zeal and piety as not to regard anything in the world in comparison with God's Almighty glory, the salvation of his soul and the conversion of our kingdom which has a long time been oppressed and miserably harassed with heresy and schism.'

Oates was too cunning, or too stupid, to accuse James of knowledge or complicity in the Popish Plot. But the damage to the Duke of York was real and serious. He swore on his honour – on his sword – that certain friends were lying when they insisted they had faithfully recorded his philosophy of affairs. Perhaps they incriminated him in the hope of saving themselves: who would dare behead the heir-presumptive? And how could anyone else be beheaded if he were not? Perhaps James was lying. Whatever: he persuaded Charles of his innocence. He persuaded the Privy Council. He persuaded

the Lords. He could not, though, persuade the Commons.
James had once again been publicly linked to 'Popery and
arbitrary government', and frightened men who had hitherto
hung back from attacking the august prince now rose in
determined effort to block him from the succession.

James had still sufficient standing to resist immediate
marginalisation. The Lords rejected calls that he be sent from
court. More: he won exemption from the severe new measure
now excluding Catholics from both Houses of Parliament.
James's dignity, though, was not enough to overawe his
brother. At Charles's orders the duke had to stop attending
the committee on foreign affairs; stop attending the admiralty
board; stop any public part in English public affairs. Charles,
too, was thinking aloud about still more biting anti-Catholic
measures, if only to appease the multitude. Things grew even
more serious when Oates began to accuse Queen Catherine of
Popish Plot involvement; if she were removed from the scene,
by divorce or worse, then Charles might yet remarry and sire
children. And, of course, there was the Duke of Monmouth,
who was fast distancing himself – very visibly – from his
beleaguered uncle. The best story of this foolish, mean-
tempered time concerns Nell Gwyn; returning, perhaps, from
some tryst with the king, the mob mistook her carriage for one
of the king's French Catholic mistresses. Stones and filth flew.
Nell sensibly ordered a halt, lowered the glass, and shouted,
'Don't stone me, good people. I'm the *Protestant* whore!'

Among the Stuart bastards – such as the Wolf of Badenoch,
the Earl of Moray, the Duke of Berwick – Monmouth cuts a
poor figure, and much less straightforward than Nell Gwyn.
He was vain, cruel, loose-living, and an ingrate. He was, as we
shall see, a coward. He lacked discernment in his dealings
with men, guile in statecraft, or much grasp of political reality.
In his last years he would resort to crazy accusations: that
James had started the Great Fire; that James had poisoned
Charles II. Much as Charles loved his son – and he did – he
refused, in 1662 or ever, to put away his wife and repudiate
his brother and own Monmouth as his legitimate heir-
apparent. All his days he denied adamantly he had ever

married Lucy Walters; in the end Charles was so exasperated by his son that they severed relations completely, and the old king had no word of blessing for Monmouth – no word at all – even on his deathbed.

But, in 1679, Monmouth could do James great harm. His ostentatious avoidance of the duke – whose service to the realm had been long, meticulous and loyal, and who had shown his nephew much co-operation and kindness – only excited others to press yet more vicious attacks. The Duke of York's nerve now broke. Men in this position, bearing the brunt of wild accusations in an irrational and paranoid atmosphere, are best advised to keep calm, dignified silence. Instead, fearful for the nation's order, and concerned for the safety of the king, James was far too noisy in defending himself, and so determined to keep the army, and some sort of position for himself in that army, that he played into his foes' hands. At a critical moment the secret correspondence between Danby and Louis XIV was made public, and any authority Charles had in retaining James in England's public life evaporated. So the Duke of York was presented with an ultimatum: he reverted to the Church of England; or he left the court. Charles even sent spiritual counsellors to argue with his brother, and the Duke of York spent tiresome hours talking doctrine with the Archbishop of Canterbury and the Bishop of Winchester. James did not change his faith. He also insisted he would not leave court without a direct written order from the king.

The king by this point had run out of options, and patience. The command came to James, in writing, to leave court and, indeed, the country. It was softened only a little by the king's simultaneous declaration in council, yet again, that he had never been married to anyone but the queen. The king even refused to see the Duke and Duchess of York, who sailed forlornly for Holland on 3 March 1679. They spent most of the next three years in exile, while the pamphlets probed new heights of Protestant rhetoric:

Fancy, that amongst the distracted crowd you behold troops of Papists, ravishing your wives and your daughters, dashing your little children's brains out against the walls, plundering your houses and cutting your own throats by the name of heretic dogs . . . When he (as all other Popish kings do) governs by an army, what will all your laws signify? You will not then have Parliaments to appeal to; he and his council will levy his arbitrary taxes and his army shall gather them for him.

Time was on James's side. Once the emotion and terror and pamphleteering subsided, the greater part of England's vested interests would support his accession. The Restoration had heightened the political nation's view of the monarchy: they saw absolute, implacable primogeniture both as a providential instrument of God in government and as a principle underpinning their own rights in Church, lands and property. Most Anglican clergy held primogeniture near-sacrosanct. Anyway, James was old, by the standards of their day, and would not live long; he might not even survive his brother, and the duchess had yet to bear a healthy child. There was always Mary and William. So Charles, astute enough in politics, reasoned in himself. His immediate priority was to regain control of the country and of affairs and to win back the capacity to govern, for a good stretch, without parliament. That meant quietening the multitude and keeping his nations out of war. Assurances and executions as necessary would placate the mob; James could be usefully employed abroad. The best chance of weathering the Exclusion Crisis was to manage without parliament.

James was at first bored. Naturally, he and the duchess first spent time with his daughter at The Hague. He went the rounds of houses and met assorted old acquaintances from the last exile. His mother-in-law stayed for a while. Funds were tight and the household had to make economies. He passed time by reading turgid devotional books and going out a-hunting and killing things. He studied his son-in-law closely and wrote of his fears to Charles. It was apparent even to James that William's priority, then and always, was to defend the interests of the Dutch against the French. He wanted as much English aid as possible, and so was eager for Charles to get along with parliament. If parliament continued to demand his father-in-law's exclusion, and charged that price for troops in Flanders fields, it was a price William would happily pay.

James was much encouraged when, late in August, Charles fell seriously ill. There was general panic in London and the Duke of York was secretly sent for, ministers all the time, of course, denying any knowledge of it. There was general fear of Monmouth and true fear of civil war; only the heir-presumptive had sufficient standing to calm the city. To general surprise James's brief return was unremarkable. There were no riots in the streets; blood did not run in the gutters; the heads of infants were not dashed against walls. London's mayor and aldermen paid court to the Duke of York. Almost all knelt, bowed, and showed him due respect. His stolid, dull virtues were suddenly much valued. He played halting but careful politics as Charles grew better. Friends of James were encouraged for favours. The bishops were softly assured that, should James be king, he would never try to establish Catholicism by force.

After a month he had to leave briefly for Brussels, but with some satisfaction. The mob had not taken to the streets against him; and if they cried for Monmouth in the taverns the men who really mattered in the kingdom were flocking to his own star. They were men of ambition, fearful for order, and their wealth and strength lay largely in the shires, and their hearts in the land and in the principle of lawful, assured inheritance. Men whose wealth is in land, rather than commerce or gold or jewels (as, even in our day, the long-harried Jews still pursue the diamond trade followed by their insecure ancestors) prize order above all else. So they formed a party behind James, determined on his lawful succession; and this party of 'Church and king' men, by the end of 1680, was already known to their opponents by the tag of freebooting Irish Catholic bandits. James, you could say, was the first leader of the Tories.

When he came back to London, two weeks later, there were

more little triumphs. Shaftesbury, Lord President and his most prominent enemy, badly overreached himself: by his own authority the Lord President called the Privy Council to discuss the wisdom of James being trusted with power in Scotland. England's council had no authority in Scotland, and Shaftesbury had no right to convene it without the king. Charles was furious and Shaftesbury was stripped of office. A week later Titus Oates and a henchman tried to disrupt a dinner James was enjoying with the gentlemen of a London militia, with cries of 'A Pope, a Pope,' until a guard pointed a gun at them; then they croaked, 'No Pope, no Pope; God bless His Highness!' and scuttled off. There was a good turnout for the meal and James was pleasantly treated. Serious as his plight remained, he and the duchess left for Scotland on 27 October, in good spirits, not greatly minding the petty snubs they encountered on their route through England. The Duke of York reached Edinburgh on 24 November, and readily took his seat on the Scottish Privy Council; he could use his rank and authority, as the king's brother, to duck the oath of allegiance.

James ran Scotland's government until 1682. He approached its problems with caution. The immediate problem was Lauderdale, effectively the governer of Scotland, whose powers were failing, and who was threatened by powerful factions in the nobility; James had to bolster the earl while living on easy terms with the factions that mattered. 'I live as cautiously as I can,' he wrote, 'and am careful to give offence to none and to have no partialities and preach to them laying aside all private animosities and serving the King his own way.' In his political dealings, and his social conduct, James was prudent and friendly.

He was also keen, of course, to secure his own prospects. When Scotland's feeble parliament was called in 1681, it readily passed an Act guaranteeing James's succession to the Scottish throne. The Duke of York also spent much energy building up the militia, both to keep order in the land – he was determined that the king's writ would be upheld in all things of Church and state – and to give him serious clout if things grew worse in England. The Exclusion Crisis raged on, with Charles under the most intense pressure to alter the succession, and each new crisis and confrontation caused James acute anxiety, especially as by the time any London news reached him it was already a week old. Scottish affairs were less sophisticated. In large parts of the land, such as the Highlands, the government's writ barely ran. Edinburgh itself was a crowded, stinking city. The nobility still exercised power and privilege in Scotland they had long lost in England. The culture, too, was much more violent. Assassination, clan feud, Borders vendetta, armed uprising, murderous street riots: these were realities; and the government had to resort to armed force to maintain order, with a viciousness never necessary, nor practicable, in England.

Religion was a high issue here, but the divide was between Presbyterianism and episcopacy; Scotland's Catholics hardly mattered. There is no doubt that the great mass of Scots wanted a Presbyterian order, and especially their pulpit-centred liturgy. At the same time, most Scots had accepted the modified episcopacy of James VI, where bishops served as president of the diocesan synod, with ordination a function of Presbytery. Charles I's antics had led to the destruction of this order and provoked an extreme, theocratic Presbyterianism, which had never majority support in Scotland. By 1680 most Presbyterians could be described as 'Resolutioners', a moderate party prepared, for the main, to accept a moderate episcopacy on the lines of government policy prior to 1638. The 'Protestors', who would not tolerate episcopacy in any shape or form, and who thought the Kirk should run the country in every sphere, should have been an unpopular minority. It was the Stuart insistence on imposing an alien, liturgical, tyrannical episcopacy upon Scotland that caused so much ill-feeling, disorder and bloodshed.

There were still the Covenanters, of whom the Cameronians were the most dangerous. These followers of Richard Cameron, a cleric from Fife, in June 1680 declared open war on Charles II and the state.

We for ourselves do by thir presents disown Charles Stewart, that has been reigning (or rather tyrannising as we may say) on the throne of Britain these years bygone, as having any right, title to, or interest in the said crown of Scotland for government as forfeited several years since by his perjury and breach of covenant both to God and his Kirk . . . As also, we being under the standard of our Lord Jesus Christ, Captain of salvation, do declare a war with such a tyrant and usurper and the men of his practices, as enemies to our Lord Jesus Christ, and his cause and covenants.

English historians portray Cameron as an extremist, a revolutionary who would have been as brutal in power as the men who oppressed him and his followers. They insist on seeing their 'offence' as political rather than religious; a threat to the public safety.

The truth lies somewhere between southern incomprehension and the wild hagiography of nineteenth-century Presbyterian writers such as Alexander Smellie and the younger Thomas McCrie. There were bloodthirsty, vicious men among the Covenanters, as there are in any desperate movement. But there were only outlawed, desperate Covenanters because of stupid and brutal Stuart policy in Scottish religion. The Covenanters took up arms because they were compelled to defend themselves against religious persecution. And if they disowned, like Cameron, the authority and rights of Charles II, they had abundant moral and legal cause. He had broken faith, in infamous fashion, with the solemn vows of the 1651 coronation. So there were Cameronians, in armed rebellion; and there were the 'Killing Times', under James, Duke of York. It is a little hard to sit in placid judgement upon men prepared to die for peace of conscience, especially if you are a historian not prepared to die for anything.

James arrived in the aftermath of the Covenanter rising which Monmouth had crushed at Bothwell Brig. Most of the rebels had been spared, and Monmouth had further, and wisely, granted a degree of toleration: religious dissenters could worship in their houses, which he deemed less of a

threat than the large open-air conventicles. Many of the
nobles opposed this, but James saw no reason to reverse
the policy. It calmed the situation sufficiently to satisfy the
bulk of Covenanters and leave only the Cameronian hard
core. They were then readily isolated from popular support
and could be dealt with as a political rather than religious
threat. They proved little of a military one. After 5,000 merks
were put on Cameron's head, he was caught and killed in a
messy skirmish with government troops at Airds Moss, in
Ayrshire in 1679. Covenanting leadership passed to Donald
Cargill, who in turn was caught and hanged; then to James
Renwick, who would die in the last year of James VII's reign,
the last martyr to the Covenant.

There is no doubt that James smashed the Cameronians
with will and brutality. He spoke merrily of the 'hunting
ground' of Lowland Scotland; he directed the search operations, and was present at several interrogations, witnessing
such tortures as the thumbscrews and the 'boots'. He was not
a brutal or vicious man, but he loathed the Covenanters, and
had a soldier's toleration for cruelty and pain. He does not
seem to have taken sadistic pleasure in such exercises, and was
quite shaken by the courage of some prisoners, who refused
utterly to betray comrades or repudiate the Covenants or take
the oath of abjuration, even as their legs were crushed in the
boots. 'Take them away,' James said at length, after one
fruitless torture session, 'else they will say what will hang
themselves.' So the Killing Times ground on, with pot-shot
peasants and tormented ministers and drowned girls; but the
suffering was now marginalised and of little concern to the
political nation.

The Scottish parliament met in the summer of 1681 and did
all James wanted: it approved taxation to fund the army;
vouchsafed his succession; and passed a Test measure, for
James wanted the measure of loyalty in the Scottish nobility.
Apart from loyalty to crown, succession and so on, this Test
committed the oath-taker not ever to attempt any alteration in
Church or state. James was satisfied when the Duke of
Hamilton – the most pro-Presbyterian peer – finally, after

great squirming, took the Test in March 1682, on pain of losing all public offices. The Earl of Argyll, son of the poor marquis, fussed, demurred, and finally refused to take the Test; worse, he published his reasons, which were principally his ecclesiastical views. James was not amused. Argyll was soon arraigned for political crimes and at length convicted of treason. James was not eager to see him executed – he wanted merely to break Argyll's power in the West Highlands – and the matter became academic when the earl escaped, in his daughter's clothes, and fled to Holland.

By the spring of 1682 James felt his work in Scotland quite accomplished: the land at relative peace, the law respected, the king secure and the Church upheld. It all served gratifyingly to impress the English Tories. He returned modestly to England, not pressing for any high place, and a much-mollified Charles granted him leave to return permanently. James sailed back to Scotland to fetch his wife, and had one of those narrow squeaks that occur so often in the Stuart story: his ship foundered in a storm, and the Duke of York was fortunate to escape with his life. A hundred and fifty others drowned. Had he, too, been lost, his daughter Mary would have succeeded Charles II; there would have been no Old Pretender and no Jacobites, and a very different order of succession.

So, after all the alarm and controversy, the Duke and Duchess of York enjoyed three serene years back in England, with Charles II firmly in control, the Tories consolidating support, parliament unwanted and unmet. James still had many enemies; they, the Whigs who dominated the Commons, still agitated against 'popery and arbitrary government'. But the Tories wanted an exalted Church of England and saw the main threat to order as the Dissenters, not the Catholics. To them only the monarchy would defend the Church of England, and James's record in Scotland suggested he would defend it vigorously, whatever his private faith.

The other problem, apart from the Whigs, was Monmouth. In 1683 the Rye House Plot was exposed: a bizarre scheme somehow to overthrow the succession, by kidnapping or even murdering Charles II, recalling parliament, and eliminating James. The conspiracy was uncovered before it had gathered much organisation or momentum; it was really a vague opposition movement of a dozen assorted plots and ploys, most fanciful and extreme. Charles came down on it savagely. There were trials and executions. Monmouth was thoroughly implicated, but travelled to Whitehall to throw himself at the king's feet and pledge his innocence and beg forgiveness for foolish company. Naturally this confession was published as proof of the wider plot; when challenged by the Whigs, Monmouth hesitated, then withdrew it.

Now the king broke with him utterly, exasperated beyond endurance. Monmouth, having been pardoned, could not be proceeded against; but life was made throughly unpleasant for him, and early in 1684 he fled to Holland, where William treated him very nicely, even as the Prince of Orange's relations with his uncles continued to deteriorate. William could not grasp how detested Monmouth now was at court, and so the royal bastard continued to cause yet more trouble.

In May that year James resumed his seat on the Privy Council. He took up the reins of office again at the Admiralty. His old foe, James Butler, Duke of Ormond – almost the last of the original Cavaliers – was removed from office as Lord Lieutenant in Ireland. The government, more absolute than ever, had grown markedly more pro-Catholic in policy when John Evelyn sourly recorded, of a January evening at White-hall, the atmosphere at court:

> I can never forget the inexpressible luxury and profaneness, gaming, and all dissoluteness, and, as it were, total for-getfulness of God (it being Sunday evening) which this day (25th January 1685) I was witness to, the King sitting and toying with his concubines – Portsmouth, Cleveland, and Mazarine, etc.; a French boy singing love songs in that glorious gallery, whilst about twenty of the great courtiers and other dissolute persons were at basset round a large table, a bank of at least £2,000 before them, upon which

two gentlemen who were with me made reflections with astonishment. Six days after, all was dust.

Charles II had cackled that his brother would not last four years as king.

Historians are often accused of wasting their energy in demonstrating something was inevitable, long after it has happened. It would be wrong to suggest the failure of James VII and II was inevitable. He inherited a parliament, dominated by the Tories, markedly supportive of him and the monarchy. The bishops trusted him. The three kingdoms were stable. The land was not entangled in European war.

> I shall make it my endeavour to preserve this government both in Church and state as it is by law established. I know the principles of the Church of England are for monarchy and the members of it have shown themselves good and loyal subjects; therefore I shall always take care to defend and support it. I know too that the laws of England are sufficient to make the King as great a monarch as I can wish; and as I shall never depart from the rights and prerogative of the Crown, so I shall never invade any man's property.

The Privy Council loved this speech so much they begged King James to publish it.

The Church of England was expressly assured that James 'would never give any sort of countenance to Dissenters'. Loyal addresses flowed in from all over the country; many, Miller observes, specifically praised the accession of a king pledged to preserve the established order of Church and state. As for the administration, all Charles's officials were confirmed in their appointments, though a few trusted and minor retainers were advanced to places in the royal household, such as John Churchill. James exuded magnanimity. He assured some who had once opposed him that he had forgotten the past. Only the most offensive of these were declined leave to kiss the king's hand. He rejected a silly proposal that all who had publicly called for Exclusion should be debarred from parliament.

He cleaned up the court; he worked conscientiously, putting in much harder hours than his brother. King James paid new and close attention to the royal accounts, demanding weekly figures of income and expenditure. He cut back household expenses, and eliminated waste where he could detect it. He made a very good impression by, as a point of moral and political principle, paying off all the late king's many debts. He paid servants and staff promptly. He forbade the sale of employments. He declared blasphemers, drunkards, gamblers, debtors, adulterous husbands and recalcitrant sons would be given no place at court. He also worked fiercely to repress duelling, a fashionable – and murderous – new custom. Some of these declarations were more for effect than enforcement; Rochester, for instance, whom James now made Lord Treasurer, was a notorious boozer. But court life did markedly improve. James remained as accessible to men as his brother; but bad language, blasphemy, gross drinking, lascivious caresses, and all the beyond-parody licence of his brother's era ceased. James himself had never been much of a drinker and, in his latter years, scarcely drank at all. Even his tastes at table were simple: the mouth does not water when you hear of James's 'universal sauce', which he ate with fish or fowl or flesh, and of which he was so proud he confided the recipe to Samuel Pepys: 'made of some parsley and a dry toast beat in a mortar, together with vinegar, salt, and a little pepper'.

The 'men of pleasure' who had diverted King Charles with their wit and bawdiness were not now welcome. James was too solemn to enjoy their company and dim to understand their jokes. He had more difficulty eschewing women; comely as the queen was, and old as he himself was now, his appetites were as strong as ever. Whores were still smuggled to his chamber by a privy stair. His chief mistress, Catherine Sedley, was sent away when he took the throne; but in 1686 she was brought back and created Countess of Dorchester. There was a to-do; the queen wept and stormed, and the countess had to leave court again. But James still saw her and other obliging ladies, in furtive circumstances and childish arrangements. He compensated for this sexual industry by applying himself all the more feverishly to Roman devotions, when less pleasurably engaged.

The queen was losing popularity. As Duchess of York, Mary had won friends and regard with her uncomplicated charm. She now put on great airs and was bitterly described as 'much changed to stateliness'. She fell prey to faction, having her ear much bent by flattering tongues, and tried to influence her husband in policy; as a fanatical Catholic, and really rather ignorant of her adopted land, the advice she gave was usually stupid. She was very ill for a time in 1685 and in 1686 had another miscarriage, after which she concluded despairingly she would never bear a child again. So Queen Mary nagged and fussed and bore herself haughtily about and played cards with the court ladies. She had got on well with her step-daughters. Now the Princess Anne, who had married the bovine Prince George of Denmark and was enduring constant pregnancy, developed a great dislike of the queen, and this had grave consequences.

He was destroyed by two other factors. One was bad counsel: that of Robert Spencer, Earl of Sunderland, who wormed his way into the king's confidence after a succession of misjudgements: this Sunderland, for instance, had spoken strongly in support of Exclusion. He curried James's favour now by insisting it was entirely possible to achieve the king's dearest wish: the conversion of the kingdoms to Rome. Sunderland was a strong personality and soon won the king's confidence. Having embarked the reign on this ruinous strategy, it was quite impossible for Sunderland to reverse his advice, even as more and more outrage mounted in the land and James dug himself into yet deeper trouble, at home and abroad. There was one final, but essential death-blow for the reign: the arrival of a healthy Roman Catholic son.

Now there is not the least evidence that James wanted, or intended, to promote Roman Catholicism by force. His subjects, of course, concluded otherwise, and feared the worst by way of sword and fire and *auto da fé*. All he desired was to put Roman Catholicism on an equal footing with other faiths. Critically, that meant removing the legal barriers on Roman Catholics as subjects and citizens. They should be allowed freely to worship, to build churches, to train priests and to run convents and monasteries and schools. And they should be allowed to hold public office and sit in guilds, corporations and in parliament. He claimed, all his life, to be against persecution for conscience's sake; it is ironic that, writing from Scotland – of all places – in 1680, he told his brother that 'though he wished all men alike in his religion, yet thought it unlawful to force any man, much less a kingdom, to embrace it.' His modern defenders insist that when he harassed Dissenters, as he had done so busily in Scotland, it was always on political grounds. They miss, perhaps – he was certainly such a dullard that he missed it himself – the troubling point that, too often in the career of James, he had held religious dissent and political sedition to be axiomatic. Though he had repudiated the Anglican communion, he still thought the Church of England a Church, if flawed and erring. Presbyterians, Anabaptists, Quakers and so on were to him but a ludicrous and dangerous rabble.

Yet he did not have the force to enthrone Catholicism. Barely two in a hundred English subjects were Roman Catholic. His accession did not produce mass conversion by the thousands. His army and navy were small and the great bulk of their fighting men Protestant. And – all Protestants took comfort in this – there was no Catholic heir. There were priests about him eager to encourage him in, perhaps, altering the succession; but they could not shift James in his tedious integrity. Such talk of alteration with the dictates of Providence he deemed blasphemous.

He believed in God and the support of God. Judge Jeffries, as the regime collapsed and James continued piously to look for a miracle, sighed in scorn that 'the Virgin Mary is to do all.' To James Catholic truth was so self-evident that its rightness to any fair mind must be immediately apparent. 'Did others enquire into the religion as I have done, without prejudice or prepossession or partial affection, they would be of the same mind in point of religion as I am.' So he resolved to lift the various penal laws that so hindered Roman Catholic worship, education and evangelism. Once Roman clergy could compete with vicars and ministers on equal terms, the true Church would increase mightily. And then there was that great obstacle to conversion: the loss of standing, privilege, power, lands, offices. James had a cynical view of the Anglicanism of the gentry; most, he once observed, seemed to have no real religion at all. He was also aware that many Protestant gentry feared for their estates, once monastic land long since seized by the crown and conferred on their favoured ancestors. They had to be reassured. So, of course, had the Anglican clergy, fearful they might be evicted from their livings. Yet he was determined to abolish the Test and Corporation Acts. They were blasphemous; they required men to repudiate the holy doctrine of transubstantiation. And they deprived him of the services of loyal Catholic subjects.

He was, in this, ahead of his time and quite beyond the views of the majority in the land. Men in the late seventeenth century had genuine difficulty in seeing king and law grant toleration to religious errors; errors, they believed, that consigned their dupes to the flames of hell. Besides, conventional wisdom taught that Catholics were a grasping, acquisitive, ruthlessly ambitious lot, who if freed from legal fetter would rapidly climb to power at every level. They would use that power to exterminate Protestantism and, like King Louis, would do so by force.

James also made two fatal political misjudgements. For one, he grossly overrated the support he could expect from the Anglicans. The parliament elected in 1685, after his accession, was full of Tories and Anglicans. They were good king's men, in no mind for revolt or deposition. But they would not accept any measure of legal tolerance for Catholicism. 'I must tell you,' bemoaned the king, 'that in the King my father's time the Church of England's men and the Catholics loved each other and were, as t'were, all one but now there is gotten a new spirit among you which is quite contrary.' That spirit he could not shift; it was, in any event, far from new. James could have waited for easier times, instead he abandoned his wooing of the Anglicans and began to flatter the Dissenters. In the meantime, by royal prerogative, he suspended the Tests, pending their formal repeal by a new parliament. This, of course, invited accusations of 'arbitrary government'.

The other blunder was his pathetic friendship with Louis XIV. To James he was a Catholic prince, His Most Christian Majesty, sure partner in supporting the advance of the true faith in England. To Louis, James was a pious ass. King James was a weakling of a king who could only make war if his parliament allowed him pocket money. Louis cared only about the security of his own frontiers and the stability of regimes in wider Europe; he was especially fearful about the Spanish succession. Louis would scarce have noticed if the English had converted wholesale to Hinduism. He paid lip-service, now and again, to James's religious aims; but, when it came to the crunch, James would be on his own. England was always France's enemy, and long would be, whoever reigned and however he and his people prayed. James, however, plodded on his obstinate course, convinced he had the might of France behind him.

He forgot, too, his son-in-law William, who would not lightly stand by and see James ham up things so badly that parliament might strip the monarchy of effective power, or abolish the monarchy altogether. William himself was not secure. He was a prince in name only, and by power a Stadtholder, a president of sorts over a bickering, virtuous coalition of seven tiny Dutch provinces, each with very different economies, legislatures and priorities, and with much autonomy from the central legislature, the States General: it could decide nothing of importance without the approval of every single province. And within each province, towns and villages enjoyed similar autonomy; a minority of delegates from one town could block a scheme supported by the majority in the state. Actually, the United Provinces worked a good deal better than you might think. Holland itself was the biggest, and by far the richest and most economically advanced province. Other provinces tended to combine against it, so William usually faced only two factions at loggerheads in the States General rather than seven. But he was hampered continually by another element in the bizarre constitution, the regents, who ran the different towns and cities as mayors, and enjoyed both enormous influence in the States General and widespread popular support. Things were made still livelier by the Dutch press, the most outspoken and uncensored in Christendom. It would take a great deal to persuade this godly, pragmatic, talkative, coffee-sipping conglomerate to unite their efforts and abandon parochial concerns to fight for a common good. William had immense difficulty persuading them of the necessity to keep him armed against France. He could not convince them that King Louis was a perfidious man, a ruthless tyrant, whose words of peace could not be trusted. In 1685 the Dutch were as stubbornly pacific as ever. Then there came a Catholic king in England. By 1688 an Anglo-French alliance seemed imminent and at that point, terrified, for their own fate and his, the Dutch united to arm William.

James's fate was sealed because he and William could not get on. They were both stubborn men, of wildly different religion, and both princes. William resented being treated like a subordinate youth. He was cleverer than James, and knew it. He wanted England to grasp the scale of French ambition and unite with the Dutch to block it. He also feared for Mary's rights of succession, and his own, and that James's antics might spark such a rebellion that there would be nothing left to inherit. James wanted William to expel all Scots and English political refugees from the Netherlands. William refused. Among these was Gilbert Burnet, whom James was determined to arraign in Scotland for treason; Burnet feared for his very life, and that is why his record of James is so hostile. More immediately, he badly coloured William and Mary's view of the state of affairs in court and Britain. Assorted ambassadors and spies further muddied the waters, with tales and tittle-tattle that alienated king and prince, father and son-in-law further.

*   *   *

James was barely king when he had to face – and fought down utterly – a revolt, and so greatly increased his authority, a coup he quite failed to exploit. It was Monmouth, of course, still convinced the crown was his by rights, still in the grip of flatterers and adventurers. He launched the expedition in cahoots with Argyll; and they launched it from Holland, at a time when William and the States General were trying mightily to ingratiate themselves with King James. Argyll left the Netherlands in May 1685, making for Scotland with three ships, laden with arms; Monmouth, who had been expelled from The Hague as soon as word came of Charles's death, quit for England in four similarly burdened ships a month later. It was not, in fact, William's fault; the ineptitude of officials on the ground, the Byzantine requirements of Dutch bureaucracy, and the risks of attacking armoured vessels in the tortured waters of the Zuyder Zee had let Argyll and Monmouth escape easily. Everyone wanted written orders from the proper authority and, by the time these were had and the vessels' whereabouts were accurately known, they were lost. It is most unlikely that William was involved in Monmouth's plot. He had nothing to gain from it. He offered James every assistance in quelling the rebellion and sent home the three English regiments stationed in the Netherlands. If he was initially hesitant, it was not because he had some part in Monmouth's design, but rather his incredulity – William being the most honourable of men himself – that the duke would so betray the most solemn oaths of loyalty.

The rebellion came to nothing. Argyll and his 300 men landed in Scotland to find its army mobilised and the likeliest Covenanting supporters interned in castles at Blackness and Dunnottar. He could raise no further support. At Inchinnan, near Renfrew, he was arrested; the earl, like his father, was tried for treason, and in due time executed. Monmouth landed in what was, relatively, a remoter region: the south-west of England, where there had been considerable support for him during the Exclusion Crisis. The king's army in England was scattered in assorted garrisons, and numbered only 9,000 or so. The militia could not be risked in pitched battle, even if Monmouth's troop amounted to little more than armed peasants. One group of Somerset militia actually deserted to Monmouth's cause. Any military defeat could be disastrous, and of political consequence. James now showed a guile and tactical skill quite lacking in 1688. He used the militia to spy on Monmouth, to pad after him, and deter recruits; further, the king ordered the destruction of the bridge at Keynsham, lest his nephew take Bristol. On 5 July the prince's nerve snapped first. He launched a night attack on the royal forces at Sedgemoor, which went quite wrong, despite the advantage of surprise. A host of peasants and hot-headed idealists, armed with staves and scythes and pitch-forks for the most part, were no match for trained and seasoned troops. The army of Monmouth was quickly scattered. Two days later Monmouth was captured, disguised as a shepherd and quavering under a hedge.

He wrote desperate letters to James and Mary, begging for his life. Admitted to the presence, he threw himself at the king's feet. Raving as one possessed, he disowned the declaration of his own kingship as a trick – he had been tricked into it – and who was James? Why, James had poisoned the king his father – and so on. It was not his lies that condemned Monmouth quite as much in the king's eyes as his cowardice. He wrote to William in disgust, saying that Monmouth's behaviour ill fitted one who would be king. There was already an Act of Attainder against Monmouth, so there was no need of a trial, and he survived his poor soldiers by barely a week. The senior bastard of Charles II was beheaded, badly, on 15 July; it 'took five choppes'. Somebody pointed out how few accurate portraits there were of this quasi-prince. After discussion they sewed his head back on and made one last painting of him.

It was the high point of the reign of the last Stuart king. What was left of James's brief monarchy unravelled steadily like a disaster waiting to happen, as much farce as grand opera. He had briefly some standing in Scotland, where parliament voted him a substantial revenue, and passed yet more severe laws against the Covenanters. But the land

refused to quieten. Cameron was more dangerous dead than
alive; he was followed by Donald Cargill, then James Renwick, and still the Covenanters prayed and fought and died.
Once the English parliament had refused to repeal any anti-
Catholic legislation, the dispensations James then issued not
only excited cynicism among Presbyterians; they cost him the
support of his most faithful block, the High Anglicans.
Parliament was prorogued in November 1685 and James
never held another.

The defeat of Monmouth was soured by the 'Bloody
Assizes', under 'Hanging Judge' Jeffries; the executions were
so plentiful, and so brutal, that the populace were all the more
reminded of 'popery and arbitrary government'. The army
grew bigger; at its head appeared more and more Catholic
officers. Without parliament, James continued clumsily to
wield the royal prerogative, powers ill tested since the Restoration and requiring much shrewdness, tact and judgement. These skills James did not have. But he tried to use the
'dispensing' power, which allowed him to exempt given
individuals from the writ of a stated law; and the 'suspending'
power, which allowed him to suspend that law altogether.
Meantime a great army, some 13,000 men now, was stationed at Hounslow Heath, adding menace to James's good
intentions. So he did what he had always been determined to
do. He stacked the land with Catholics and with Roman
Catholicism. By the dispensing power he planted Catholics in
high positions, in the universities, and in the Church, and in
government, and in the army and navy. Across the land he
dismissed justices of the peace who would not support these
appointments and defended vigorously the Test Acts and
penal laws. Most of them were replaced by Catholics. Meanwhile Robert, 2nd Earl of Sunderland re-established diplomatic links with the papacy. A Catholic Council was
appointed, to guide the king in affairs spiritual. After an
arcane legal debate, the Court of King's Bench, in April
1686, upheld the crown's policy and supported such exercise
of the royal prerogative. But James's support, throughout the
political nation, was haemorrhaging.

In April 1687 the king issued a Declaration of Indulgence. It suspended the operation of all laws impeding Catholics and Dissenters. There was widespread condemnation and anger. Few Anglicans – for that matter, few Dissenters – really believed James's protests of tolerance for all. It was, to them, but the first step towards enforced popery and, of course, arbitrary government. William and Mary grew anxious. Even Sunderland, ever more enmeshed in the folly, whispered his doubts. At some point early in 1688 William's concerns hardened into resolve. He let it be known, very discreetly, that if men of goodwill and honest standing wanted him to sail over and help rescue England's religion and nationhood, he might be ready by September. William feared for more than his wife's prospects: he could see no Dutch succour in a realm enthralled to popery and all but enthralled to Louis XIV. What might James do next? Time was on his side. He might purge the army of Protestants. He might call a parliament packed with Catholics.

Yet, on 27 April, King James reissued his Declaration of Indulgence, and commanded that all bishops of the Church of England distribute it and that it be read in all pulpits of the Church on two consecutive Sabbaths. He was no doubt emboldened – though, by this stage, he had no grounds for obstetric optimism – by the knowledge his queen was, yet again, in an interesting condition. But many queried the validity of this latest order-in-council. And seven bishops, including the most important, William Sancroft, Archbishop of Canterbury, denounced the declaration so loudly they were arrested and charged with seditious libel. As they languished in the Tower, news broke in London like a thunderclap. The queen was safely delivered of a prince. When King James heard the news it is said he fell on his knees and thanked God; for most of the night he laughed and wept in joy. Barely reconciled to a popish king, the English now faced a popish dynasty.

Everyone knows the tale of the 'warming-pan baby': that the true child was stillborn, and some tiny male bastard smuggled beneath the lying-in sheets in a warming pan.

The tale is preposterous. Royal births were as public as royal deaths. At one point, as Charles II gurgled away his last hours, his chamber held seventy-five people, including six bishops. So the birth of Prince James Francis Edward had taken place before a large audience; in any event, the Old Pretender grew up to resemble both his parents closely. But James was quite lost. No one now believed anything for good. The queen had been playing cards only the night before, so folk whispered the child came 'suspicious early'. Princess Anne spitefully spread a tale that, learning of the looming happy event, she had tried to study the queen's figure as she dressed in her chamber, and the queen had rudely hidden behind a screen. (This, if we know queens at all, sounds entirely reasonable.) Still the lies spread and daft pamphlets of improbable substitutions and scandal caused excitement in the Netherlands.

The trouble was that Protestants simply did not want to believe the king now had a son – a Catholic son. 'Be it a true child or not,' said a cynical observer, 'the people will never believe it.' Someone else said sweetly everyone would believe it once the child had followed its siblings and died. To this end the royal doctors certainly seemed to direct their curious energies. They announced that milk was bad for babies, and for a time the infant languished: not too surprising, on a diet of gruel, boiled bread, Canary wine, and the unknown horror of 'Dr Goddard's Drops'. The pope, that old celibate, expressed horror: he and Louis XIV argued forcefully that a wet-nurse made far more sense. The doctors wasted more time trying to find a wet-nurse of suitably blue blood. In the end – after the prince nearly died, in August – he was given to a tiler's wife to suckle, and never looked back. How much hung on the life of this baby; how strange a Providence it seems that, preceded by so many weak and short-lived siblings, the king without a crown would live to his seventy-eighth year.

The father rejoiced; the king fast languished. When the 'Seven Bishops' came to trial, the judge unequivocally condemned the king's dispensing power, and the jury found the bishops not guilty. There was a paroxysm of rejoicing and glee throughout the land; it is said that even the soldiers on Hounslow Heath 'could scarce forbear to cheer'. Within days seven great dignitaries, Whig and Tory – they included even Danby, sometime Lord Treasurer – sent word to William: 'nineteen parts of twenty of the people', they insisted, begged for change. At this bidding William moved; meantime, King James issued writs for a new – and packed – parliament.

It took him weeks to realise a serious invasion was on its way. When James finally grasped the threat, his reactions were clumsy and in some ways inexplicable. He should have stood his ground and played the king. But instead he dismissed Sunderland. He withdrew the writs for parliament. He dismissed Catholics from office. In crisis, all such concessions drastically weaken your authority. No one trusted James now and, worse, no one now feared him. William, who made known only that he was come to allow the meeting of a 'free and lawful Parliament', left the United Provinces on 12 November, his sails filled by an east and very Protestant wind. Four days later he landed at Torbay; his accompanying bodyguard numbered 10,000 men.

James still had his army. He still had the palaces; the government pay-roll; the trappings of office. All waited to see how events would move. Instead of rising to the occasion, he sank from it, into timidity, indecision and melancholy. He withdrew from affairs and affairs slid away from him. John Churchill, Princess Anne and hundreds more fast deserted his cause as William moved towards London. On 9 December what remained of the king's credibility vanished when the queen and his baby son were bundled off to France. He moaned over the rosary and cried to God for his sins. On 11 December the king himself tried to escape. He was caught by three fishermen in Kent, who were having great sport harassing fleeing Catholics, and James spent three miserable days as a captive. On the 15th he was hauled back to London, where he was no longer held to be a threat, but an embarrassment. No one, least of all William, wanted to cut off his head. James was taken down to Rochester, and – not without a good deal of prodding – allowed to escape, two nights before Christmas. He dropped the Great Seal of England in the Thames. It was more likely a gesture of self-abasement than a calculated effort to decry the legitimacy of the new regime. He was shortly in France, where, hearing his mumbled complaints and imprecations, the wise shook their heads and said, 'When you listen to him, you know why he is here.'

12

DE FACTO; DE JURE

William; Anne; Pretenders

As King James thumbed his missal in France, London was left to grope in a curious new vacuum of power. For some days no one knew where the realm stood. Was James still king, or no? And if he were not now king, how was that to be explained? And, the throne being vacant, who now should succeed? And, whoever now reigned, how best might the Protestant religion be bolstered, the order of parliament upheld, and all the rights and interests of the political nation established?

So there unfolded the last rites of the Glorious and Bloodless Revolution. The steps were prudent, popular, and in strict law quite illegal; but not a drop of blood was shed, and a political order was created that, though much threatened for another sixty years, would never be overthrown. It has survived and evolved to our own day, which is more than can be said for the Stuarts.

King James had vanished to France. He had absconded from the kingdom and therefore it could be given out – falsely – that he had abdicated. Most knew this was not true, but for the sake of stability they were happy to believe it. The logical heir, then, was his infant son: but he was abroad; he was papist; and he was secure in his father's custody. Few expected the child to survive long in any event. The Stuarts had not lately been tended by paediatric fortune. So Mary, Princess of Orange, was the most patent and acceptable occupant for the throne. She refused, though, to serve without her husband; and he as joint monarch, not merely as consort. William, for his own part, said coldly that he wanted to be a monarch in his own right; to reign as monarch for the rest of his life; and not merely to serve as 'his wife's gentleman usher'. Mary was not gifted for government and was, in any event, in a difficult position of conscience in assuming a throne still warm from her father. Her claim, though, was dynastically better than William's, who stood behind her and Princess Anne and whatever sickly infant Anne was nursing at the time. William and Mary needed each other and the country needed William, and order.

On 22 January 1689 a convention, assembled in London, agreed the appropriate legal rhetoric. James II had 'broken the original contract between King and people', and his flight deemed an abdication. A Declaration of Rights was issued, most of which was enshrined in the Bill of Rights parliament enacted later that year. Its main plank was to stress the primacy of parliament in government. No laws could be suspended, no monies levied, no standing army maintained without the consent of parliament. The Commons were to have free election (on the basis, of course, of the very limited franchise) and entire freedom of speech; parliament was to meet frequently. No Roman Catholic, nor spouse of a Roman Catholic, could hold the crown. On acceptance of these terms, William and Mary could reign. They were duly proclaimed, on the nomination of parliament, King and Queen of England and Ireland, on 13 February 1689.

It is the only time in England's history that the land had two sovereigns, and a special orb had to be made for the coronation, for Mary; it has never been used again. William was the monarch who mattered, of course, and Mary's executive role was exercised only when he was out of the country – as he frequently was, at war with one or both Catholic powers – and that in the most nervous, biddable fashion. The succession, for the moment, was left in abeyance. Mary was still only twenty-six and might yet have a child. Anne might yet produce one that would see its first birthday. The warming-pan baby might die.

It was 1689 before the Revolution was paralleled in Scotland. (It is one of the mysteries of James's last days as king why he did not fly to his northern realm, where he had friends and an army.) On 10 December 1688, as the queen and the tiny prince sailed for France, word reached Scotland of the developing turmoil in the south, and the news excited that most colourful element in Scottish politics, the Edinburgh mob. Under the distinguished leadership of the Lord Provost and the Town Guard, they sacked the Palace of Holyroodhouse, killing a good many of its soldiers. The houses of prominent Catholics were also attacked. Through Christmas and the turn of the year the Lowlands echoed to assorted raids and 'rabblings'; some by the Cameronians, some by assorted gangs. Christmas Day itself saw a sustained, synchronised onslaught on the detested parish ministers. Over 200 were driven from their charges, their manses wrecked and their families terrorised.

Once it became apparent that the king was abroad, the Scottish Privy Council was hastily convened. After some argument an enthusiastic address was despatched to William of Orange, modified after protest by the Episcopalian party. Deputations, from both camps, went to London, and on 7 January William was formally invited to take temporary charge of Scottish affairs and call a convention of estates in March. In the meantime, William probed the ecclesiastical waters of the north. He was by temperament as Erastian as any of the Stuarts; he believed that the Church should be a department of the state, under the crown's authority at all levels, and much preferred episcopacy to Presbyterianism. It did not take him long to grasp, however, how little popular support the episcopal order had in Scotland. It also became plain that the bishops, and the bulk of Episcopalian clergy, felt bound in conscience to the cause of King James. Even in England Archbishop Sancroft, and seven other bishops, refused to take the new oath of allegiance, and many other Anglican clergy; all were deposed.

Bishop Rose of Edinburgh was granted an interview with William, who said carefully, 'I hope you will be kind to me, and follow the example of England.' Rose, an honourable man, said with equal care, 'Sir, I will serve you as far as law, reason and conscience allow me.' William turned away without speaking, and that was the end of an Episcopal Church of Scotland. The estates met in March. It was well attended, with a strong Jacobite presence – they had won leave from James – and even some Catholics; the Test was disregarded for the occasion. There were thirteen Scottish bishops, of whom only one – after every inducement from William – would espouse his cause. A letter was read from William. It was courteous and concessionary, and while pressing hopefully for 'ane union of both Kingdomes', it pressed all the right religious buttons, with talk of 'secureing the Protestant Religion, the ancient Laws and Liberties of the Kingdom'.

The communication from King James was not read until all present had signed a bond declaring themselves to be a 'frie and lawful meeting'. (After all, he was still by law and right King of Scots, and the letter might consist of a plain order to dissolve the estates.) In fact it was a typical, crass, tactless, woolly statement from James, heavy with threats and ominous in language; he demanded:

> from you what becomes loyall and faithfull subjects, generous and honest men . . . That you will naither suffer yr. selves to be cajoled nor frightened into action misbecoming true hearted Scotsmen, and that to support the honour of yr. Natione you will contemn the base example of disloyall men and eternise your names by a loyalty suitable to the many professions you have made to us. In doeing whereof you will choise the safest part, since thereby you will evite the danger you must neids undergo. The infamy and disgrace you must bring upon your selves in this world, and the Condemnation due to the Rebellious in the nixt. And you will likeways have the opportunity to secure to yourselves and your posterity the gracious promises we have so often made of secureing your Religion Laws Property libertys and rights which we are still resolved to performe.

After this barely comprehensible bluster, the soggy centre of the convention swung towards William. The Jacobites, as they were already known (they supported King James, Iacobus in Latin) withdrew from the convention; John Graham of Claverhouse, Viscount Dundee, galloped away and north to organise an armed rising. What was left of the convention discussed, and dismissed, proposals for a parliamentary union, advocated by the man emerging as William's Scottish governor, John Dalrymple. It was apparent that Presbyterianism would not be imposed in England and they still feared episcopacy might yet be imposed on them. Further word came from James, who had now appeared in Dublin: he promised to maintain the Protestant religion, and offered a general amnesty. By now the mass of Scots refused to believe a word he said, and on 4 April only four of the commissioners voted against Dalrymple's bill, which declared that:

> King James being a profest papist did assume the regall power and acted as King without ever taking the oath required by law [to maintain Protestantism, and] did invade the fundamental constitution of this kingdome and alter it from a legall limited Monarchie to ane Arbitrary Despotick power and by publick proclamatioun asserted ane absolute power to Cass annull and Disable all the Lawes and . . . did exerce that power to the subversion of the protestant Religion . . . by Erection of publick schooles and societies of the Jesuits and allowing mass to be publickly said.

And so it went; the wicked king had employed papists in high office; allowed popish books to be printed; funded popish schools abroad; imposed illegal oaths; imposed martial law; raised funds and a standing army without parliament; used torture in the probation of crimes; persecuted under obsolete laws; interfered with the course of justice: wherefore he had 'forefaulted his right to the Croune, and the throne vacant'. On the Duke of Hamilton's motion the Scottish crown was offered to the 'Prince and Princess of Orange, now King and Queen of England'; on 11 April William II and Mary II, being joint sovereigns, were proclaimed at the Mercat Cross in Edinburgh. For the last fortnight of the estates a committee worked on a Claim of Right, which the Scottish parliament adopted. It further denounced King James, and acknowledged the succession to William and Mary, and thence to issue of

Mary, and thence to issue of Anne. Various grievances were listed, including the marriage of a sovereign to a papist, and ended with a ringing endorsement of Presbyterianism; prelacy 'and superiority of any office in the Church above presbyters is, and hath been, a great and insupportable grievance and trouble to this Nation and contrary to the Inclinationes of the generality of the people . . . and therefore ought to be abolished.'

Before the convention rose it further ordained that 'None presume to own or acknowledge the late King James the Seventh for their King . . . upon the highest perrill by word, writing, In Sermons or any other manner of way to Impugne or dissoun the Royall authoritie of William and Mary King and Queen of Scotland . . . that all ministers of the gospell within the Kingdom publickly pray for King William and Queen Mary.' It was, apart from an ingratiating measure with the new order, a clever device to marginalise the Episcopalians. Presbyterian ministers fell in with a will and prayed exuberantly and inordinately for William and Mary. The Episcopalians refused, and many in the Lowlands were as a result quickly deprived of their livings. The Claim of Right was presented to William on 11 May, and he readily accepted its terms. He and Mary never had a Scottish coronation, but he did take the distinctive coronation oath. Neither ever set foot in Scotland, nor would any future monarch, until George IV visited Edinburgh, in tartan state, in 1828.

The first Jacobite rising was well under way. James had landed in Ireland in March, at the orders of Louis XIV, aiming to subdue that island and then invade mainland Britain with a vast Catholic army. The southern mass of the country was soon under Jacobite control, but the Protestants of Ulster made plain they would fight to the death. The Jacobites were soon hampered by inept leadership, dreadful organisation, and their lugubrious, despairing monarch. In Scotland the convention did not adjourn before pronouncing Dundee a rebel; and as William and Mary were proclaimed in Edinburgh he raised the royal standard in the city of his title. Then Dundee went west and raised the clans, marshalling a force of

2,000 at Glenroy, and led government forces a merry dance all summer, through the Highlands, while he waited for reinforcement from Ireland. Meantime the Church parties fought to the death, and the Presbyterian cause made a further advance when, late in July 1689, all the past Acts in favour of episcopacy were rescinded. It would be 1690, with the realm at peace, before William would conclude the 'Revolution Settlement' in Scotland. The Church in Scotland was established as Presbyterian. Patronage was abolished. So was the Act of Supremacy, which had made the king almighty in religious affairs. The settlement, though, fell well short of the terms of the National Covenant, and – in south-west Scotland especially – many Presbyterians refused to associate with the newly reformed Kirk. It was 1745, though, before the Cameronians could muster two clergymen and hold a presbytery to inaugurate the Reformed Presbyterian Church of Scotland, which still exists.

When Dundee's reinforcement arrived from Ireland it was a shock and an embarrassment: only a single regiment, which was worse than nothing, for it pitiably exposed Jacobite weakness. He needed a quick battle now, victorious, to preserve his cause, and on 27 July the Jacobite and government forces met at the Pass of Killiecrankie, in Perthshire, as General Hugh MacKay led the troops of King William to Blair Atholl. Though outnumbered – MacKay commanded 4,000 men – Dundee's deadly ambush in that narrow defile quite routed the government army, of whom 2,000 were killed or wounded. But Dundee himself was shot, mortally; it is said by a musket loaded with a silver button. He lived long enough to know he had carried the day. A soldier told him, 'Well for the King, but I'm sorry for your lordship.' 'The less matter for me,' said Dundee, 'seeing the day goes well with my master.' Shortly he died, and the Rising of 1689 with him, for the Jacobites had no general of calibre and skill to replace him. They were finally scattered, at Cromdale on Speyside, on 1 May 1690.

Six weeks after Cromdale, King James and King William met in pitched battle at the Boyne, in Ireland, on 12 July. It was a triumph for William and James fled once more to France. When news of his defeat reached Rome, the Pope ordered a torchlit procession of rejoicing; he was as much a secular prince as a holy pontiff, and the Pope had no desire to see an ally of Louis XIV prosper. In Ulster and Scotland, to this day, the Battle of the Boyne enjoys a place in Protestant mythology that is preposterous and absurd. The war in Ireland ground on till the end of 1691, with such horrors as the siege of Londonderry; but William crushed it in the end, and for a quarter-century there was no serious military challenge to the new Protestant order.

William III and II ruled until February 1702. In 1694 Mary died of smallpox, and all were taken aback by the depth and bitterness of his grief. They had rebuilt much of Hampton Court for a palace – he hated central London; the coal-smoke provoked his asthma – and, between the genius of Sir Christopher Wren, the lovely pieces of blue and white Delft porcelain Mary collected, and the magnificent formal gardens they laid out, they made a fine palace of it. Mary had also initiated the building of Greenwich Hospital, for retired sailors of the Royal Navy; this was finished, and is today one of the finest buildings in London. But the Hampton Court improvements ceased in 1695. It was too evocative a place for William and he went there seldom.

He continued his campaign against France, and in John Churchill found a brilliant general, duly ennobled as Duke of Marlborough. But William's vision of an effective, rather despotic if just monarchy was inevitably choked by parliament. Inexorably parliament assumed more and more power, especially as the king needed ever more funds for warfare. The Triennial Acts, passed against his will, forced a general election every three years. The economy, too, expanding in empire, required an ever bigger army and navy. William's reign saw the birth of things now part and parcel of British governance: the Bank of England; a civil service; a funded National Debt; even insurance companies. And party politics were well established. The Whigs, who dominated affairs for most of the next century, believed in money. So did the Tories. But the Whigs wanted a limited monarchy and a strong parliament and much greater toleration for Protestant Dissenters. The Tories did not, and preferred a patriarchal order in the land, centred on squire and vicar, rather than the commercial hegemony of nasty London. Many Tories inclined to the Jacobites.

William kept his word in Scotland. But Scotland nevertheless languished. It was frozen out of the English market and a succession of bad harvests and viciously cold winters caused recession, widespread famine, and indeed many deaths. Squeezed inexorably towards union, it sustained the humiliation of the Darien venture: an attempt to colonise this region of Panama with Scots was defeated by mismanagement, disease, native massacres, and English hostility. Most infamous in William's reign, though, is the Massacre of Glencoe, when by obscure government authority a troop of billetted Campbells rose in the night to slaughter their hosts, the MacDonalds of Glencoe, a harmless little clan of kindly Episcopalian cattle-rustlers whose only fault was that their chief, MacIain, through no fault of his own – he had marched innocently to the wrong garrison, after waiting on tardy permission from King James – had not taken the new oath of allegiance to William and Mary until some days after the proclaimed deadline. For this the Campbells of Glenorchy fell on them, in February 1692, with orders 'to put all to the sword under seventy'.

By Highland standards it was a small massacre. Government forces had neglected to block escape-routes from the glen and the swirling blizzard caused such confusion that most of the clan escaped. But the thirty-eight dead included two women and two children. MacIain himself, an old man, was killed in his bed; his aged wife had her rings torn from her fingers by an officer's teeth, was stripped naked, and thrust into the snow to perish. There is some evidence to suggest King William had prior knowledge of the massacre and that it went ahead with his full approval. He took three years before, in the face of widespread outcry, a commission of enquiry was held in Edinburgh. It fixed full responsibility on his Secretary of State in Scotland, John Dalrymple, Master of Stair. 'All I regret is that any of the sort got away,' Stair had written, in March 1692, 'and there is a necessity to prosecute them to the utmost.' After the commission of enquiry had published its findings, King William did nothing. Except, before his death, to make Stair an earl.

James sulked and prayed at St Germain-en-Laye. His son continued to wax in health and strength. In 1692 his exile was further brightened when Mary bore him a daughter, Louise Marie, whom he adored; he called her 'La Consolatrice'. He lapsed into fatalism, ever more maniacal religious exercise, and senescence. Half-hearted naval efforts to restore him were scattered by winds, or contemptuously shot to bits by the Royal Navy; a plot to assassinate William failed. James greeted these reverses with such hopeful lines as 'the good lord did not wish to restore me.' He wrote a *Memoir*, largely about religion. He greeted Mary's death in 1694 with sick pleasure. She was his daughter, his eldest child; but he forbade any gestures of mourning, and showed not the least personal sorrow. He was much more moved in 1697, at the Peace of Ryswick, when Louis XIV formally accepted William III as *de facto* king, and pledged not to support any who sought to overthrow him. 'God's will be done,' said James with legal patience. He now took mass twice a day, regularly stayed in the Trappist monastery, had the pleasant habit of scourging himself with cords to take away his sins, and began to wear spiky chains around his legs. Only under anxious pressure from those about him did the old man refrain from yet more extreme measures of self-abasement.

It was not a starving court; King Louis granted the *de jure* king some £45,000 a year. But it was increasingly a gloomy one, brightened only by squabbling factions and much fantastic talk. In 1698 it was noted that the central actor 'looks mighty old and worn and stoops in his shoulders; the Queen looks ill and melancholy.' As for their son, he had a dull time of it. The old king reminded him to 'consider that you are come into the world to glorify God, not to seek your pleasure', and, again, 'Kings not being responsible for their actions, but to God only, they ought to behave themselves in everything,' and, with morbid hypocrisy, 'Nothing is more fatal to man, and to the greatest men (to speak with a deep-bought experience) than to be given over to the unlawful love of women.' And, of course, James Francis Edward was indoctrinated utterly in Roman Catholicism and the divine right of kings.

In March 1701 King James was badly disabled by a stroke. Tormented with stomach ulcers, he declined rapidly, and on 5 September, worn out by convulsions, James died. He was in his sixty-eighth year, the best age attained by any Stewart monarch.

A mad cult of veneration surrounded the dead king; serious lobbying began to have him canonised as a saint, and men searched for evidence of suitable miracles. He had self-effacingly ordered burial in the parish church at St Germain, with as little fuss as possible, but King Louis ordered otherwise, and in the end the burial of James VII and II was remarkable indeed. Some of his bowels were buried at the church. The rest of his viscera went to the English Jesuit college at St Omer. The Scots College, in Paris, got his brain. His heart was deposited at a nunnery in Chaillot where he and his queen had spent time on spiritual retreat. The rest of his body was interred at the church of the English Benedictines in Paris. Amid all this butchery admirers went away with other tiny scraps of tissue, or dipped handkerchiefs in Stuart blood. One handkerchief sold for some thousands of pounds at auction in 1997. Nevertheless every bit of the royal corpse – the heart, the brain, the guts, the embalmed cadaver – disappeared without trace in the French Revolution.

The succession pressed on men's minds with new urgency; James had hardly rattled his last when Louis XIV recognised his thirteen-year-old son as king. We have a vivid portrait of William's fury at the news; he went 'red in the face and pulled his hat down over his eyes'. In the summer of 1701 he had already been forced to a radical new policy in the succession that was much mocked and unpopular. The trouble was the lack of a Protestant successor in the linear descent of James. William and Mary had produced no offspring. Anne and Prince George had toiled valiantly; the wretched woman endured eighteen pregnancies, seventeen in the first seventeen years of marriage. Twelve babies were miscarried, or still-born; only a handful survived into early childhood, and only one, William, Duke of Gloucester, made his second decade. William was a bright and engaging child, but hydrocephalic; he could hardly walk without others supporting him, and was an acute embarrassment as reports came of the vigour and health of James Francis Edward. The Duke of Gloucester was eleven years old when he died in July 1700. It was a shattering blow to the regime, whose legality was still held in honest doubt by many; the promised succession of the staunchly Anglican Anne, then William, had kept the Church of England largely loyal. No one now believed either William or Anne would beget more children. It was widely held that William was physically incapable of fathering a child. His government was unpopular and everyone was sick of war. James and the 'Pretender' – Anne had thus dubbed him, and still tried to believe he was no true kin – presented a serious problem.

So, in the summer of 1701, and after much discussion in high places, parliament passed the Act of Settlement. It conferred the thrones of England and Ireland, after the death of William, Anne, and any child they might yet produce, on the Electress Sophia of Hanover and her heirs. She was a sprightly old German lady, granddaughter of James VI and I by his daughter Elizabeth. The electress had a son, George, now forty years old, whom Anne had rejected as a potential husband. The house of Hanover were worthy, dull, fecund and, most importantly, Protestant; under the Act they were required 'to joyne in Communion with the Church of England as by law established'. The Act further and violently repudiated any Roman Catholic, or spouse of a Roman Catholic, from the succession 'whereas it has been found inexpedient with the safety of this realm to have a Popish monarch'.

Its name is really a misnomer; its full title was 'An Act for the further limitation of the Crown and better securing the Rights and Liberties of the Subject'; and in many ways its terms were deliberately offensive to King William; for instance, it legislated that an English monarch who was of foreign birth could not take England into 'any Warr for the defence of any Dominions and Territories which do not belong to the Crown of England'. As William's prime aim in foreign policy seemed to be the protection of the Dutch, the rebuke was obvious; the king suffered that clause, and others, to pass, because the Act was entirely inoperative until after the death of William, Anne, and heirs of their bodies. Most of its provisions, apart from those bearing on the succession, were abolished in the time of the Georges. It was worth pointing out that, by 1701, Sophia was well distant from the throne by the rules of primogeniture; there were other cousins nearer William and Anne by blood, and some Protestants among them. By the time Anne died, in 1714, at least forty-eight people had a better claim to the throne than George I.

We might remember that John Balliol had a stronger case for the Scots crown than Robert Bruce; but the Hanoverian succession would be distinctly difficult to sell to the people. The Guelphs, as they were known by name, were selected because the German connection best suited William's purposes abroad. Meantime the Scots succession remained unaltered. If William and Anne died childless, the Pretender would inherit. There is no evidence for the recurring legend that William offered the succession, by secret diplomacy, to his young brother-in-law if he would but embrace the Protestant faith.

William did not long survive his tough old father-in-law. His war with France had been weary and accomplished little, and from 1697 he tried by desperate diplomacy to avert the advancement of France by the death of the childless Spanish king, Charles II. His work failed and the Spanish throne passed to Philip of Anjou, who stood very near the French throne too; the appalling spectre was raised of a popish *Anschluss*. Early in 1702 William was already planning renewed warfare with his old enemy, the French; then, on

21 February, out riding in the parkland around Hampton Court, the king was thrown by his horse when the mount tripped on a molehill. The fall broke his collarbone and the shaken, battered monarch was removed indoors, in great pain.

'O Almighty God,' he prayed, or is said to have prayed,

the Creator and Preserver of men, from everlasting to everlasting Thou art God. But time and chance happeneth to all that are under the sun, and, in the midst of safety, we are in danger; yet, O Blessed God, it is still in Thee we live, move, and have our being, and our times and lives are wholly in Thy hand. A sparrow falls not to the ground without Thy leave and direction; much less are the persons of Kings shut out from Thy rule and government. I desire to adore Thee in the depths of Thy overruling Providence, which I am not able to fathom. I believe that affliction springs not out of the dust. I humbly submit to Thy fatherly discipline, for Thou correctest in mercy and for my profit. Thou, O Lord, hast exercised me from my youth up until now with troubles and difficulties, and hast hitherto carried me safely through the manifold chances and changes of this mortal life. O, be Thou still my God and my Guide. Preserve in me always a due sense of the instability of earthly things. Let my heart be fixed where true and everlasting joys are to be found, and grant that I never may be unprepared for death and judgment. Sanctify, I beseech Thee, in a particular manner this, my present affliction; give me patience under it, and happy issue out of it. Let Thy Fatherly hand ever be over me, and Thy Holy Spirit ever with me. Whilst I live give me grace to serve Thee faithfully in the high station in which Thou hast placed me; and when I have served my generation according to Thy will, vouchsafe me an easy passage to everlasting rest, through Jesus Christ our Lord. Amen.

The prayer is a fine example of Calvinist exercise; it was published many years later by Rev John Glover of Trinity

College, Cambridge, who found it in an old manuscript in the library. It attests either to the spirit and presence of mind of a frightened old body, or to the credulity of Protestant hagiographers. William III was not, though, spared longer to serve his generation. The doctors made a mess of his fracture; bronchitis set in, and he died on 8 March. William is remembered with more respect than affection. The Jacobites, nastily, commemorated the mole in ciphers and cartoons; for many years they proposed toasts to 'the wee gentleman in velvet'.

Anne is a monstrous figure whose short life – she died before she was fifty – was marked by misery, illness, and suffering. She could hardly remember her mother and relations with her stepmother had broken down before the Revolution; she fell out with her sister Mary, too, and if they were ever reconciled it was only on Mary's deathbed. She deserted her father, with some brutality, in the last weeks of his reign. Anne was a grossly uneducated woman; apart from instilling the catechisms and merits of Anglican religion, the sisters learned little more than basic English – their spelling was dreadful; and assorted card-games and mindless pastimes. They were raised largely apart from their father in a loveless, empty environment; both Mary and Anne poured their sad hearts, and romantic energies, into violent schoolgirl crushes; most famously, on Sarah Jennings, who married John Churchill and rose to be Duchess of Marlborough. The intensity of relations between the three, their gossip and flirting and passion and fallings-out, makes the intimate life of the late Stuart court resemble nothing as much as an Angela Brazil account of the Lower Fourth. Those who have read too much Freud immediately see explicit sexuality in all this: lesbian tendencies. They see too much, though the friendship of Anne and Sarah certainly advanced the Marlboroughs and their son-in-law. Later Anne cooled on the duchess and grew close to Abigail Hill, who inclined the queen to Toryism, and encouraged her loathing of Lord Wharton, a debauched atheist who had been one of the Whig 'Junto' prominent in the government of William.

Anne had been married to Prince George of Denmark, and the match was happy; he was tall, fair and handsome, though soon grew fat, and his only fault was his great and extreme stupidity; one of the dimmest individuals ever to enter the royal family. Charles II said famously, of this George, that he had tried him drunk, and tried him sober, 'and there's nothing in him.' He was not made king consort when she acceded, and was not greatly moved by it; it set the abiding precedent that the consort of a queen regnant is not crowned or styled king. But Anne's constant and wretchedly fated pregnancies quite broke her health. At her marriage she was deemed large and handsome, with remarkably beautiful hands. By 1702 she was a vast, pitiable, rather alarming creature. Like her mother Anne had become grossly fat, huge of girth, big of hip, multiple of chin. She was extremely short-sighted, and so would frown aggressively when some stranger entered her presence, in a determined effort to focus her vision. The effect on visitors was alarming.

Smallpox had scarred Anne's face. Her complexion was further spoiled by red blotches, which have been attributed to erysipelas. She suffered dreadfully from gout, and her hands were twisted with arthritis, which latterly made it almost impossible for her to write. The queen, who seems to have had some pelvic weakness – which would also explain her obstetric tragedies – could hardly walk. She may well have suffered from porphyria, which had haunted earlier Stuarts and would indeed haunt the house of Hanover; it would account for her alarming mood swings, and her unsightly skin rashes. Her health, especially her limited mobility, and lack of intellect had political implications. She was never going to be much of a force in affairs and, as really our first constitutional monarch, with the men of parliament quite in the ascendancy, she earns that status as much by her limitations as by her acceptance of the new order of things.

It is tempting to pity this poor, tortured woman, but Anne deserves a measure of respect. She was a survivor. Through acute suffering she drew comfort from her husband – his death in 1708 was a considerable blow; and from her intense, often melodramatic friendships with women; and from Anglican devotion, being of sincere faith. She also liked sweets, and ate them in great quantity. Above all, she was ardently nationalist. She was the most English monarch, by blood and attitude, in British history. She had little care for Scotland and Ireland, and never visited them – it was all the lady could do to visit the House of Lords – but she loved England, and enthusiastically supported the Union of Parliaments, which – duly lubricated by gold – was encompassed in 1707, and is the most important event of her reign.

The Union was unpopular with the mob in Scotland, but it had the majority support of the political nation in Scotland, and, critically, brought Scotland under the terms of the Act of Succession. It opened new markets to Scots trade and offered Scots far greater opportunities abroad, while securing the autonomy of its two distinctive institutions: the Kirk and the Scots legal system. The Union was the best advancement of Scotland's interests for that time, and provided security against the Jacobite threat and return of 'popery and arbitrary government'. It is silly to regard those who fostered the Union as traitors to their country, and only since the Second World War has it become possible credibly to argue – as Scots today increasingly believe – that the Union has served its purpose. In a foolish move – and expressly against the articles of the treaty – patronage, English-style, was imposed on the Kirk in 1712, for the first time since the Revolution. It was not repealed until 1874 and led to repeated secessions in the Kirk, and the fragmenting of Presbyterianism, most notably in the Disruption of 1843.

Anne could be difficult. She insisted that her ministers conducted themselves as if they were her own servants, and liked to think she had in truth chosen them herself. She was the last British monarch to deny the royal assent to an Act of Parliament. (It was not a very important Act, and she got away with it.) She was no wimp. Like Elizabeth, she could stand up for herself; George was as submissive to Anne as William had been to Mary. (Perhaps he was afraid she might sit on him.) George was a 'kindly, negligible mortal', as

Trevelyan called him, but even men as formidable as the Whigs Godolphin and Harley found the queen a considerable opponent. Like her father, Queen Anne could be extremely stubborn; and of decided independence of mind. Like Elizabeth, she could be astoundingly petty. She could even be ruthless: Godolphin and Marlborough, who had served the crown for years with great industry and fidelity, were sacked in heartless, though politically justifiable, fashion. So there was a core of iron in that great bag of blubber.

Limited as she was, Anne was yet a force, for she worked hard, and was durable. While her ministers could take control of detailed legislation and foreign policy in a way unthinkable under William, they could make no major decision, or any stand on a great issue, without Anne's consent. She read – or had read to her – reams of paperwork, and kept track of what her ministers were doing as best she could; she hauled herself courageously to important debates in the Lords and major meetings of what men were beginning to call the Cabinet. Others came and went in affairs, in that twelve-year reign, but she abode; and thus Barry Coward, in his recent history of the Stuart age, describes Anne bluntly as 'the most important political character of the reign'.

> All I desire [she wrote in 1706], is my liberty in encouraging and employing all those that concur faithfully in my service, whether they be called Whigs or Tories, not to be tied to one or the other. For if I should be so unfortunate as to fall into the hands of either, I shall not imagine myself, though I have the name of Queen, to be in reality but their slave, which, as it will be my personal ruin, so it will be the destroying of all government; for instead of putting an end to faction it will lay a lasting foundation of it.

In one compelling recollection we read of her poring dimly over paperwork in midwinter, by a blazing fire in a great hall, dipping her arthritic knuckles into a basin to ease the pain, when they were not pedalling sweets into her prim, unhappy mouth.

Anne refused utterly to treat with her half-brother, who wrote to her with such pleas as 'meet me in the friendly way of composing her difference'; but she was not above flirting with his hopes. She let the Jacobites know she would favour their cause 'at the proper time'. She refused, in blunt terms, to let the Electress Sophia, or Prince George, set foot in Britain all her lifetime. Ministers, such as Bolingbroke, were tacitly allowed to visit the Pretender in France. Like Elizabeth, she delighted in a degree of uncertainty, and the possibility of an altered succession was a good weapon for reminding ministers not to take their sovereign too much for granted. No doubt she seriously considered recognising James Francis as her heir. And she must have felt the passing of her house from the throne with a certain emotion. But, when she fell ill in December 1713, and as it became apparent she would not recover, she appointed ministers all knew – and she knew – would invite George to assume the throne. From March 1714 she resigned herself to be the last of her house to rule. Anne lapsed into a coma on 30 July 1714, and this strange, spiteful, wistful queen died the following day. She was forty-nine years old, and so obese she was buried in a coffin almost square.

Anne had one dark little triumph in death: she had survived Sophia, whom she greatly disliked, by a few weeks. It took seven before King George I at last accomplished the journey from Hanover to land, to less than enthusiastic reception, at Greenwich. There was much popular feeling against him, so remote was his claim by blood to the throne. Someone has declared that, had James Francis been in London on the day Anne died, he would have been carried to the throne by force. A Jacobite student quarrelled with a Hanoverian classmate at the University of Oxford; it came to pistols, and the Jacobite was shot. In Somerset, defiant subjects rang church bells, and toasted the health of King James. In Bath, Lord Lansdowne was busy collecting cannon, muskets and pistols, and laying plans for James to land near Plymouth. This West Country rebellion was only throttled when its leaders were arrested. They included six members of parliament, proof of Jacobitism as a significant force, with powerful backing in High Anglican circles, in Oxfordshire, in the 'squirearchy', among the Tories.

In Scotland there was open outrage. It was not long before a popular song had, as its refrain: 'Wha the de'il hae we got for a King, But a wee wee German lairdie?' In Inverness, the luckless town crier could scarcely be heard proclaiming the new king, for the roaring and barracking of those about him – and that was not a mob of Highland peasants, but the assembled town magistrates. Heroically he cried, 'God save the King!' 'God damn them and their King,' cried everyone. When word of Anne's death reached Edinburgh, the garrison of the great castle quite panicked. They knocked down the bridge at the gate; they dug a moat, and erected a drawbridge. The government in Scotland felt besieged, and launched a purge of Jacobites. Almost a fifth of Scotland's justices of the peace were stripped of rank and title. Even Presbyterians could be found who supported James, though the bulk of Jacobite sympathy lay in the Highlands, and especially in the north-east Lowlands, where episcopacy was strongest. William had shrewdly rehabilitated the Episcopal Church, allowing free worship and the construction of churches as long as its clergy took the oath of allegiance. Those who refused – the 'non-juring' clerics – were many; and they, and their people, were overwhelmingly Jacobite. And then Scottish nationalism was a force; those who hated the Union – which was much less popular now than in 1707; the Scots felt betrayed and let down by its results – were prepared to back James if he would restore their nationhood. And there were adventurers: place-seekers and disappointed men, who had no standing in the Whig order and were prepared to support anything that might overthrow it.

But where was James?

The Stuarts had survived, through much ill-luck and disaster, because they were apt to be charismatic; the family characteristics might have included melancholy, obstinacy and exuberant libido, but they also enjoyed wit, courage and dash. There had also been a remarkable pattern of shrewd, decisive

Stuarts rising just in time to repair the ruin of an inept predecessor. James I, James IV, James VI and Charles II all recovered the monarchy's authority from the débâcles they inherited. The final Stuart tragedy, which cost them the throne, was one of fertility; at a critical point in family fortunes, after the Restoration, they failed to produce healthy heirs in sufficient number (and wasted two by marrying William and Mary to each other). But it was more than that: the line ended in a resounding bore. The last of the line, his sons, were, respectively, an unstable drunkard and a prim self-righteous homosexual.

James Francis Edward, 'James VIII and III' – who latterly styled himself the Chevalier de St George – lived to be a very old man; he died in 1766 in his seventy-eighth year. Humane, gentle, kindly, and above reproach in his private life, he would have made a fine constitutional monarch. The trouble was that James had none of the gifts and drive, none at all, necessary to recover his throne in the first place. To the Scots, he was first known, rather affectionately, as Jamie the Rover; then they had a look at him, and he was remembered ever after as Old Mr Melancholy. James was in dire need of a charisma transplant. He was deeply religious. He was moral to the point of being priggish. He was acutely shy, like his grandfather; like his father, he was very stubborn, and had absolutely no sense of humour.

James was tall and thin with a big nose, strong chin and a full mouth; but he had his mother's huge, lustrous eyes, and was very dark and Italian in appearance. His father had botched his education, concentrating on the worthy and the devotional. Once he was orphaned, James came under the supervision of King Louis, and – rather late in the day – was introduced to more masculine accomplishments: riding, dancing, swordplay and shooting. He did not enjoy them and was never good at them. And his gloomy background had done more than render him socially awkward. James had no knowledge of the ways of men, little judgement of character, little sense of psychology. He was, as Ross damningly puts it, 'a worthy bank manager, not a history maker'. His close relationships were a disaster. His marriage would disintegrate and his elder son grew to hate James so much that, from 1744, they never met again. He despised the one man with the gifts and ability to restore him, the Duke of Berwick; like another illegitimate brother, the Earl of Moray, Berwick was a fine general and an ardent Jacobite who commanded great respect in Europe. James refused to listen to a word Berwick said about anything; when Berwick warned of the folly of a Scots rising, the Pretender stupidly declared him 'a disobedient servant and a bastard too'.

There were various half-hearted efforts made to restore James to his kingdoms throughout Anne's reign. A scheme in 1702 came to nothing. As the War of the Spanish Succession mounted, though, the French were eager to support a Jacobite effort, and there seemed enough unrest in Scotland to make another effort worth while. In March 1708 James was sent to Scotland, with a fleet of twenty-eight French vessels and 5,000 men. He was to land in Edinburgh, seize the castle, raise an army and invade England. Everything went dreadfully wrong. The French organised the expedition badly. The commander of the naval force was incompetent. On the voyage, James fell ill with measles, and was horribly seasick. The Protestant winds delayed the expedition and the flotilla reached the Firth of Forth too late to effect a strong enough rendezvous with Jacobites ashore. Meantime the Royal Navy hoved in sight, and under fire from Admiral Byng's guns the French were driven out to sea. As the fleet scattered in storms James, not yet twenty, begged bravely to be allowed only a small boat: he would land in Scotland himself and do what he could. He was ignored. They all landed, back in France, 'more like rats than men'.

James gave it a rest for a time. He learned some soldiering in the French army, showing little gifts for command but an ability to enjoy the rigours of camp life and combat. Another effort in 1712 was aborted; that same year, to his great sorrow, his sister died. And then came August 1714, his hour, and where was James?

It was probably the most disastrous timing in the history of the dynasty. It was a full year before the Jacobite standard was raised, by the Earl of Mar, at Braemar in Deeside in the Highlands; it was December 1715 before James sailed for the British Isles. There were mitigating circumstances. For one, mindful of the security implications, there had been little warning of Anne's demise: her ministers and the court had kept the gravity of her health throughout 1714 to themselves, and the ports were closed when she died; it was some days before even some members of parliament knew she was dead. 'Dead! She is as dead as King Arthur,' one late hearer of the news was mockingly told, and the jibe, 'Queen Anne's dead,' has long teased the out-of-touch in the English language. Further, the Whig regime had established a masterly intelligence network; spies were everywhere, in each European court and in James's household itself, and spies had brought the London government full details of the 1708 expedition before it even sailed.

The Jacobites in 1714 had their best ever opportunity of restoration. George I could barely speak English; he addressed his ministers in dog-Latin. He had locked up his adulterous wife in a Hanover tower till her dying day. People spoke of this in shocked tones. There were Jacobite riots round the country. Bishops and members of parliament and squires and aristocrats everywhere supported a Stuart restoration. But nothing happened, and as months went by the Whigs reasserted their grip. They raised the price on James's head, to £10,000, and clamped down hard on the realm. By the summer of 1715 the riots had stopped and most Jacobite ringleaders were in custody. Meantime James wasted time. His blundering diplomacy, and the loud uninterest in European courts, exposed the weakness of his cause. He lacked the will or even the authority to control the Jacobite movement itself, a clumsy clutter of interests, ideologies, religions and nationalisms and petty criminals and cynical mercenaries and the sort of inadequates and psychopaths all forlorn causes attract.

The 1715 was an ill-timed rising with leadership of astonishing ineptitude. In a crowning blow of mistiming, Louis XIV died early that year, leaving his tiny great-grandson the throne; the brilliant old devil upset Stuart plans even by his demise. The rising's main strength was in the north-east Lowlands of Scotland, where Episcopal and Roman Catholic lairds and nobles gladly backed the Stuart cause. Nationalism was such a force that many Presbyterians rallied to Mar's standard in September; the big Highland clans came out too. All that was missing was gifted, compelling leadership. James was not compelling and Mar was not gifted. He was a hopeless general. Braemar was a bad point to start a rebellion: it was a little too remote from the north-east towns, and much too far from the West Highland base of clan Jacobitism. Bad communications bedevilled the whole rising. The advance of the clans down the West Highlands was hopeless. By October they had failed to take Inveraray or even Fort William. They gave up and joined Mar's main army in Perthshire. He had taken Perth, then Inverness, and all Scotland north of Forth was under his control. But at Perth he waited, and waited, and waited, with Edinburgh defenceless before him and all Scotland for the taking. The dramatic battle with dramatic Jacobite victory never came. There was a battle at Sheriffmuir on 13 November, against a tiny government force: 1,000 troops under yet another Campbell chief, the Duke of Argyll. The battle was effectively a draw, but in political terms a victory at last for an Argyll. The momentum was lost and Mar's army began to disintegrate. By now his own men were calling Mar 'Bobbing John', vexed at his procrastination and indecision; proof, as always, that good politicians make lousy soldiers.

Far too late, James disembarked at Peterhead on 22 December. An English rebellion in the north-west had just collapsed, the Jacobites defeated at Preston. James made an appalling impression on his Scottish supporters. He offered no plan of action. He brought no troops and no cash. Like his grandfather, his crippling shyness came across as callous indifference; he seemed to care nothing for the men fighting in his cause. Soldiers eyed each other in wonder as the glum, taciturn, periwigged kinglet went about with big cold eyes and not a word for anyone. 'We saw nothing in him that looked like spirit,' wrote an angry officer. 'Our men began to despise him; some asked if he could speak.' James could not even stay well; he caught a bad ague, and huddled in chairs most of the time, shivering, looking miserable. At Scone, where he kept dreich court, he gave the air of one who expects nothing in life but misfortune. As the rising died a death and government troops closed in, he scurried east to Dundee, then north to Aberdeen, and sailed for Flanders in February. James had snatched defeat from the jaws of victory. Though he had fifty more years to live, he never set foot in the British Isles again.

There was another rising in 1719, which consisted of a continental expedition to Lewis and from thence to launch their revolt in the West Highlands, with the support of Spanish ships and men and none other than Rob Roy Mac-Gregor. But the Protestant wind scattered the good Spanish fleet: twenty ships and 5,000 men were blown away to disorder at Corunna. The Highland advance party knew nothing of this disaster and berthed at Stornoway, to collect eminent Scottish Jacobites. Then the command fell out: George Keith, tenth Earl Marischal, and the Marquis of Tullibardine. They were both able men but they were pig-headedly proud and could not get on. Vital councils of war were reduced to crazy shouting matches. They could not even decide on a route to Inverness. Their 300 fighting men – Spanish – were besieged at Eilean Donan Castle, on Loch Duich, and forced to surrender. On 9 June there was a tiny battle at Glenshiel, which killed the rising altogether. Like a small earthquake in southern Chile, there were not many dead. The Spanish were treated kindly and, after a few months in captivity, allowed to go home.

There were many more petty putative risings; abundant plots of London coup or Hanoverian assassination, involving such foreign potentates as the King of Sweden and the Tsar of Russia. But for a quarter-century nothing came of them. They were betrayed by spies, frustrated by the reliable Protestant wind, torpedoed by court factions, or pure mischance. (At one critical moment, when a scheme of genuine might was about to begin, the King of Sweden, its main backer, was killed in battle.) There were other difficulties. James was one in himself. The star of the Jacobite cause was its greatest liability. In 1719 he consoled himself after the latest Scots reverse by doing something rather exciting. James got married, to Clementina Sobieski, a minor Polish princess of demure appearance and featherweight brain, who was brought to her groom only after a series of hair-raising and at times hilarious adventures; British agents dogged her journey at every course, and at one point she was held hostage in Innsbruck, and at another rattling through the Alps in a carriage in wildest winter. That she made Rome at all was a tribute to the gallant Charles Wogan, a plucky Irishman who was one of the few truly able men the languishing Jacobite court enjoyed.

That James was in Rome in the first place was a British trump; it had taken them years of gunboat diplomacy to turn him *persona non grata* everywhere else. He had been forced to quit St Germain; forced even to quit Avignon. The Pope was good to him and granted a pension and a fair-sized palace, more forbidding than cosy. But Roman residence was politically disastrous for James, and even he had the sense to understand that. Protestant fervour had lost none of its force in Britain. There were thousands of violent men prepared to fight against popery, as one joked, 'though they knew not whether it was a man or a horse'.

It was also apparent that no European court was prepared now fully to back a Jacobite enterprise. For one, kings of Spain or France were reluctant to commit forces and funds until a rising was well under way in Britain; in Britain, Jacobites would not rise until foreign forces had been committed and had invaded. It was a double-bind that would have frustrated better men than James. For another, what hard-headed kings of France or Spain wanted were Jacobite side-shows, not Jacobite revolutions. It was much more in their interests to have the British government distracted by a Highland rebellion, or weakened by prolonged civil war, than to see a swift change of monarchy which would make little real difference on the diplomatic map. Whoever reigned in Britain, the same sort of clever men would still rule and, in the long term, in British interests.

The royal marriage was not a success, and its failure another political reverse. James was very pleased with Clementina. She was far from pleased with him, and even her dim intelligence was stupefied by his boring, spiritless ways. Within a year they were quarrelling. She had borne him only two sons before the marriage, in 1725, crumbled completely. Clementina developed neurotic depression and what was plainly, to our modern knowledge, anorexia nervosa. She grew so thin she ceased to menstruate. She ranted and raved at her husband, accused him absurdly of adultery (James was not capable of anything as interesting), and at length retreated within a convent. The Pope meddled, unhelpfully. The British laughed mightily and the state of the Pretender's marriage became the joke of Europe. Clementina survived till 1735, demonstrably insane. It destroyed what remained of James's interest in life and destroyed the lives of their sons, who grew warped and fragmented of personality, with serious psycho-sexual difficulties.

The '45 was the last significant Stuart rising and, against all the odds and from a much weaker political and military base, came the nearest of any to success. Its hero is the man generally remembered as Bonnie Prince Charlie, elder son of James Francis. Charles Edward Louis John Casimir Silvester Severino Mario Stuart was born on 31 December 1720 and had been baptised by the Pope himself, who had also married his parents. Charles Edward is one of the most overexposed and least understood figures in popular Scottish history. He has been demonised by some and idolised by others. He was not the rash fool who wasted much life and blood and by his carelessness hugely advanced the destruction of Gaeldom. Nor was he the young genius who, but for wicked and jealous men, would have marched from Derby to take London and preside over a British Arcadia that never was. He was a deeply flawed man; but he is a fascinating figure to study: infinitely more interesting than his father, essentially modern in attitudes and spirit, and impossible – on close study – to dislike.

He was highly accomplished. He never learned to swim, but mastered almost everything else. From earliest childhood Charles Edward won such praise from visitors – he had charm, guts, wit and vigour – that his father grew deeply jealous, and James and Charles grew to be bound by deep and largely unconscious ties of profound hatred; everything good in Charles reminded James of his own inadequacy. His nagging letters of rebuke, his endless homilies, his inability to bestow meaningful encouragement or love estranged the two men completely. Yet Charles had more brains; his own letters, though dreadfully spelled (he was probably dyslexic) show good judgement and powers of argument; his recorded conversation shows wit and charm. He reached manhood fluent in French, Spanish and Italian. English was his first language and he spoke it in an attractive Scots-Irish brogue. He left Scotland able to converse in Gaelic. He was tall, fair, and very handsome, apart from a slightly weak chin. He could handle horses, falcons and dogs. He was a brilliant shot. He loved tennis and badminton. He played the cello most sweetly and was an elegant dancer. He had charm; the power to make anyone he met feel good about himself. He was irreligious, probably an agnostic; in the shambles of late life he developed a strong scientific bent, like his grand-uncle, and acquired a laboratory and even a microscope. (In 1750, when it scarce mattered any more, he converted to Anglicanism; he was received back in the Roman communion before he died, and was probably not aware he had done so.)

There were only three problems. One was his dreadful relationship with his father: it meant Charles had great difficulty coping with criticism or advice, however well intended, that threatened his view of things and especially his ambition. One was drink. It became a chronic problem after the '45; by 1750 Charles's boozing was a serious embarrassment to the Jacobite cause, and by 1770 he was a true alcoholic. But the heavy, dependent drinking was already evident – if only in bouts – years before he sailed for Scotland.

The third problem was women. When he came to Scotland all the evidence suggests he was a virgin. It was after Derby before we know of any sexual episode, with Clementina Walkinshaw, who later bore him an illegitimate daughter, Charlotte; the prince loved Charlotte, but treated Clementina abominably. In Edinburgh and elsewhere his tendency to avoid the company of women – even socially in banter and at concerts and so on – attracted comment. Like a coiled spring, it could be argued, he was abstaining from fleshly distraction in his questing crusade for restoration. But it indicates, really, a much deeper problem. Perhaps, like his brother, he was at heart homosexual.

The story of the '45 has been told so often that it bears little repeating. In 1744 a serious French-backed Jacobite expedition was pulled at the last minute, the Protestant wind starring yet again in the destruction of a marshalling fleet; twelve ships sank, and seven with all hands. Charles, who had come to France without his father's knowledge to join this venture, pled unsuccessfully for further French help. He gave up, went to a venture-capitalist in Paris, pawned the family jewels, bought two ships, hired some men, loaded some arms, and sailed to Scotland in the summer of 1745. An English warship met them in the Channel and one of the ships – with all the soldiers and much of the weaponry – had to turn back. The prince proceeded on the other.

In July 1745 he landed at Eriskay, in the Outer Hebrides, and made his way to Catholic country on the mainland, at Moidart, and, despite initial discouragement, won the backing of several important clans and their chiefs, two of whom the prince had to indemnify lest they lose all. (They did, of course, but he kept his word, and won them rich positions in France.) The speed and triumph of the '45 is part of Scottish legend. The standard was raised at Glenfinnan, the Highlands fast traversed, a lumbering government army outwitted and bypassed, and by December the prince was in Edinburgh and master of Scotland. The government was slow to realise the scale of the threat; the speed of the prince's campaign took everyone by surprise, and in a cynical and corrupt land not many really cared who sat on the throne, as long as there was no great disruption or war, and fewer still were prepared to fight to defend the house of Hanover. At Prestonpans, east of Edinburgh, the prince's army won an astonishing victory over a superior government force.

Convincing his council that he had pledged support both from English Jacobites and King Louis XV, Charles persuaded them to invade England. He was lying, but guessing well; there was a Jacobite force being raised in England, under Watkins Williams Wynn, and King Louis did react to news of Prestonpans by commissioning a major expedition. The tragedy was that this was an age when news travelled no faster than a man could move, by horse or sea. Louis was at least a fortnight late with news from Edinburgh and everyone blundered in a vacuum of ignorance and fear, further confused by spies and double-agents. Twenty-seven days after crossing the Border, Charles Edward and his army were at Derby. But few Englishmen had flocked to their cause and his chiefs and generals demanded a council; the Jacobite ranks, too, were being thinned by desertion. George II was preparing to run, but they did not know that. Louis was loading his ships, but they did not know that. London was defended by a militia barely more than a rabble; the two government armies had not the least idea where the prince's army was; Wynn was on the way, but of this Charles and his council knew nothing.

He argued, rightly, that they should press on to London. They refused to take the risk and were in little doubt now that Charles had lied to them. At a critical moment a man was introduced to the room to assure the council of a third – and fast-approaching – government force. There was no such army. He was a Hanoverian spy. The council voted unanimously against Charles, and demanded retreat to Scotland. It was his moment and he blew it. Charles had the passion and the trust of his force and he could have left the council and gone out and called his men and marched on London himself. He did not. His confidence went. The rest of the campaign, and his life, was pitiless decline, morally and mentally. But he, unlike his council, understood the folly of retreat.

At some point, that night, at last, he was alone. And we may think of him looking to the bottle, and draining that bottle, and perhaps another, and disappearing at merciful and fatal length to that strange realm between anaesthesia and Hell. It was the end of Stuart fortune; deep within his being, Charles Edward knew it, and knew he should care, and did not care.

The rest of the '45 and of the Stuarts is as an opera in its last act with the scenery falling down. The Jacobite commander, Lord George Murray, led the Highland army back to Scotland with speed and skill and skirmish, such as a triumphant action at Penrith in Cumbria; but this Murray could not see what we would now call the big picture. He never grasped, as Frank McLynn observes, the most vital military principle: concentration of force. Nor could he perceive the power of perception itself. The army, from the moment they were in retreat, was one of lamentation and fear. London and George II were rejoicing, and Charles Edward knew it; he knew what such as the diarist Horace Walpole wrote in London of London as the Jacobites reached Derby: 'There never was so melancholy a town . . . nobody but has some fear for themselves, for their money, or for their friends in the Army . . . I still fear the rebels beyond my reason.' And Charles Edward, who now slept late, and sometimes did not bother to shave, and who could hardly speak to Murray or the chiefs in their thrawn fearfulness, must have known what Walpole would write when news of retreat reached him. 'No-one,' wrote Walpole exuberantly, 'is afraid of a rebellion that runs away.'

There is a persistent Highland tradition: improbable as it may seem, it is heard too often in little corners of Lochaber and the Isles to ignore, and it is that this Lord George Murray, who more than anyone else sought retreat from Derby, was a Hanoverian agent.

They had lost Edinburgh upon quitting it. News of the retreat reached Wynn: he cancelled everything. News reached Louis. He unloaded the ships. The London mob danced in anti-Scottish frenzy; though, in strict truth, only a minority of Scots supported the cause now, and more Scots fought against

Charles Edward than for him. The Jacobites won a battle at Falkirk, between Edinburgh and Stirling, in January 1746. The triumph was not followed up and counted for nothing. Murray pursued a rearguard action, trying to secure a base in northern Scotland: it was a tactical wisdom necessitated by strategic absurdity. Meanwhile the Jacobites were being pursued by the vast, Teutonic figure of William Augustus, Duke of Cumberland, younger son of George II. He was German by temperament, cruel by nature to his own troops, and with only genocidal contempt for Scots and all Highlanders; but, in the German manner, he was efficient, and studied Highland tactics in battle closely, and drilled his men by lash and bawling to master counter-tactics. At Inverness, in April 1746, the Jacobite army's commissariat had collapsed – it was under a self-pitying Edinburgh incompetent – and the starved, ill troops failed to reach Cumberland's camp at Nairn, on the night of 15 April, in time to mount an effective dawn assault.

Cumberland's force came after them. Charles Edward, against all advice, took personal command of battle, for the first time, and committed his men to a cramped high pitch on Drummossie Moor, by the house of Culloden, where they proved easy meat for government artillery. He managed to position his biggest clan troop, the MacDonalds, elsewhere than their traditional stand in battle at the right of the army, and many refused to fight at all. Finally he positioned himself where he was unable to see anything that was happening. Cannon and grapeshot had cut his force to ribbons before, finally, they received the order to charge. Charles Edward later insisted he had made the order eight times before his men finally charged.

It was not an utter military defeat. With remarkable discipline what was left of the Jacobite ranks rallied at the Ruthven barracks, on the road south from Inverness; they were joined by still more Highlanders, and a continuing campaign was entirely feasible. Charles Edward pulled the plug. He did not appear at Ruthven. He sent word to disband; he was making for France, and would come back as soon as possible with a mighty continental army. Cumberland proceeded to pacify the Highlands with incredible cruelty. Charles Edward, after months of hardship – he was chased up and down the West Highland seaboard; often hungry; often cold; eaten alive by biting insects; often drunk – escaped to France, at last, from Loch nan Uamh, at almost the same cove where he had made mainland landfall on Scotland a year before. He never returned. The tale of his flight, and of those who harboured him at the risk of all they had, including their lives, is still a good story.

His brother, Henry Benedict, titular Duke of York, in April 1747 took a cardinal's hat at Rome. He announced further that he would shortly be ordained a priest of Rome. It was a plot, arranged by James and the Pope and kept entirely secret from Charles; a plot agreeable to Henry, who had a morbid horror of women and was already in the habit of sharing his bed with pretty boys and vigorous young men. It was a calculated slap in the face for Charles Edward and the last ruin of Jacobite hopes. There were more, and ever more fantastic schemes. But Henry's perfidy was a death-blow. Charles Edward said it was like a 'dagger through my heart'. The gloating Walpole wrote that the Stuarts had done more to extinguish their party 'than would have been effected by putting to death many thousands of deluded followers'. At the end of 1748 Charles Edward was ordered to leave France, where he was a diplomatic embarrassment. He refused, and remained conspicuous and defiant, ignoring all warnings; at length French troops seized him by night, and he was bundled safely over the border.

James Francis died in 1766, quite senile and harmless. Neither the Pope nor anyone else formally acknowledged his elder son as King Charles III. He was now a loathsome, pathetic figure, who wept and stormed if anyone reminded him of Scotland and the Highlanders. He travelled much, often disguised and always incognito; it is even said he attended the coronation of George III. He made a disastrous marriage to a silly and very poor German princess, Louise of Stolberg; the marriage was childless. He beat her and subjected her to unnatural practices, and drank, buckets; he was flatulent, obese, almost always drunk, often seen to vomit at the opera; tormented by piles. Within a year Louise had found a lover. The marriage collapsed amid the hilarity of Europe. In his last years, in moments of rare sobriety, Charles Edward enjoyed his scientific hobbies, and delighted in the rise of the United States of America. At the end, his daughter lived with him and created some comfort and dignity around him. Charles died, old and broken, on 30 January 1788.

'Henry IX' used that title only on a medal he struck on his titular succession; in Latin, he was described on the obverse as Henry IX King of Great Britain, but on the reverse Not By The Will Of Men But By The Will Of God. It was a nice compromise and much appreciated in Britain. Cardinal Duke of York had made a very pleasant life for himself and taken a measure of schadenfreude in the sick joke of his brother's career with the 'nasty bottle'. He held high office at the Vatican and threw opulent banquets at Frascati. He acquired a wonderful library, fine antiques, magnificent paintings; nor was the old queen ever lacking for obliging boys. But he also devoted much wealth to the poor, supporting religious foundations, hospitals, soup-kitchens and so on. Apart from the commemorative medal, he made few concessions to his claim of monarchy. He 'touched' for the King's Evil – scrofula; a tubercular infection of glands in the neck – and expected his servants to address him as 'Your Majesty'. He also altered his official style, making known he should now be dubbed 'Cardinal calling himself Duke of York'. It implied, delicately, and with exquisite taste, that 'Duke of York' was but a self-effacing incognito.

The early campaigns of Napoleon caused the old man much hardship; he was forced at one point to flee for his life, and lost almost all he owned. He gave most of his banked assets to the Pope to pay Napoleon's enforced tribute in 1796. Napoleon's troops rewarded him by sacking his diocese. But the cardinal king lived to return to Rome in 1800 where the people hailed him as 'Protector of the Poor'. Meantime, an

English member of parliament now espoused his cause. 'It is greatly afflicting to see so great a personage, the last descendant of his Royal House, reduced to such distressed circumstances,' wrote Sir John Hippisley, and *The Times* was moved to editorialise on the pathos of the cardinal being 'exposed to the shafts of adversity at a period of his life when least able to struggle with misfortune'. Britain actually owed the cardinal king a great deal – for a large chunk of Mary of Modena's dowry, due to James VII, was withheld by William II's government – but Henry did not know that, nor did George III, and he granted his ageing cousin an annual pension of £4,000. Henry, cardinal calling himself whatever you saw fit, said delicately, 'I am in reality at a loss to express in writing all the sentiments of my heart.' He lived to become one of the 'sights' of Rome for gentry doing the required tour; he even met sons of George III, such as the Duke of Sussex, who gave him much prim pleasure by solemnly addressing the cardinal as 'Your Royal Highness'.

He lived to the grand age of eighty-three, and died in Rome on 13 July 1807. In 1819 the Prince Regent, later George IV, commissioned Canova to build a tomb; and in this Stuart monument, at the Chapel of the Virgin in St Peter's Church, Rome, lie the remains of the last three Pretenders.

There was no legitimate issue: Napoleon made an exhaustive search, when he fancied a Jacobite adventure of his own, and found none. Had a baby resulted from Charles Edward's marriage, he would certainly not have kept it secret. The 'Sobieski Stuarts' who brightened Scottish life last century were charlatans, as was the Frenchman who styled himself Michael Stuart and made similar claims in the 1980s, winning a job in the Edinburgh tourist industry. Charlotte, Charles Edward's illegitimate daughter, survived her father by mere months. She had two illegitimate children by her liaison with the German Cardinal Rohan. The son of that union, who styled himself Charles Rohanstart, was killed in a coach crash in the Highlands in 1854, an old man; he is buried at Dunkeld. There is no trace of his sister who died very young.

The senior line of Stuart descent is that of the royal house of

Sardinia; as a crucial link, though, is an uncle-niece marriage in the late eighteenth century, the claim is null under British law. The present Duke of Bavaria, now very old, is generally recognised as the valid occupant, by strict primogeniture, of the throne. An ancestor, last century, sarcastically acknowledged the claim by decorating his *schloss* in tartan wallpaper.

In 1974 a young woman was arrested outside the Palace of Westminster. She was protesting, in noisy and abusive fashion, that no parliamentary legislation was valid in law, nor had been, since December 1688, nor could be, until King Franz, Duke of Bavaria, was restored to his lawful throne.

In 1960 the Reformed Presbyterian Church of Scotland, descended from the Cameronians, finally lifted its rule of political dissent; ministers, members and office-bearers were at last allowed to vote. The big sister, though – the Reformed Presbyterian Church of Ireland – still enforces the law, to this day. None who sits at the Lord's Supper can vote in a parliamentary election; nor can they, until parliament ratifies, and adopts as strict policy, and enforces throughout its dominions, the Solemn League and Covenant.

BIBLIOGRAPHY

Bingham, Caroline, *Darnley: A Life of Henry Stuart, Lord Darnley, Consort of Mary Queen of Scots*, Constable, London, 1995

Brown, P. Hume, *A Short History of Scotland*, new revised edition by H. W. Meikle, Oliver & Boyd, Edinburgh, 1955

Cameron, Nigel M. de S. (ed.), *Dictionary of Scottish Church History and Biography*, T & T Clark, Edinburgh, 1993

Coldwell, Christopher (ed.), *An Anthology of Presbyterian and Reformed Literature (vol. V)*, Naphtali Press, Dallas, 1992

Coward, Barry, *The Stuart Age: England 1603–1714*, second edition, Longman, London, 1994

Fleming, D. Hay, *Mary Queen of Scots*, Hodder & Stoughton, London, 1998

Fraser, Antonia, *King Charles II*, Weidenfeld & Nicolson, London, 1979

Fraser, Antonia, *Mary Queen of Scots*, Weidenfeld & Nicolson, London, 1969

Hamilton, Elizabeth, *William's Mary*, Hamish Hamilton, London, 1972

Johnson, Paul, *A History of the English People*, revised edition, Weidenfeld & Nicolson, London, 1985

Lenman, Bruce, *The Jacobite Risings in Britain 1689–1746*, Eyre Methuen, London, 1980

Lynch, Michael, *Scotland: A New History*, Century, London, 1991

McCrie, Thomas, *The Life of John Knox*, Edinburgh, 1811; modern edition: Free Presbyterian Publications, Glasgow, 1991

McCrie Jnr, Thomas, *The Story of the Scottish Church from the Reformation to the Disruption*, Edinburgh, 1874; modern edition: Free Presbyterian Publications, Glasgow, 1988

MacKenzie, Agnes Mure, *The Passing of the Stuarts*, Alexander Maclehose, London, 1938

Mackie, R.L., *A Short History of Scotland*, revised edition (by Gordon Donaldson), Oliver & Boyd, Edinburgh, 1962

Macleod, John, *Highlanders: A History of the Gaels*, Hodder & Stoughton, London, 1996

McLynn, Frank, *Charles Edward Stuart: A Tragedy in Many Acts*, Routledge, London, 1988

Miller, John, *James II: A Study in Kingship*, revised edition, Methuen, London, 1989

Pagan, Anne, *God's Scotland?: The Story of Scottish Christian Religion*, Mainstream Publishing, Edinburgh, 1988

Paton, H.J., *The Claim of Scotland*, Allen & Unwin, London, 1968

Plumb, J.H., and Wheldon, Huw, *Royal Heritage: The Story of Britain's Royal Builders and Collectors*, BBC, London, 1977

Ross, Stewart, *The Stewart Dynasty*, Thomas & Lochar, Nairn, 1993

Scott, Otto, *James I: The Fool as King*, Ross House Books, California, 1986

Smout, T.C., *A History of the Scottish People 1560–1830*, William Collins, London, 1969

Spencer, Colin, *Homosexuality: A History*, Fourth Estate, London, 1995

Steel, Tom, *Scotland's Story*, William Collins, London, 1984

Watson, D.R., *The Life and Times of Charles I*, Weidenfeld & Nicolson, London, 1972

Wormald, Jenny, *Mary Queen of Scots: A Study in Failure*, Canongate, Edinburgh, 1989

Youngson, A.J., *The Prince and the Pretender: Two Views of the '45*, Croom Helm, 1985; reprinted: Mercat Press, Edinburgh, 1996

INDEX